The Rose in Contemporary Italian Poetry

Thomas E. Peterson

University Press of Florida
Gainesville/Tallahassee/Tampa/Boca Raton
Pensacola/Orlando/Miami/Jacksonville

Copyright 2000 by the Board of Regents of the State of Florida
Printed in the United States of America on acid-free paper
All rights reserved

05 04 03 02 01 00   6 5 4 3 2 1

Library of Congress Cataloging-in-Publication Data
Peterson, Thomas E. (Thomas Erling)
The rose in contemporary Italian poetry
p. cm.
Includes bibliographical references and index.
ISBN 0-8130-1751-3 (alk. paper)
1. Italian poetry—20th century—History and criticism. 2. Roses in literature. I. Title.
PQ4223.R67 P48 2000
851'.9109364—dc21   99-056588

The University Press of Florida is the scholarly publishing agency for the State University System of Florida, comprising Florida A&M University, Florida Atlantic University, Florida International University, Florida State University, University of Central Florida, University of Florida, University of North Florida, University of South Florida, and University of West Florida.

University Press of Florida
15 Northwest 15th Street
Gainesville, FL 32611–2079
http://www.upf.com

CONTENTS

Preface vii

1. In the Garden of Italian Literature 1
2. Roses and Violets, or the Problem of Wonder 19
3. Le Mystère d'un Nom 35
4. Gozzano and His Contemporaries 56
5. The Pathetic and Mannerist Rose 67
6. The Votive and Hermetic Rose 87
7. The Anacreontic Rose 109
8. The Idea of Liguria 128
9. Of Rarefaction and Rhetoric 144
10. The Encyclopedic Rose 161
11. The Feminine Voice, and Other Alibis 184
12. The Rose of Advent 205
13. The Otiose Rose 223

Notes 239
Bibliography 317
Index 337

PREFACE

Walter Benjamin was tempted to write a book entirely of citations, so well chosen as to render any linking commentary unnecessary; there is something of that ambition here. While a reasoned catalogue of the "rose" in modern Italian poetry obviously requires commentary, the sample is largely self-organized. Seeking out poetry's endogenous patterns of sound and sense, I have seen my primary responsibility as that of placement or *dispositio*. The commentary is in no way exhaustive or definitive. Benjamin was aware of the difficulties of his project, but found them justified

> so as not to ruin everything with explanations that seek to provide a causal or systematic connection. In so doing he was aware that this new method of "drilling" [rather than excavating] resulted in a certain "forcing of insights . . . whose inelegant pedantry, however, is preferable to today's almost universal habit of falsifying them"; it was equally clear to him that this method was bound to be "the cause of certain obscurities."[1]

To study a *topos* is also an act of critical drilling. The *topos* is "a motif which has been codified by the cultural tradition so that it can be employed as an argument"; its study requires a deep knowledge of that tradition, and of the musical and aesthetic basis of motifs.[2] Nor in drilling is the criterion of mystery to be overlooked, or the potential of poems to be "as shadows illuminated by their own light."[3]

In his recent chapter on *topoi* or commonplaces, Giovanni Pozzi notes their antithetical nature: "situated at the lowest level of literary-critical activity," they are also "the cornerstones and subject matter of literature":

> The contradictions that emerge from the two antithetical positions . . . clarify the diverse type of difficulties that a study of *topoi* encounters: the extension of the material, uncircumscribable and unclassifiable, and the equivocalness of terms, in which different meanings are superimposed. In fact, in the use of the concepts of theme, topos, motif, one passes from the idea of content-related elements to the idea of formal elements; from the idea of a constant to the idea of mutation and evolution; from the idea of a polysemic entity to the idea of an asemic entity; from the idea of the calque to the idea of the archetype. Extremely diverse things are observed in each datum: the semantic polyvalence of a concept, verbal or figural symbolic forms, social and linguistic conventions of the modes of communication; the practices of persuasion, techniques of memory, intentional stylistic forms.[4]

Implicit in this appraisal of the problem is the need to adopt a method sufficiently broad and heterogeneous so as not to anticipate what the *topos* might tell us. Thus, while acknowledging the importance of formalistic analysis (including poetic sources and derivations), our concern is the overall picture. As Ernst Curtius writes,

> When we have isolated and named a literary phenomenon, we have established one fact. At that one point we have penetrated the concrete structure of the matter of literature. We have performed an analysis. If we get a few dozen or a few hundred such facts, a system of points is established. They can be connected by lines; and this produces figures. If we study and associate these, we arrive at a comprehensive picture.[5]

Let me then present the "picture" of this volume and some of the connecting lines. Chapter 1 establishes the centrality of the rose *topos* in the Italian and Romance traditions, along with their densely intertextual and self-referential nature. Chapter 2 studies the conventional pairing of roses and violets as a function of poetry's engagement of the problem of wonder. Chapter 3 is a survey of the rose in modern French poetry. Chapter 4 concerns the early part of the century, when various strands of fragmentism, moralism, and experimentalism marked an epochal transition in Italian poetry. Chapter 5 traces the pathetic and ludic use of the rose as a figure for the fragility and evanescence of life. Chapter 6 explores the votive rose, primarily during the extended period of hermeticism, whose linguistic experimentation and use of analogy proved comparable to the sacramental literature of the liturgical tradition. Chapter 7 exposes the transgressive rose, also in terms of a contemporary baroque. In chapter 8 the rose is examined through the lens of one Italian region whose poets resisted the eloquence of the center and provided from the periphery great impetus toward change. In chapter 9, the rose is viewed theoretically in the guise of two rhetorics: one which employs citation to attenuate the rose's status as stylistic token, and the other which avoids the rose altogether, in order to attenuate rhetoric's ornamental function. In chapter 10, the encyclopedic rose is defined and situated within a discursive mode, amidst the heteroglossia and realism typical of the "open work." In chapter 11, the feminine voice is seen to engage the flower as an alibi or alter ego in what Aldo Gargani calls the "space of contingency, intention and sense." In chapter 12, the rose is projected into the future in a sometimes prophetic modality that ranges from the utopian to the pragmatic. In chapter 13, poets are seen to explore the rose from the position of solitude, leisure, and contemplation.

While each chapter possesses its own internal coherence, the themes are interpenetrating. The use of rapid critical comparisons is intended to delimit the overall ethos of the poets. As suggested above, the positioning of citations is undertaken with respect for the specific coherence of poetry, the unity of facts and values it comports, and the need for readers to bring powers of inference to the poetry and sort through fertile ambiguities. One seeks in vain for inexorable historical or stylistic categories. Rather, in line with anthologists such as Mengaldo and Fortini who minimize the importance of "lines," poets are studied on an individual basis.

Given the scope of the project, I have chosen to limit the length of citations to one "unit" of rhythm, or *rhythmeme*. Though some poems appear in their entirety, I am generally content to render the phrasing, the lexical-syntactic frame or setting of the rose. This allows me to blend discussions of poets, movements, and themes and to allow emphases between the diachronic and synchronic properties of poetic language. Gianfranco Contini describes such an alternation as a kind of staircase pattern that moves "successively and periodically from a horizontal synchronic approach to a vertical diachronic approach and then again to the synchronic landing and so forth"; the alternating phases are those of "structure and growth."[6] In addition to the criteria of growth and structure, the organization of my chapters reflects the heterogeneous nature of *topoi*, in which one always finds the antithetical qualities of arbitrariness and necessity moving back and forth, like a shuttle on a loom, "from the idea of the calque to the idea of the archetype."[7]

The cited poetry is translated in the notes; unless otherwise indicated, the translations are my own. The notes contain the original titles of the poems, while titles appearing in the text are usually translated. Translations contain stanza and line breaks when those are essential to a clear understanding of the text. Secondary sources present in the text have been translated; those in the notes are left in the original language.

1
IN THE GARDEN OF ITALIAN LITERATURE
Quegli prese la rosa e pianse.
SILVIO PELLICO[1]

A synoptic study of the noun *rosa* in twentieth-century Italian poetry must approach the traditional use of that "most abused of metaphors" within the Italian and romance traditions.[2] The word which for centuries was a paradigm of the momentary and ephemeral, the beautiful, healthy, and perfect, has acquired a more diverse and less univocal status as keyword. Once relatively constant as a rhetorical convention, the commonplace is now a chimera functioning at different moments in different hands as image, symbol, or theory, expressing tonalities from naive to sophisticated, from the ironic and contentious to the self-conscious and exquisite.

As empirical object, or referent, the rose matured with Europe: the humble bush-flower was cultivated into countless varietals and hybrids of exquisite shape, color, and texture. As poetic form, or signifier, the melic /roza/ was a frequent candidate for rhyme, homophony, and other figures. As poetic content, or signified, *rosa* underwent countless metaphorical contaminations (simile, symbol, allegory, personification) in diverse thematic registers (amorous, pastoral, religious, patriotic). Its genericness—in Latin *rosa* stands synecdochically for the entire class "flowers"—contributed to its use as a reminiscence of classical prosody. At the same time, such deliberate archaism allowed the rose to become an emblem of semantic multiplicity and indistinction. The unified Saussurean sign was compromised so that the acoustic-graphic signifier often assumed a space of its own, even in poems of a referential-discursive nature. This tendency can be traced to the early part of this century, when the relation between poetic form and content, between the facts of language and those of theme, was profoundly altered, and traditional assumptions gave way to an emphasis on poetic process, and the concept of literary genres was relaxed or even abandoned.

Given the nature of this transition, one cannot rely on a single (semiotic, stylistic, linguistic, sociological) means of exegesis. Rather an "endogenous" criticism is required that is sensitive to a poem's interpretive needs on a case-by-case basis. Two concepts used in communication theory will be helpful in this regard: the *report message* or enunciation, "that part of the message containing the content or substance"; and the *command message,* or the instructions for use of that enunciation, "that part of the message that refers to the relationship between the communicants."[3] If one considers the above epigraph, taken from Pellico's *Le mie prigioni,* the rose is the gift of the amputee Piero Maroncelli (Pellico's collaborator and fellow inmate and *carbonaro,* who served ten years at hard labor in Spielberg for anti-Austrian activities) to the surgeon who has just removed his leg. The lyric brevity and pathos of the report message is enhanced by the command message, the larger context of a prison memoir addressed to the Italian aspirations of nationhood and Christian piety. For this reason the passage has acquired canonical status in the Italian ethos. The use of this communicative model frees us from the constraints of formalist criticism, with its unique focus on the report message, and from those of historicist-philosophical criticism (deriving from Benedetto Croce), which focuses on the command message and evades the discussion of rhetoric. It will enable us to approach a recursive semiotic relation that requires a means of analysis unlike Saussure's that does not assume a priori an underlying order to the linguistic system.

In other words, a study of the report message of the rose (for example, its use as a figure of beauty, youth, perfection, the ephemeral, the transitory) would in itself fail to reveal the "comprehensive picture" we are seeking, as would a mere discussion of the command message (the communicative implications of its usage), which would reveal a series of cultural discontinuities and aporias alongside a largely conventional thesaurus of usage. To understand this crisis, one must first acknowledge the general sense of uncertainty and negativity that has prevailed during the century. Under this negative sign, the ideal of unity itself often survives only as an absence, as poetry is reduced to its own virtuality. If the rose continues to be an icon of poetry, it is fair to say that the sign it now refers to is one of non-meaning.[4] To ask what the rose "is," as Umberto Eco reveals in glossing the title of his famous novel, can only lead to semantic dilution and insignificance:

> The idea of calling my book *The Name of the Rose* came to me virtually by chance, and I liked it because the rose is a symbolic figure so rich in meanings that by now it hardly has any meaning left: Dante's mystic rose, and go lovely rose, the Wars of the Roses, rose thou art sick, too many rings around Rosie, a rose by any other name, a rose is a rose is a rose is a rose, the Rosicrucians.[5]

In terms of our communicative approach, however, the non-meaning of "rose" as a report message remains a meaning on a command level, since poems (and novels) continue to communicate to readers.

Croce's division between "poetry" and "non-poetry" was crucial to a generation of poets who came of age under the shadow of logical positivism. The notion of poetry as intuition, liberated from constraints of genre, led naturally into

> the passion for "fragments," the splendid *fragmentism* of Ardengo Soffici and of Papini [and] hence the anti-traditional, uncanalized, uncontrolled character of the new lyrical poetry, where the enduring empirical personality of the artist is lost sight of in the consideration of the succession of his lyrical moments and visions, as in Govoni, Gozzano, Corazzini, Palazzeschi.[6]

These poets and others associated with the international avant-gardes permitted themselves to construct poetry as a kind of palimpsest, a text of fragments overwritten on other fragments. With World War I and the advent of fascism, poets educated to the Crocean aesthetic came to define a post-Crocean sensibility and a marginal poetic language whose raison d'être is the expression of its own autonomy.[7] Such a sensibility recognized developments in philosophy and science, leading to poetry that might variously be described as ecological, epistemological, or encyclopedic.

A growing awareness of poetry as communication and not simply expression led to a "deprovincialized" literature in which local-dialectal, national, and international features could interpenetrate. The status of popular poetry and dialect poetry was also changing, conditioned by such factors as internal and external immigration, more accurate research and documentation, and a greater interregional awareness of dialectal practice and texts. Gramsci's advocacy of a "national-popular" literature (by definition, unrealized) offered an alternative to the aulic and elitist practices which held sway in large sectors of Italian literary society.

The rose is prominent in the earliest romance tradition, from *Le roman de la rose* to Ciullo d'Alcamo ("Rosa fresca aulentissima"), to Giacomo da Lentini, to Guido Cavalcanti ("Fresca rosa novella"). It is central to Dante's *Divina commedia* (as well as the *Detto d'amore* and the *Fiore*, attributed to him), the anonymous *Fioretti di San Francesco,* and Petrarch. Even the briefest attempts to describe the rose's role in that tradition run across difficulties of attribution, influences, and linguistic drift. The plethora of symbolic and religious associations results in semantic dilution, even when the botanical name of a species or varietal is used. The rose's use always implies a certain degree of stylization, of artifice. As *the* poetic flower by antonomasia, its definition is categorial: whether as the sublime flower, noble and sanctified, or the embodiment of passion and aspirations, vain, opulent, and ephemeral. In fact, the qualities of tenderness, nostalgia, and loss of the Marian rose are simultaneously regal and humble, chaste and passionate.

Dante's use of *rosa* is central. In his arduous early canzone, "Tre donne intorno al cor mi son venute"; the "cut rose" ("succisa rosa") is of Virgilian origin and represents the weeping head of the first of three women in the allegory. As Contini writes, "The first woman pours out laments and leans head on hand like a severed rose: her naked arm is the column of sorrow, it feels the rain from the tear-filled face that the other hand is lifted to conceal."[8] In the *Commedia* the use of *rosa* is limited to the *Paradiso* (except for one earlier reference to its color), where the white rose is the final and dominant configuration, the "one" in which the "many" blessed are situated, and the point of arrival of the entire journey. As a simple round structure containing within it the more detailed figurations of Paradise, Dante's rose "overturns the usual relation between poetry and structure. . . . [R]ight when we expect a return to non-poetry, the poet's availability to the image becomes total."[9] The *candida rosa* is named and alluded to in Cantos 30–32 as "circular figura," "gran fior," "fior," "fior venusto," "città," "sicuro e gaudioso regno," "regno," and "reame."

Petrarch's customarily plural usage (*rose*) adds to the generality and abstractness of his iterative landscape, in which the rose is an emblem of passion and potency. It occurs as one in a "garden" of flowers appropriate to classic versifiers: "roses, violets, irises, crocuses, hyacinths, and narcissuses."[10] His use of "candida rosa" recalls Dante and is one of only two singular uses of the noun in the *Canzoniere*. The widespread imitation of the poet gives rise to Petrarchism, in many respects the central line of the Italian poetic tradition, a poetry of form over content, of iconicity over realism.[11] For virtually all Petrarchists, including Shakespeare, the rose is a simulacrum of the beloved, though, in general, the English poetic tradition casts its lot with substance and specificity, and lacks the nimble play of melic surfaces, essences, and generic conventions that develop in the romance lyric.[12]

Giovanni Pozzi's study of the rose in the Italian lyric poetry of the sixteenth and seventeenth centuries focuses on the synchronic stylistic practices that prevailed during Petrarchism, in which the rose expresses a symmetrical relation between connotation and denotation: "Every connotation can be considered as a transmutation of a hypothetical denotative model, a variant in relation to an invariant."[13] Within this stable, aulic arrangement the motifs of "color" and "transitoriness" stand respectively for the rose's figuration of "cheeks and mouth" and "the unpredictability of fading when one's eyes are set on the glory of blooming."[14] Pozzi dismisses the notion of literary evolution as tending toward tautology and ellipsis; however, in the final analysis, we may say with Maria Corti that Pozzi does trace an evolution:

> Pozzi has followed the structural transformations of the trope of the rose. Starting from an examination of the "thematic and figural seminary" rather than from the single theme or single "figure" of the rose, he arrives not only at an individuation and classification of literary *topoi* but at a sense of the evolution in a genre of poetry of a *topos* that sometimes becomes a little plot in miniature, a minuscule allegorical fable with the rose as protagonist.[15]

After the experience of mannerism and the Copernican revolution, such a symmetry between connotation and denotation in poetry becomes problematic. The marvel of a subject for an object external to itself (extensional wonder) and the marvel that subject projects internally (recursive wonder) diverge; poetic language too is stretched. In the earlier periods the rose typically expressed wonder for some aspect of objective reality (woman, nature) and for the transcendent order underlying it (God, the Virgin, the blood of Christ). The poems exploit this duplicity and express in their synchronic structure a kind of isomorphism, so that topical variances are slight and are carried out within well-defined parameters. With the Enlightenment came a greater gap between the theistic and empirical (or mechanistic) visions of the cosmos. Yet the root problem of interpretation remains: to reconcile the poetic function of language and its philosophical-cultural content, that is, the polyvalence of the poetic text as communication, as an event-in-process having its own origins and destinations.[16] With the advent of romanticism and nationalism, the same literary-semiotic system that accorded the rose the role of expressing extensional wonder now calls on it as an object of recursiveness, that is, as a figuration of the historical condition of poetry and language itself. Perhaps Johann Wolfgang von Goethe (1749—as with authors throughout the book, this indicates date of birth) was the first to indicate carefully the historical nature of the problem. Goethe cannot innocently engage the rose in its classical garden or seminary: it is now the ideal of an all-subsuming unity, as well as the suspicion of such a unity.

> And what is a rose, now we know;
> now that the age of roses is past.
> One last one is shining among the thorns
> and alone it has within it all flowers.[17]

This same awareness is evident in Goethe's admirer Alessandro Manzoni (1785), who employed the mystic Rose of the litanies as a figure of praise for the Virgin Mary: "Salve, o degnata del secondo nome, / O Rosa, o Stella ai periglianti scampo, / Inclita come il sol, terribil come // Oste schierata in campo."[18] The conventional nature of the hymn is problematized by the simile adopted, in which the "terrible" Rose fearfully connotes the armed power of the Church Militant.

For a Christian romantic like Novalis, flowers embodied the human potential for self-realization: "Flowers are allegories of the consciousness or of the head. A higher propagation is the purpose of these higher blossoms—a higher preservation. In human beings it is the organ of immortality—of a progressive propagation—of the personality."[19] Such an aspiration is seen in Niccolo Tommaseo's (1802) "Faith and Charity": "Come al verme che striscia in sulla rosa / ala d'uccel canoro alta sorvola; / alto sovrasti, o Fede, all'incresciosa / dotta ignoranza dell'umana scuola."[20] The elaborate metaphor, in which the rose stands for a human potential threatened by the "worm" of "ignorance," expresses a threat of disharmony between the natural and theological orders, and an equally perilous symmetry between the denotative and connotative modes of signification.

The full understanding of the flower's genericness was approached in Italy only by Giacomo Leopardi (1798), a great avoider of the rose who opposed the sterile cult of form still at work in a Monti or a Tommaseo. In response to the De Staël controversy, the twenty-year-old genius reframed the romantic debate over translation, imitation, and the classics. His willingness to translate foreign texts—as the author of *Corinne* had advocated—was demonstrated in "Imitazione" (a version of "La feuille" by Antonio Vincenzo Arnaut):

> "Lungi dal proprio ramo,
> povera foglia frale,
> dove vai tu?
> . . . .
> Vo dove ogni altra cosa,
> dove naturalmente
> va la foglia di rosa,
> e la foglia d'alloro."[21]

Leopardi classified the flower as a mere member of the class "things." The metaphor of the rose's transience, which in the original stood for political exile, is converted by Leopardi to a metaphor for his own sense of exile. For Leopardi the wonder one senses in extensive forms is in actuality occurring "in here," within the intensive realm of personal reflection and meditation.[22] The final result is his "The Broom Plant, or the Desert Flower," with its imposing civic message for the future.

The Tuscan classicalist Giosuè Carducci (1835) drew inspiration from Leopardi's civic poems. The son of a Republican and *carbonaro*, Carducci would become the great national poet after the Unification. While respectful of the classical divisions between registers and genres, his proposal of a "metrica barbara" opened the way to free verse. In his posture as Vate, or poet-prophet, he presumed a deeper insight into the destinies of man and the ways of nature, as seen in the sonnet "On Writing a Commentary of Petrarch's *Canzoniere*," which conflates the amorous and patriotic registers:

> De le canzoni vostre è il dolce coro
> cui da un cerchio di rose a pena doma
> va pe' bei fianchi la cesarie d'oro
> in riposo ondeggiante. Ahi, che la chioma
> scuote e 'l placido labbro una di loro
> apre al grido ribelle: Italia e Roma.[23]

The cumbersome nature of the neoclassical is even more apparent in Arturo Graf (1848), who writes of his natal city of Athens: "Ebbra d'aria e di sol, tacitamente / sogna un'antica visïon divina, / e fra le rose, e fra gli ulivi sente // fremer non morta la sua gran rovina."[24]

Far from this falsely antique and heraldic style, the symbolism of Giovanni Pascoli (1855) and Gabriele D'Annunzio (1863) engages the reader as a collaborator in the artistic process. One sees this awareness in Pascoli's pastiches and "poemetti" and D'Annunzio's voluntaristic cycles of verse. Both are manipulators of classical myth and radical deformers of language. D'Annunzio's rose is a figure of *vanitas* and luxury, recalling Marino's "Elogio della rosa" (in *Adone*, 1623). His hedonistic cultivation of the *ars poetica* emphasizes the mythic prowess of the first-person subject. Pascoli's classicism, as suggested by the bucolic title *Myricae* (Tamarisks), employs an intimist and elegiac style in support of a second- or third-person subject, rich in the particularity of its references. Pascoli embraces a "poetry of things" and an interest in phenomenal contingency; he collapsed the separation of poetic styles (high, medium, and low) into a mixture of styles, erasing the distinction between the lofty "hundred-petalled rose" and the various common roses (rosa boschiva, *rose d'ellébore,* rosa canina, rosa tremière):

> Rosa di macchia, che dall'irta rama
> ridi non vista a quella montanina,
> che stornellando passa e che ti chiama
>   rosa canina;
>
> se sottil mano i fiori tuoi non coglie,
> non ti dolere della tua fortuna:
> le invidiate rose centofoglie
>   colgano a una
> a una[25]

Pascoli's status as "the greatest metricist in the Italian tradition" is enhanced by his refusal to be constrained by any orthodox system of formal organization of the poem.[26] This novelty is apparent in the following dramatization, in which the pathetic idea of a mutilated beauty—the rose as it is plucked apart—is magnified by the double meaning of "femminelle" (women, buds) and the double use of "alba" (clean, dawn), and enhanced by the botanical specificity of "colchicco" (meadow-saffron), "sparagio" (asparagus), and "ruta" (rue):

> E dice la rosa alba: Oh! chi mi svelle?
> Son mesta come un colchicco: dal ciocco
> tanto mi germinò di femminelle!
>
> Erano come punte tenerine
> di sparagio: poi fecero lo stocco:
> buttano anch'esse e s'armano di spine.
>
> Vivono de' miei fiori color d'alba,
> d'alba rosata; e tu non giovi, o ruta.
> Mettono un boccio: una corolla scialba,
> subito aperta, subito caduta.[27]

While initiating a more exact naming of natural phenomena, Pascoli is the domestic poet par excellence. In "The Magician," the roses are invoked as a figure of the uncanny, yet kept safely within the confines of the homestead as demarcated by the hedge ("siepe"):

> "Rose al verziere, rondini al verone!"
>
> Dice, e l'aria alle sue dolci parole
> sibila d'ali, e l'irta siepe fiora.
> Altro il savio potrebbe; altro non vuole;
> pago se il ciel gli canta e il suol gli odora;
> suoi nunzi manda alla nativa aurora,
> a biondi capi intreccia sue corone.[28]

For both Pascoli and D'Annunzio, the acoustic signifier /roza/ remains compatible with the descriptive phonetic precepts of a Dante or Bembo that qualify it as "leggiadro," "soave," and "melico." However, in the work of both writers the signified *rosa* has been complicated by irony and violence. Pascoli's rose may imply, at one and the same time, a moribund eros and a will to transcendence: "Pallida Psyche, prendi tra le labbra / che sembrano due petali appassiti / di morta rosa, un obolo, e leggiero / tienlo, così, che te lo prenda il vecchio, / nè tu lo senta; e chiudi gli occhi, e dormi."[29]

Like Pascoli, D'Annunzio had a foot in either century and found in the rose a harbinger and portent, a fragment of literary memory that could stir up pathos, blooming in the bursting sun of June or fading in September: "D'un pensoso dolore / Settembre il ciel riempie. / Gli languon sulle tempie / le rose dell'està."[30] But unlike Pascoli, D'Annunzio favored an "unnatural rose": "Io—dice—son l'innaturale Rosa / generata dal sen de la Bellezza. / Io son che infondo la suprema ebrezza. / Io son colei che esalta e che riposa."[31] This rare use of the singular noun (following Petrarch, fifty-five of sixty-two uses in the *Chimera, Poema paradisiaco,* and *Isottèo* are plural) reifies the flower as a figure of literary inspiration, as the unnatural muse. D'Annunzio's overt manner and tone are remote from the recondite symbolism of Stephane Mallarmé, to whom he has been compared: "Sono spogliati tutti i miei rosai. / Non più ghirlande! E la mia coppa è vuota."[32] His taste for allusive quotation is a means to explore the virtuosity and plenitude of his vein, as in this self-projection into a suffering figure of Saint Francis. "Anche vidi la carne di Francesco, / affocata dal demone carnale, / sanguinar su le spine delle rose."[33]

D'Annunzio is drawn to the rose as a lavish and perfumed accessory to a mise-en-scène; here "Mona Francesca" is compared in her nobility and grace to the Este court, in a sonnet that closes with a line from Petrarch:

> Tante rose portò ne la sua veste
> Mona Francesca all'ospite in pastura
> quante mai n'ebbe il Ciel per avventura,
> bianche angelelle, a cingervi le teste.
> . . . .
> Un verso del Petrarca a l'aria sorse:
> "Così partìa le rose e le parole."[34]

In D'Annunzio's "Le armonie," an imitation of Ugo Foscolo's "Le grazie" (discussed in Chapter 2), the brows of the neoclassical Graces are adorned with roses; the sonnet in octonaries is addressed to the Villa of Bellosguardo in Florence, where Foscolo's work was drafted. In the incontinent use of roses one has a sign of D'Annunzio's libertinism:

> Bellosguardo, io certo dimane
> verrò ne' rosai che tu porti
> carichi di rose ancor chiuse.
>
> Ben so che i bocciuoli saranno
> come i capézzoli gonfii
> della pubescente. Ma forse
> bianca sarà la tua prima
> rosa fiorita su pel ferro
> onde pende nel pozzo
> la secchia loquace. O collina
> dell'Incontro, per la finestra
> ti veggo tutta rosata
> non come le rose ma come
> i fiori dell'erica . . .[35]

In the following example the poet is crowned at dawn by Arethusa. The Naiad, who was transformed into a spring when pursued by Actaeon, exclaims, "The triumphal laurel shines with roses!" The tercets are written in irregular terza rima:

> E così della rosa e dell'alloro
> parlò quell'Aretusa fiorentina,
> mutevole onda con un viso d'oro.
>
> La sua voce era come acqua argentina
> che recasse lavandula o pur menta
> o salvia o altra fresca erba mattutina.
>
> Tutto rigato dalla schietta vena
> "Sol d'oleandro voglio laurearmi"
> io dissi. Ed Aretusa era contenta;

> e recise per me altri due rami
> e fe' l'atto di cingermi le tempie
> dicendomi: "Pe' tuoi novelli carmi!
>
> Che la cerula e fulva Estate sempre
> abbia tu nel tuo cuore e in te le rime
> nascano come le sue rose scempie!"[36]

Pascoli and D'Annunzio found in the lyric poem an occasion to encompass a greater cognitive moment and cultural aperture than was allowed by Croce and his followers. They exacted a return to the "word," that is, to an elaborate system of encoding by figures and genres present in the *ars poetica* of the classical, medieval, and humanistic legacy, yet rich in the poetic logic of the new century, within which the rose came to stand for mutability and self-reflexivity. Not only was this *topos* a means of self-definition and a rite of passage, but it served in its recursiveness as a stylized comment on the tradition.

While Pascoli and D'Annunzio worked in isolation, a group of bohemian artists and writers called the *Scapigliati*, who were centered in Milan, applied an oneiric symbolism to traditional amorous and patriotic themes. One of them, Gian Pietro Lucini (1867), a disciple of Carducci and compatriot of Carlo Dossi (author of the early novel *La villa delle rose*), presents a "love dance" in which a "Knight" emerges from a dream world of erotic splendor to encounter a "Lady" and deliver her from sorrows and disillusionment. The roses are but the agent of a momentary bliss.

> La Dama e il Cavalier vanno lontano
> lontan sotto alla volta verde dei laureti:
> e nei miti splendori
> delle notti serene
> la danza e il ritmo sperdonsi sonori,
> sulle rose,
> amorose,
> sbocciate tra i cespugli e appassite tra i seni
> candidi e sodi:
> La mia nota si muore.[37]

As an advocate of both symbolism and futurism, Lucini expressed ambivalences between the "occult" and the "revolutionary," between modest "reserve" and "titanism." In his "restless Europeanism: socialistic, esoteric, and estheticizing," Lucini manifests the general truth that Italian poetry in the twentieth century is conservative in its foundations in the past and revolutionary in its insistence on poetry as a liberating spiritual act.[38] There is in Lucini a newly dialogued or diaristic element, a relation to the Other and to the society at large. This supplementary plane of intentionality represents a new means to manipulate the traditional poetic object, a sea-change normally associated with the name of Mallarmé.

The advent of free verse, marked in Italy by Lucini and in France by Jules Laforgue, was an attempt to reconcile the cadences and tonal and syllabic versification of the literary tradition with the rhythms and usages of contemporary prose syntax and speech. Mallarmé's most important successor as exponent of *poésie pure* was Paul Valéry. Together with Laforgue, these two had a strong influence in the 1920s and 1930s on those poets Francesco Flora would label "hermetics." While surrealism made little headway in Italy, the idea of a "pure poetry," deriving from the blend of the musical and the metaphysical found in Mallarmé and Valéry, assumed great importance. The indeterminate nature of symbolist and then hermetic practice exemplifies a crisis in representational language that occurred when simplex structures (such as the monologue, or the sonnet form) were replaced with duplex structures, including the creation of doubles (Valéry's Monsieur Teste) and sustained internal dialogues. A parallel phenomenon was the use of negation, enantiosis, and paradox, as evident in such titles as Diego Valeri's *Le gaie tristezze* (Gay sadnesses, 1913), Giuseppe Ungaretti's *Allegria di naufragi* (Joy of shipwrecks, 1919), Eugenio Montale's *Ossi di seppia* (Cuttlefish bones, 1926), and Salvatore Quasimodo's *Oboé sommerso* (Submerged oboe, 1932).

Of all the great poets of modernism, Rainer Maria Rilke (studied in chapter 6) is the most prodigal in his use of the rose. In these lines from the first of the *Duino Elegies,* the rose stands for the human ability to make ritual symbols and to dispatch auguries: "True, it is strange to inhabit the earth no longer, / to use no longer customs scarcely acquired, / not to interpret roses, and other things / that promise so much, in terms of a human future."[39] When Rilke reflects back on his life and on the use of roses as propitious signs, he refers not only to his own death but to a transformation in the human capacity for wonder, for spiritual awakening.

Another German who addresses the historicity of the *topos* is Bertolt Brecht (1898), like Rilke a student of Novalis mindful of the rose's status as an emblem of custom and ritual. In "The Little Rose, Oh How Should It Be Listed?" Brecht assesses the limits of the rose's signification as being essentially those of human perception and knowledge. He juxtaposes presentation and representation, the retinal perception of the rose and the gestic act of naming it:

> The little rose, oh how shall it be listed?
> Suddenly dark red and young and near?
> Oh we never knew that it existed
> Then we came, and saw that it was there.
> Unexpected till we came and saw it
> Unbelievable as soon as seen
> Hit the mark, despite not aiming for it:
> Isn't that how things have always been?[40]

Though the rose was unexpected and defies belief, the very wonder it creates is part of history. That is, for Brecht the rose is an enigma because it represents both sides of the duality of essence and experience.

What one finds in the modern era is that the formerly stable tropes have become the object of experimentation and *mise-en-abîme*. As poets become willfully elliptical and tautological, previously unquestioned hierarchies and selectivities become the subject of irony, farce, and satire. Poets blend the demands of "poetry" and "nonpoetry," of technique (versification, rhythm, lexis, tropes) and process (the impurities of prose, the fragment). As stated above, the stable relation between connotation and denotation is altered. An extreme instance of this is found in Ezra Pound (1885), who invited "history" into the poem, spatially juxtaposing its multiple codes on the page, creating new associations and an absolutely novel depiction of the passage of poetic consciousness through time. The early Pound, imbued with pre-Raphaelite taste, praised the rose for its permanence: "I would bid them live / As roses might, in magic amber laid, / Red overwrought with orange and all made / One substance and one colour / Braving time."[41] Years later, in the longest of the *Pisan Cantos*, he again evokes the permanent "substance," as opposed to "accident," of the rose pattern formed in "steel dust" by a magnet:

> This liquid is certainly a property of the mind
> nec accidens est but an element
>   in the mind's make-up
> est agens and functions dust to a fountain pen otherwise
>   Hast 'ou seen the rose in the steel dust
>   (or swansdown ever?)
> so light is the urging, so ordered the dark petals of iron
> we who have passed over Lethe.[42]

The rose pattern embodies for Pound the "poetic image" as he described it thirty years earlier: "a radiant node or cluster; ... what I can, and must perforce, call a VORTEX, from which, and through which, ideas are constantly rushing."[43] If Mallarmé's pursuit of a metaphysical truth was Orphic, Pound's radically diachronic experiment to "include history" was founded on the concrete things of this world. While attributing the property of permanent substance to poetry, Pound no doubt understood from his prison cage in Pisa that such a rose pattern was perceptible only to those "who have passed over Lethe." Pound's vorticism suggests how the rose constitutes an array; more generally this pattern will be seen in the "rosa dei venti" (compass-card) and the circular design of a rose window. *Rosa* is also the grouping of members of the flower: an assortment of petals, a garland, a set of candidates, a pattern of buckshot. As such it lends itself to an idea of spatiality, deixis, and stochastic events. This is apparent in various references to Dante's "In forma dunque di candida rosa" (*Paradiso* xxxi,1: "In the shape then of a white rose") discussed later in this book. Such poets do not understand the rose's shape as a geometrical essence or Platonic idea of the circle, but as the unity of the ideal and the real, of essence and experience. Thus in our later chapters the evocation of the rose shape will stand as a figure of the recursive wonder (interiority, the Other) as continuously coterminous with one's physical extension in space.

Maria Luisa Spaziani demonstrates this figure by comparing the moonlit Roman Colosseum to a fragmented rose whose ruins can only be reordered by poetry. The architectural hub from which spokes irradiate is a figure of extensive wonder, while the analogy drawn between that "reconstituted" structure and poetry, the Colosseum-rose, is an example of recursive wonder: "È una rosa disfatta, stanotte, il Colosseo / e la vita si disfa con lui sotto la luna. // Io cerco il verso unico, lo stelo, il sortilegio / che ogni franta immagine ricostituisca in una."[44] These lines are symptomatic of a shift in the Novecento from aesthetic formalism to an openness to contingencies. If, within the earlier paradigm, the conventional signified *rosa* had lost all touch with its referent, now, by engaging the forces of destruction and disintegration, that same signified recurs as a signifer, whose signified is that of "non-meaning." In this way previously intact boundaries of affective and intellective discourse are eroded until negativity itself becomes a means to reconcile essence and experience.

Leopardi is the original catalyst of this development. Through the various forms of Leopardism one can sketch out a profile of the poetry of the Novecento. Pier Vincenzo Mengaldo writes of three types of Leopardism—the "intellectual" type of Montale, the "mythic-fabulous" and "idyllic" type of Ungaretti, and the "rhetorical" type of Cardarelli. One could add several others: "civic," "philosophical," "empirical," "metaphysical," and so forth.[45] The additional names that must be mentioned are Camillo Sbarbaro, Sergio Solmi, Carlo Michelstaedter, Diego Valeri, Clemente Rebora, Antonia Pozzi, Franco Fortini, Pier Paolo Pasolini, Elena Clementelli, Alfonso Gatto, and Leonardo Sinisgalli.[46] The point is that models and lineages are a fact of poetic recursivity and thus a useful means of ordering the sample.

To study the rose is to confront the semantic emptiness of commonplaces, their belonging to a thesaurus of generic conventions and their constant emergence as a new tabula rasa. In discussing the recursivity of *topoi*, Curtius treats this duality as an alternation between continuity and creativity, remembering and forgetting.[47] The emptying out of the "garden" initiated by Pascoli and D'Annunzio takes heed of the Mallarmean merger of music and metaphysics, and the so-called "verbal" poetry associated with Rimbaud. The hollow rose is above all a catalyst, the result of an ontogenesis and not an ontology. Its hollowness is also an incarnation. As Norman Brown writes, "A pregnant emptiness. Object-loss, world-loss, is the precondition for all creation. Creation is in or out of the void; *ex nihilo*."[48] In modern poetry one witnesses "the over-determination of a lexeme by multiple meanings which it does not carry in ordinary usage but which accrue to it as a result of its occurence in other texts; syntactic irregularities such as ellipses, non-recoverable deletions, indefinite embeddings, etc."[49] As Julia Kristeva writes, modern poiesis is a "hetereogeneous process" which is centered on the "speaking subject"; by registering the "status" of that subject over time one can arrive at a "historical typology of signifying processes."[50] Seen in this light, the rose persists as a kind of emblem of the mystery of poetry, standing at the boundaries of the codifiable. It is at once a marker of earlier linguistic practices and a necessary point of departure. When a new class of stylistic options emerges at the end of the nineteenth century, poets require a lyric code that can look backward to the tradition and forward to the new century. At the center of that code is the rose, abstract and concrete, singular and multiple, a brake on hubris and a means of updating the former enclosure of literature by rhetoric, the "garden" or *hortus conclusus* of poetry.[51]

2
ROSES AND VIOLETS, OR THE PROBLEM OF WONDER

The classical relation between roses and violets is one between the lusty and lofty, blood-colored flower of summer, soon to fade, and the humble, smaller flower of spring, a figure of modesty and endurance. Maria Corti has explored this antinomic relation in the genre of the *contrasto* and specifically the *Disputatio rosae cum viola* of the thirteenth-century poet Bonvesin da la Riva, demonstrating how that poet, in order to make a social critique of his times, creates a "break" between the thematic level of roses and violets and the corresponding symbolic level of vices and virtues. This breadth of allusivity exploits the fact that color, like shape, is both an idea and a perception, and that the rose and violet have been, since classical times, "proverbial equivalents, by antonomastic indication, of a state of delight."[1] Dante's pairing of the flowers (the only non-*Paradiso* use of *rosa* in the *Commedia*) concerns the median color of the tree of knowledge—of good and evil, and of God's justice—which stands between the colors of these two opposites. This tree wondrously renews itself before the pilgrim's eyes in the Earthly Paradise: "men che di rose e più che di viole / colore aprendo, s'innovò la pianta."[2] Extending this opposition, we might say that the *rosa-viola* dyad represents the problem of wonder.

In Ugo Foscolo's (1778) "Le grazie," the birth of Venus involves, in the words of Domenico De Robertis, "the complete overturning, at the very origins of the world . . . of the classical fable of the roses."[3] In this passage, once the roses have seen the violets—the flowers of shame and first message of spring—they spontaneously renounce their lustful passion and become glad supplicants at the altar of classical harmony and beauty:

> . . . un'ignota violetta
> Spuntò a' piè de' cipressi; e d'improvviso
> Molte purpuree rose amabilmente
> Si conversero in candide. Fu quindi
> Religione di libar col latte
> Cinto di bianche rose, e cantar gl'inni
> Sotto a' cipressi, ed offerire all'ara
> Le perle, e il primo fior nunzio d'Aprile.[4]

Foscolo's use transposes modern values onto the language of myth. Beneath the theme of serenity lies that of sorrow and struggle, just as behind the candid roses of the classical stereotype one finds allusions to Foscolo's amorous exploits. Aware of the anachronistic nature of the myth he espouses, Foscolo makes the flowers, and thus the Graces, into figures of both extensive and recursive wonder. As a neoclassicist, Foscolo finds in them a model of the chastity of form, and the moral benefits of exposing oneself to beauty. As a romantic, Foscolo is responsible for investing in these female figures and flowers the recursive wonder of poetry itself, as well as repressed sexuality. The roses' sudden and miraculous transition from scarlet to white has been linked to Foscolo's desire to "give his poem a prodigiously rapid impulse and rhythm," an intention that results in his "reversal of an ancient mythic tradition . . . according to which Venus in running to the fatally stricken Adonis was wounded on her foot with rose thorns, which bathed in her blood, caused the white roses to become red." (As the critic notes, the presence of violets and cypresses recalls Foscolo's most famous poem, "De' Sepolcri," where, instead of roses, red amaranths are planted with violets on the ancient grave sites.) The change to white roses—more appropriate to the Graces than red—possesses the "symbolic significance of an implicit infraction."[5] By modifying the staid opposition of the flowers within a tradition he is yet eager to maintain, Foscolo has inserted a strong Vichian and Dantean, historicist position within a poetics long dominated by the synchronic tendency reflected in Petrarch's presentation of roses and violets as approximate synonyms: "cosí rose et vïole / à primavera, e 'l verno à neve et ghiaccio."[6]

Leopardi's only original use of the rose appears together with the violet in the incipit of the idyll "The Village Saturday":

> La donzelletta vien dalla campagna,
> in sul calar del sole,
> col suo fascio dell'erba; e reca in mano
> un mazzolin di rose e di viole,
> onde, siccome suole,
> ornare ella si appresta
> dimani, al dì di festa, il petto e il crine.[7]

The mixed bouquet of freshly picked flowers is a figure of beauty and plenitude. The young woman who will wear them on her breast and hair is a foil for the estranged poet. In objecting to the line "un mazzolin di rose e di viole" in his 1912 essay "Il sabato," Pascoli opens a new chapter in the history of this convention: "Roses and violets in the same country bouquet gathered by a peasant girl, I don't believe Leopardi could have seen. In one bunch we can imagine March violets, and only in another May roses."[8] As Claudio Varese writes, Pascoli "did not mean to imply or even really dispute a world or a linguistic measure, but to vindicate the new, in style as well as in theme, in defense of his cherished sense of the exact, at once objective and ambiguous. . . . Unfamiliar at that time with Leopardi's *Zibaldone,* he couldn't realize how the poetics of the infinite corresponded to the theory and linguistic choice of the vague and indeterminate."[9]

Giosuè Carducci evoked the passions associated with the flowers—of love and rebirth—as one whose nostalgic and mournful voice was deprived of them: "Ma ci fu dunque un giorno / Su questa terra il sole? / Ci fûr rose e vïole, / Luce, sorriso, ardor?"[10] He also employed the pair synonymically as a *topos* of fragility: "E un desio dolce spiran le vïole / E ne le rose un dolce ardor s'accende."[11]

Pascoli is prey to a spiritualism to which Leopardi is not. Indeed, in Pascoli too there is a strong element of lexical indeterminacy and artifice. On one occasion Pascoli uses *rosa* and *viola* together, as his sister Maria's innocence and her companion Rachele's susceptibility to passion are seen through the filter of their memories, perfumed with the "odor of bunches of roses and violets":

> Vedono; e si profuma il lor pensiero
> d'odor di rose e di viole a ciocche,
> di sentor d'innocenza e di mistero."
>
> . . . .
>
> Sola
> ero con le cetonie verdi. Il vento
> portava odor di rose e di viole a
> ciocche.[12]

The poem ends on the note of wonder, the "stupore" of the virginal Maria upon hearing Rachele's "floral" memories of love. Pascoli also uses the name "Rosa" with "viola," here in an erotic key:

> Ma tu ti sganci il candido corsetto,
> o bionda Rosa. Fuori è chiaro il sole,
> e due colombi tubano sul tetto
>
> Ti slacci il busto. Odore di vïole
> bianche è nell'orto. Oh! lascia come prima.
> Bello è come è. Non altro fior ci vuole.
>
> Ci son due bocci ch'hanno il rosso in cima.
>
> Non chiudere dentro il bianco petto, o Rosa,
> il fior del sonno. Non la notte e il giorno
> costì si veglia e mai non si riposa?[13]

In the following *strambotto* Pascoli draws on a popular tradition in which the flowers are metaphors for the woman's sexuality:

> Deh, Lévate la stringa dallo petto
> e lassame mirar quelle vïole:
> e lassa stare el paradiso aperto,
> dove se leva la luna e lo sole!
> El sol se leva e la luna se posa,
> dagli la bona sera a quella rosa.[14]

The onomastic sisters "Rosa" and "Viola" are protagonists in Pascoli's *Primi poemetti* and stand for the poet's sisters, Ida and Maria. The former, his "great love," would eventually leave the family home to marry at age thirty, while the younger would reside with Giovanni until his death. Such an onomastic usage is also seen in Antonio Fogazzaro (1842), for whom "Rosa" is a figure of rural domesticity: "Pur l'aëre mutò, su per le spalle / Delle montagne si ritrae la neve, / Si vede nelle nubi nereggianti, / E nella piova tepida si sente / La novella stagione. Il figliuoletto / Della Rosa portommi le vïole."[15]

Pascoli's greatest admirer in the next generation was Arturo Onofri (1885), here cited in a 188-line paean to love with a markedly anti-d'Annunzian title, "Il trionfo della vita." The Orphic prayer is that the flowers be used as a garland for love's elect:

> Noi, che sappiamo l'amore, precingano
> in sulle tempie floride ghirlande
> di rose, di gigli e vïole.
> E ovunque d'intorno
> superbi cantici di desiderio
> dall'Anima erompano come
> propagini alate
> ai freschi favonî dell'alba.[16]

In Enrico Thovez's "Inverno," the two flowers are not mentioned, but their homonymous colors are reversed in value: the normally cool purple ("viola") is set in the hot sexuality of a forest, its flames extinguished "in shadows of pink" ("rosa") by the implacable "candor" of winter: "Roseo un fulgor di vïola, / tenero, molle, qual fiato caldo di un'umida bocca, / fiammeggia sul verde cupo, divampa tra la boscaglia, / si frange qui sul candore intatto, in ombre di rosa."[17]

Gabriele D'Annunzio's tracing of the conflict between rose and violet in his first book, while reminiscent of Carducci, is playfully ironic in imagining the miniature actors in this garden rivalry:

> Pallida rosa, che da 'l verde céspite
>   ridi con disìo placido
> . . . .
> Ecco, il tuo stelo trema a 'l bacio languido
>   d'un'amante libellula,
> e le viole invidïando guardano
>   i tuoi divini gaudii[18]

D'Annunzio accepts the floral cliché as a raw material in his eurhythmic-melic fusion of eroticism and panic exultation. His cloistered sense of artifice is apparent in the following lines, set over the grid of the Petrarchan rhymes *lembo / nembo / grembo:*

> Sembri Ermione, sola come lei
> che pel silenzio vieni incontro sola
> traendo in guisa d'ala il bianco lembo.
> Sì le somigli, ch'io m'ingannerei
> se non vedessi ciocca di viola
> su la sua gota umida ancor del nembo.
> Ha tante rose in grembo[19]

D'Annunzio seems to have acknowledged Pascoli's point about "rose e viole," while keeping the memory of the pure trope alive in exquisitely artificial scenes:

> Pio pellegrino, le rose
> del laurigero oleandro
> e il fior violetto dell'agno-
> casto io colsi tra le ruine.[20]

* * *

> Com'api armoniose
> uscenti a 'l novo sole
> per le felici aiuole

> de' gigli e de le rose
> . . . .
> su le chiome odorose
> che Amor cingere suole
> di sogni e di viole
> spìrino dolci cose,
> com'api armoniose.[21]

In Guido Gozzano (1883) the conscious use of the rose and violet cliché is one of the healthier means used to combine the extensive wonder and the recursive, and thus to exceed the symbolist impasse. In fact, the attributions of modesty and mortality, to rose and violet respectively, are exactly opposite the traditional symbolic associations.

> Muto mi reclinai sopra quel volto
> dove già le viole della morte
> mescevansi alle rose del pudore . . .
> Disperato dolore!
> Dolore senza grido e senza pianto![22]

Gozzano's direct confrontation with his source bespeaks an awareness of the crisis in representational language denounced by the symbolists, a crisis he tends to parody. Gozzano's friend Massimo Bontempelli (1878) devolves a similar irony onto an eerily frozen and fantastic war landscape. The slow rhythm and allusiveness of the passage, including homophony and internal rhyme, accentuate the violence and intensity of the wartime disintegration:

> Piccoli uccelli dell'Ovest
>   spinti dal fumigare delle rose
>   dentro un piovere di petali fitto,
>   di là dalla pioggia son veli di sole.
> . . . .
> Una penna è caduta su una zattera
>   un'altra posa sul fumo rosa
>   una naviga in mezzo alle viole
>   ma l'ultima penna serpeggia tra i primi veli di sole.[23]

In the later futurists, the pairing of roses and violets disregards the externally probable in favor of an internal violence: the flowers are allies of the poet pitched in battle against a hostile world. Giovanni Gerbino personifies the two flowers as spitting out their bitterness, while Bruno Corra (1892) invokes them as a kind of archaic talisman whose "essences" preserve for modern man some recollection of a calmer and less brutal past.

> La piazza? Una gabbia incantata,
> ove, a sera, le rose e le viole,
> i garofani rossi, i tulipani,
> sputano a terra ogni amarezza[24]

* * *

> Ma certamente per molte notti
> soffocheremo con brutalità
> la nuova nostra orribile anima moderna,
> e spargeremo con avarizia
> in vecchissime alcove
> qualche goccia delle essenze di rose e di viole[25]

In the wake of the above examples, one might speculate that any later use of *rosa* with *viola* will be ironical, excepting that in the popular or dialectal register. But this apriorism would ignore the often-ironic nature of popular poetry and the sophistication of much poetry in dialect. In the "popular" Veronese poet, Berto Barbarani (1872), and the more "aulic" poet of Ancona, Franco Scataglini (1930), both writing in dialect, one finds a compromise between low and high forms of content and expression. The former's "Strolling with the roses" is a five-part pastoral fable, each part involving a dialogue with a varietal of the rose in which the deceitfulness and hidden burning in the lover's heart is contrasted by the blithe mockery of the lowly violets:

> —Rosa rosana, 'scolta do parole:
> ti te sì una regina in primavera,
> ma le petegolone de vïole,
> le discore de ti matina e sera . . .

> Te sì nata con éle, in meso a l'erba,
> e pur, le dise, che te sì superba.—
> L'ha risposto così rosa rosana:
> che tante volte l'aparensa ingana![26]

Scataglini's *La rosa* is a version of the first 1,692 lines of the *Roman de la rose,* "the story of an enamourment."[27] The 1,853-line poem is written in ten-line strophes of septenaries *a rima baciata.* In it one sees garlands embroidered on the garments of the god of Love, in which immense roses are present and violets are absent, thus referring to the canonical polarity between carnality and modesty:

> non pervinche e violette
> non graziose spighette
>
> de ginestre odorose.
> C'era, al dritto, le rose.
> Petali vasti e grandi,
> come moltiplicandi[28]

Luigi Fallacara, a Florentine transplant from Puglia, names his first book *Primo vere* (1908), in homage to D'Annunzio. Fallacara tends to receive and adapt other sources, including the Orphic and "wretched" influences of Campana and Rimbaud, and the intricacies of the French and Italian symbolists. Fallacara's use of the rose occurs within a Petrarchan and Platonic framework, usually in short lyrics set in a voluble and ambiguous landscape. In the following lines, roses and violets are linked to an imagery that is at once morbid and erotic:

> Anseranno le rose ed un'estate
> lampo che fra i tuoi cigli umido appare,
> incendierà dolce le rocce ambrate,
> insensato di fiori bianchi un mare.
>
> Mitici nel pallore taciturno
> avranno sere di viole lente
> madidi seni traboccati all'urne
>sideree che si vuotano di vento.[29]

Another Southern voice grouped among the hermetics is Leonardo Sinisgalli. In a poem about his father's decrepitude and the celebration of "Easter 1952," the violet is literal, while the rose is a simulacrum or shape. One stands for spontaneous life, the other for pattern and transformation. The interfusion of metonymy and metaphor, the real and the virtual, recapitulates Pascoli's dual regard for "things" and "ideas."

> Aspettavo da trent'anni una Pasqua
> tra i fossi, il muschio sopra i sassi,
> le viole tra le tegole, ma i morti
> dormono nelle bare di castagno,
> . . . .
> Tutto quello che io so non mi giova
> a cancellare tutto quello che ho visto.
> I fanciulli soffiano sul carbone
> perché dal piombo fiorisca
> il simulacro della rosa.[30]

Here Sinisgalli employs the attributes of the flowers—the pride and rarity of two roses, the humbleness of two violets—to describe four sisters:

> La più rara in famiglia
> Fu la rosa Nuccia,
> La più superba
> Fu Anna tra le rose.
> Nell'orto selvaggio
> Crebbero Enza e Angela viole
> Di muraglia.[31]

Sinisgalli moved to Milan from Lucania in 1932; Salvatore Quasimodo, a Sicilian, and Alfonso Gatto, from Salerno, moved there in 1934. These southerners contributed to the milieu of the New Lyricism, which stressed the "life of poetry," its ability to resist the desolation and devastation in the world at large, the mechanization and automatism of industrial society. As such they reversed what Anceschi calls the reigning "poetry of life," "a strange indolence of taste [that] still blended the murkiness of an inert and exhausted crepuscularism with desolate residues of unjustified futurist extravagances, and the stimulants of unbelievable D'Annunzian sensuality."[32] The hermetics loosened the binds of normal prose syntax (for example, by altering standard use of prepositions and articles) so as to allow for richer lateral associations and analogies. In "The Rose" by Alfonso Gatto, the variously colored and iterated flower is counterbalanced by a singular heavy, dark violet: "La rosa se l'azzurro la colora / di sé rossa nel verde alza la rosa, / rosa di macchia fulgida la rosa / rossa d'azzurro, viola d'acqua nera."[33] The Florentine hermetic poet Mario Luzi engages the rose and violet as analogies for the absent beloved:

> dal mare (una viola trafelata
> nella memoria bianca di vestigia)
> un vento desolato s'appoggiava
> ai tuoi vetri con un piuma grigia
>
> e se volevi accoglierlo una bruna
> solitudine offesa la tua mano
> premeva nei suoi limbi odorosi
> d'inattuate rose di lontano.[34]

A fellow hermetic who chose not to appear in the Anceschi volume is Libero De Libero, a solitary rustic whose intense spiritual yearning, like Luzi's, is expressed in a kind of mystical naturalism. The two flowers here contrast by their stature: the rose is greater than us, while the violet stands for our human limitations as well as our "certainty":

> C'è da vivere ancora in altro regno
> e diciamo alla rosa una preghiera
> nata stamane e la viola strappiamo
> della sera che a tradimento odora,
> la certezza d'essere ciò che vogliamo
> non muta verso al dato che decide.[35]

In the 1971 poem "I am one of you," the opposition remains temporal but is not keyed into the opposition between dawn and dusk. The rose is nonseasonal, a symbol of the illusion of eternal fertility, while the violet is seasonal and evanescent, identified with the disillusionment of verse writing itself:

> E' stata la tua presenza una fiamma
> . . . .
> un evento perenne della rosa,
> d'essere eterna l'eterna illusione.
> . . . .
> dove già marzo arricciolava azzurre
> foglie al mandorlo e versi di viole.[36]

Among the most important heirs of the new "life of poetry" is Maria Luisa Spaziani, who in a gruesome recollection of World War II summons up the violet and rose for their symbolic values of purity and ardor:

> Tempo di viole bianche, ardua scalata
> di giovinezza ai varchi dell'istante.
> Mi abbagli ancora, scaglia di diamante,
> impero incontrastato della rosa
> in cima all'erta di trifogli freschi.[37]

In the lines following this evocation of temporal violets in harmony with the wondrous and atemporal rose, one discovers that the "Hill of the Loved One" is blossoming upon a growing mound of skulls. The rhymes of lines four, seven, twelve, and seventeen (*deschi, tedeschi, freschi, teschi*) tie the alternating hendecasyllables and septenaries into a musical unit, at once a fugue of bittersweet reminiscence and a macabre elegy at a mass grave.

The following gnomic by Giorgio Bassani (1916) deals directly with the crisis of representation we have seen develop around the pairing of the rose and violet. What role can the poetic word assume in connecting human experience to natural wonders and the occasion of death? "Dove sei? Donde chiami? Soltanto nelle cose, / solo ai vinti—

agli arresi—sei presente? E le rose / per chi dagli orti umani hanno umane parole? / Solo ai morti le viole ridon spente e lontane?"[38]

Bassani's friend Attilio Bertolucci confirms the seasonal specificity of roses and violets announced by Pascoli, by means of the exception allowed by a mild winter. Indeed the rose in Bertolucci's late works is often "reflowering" when its season is apparently past.

> Quaggiù in pianura chi si ricorda d'un inverno tanto mite
> da rifiorire rose sin sotto Natale,
> spuntare viole al finire lagrimoso
> e ridente del corto febbraio? Influenze
> e malattie poche, effetto salutare
> d'un'alimentazione povera, di guerra.[39]

This passage illustrates Bertolucci's status as an "anti-narrative poet, still dense with narrative 'material'" in whom synchronic and diachronic planes of discourse are juxtaposed, yielding an exquisite lyricism within a historical context.[40]

This latter description could also be applied to Pier Paolo Pasolini, like Bassani and Bertolucci a student of art historian Roberto Longhi. Here this continuator of Pascoli uses the two flowers as metaphors for two aspects of his boyhood memory: the birth of sexuality and the sense of transcendence. The mornings are "sorrowful and perfect as roses," and the sublime northern landscape of his dreams, penetrated by an "odor of lichens," is like that of "violets at Easter," an image reinforced by the mother's Marian purity:

> tutto accade come a una passata
>
> ora del mio esistere: misteriose
> mattine di Bologna o di Casarsa,
> doloranti e perfette come rose
> . . . .
> Da bambino sognavo a questi fiati
> già freschi e intiepiditi dal sole,
> frammenti di foreste, celtiche
> quercie, tra sterpaglia e rovi di more

sfrondati, nel rossore, quasi svèlti
dall'autunno assolato—e seni
di fiumi nordici ciecamente deserti

dove pungeva l'odore dei licheni,
fresco e nudo, come di Pasqua le viole . . .
Allora la carne era senza freni.[41]

The poetry of Giovanni Testori (1923) also tends to conflate sexual and religious images. In different sections of his series *L'amore, rosa* and *viola* stand for the sex organ of his lover. In the series *Diadèmata*, which has an apocalyptic epigraph from the book of Revelation, one finds an assortment of sexual violations and aggressions, including a brother's rape and murder of his sister, an act committed as if in a trance "raccogliendo tra le dita / la putrida rosa / dello slip fraterno."[42] Testori's tortured Catholicism reminds one of the medieval mystic Jacopone da Todi, yet it is persistently denied the transcendence in God, as in this scene of the crucifixion in which the symbol of Christ's martyrdom and Mary's purity are bitterly reduced to "rotting roses":

Vermi gridano;
lividi s'aggrappano
al relitto moribondo;
sul fondo,
tra nodi di meduse
accorrono rose marce,
luci asfittiche,
narcisi.[43]

The temporal interplay of the two flowers is found in these lines by Carlo Della Corte (1930), who, on seeing violets bloom in late winter, is able to foresee the coming of roses, love, and summer.

Molt'aria, e ormai germogliano le viole;
consunto ha i suoi colori antichi e nuovi
l'inverno; foglie si aggrumano ai nodi;

> Amore, rosa rossa, lento fiume,
> predico la tua carne, il tuo silenzio,
> l'acqua grave di foglie alle tue rive[44]

Heightened awareness of sound associations was another of the attributes of the "life of poetry" passed on by the hermetics and new lyricists, so that, for example, one can imagine the *rosa-viola* dyad within a strictly alliterative network, as theorized by Saussure in *Anagrammes*. Two poets of Anceschi's 1952 anthology, *Linea lombarda*, employ the *rosa-viola* pair together as adjectives: Renzo Modesti (1920), "e già rosa viola appar la vita";[45] and Luciano Erba (1922), "in un villino dipinto di rosa. / . . . . / Uscì un bambino da una casa lunga / o bassa, che gridava 'vedo viola!' / 'sarà il Violani,' 'ma no!, è il calomelano' / tutta sera discussero i vicini."[46] It is not far-fetched to hear the violet in these lines by Luzi: "Violavano le rose l'orizzonte, / esitanti città stavano in cielo";[47] and in these written by Dario Bellezza (1944): "sulla soglia inviolata / resti solo la paura ricercata / come una rosa profumata."[48] Michelangelo Coviello (1950) repeats the flowers in series. In the following lines that open and close his sixty-one-line poem "Marabella," the rose and violet are deliberately confused in a manner typical of the experimentalism of the neo-avant-garde:

> La rosa è la viola odorosa
> non badate se sono nervosa
> la cosa non bada alla cosa
> cosí non son nulla scusate
> . . . .
> la cosa non bada alla cosa
> non badate se sono nervosa
> la rosa è la viola odorosa
> cosí non son nulla scusate[49]

In the selected co-incidences of *rosa* and *viola* we have seen the flowers complement one another's natural and seasonal differences, and accrue their opposite symbolic identities: the rose of plenitude and opulence, the violet of modesty and chastity. The timbre of these sounded flowers is melic and sweet, suitable to the themes of beauty and grace, whether in a secular or religious key. We have seen how the poets' awareness of the conventional aspects of the pairing can highlight the problem of extensive and recursive wonder and the emerging tension existing between the synchronic and diachronic planes of contemporary poetic practice.

3
LE MYSTÈRE D'UN NOM
Dans les roses le temps se joue
PAUL VALÉRY[1]

Beginning with Gérard de Nerval (1808), the status of the poet in France was undergoing a radical change. For Nerval the rose was the negative symbol of a sanctified Eros (*eros* being an anagram for *rose*), as evident in two sonnets from *Les chimères*, a sonnet-series linked by an occult network of references. In "Artèmis" these include the pagan or local Neapolitan saints Rosalie, called the "saint of the pit" or abyss because she guards the people against the imminent apocalypse, and Gudule, whose "Rose with the violet heart" evokes the chthonic stratum of the chaste figure of Artemis.

> Aimez qui vous aima du berceau dans la bière;
> Celle que j'aimai seul m'aime encor tendrement:
> C'est la Mort—ou la Morte . . . O dèlice! ô tourment!
> La rose qu'elle tient, c'est la *Rose tremière*.
>
> Saint napolitaine aux mains pleines de feux,
> Rose au coeur violet, fleur de sainte Gudule:
> As-tu trouvé ta Croix dans le désert des cieux?
>
> Roses blanches, tombez! vous insultez nos dieux,
> Tombez, fantômes blancs, de votre ciel qui brûle:
> —La sainte de l'abîme est plus sainte à mes yeux![2]

Nerval rejects the ethereal white roses of official ecclesiastical sanctity. The spiritual longing and poetic ambiguity are just as forceful in "The Disinherited One," in which the roses, growing together with the vine, are Bacchanalian and Anacreontic. The Italian landscape near Naples is autobiographical—Nerval was saved from a suicidal depression there in 1834 by an English girl named Octavie—but also mythic, forming his self-projection as Orpheus with an allusion to Vergil's supposed burial site at Posilipo, and the legendary point of Dante and Vergil's starting point on their mission to the underworld:

> Dans la nuit du tombeau, toi qui m'as consolé,
> Rends-moi le Pausilippe et la mer d'Italie,
> La fleur qui plaisait tant à mon coeur désolé,
> Et la treille où le pampre à la rose s'allie.[3]

For Nerval the poem is an occasion for mystical transcendence through art. Many Italian poets would later cull from his esoteric imagery the potent symbols for their own brand of Orphism. They would also appreciate his directness and simplicity, as evident in more melodic pieces, such as "Chanson gothique" with its message of carpe diem:

> Belle épousée
> J'aime tes pleurs!
> C'est la rosée
> Qui sied aux fleurs.
>
> Les belles choses
> N'ont qu'un printemps,
> Semons de roses
> Les pas du Temps!
>
> Soit brune ou blonde
> Faut-il choisir?
> Le Dieu du monde,
> C'est le Plaisir[4]

For Edgar Allan Poe (1809), a contemporary of Nerval, the rose was also a nexus of spiritual and erotic longing with mortuary overtones: "My tantalized spirit / Here blandly reposes, / Forgetting, or never / Regretting, its roses—/ Its old agitations / Of myrtles and roses" ("For Annie"). Or "The happy flowers and the repining trees, / Were seen no more: the very roses' odors / Died in the arms of the adoring airs" ("To Helen").

While Poe occasioned a greater awareness of the "reader's share" in the poetic process, by anticipating the "effect" and "extent" of the poem on the reader, its "length, province, and tone," with Charles Baudelaire (1821) the reader is addressed as a "hypocrite," involved with the poet in disrupting the harmony between denotation and connotation. Poetry now generates its own distinct reality based on intrinsic structures and forms, or what Swedenborg called "correspondences." One might say that objectivity no longer exists, that all language is connotative, or, as Theodor Adorno writes concerning Baudelaire, that "Art has the potential to harbour its opposite within itself. Its yearning does not diminish as a result of that, but is made to subserve that potential whose spiritualization is akin to the moment of ugliness."[5]

Thus, in placing the rose on equal footing with the worm (the inverse position from the Tommaseo poem above), Baudelaire allows its poetic form—that of the most regal of flowers—to reach its "zero degree": "Ce père nourricier, ennemi des chloroses, / Èveille dans les champs les vers comme les roses."[6] The rhymed utterance remains vivid ("les vers comme les roses"), suggesting "greens and pinks" (les *verts* comme les *roses*) lit by the sun. The likening of worm and rose reveals a proto-modernist sensibility for which the polyvalence of the poetic Word is no longer restricted to its place within a classical structure, but is absolute in its expressive moment. Baudelaire welcomes into the poem the ugly, the disgusting, and the unnatural. His rose is the product of an antithesis (such as that of "Spleen and the Ideal") in which beauty and ugliness, violence and sanctity, connote one another by negation: "Je suis un vieux boudoir plein de roses fanées, / Où gît tout un fouillis de modes surannées."[7] This leads, in the pictorial depiction of two mythic lesbians, to the rose's equivalency to their female anatomy and bond:

> "Hippolyte, cher coeur, que dis-tu de ces choses?
> Comprends-tu maintenant qu'il ne faut pas offrir
> L'holocauste sacré de tes premières roses
> Aux souffles violents qui pourraient les flétrir?"[8]

The rose occupies the unreal land of Cythera, the allegorical land of lovers, a site with respect to which the contemporary world is a negation: "Belle île aux myrtes verts, pleine de fleurs écloses, / Vénérée à jamais par toute nation, / Où les soupirs des coeurs en adoration / Roulent comme l'encens sur un jardin de roses."[9]

Paul Verlaine (1844) carries the Baudelairean rose to an irrational extreme in the direction of "spleen" over a lost love: "Les roses étaient toute rouges, / Et les lierres étaient tout noir. // Chère, pour peu que tu te bouges, / Renaissent tous mes désespoirs."[10] In the expression of religious devotion, Verlaine's symbolism reaches an acme of musical intuitionism, complete with an allusion to Petrarch's "a passi tardi e lenti":

> Oui, tu nous dictes et fais faire d'excellents
> Actes à cause de l'excellence des causes,
> épanouissant, sur les épines, des roses
> Que la Père après vient cueillir à pas lents:
>
> Pénitence . . .[11]

Stephane Mallarmé (1842) exploits the Baudelairean disjunction or duality between signifier and signifed. As a recurrent word-image in Mallarmé's verse, the rose is a figure of nonreference or purely verbal activity, of "real absence." In the prose poem "Crise de vers" (Verse crisis), the utterance "a flower" becomes for the poet "an actual and sweet idea, the one absent from all bouquets": "Je dis: une fleur! et, hors de l'oubli où ma voix relègue aucun contour, en tant que quelque chose d'autre que les calices sus, musicalement se lève, idée même et suave, l'absente de tous bouquets."[12]

In Mallarmé the idea of the abyss becomes tangible, just beyond the ephemeral barrier of the Word. "Toast funèbre," Mallarmé's funerary ode to his mentor Théophile Gautier, who is seen to have "vanished into the ideal," was considered his "most complete statement in verse on the fundamental problems that concerned him as a poet." Subsequent poets would cultivate its purity, faith, and solemnity, its implicit religion of art. In the poem the Ideal is something other than immortality, forcing the customary funeral toast to be suspended. Up until his final death throe, the "Master" Gautier is seen to "excite for the Lily and the Rose *the mystery of a name*": "Le Maître, par un oeil profond, a, sur ses pas / Apaisé de l'éden l'inquiète merveille, / Dont le dernier frisson dans sa voix seule, éveille / Pour la Rose et le Lys le mystère d'un nom."[13]

Funerary poems, eclogues, and sonnets are important formal means to honor the poet's pact with the Ideal, as seen in "L'après-midi d'un faune":

> Aimai-je un rêve?
> Mon doute, amas de nuit ancienne, s'achève
> En maint rameau subtil, qui, demeuri les vrais
> Bois mêmes, prouve, hélas! que bien seul je m'offrais
> Pour triomphe la faute idéale de roses.[14]

Like the Faun whose "faute" implies a shortcoming or error, the poet sees his poem as based on a "perfect lack" (or "fault"), a lack known only to roses. Roses in this sense are a vestige of a higher symbolic language that transcends mimetic representation: "Je les ravis, san les désenlacer, et vole / A ce massif, haï par l'ombrage frivole, / De roses tarissant tout parfum au soleil."[15] Mario Luzi recalls that his fellow hermetics considered "L'après-midi d'un faune" as an "absolute more than a germinal text" that challenged its translators (including Luzi and Ungaretti) to "capture the lighting flash of allusions in the weave and the passage of the sentences, straining not to lose in their jagged modulations anything of the evidence and the dream."[16]

Mallarmé stood for the high, cold lights of Latinity and the abstract verbal purity of the word. In translating this most difficult of symbolists, Ungaretti maintained a fast loyalty to the word and sought to replicate the network of associations planned by Mallarmé. He abandoned the idea of literally transposing the Mallarmean poem, seeking instead to preserve its verbal values. Both Luzi and Ungaretti exceed the Mallarmé revolution, as Paul Valéry had done, by developing his genial technical insights in a "theological" dimension. Luzi "radicalizes Ungaretti's insight and makes of the shipwreck both the metaphor of existence and the agony of poetry itself," accomplishing a transformation of the symbolist aesthetic by assuming a position with respect to the self in its existential unfolding that is both "prophetic" and "evangelical."[17]

The legacy of Arthur Rimbaud (1854) is often connected to his notion of a "derailment of all the senses," advocated in a letter to Paul Démeny and demonstrative of his debts to Poe and Baudelaire. In Rimbaud one witnesses a rejection of the rose as an ecclesiastic and Parnassian symbol belonging to the constituted bourgeois society and its adoption as a symbol of the spirit alive, an expanding aura. Rimbaud's rose is alternately sacred and profane, a confusion of attributes that is patently blasphemous, whether against the Church or the Parnassian poets. "O Poëtes, quand vous auriez / Les Roses, les Roses soufflées, / Rouges sur tiges de lauriers, / Et de mille octaves enflées!"[18] It is also a trope of emphasis and word play: "Ah! la poudre des saules qu'une aile secoue! / Les roses des roseaux dè longtemps dévorées!"[19] There is a bold identification of expression with communication by this poet whose goal was "a nonconceptual and a nonverbal immediacy . . . a radical simplification of consciousness through the pictorialization of consciousness."[20] In order to reconcile form and utterance in the following passage, one must traverse the "delicious" contradictions of transgressive desire between seminarist and sacristan's wife, as ensconced in the rose of "Scripture."

> "J'effeuillais cette rose poetique! Je pris ma cithare
> . . . .
> il ravalait ma poesie! il crachait sur ma rose!
> . . . .
> mais mon coeur le comprit: c'etait la Rose de David, la Rose de Jesse, la Rose mystique de l'Ecriture; c'était l'Amour!
> . . . .
> Thimothina $\left\{ \begin{array}{l} \text{Vas devotionis,} \\ \text{Rosa mystica} \ldots \end{array} \right.$

. . . .
madame la sacristaine . . . sa poitrine cave penchée en avant
. . . effeuillait delicieusement une rose . . ."[21]

Although Benedetto Croce took a stance against Rimbaud and Mallarmé, Italian poets felt otherwise. One sees their impact on such moral writers as Giovanni Boine, Scipio Slataper, Piero Jahier, Camillo Sbarbaro, and Clemente Rebora, who published in the Florentine journal *La Voce* in the 1910s, and for whom the French symbolists had effectively shown that esthetics must begin with the ethical wholeness of the person, even if the work of art was expressed in fragments. Objecting to Croce's system of intellectualist "distinctions," they defended the extension outwards of poetry into whatever areas of human endeavor—politics, ideology, violence—would confirm that wholeness and unity were the prerogative of the artist, more than the philosopher.

The tragic case of Jules Laforgue (1860), who died of tuberculosis at twenty-seven, came to be of great interest to Ungaretti and Montale, among others. Laforgue's primary themes are sexual love, the liberation of women, wonder and praise for the cosmos, and a disavowal of formal religion. He demonstrates how irony can achieve high results; his personal sorrows and regrets, due to Hamletic hesitation in affairs of the heart and later intensified by his illness, never lapse into the pathetic. Rather there is hope in the very absence of false expectations and in the praise of beauty, however imperfect and foreign to the Ideal or the Absolute. Such a philosophy of the carpe diem is advanced by means of an audacious metrical and lexical experimentation in which the rose occupies a discreet but important place. Laforgue may indeed be considered the first great poet to write in vers libre:

[Lui]
Oui; mais l'Unique Loi veut que notre serment
Soit baptisé des roses de ta croix nouvelle;
Tes yeux se font mortels, mais ton destin m'appelle
. . . .
[Lui]
        ô défaillance universelle!

> Mon unique va naître aux moissons mutuelles!
> Pour les fortes roses de l'amour
> Elle va perdre, lys pubère,
> Ses nuances si solitaires,
> Pour être, à son tour,
> Dame d'atour
> De Maïa!
>
> Alléluia![22]

The conflict between "He," a nonbeliever, and "She," faith-bound to a marriage rite, is erased by the roses of love. If in Mallarmé's "Toast funèbre" the consummate "Master" Gautier was able to elicit the "mystery of a name" from the lily and the rose, here in Laforgue the mystery is that of a nameless and unnameable deity, able to join the groom with his "lily" and dissolve the paradox of her Christian roses and the sensual roses of "Maia." In "Dialogue before the Rise of the Moon," two voices discuss the vastest of philosophical themes in twelve witty couplets (rhymed ABBA). The Absolute and Ideal are seemingly in conflict with the Void and the Infinite, while "the Possible wails for whatever lies beyond Conceiving."

The question one ponders is how verbally to describe the experience of wonder. Laforgue's answer is to trust in a natural flow, just as the rose flower responds to its parent bush. Without attempting to establish a philosophical profile of this student of Schopenhauer, Hartmann, and Buddhism, we can say that the dialogue below between unnamed voices is a sort of paean to the recursive wonder, to the rose that is "necessary to its needs":

—Etre actuel, est-ce, du moins,
Etre adéquat à Quelque Chose?

—Conséquemment, comme la rose
Est nécessaire à besoins.

—Façon de dire peu commune
Que Tout est cercles vicieux?

—Vicieux, mais Tout!
        —J'aime mieux
Donc m'en aller selon la Lune.[23]

Laforgue appreciated Rimbaud and Mallarmé, to the extent he was aware of them. He focused more than they on the dangers of aestheticism, on the representation of actuality that threatens to control it:

(Mon Moi, c'est Galathée aveuglant Pygmalion!
Impossible de modifier cette situation.)

Ainsi donc, pauvre, pâle et piètre individu
Qui ne croit à son Moi qu'à ses moments perdus,
Je vis s'effacer ma fiancée
Emportée par le cours des choses,
Telle l'épine voit s'effeuiller,
Sous prétexte de soir sa meilleure rose.[24]

This vignette would be amusing were it not for its sense of helplessness, a feeling repeated in various forms throughout Laforgue's opus. The rose petal that falls upon the "pretext" of evening, and is caught on the thorn of the poet, contains a sadness only compounded by the poet's lack of self-pity. The rhyme words *rose* and *chose* seen in the last two examples recur in the fifth (and final) quatrain of "Esthétique": "Cueillon sans espoir et sans drames, / La chair vieillit après les roses; / Oh! parcourons le plus de gammes! / Car il n'y a pas autre chose."[25] In each case, Laforgue pairs *rose* and *chose* as members of the same immanent order. This semantic leveling is typical of a materialistic sensibility, while its opposite, the Orphic or transcendent separation of the "rose" from the level of ordinary "things," was seen above in Nerval's "Chanson gothique."

If Laforgue's God has no name, and his rose remains a pregnant and open question, for Paul Claudel (1868), a follower of Mallarmé, the "mystery of a name" evoked by the rose is that of the Christian sacrament, as in his enumerations of the Virgin Mary:

Tu les abreuveras, dit le psaume, *du torrent de la volupté!* Un écroulement de toutes sortes de bénédictions sur nous pêle-mêle et nos bras ne suffisent pas à cette brassée! Mais la rose est devenue le rosaire, cette poignée de grains agglomérée qu'épelle le doigt: *Je vous salue Marie pleine de grâce!* du milieu de la main qui prie.[26]

* * *

Les roses de Jéricho!
. . . .
La double rose incertaine
Qui s'effeuille sur la cire,
La flamme comme une haleine
. . . .
Acceptez cela, Marie![27]

Claudel uses the rose as one of several symbols of the feminine, the mother, and the sea, which, by moving from the particular to the abstract, increase ambiguity. As a proper noun, the name Rosa also becomes a principle in a Christian allegory and the *rose des vents* (compass-card) comes to stand for the cardinal virtues (quaternity being a known figure of unity). In the *Cinque grandes odes,* Claudel's rose begins by standing for a circular totality, a structural wholeness, only to then pass, tragically, into the sphere of the ungraspable and fragmentary.[28] In Claudel's *A Hundred Movements for a Fan*, a series of short calligraphic poems written in Japan, the rose has a prominent place; the first of these breath-length pieces states the ontological problem of naming reality with language: "Tu / m'appelles la Rose / dit la Rose / mais si tu savais / mon vrai nom / je m' / effeuillerais aussitôt."[29] (A similar assessment is found in Giorgio Caproni: "Buttate pure via / ogni opera in versi o in prosa. / Nessuno è mai riuscito a dire / cos'è, nella sua essenza, una rosa.")[30] Claudel's pursuit of graphic-syntactic equivalents to his experience takes on a Taoist character, an effacement of the dualism of active and contemplative lives: "Cette / nuit // il a plu / du vin / Je le sais il n'y a pas / moyen d'empêcher les / roses de parler."[31]

The visionary Antonin Artaud (1896) prevails on the spatial rose—of the compass-card, the rose window, the celestial rose—with similar latitude. Here in two exquisite variations on the language of the avant-garde, the rose provides evidence, an oneiric sign of the poet's vision:

> Des vaisseaux sur la mer tendent leurs voiles rose,
> La rosace s'effeuille à l'ombre du clocher,
> Et l'on voit dans les cieux lointains se disperser
> Les pétales errants de la céleste rose.[32]

* * *

> Je rêve un soir aux calices chargés d'oiseaux
> Où la myrrhe brûlant au sein des vasques bleues
> étincelle comme un rubis; et les cheveux
> Roses du vent s'emmêlent à la chevelure des roseaux.[33]

Another Orphic poet with roots in the avant-garde who exploits the compass-card is Jean Cocteau (1889); in his serial poem "The Crucifixion," that event is painfully anatomized into its details of ladders, nails, and a body almost anonymous, like a disanimated object, a spinning weathercock or "rose of the winds." Cocteau's is the kenotic Christ, who was made man and suffered brutally.

> Il y avait les coups. Les coups
> du fer sur le fer. Le veille rose
> des vents. Les coups. La rouille
> des coups sur l'eventail en os
> des pieds. Sur la natte
> en orteils. Sur les planches.[34]

In contrast to many of the avant-garde, Cocteau's aesthetic is not aleatory, but carefully reasoned and contemplated, a fact which connects him to Baudelaire, Laforgue, Valéry, and Mallarmé, as well as to Jiménez, Machado, and Lorca.[35]

That Paul Valéry (1871) revered Mallarmé is demonstrated by his hand-written transcription on a fan of that poet's love poem to his mistress, "Evantail," where the rose is both frigid and ardent, laughing, unfolding.[36] Valéry's rose is an iconic sign in a postsymbolist continuum, as seen in the 1917 *La jeune parque* (The young fate), a poem of 512 alexandrines intensely involved in its own musical structure. Iterations and variations on similar verses are presented as directly analogous to the psychological transformations of the Fate whose monologue this is. The carefully hewn lexis concentrates on the physicality of the young woman as a living sign of her reveries and dreams, abstract thoughts and recollections, interrogations and exclamations. The music of the poem is reflected in the four instances of rose:

> Entre la rose et moi, je la vois qui s'abrite;
> Sur la poudre qui danse, elle glisse et n'irrite [ll. 145–46]
> . . . .
> La Mort veut respirer cette rose san prix
> Dont la douceur importe à sa fin ténébreuse! [ll. 217–18]
> . . . .
> Et, roses! mon soupir vous soulève, vainqueur
> Hélas! des bras si doux qui ferment la corbeille . . . [ll. 250–51]
> . . . .
> Salut! Divinités par la rose et le sel
> Et les premier jouets de la jeune lumière,
> Iles! [ll. 352–54][37]

The flower, which from the French nineteenth century through Mallarmé had symbolized idealist perfection and feminine beauty, is now situated in a space beyond the Fate's familiar reality; at first associated with her passion for unification and self-realization, it becomes a figure of death and rebirth, of the pure recursivity of music. The flower which defined her sense of disparity between the body and the shadow returns as a sign of play and exaltation. If she is at first schizophrenic in her morbid anxiety over the Other, this disturbance is also found in the culture at large as a longing for self-knowledge. Each of the four instances corresponds to a threshold the Fate confronts as she weaves through the maze of her past and learns to think speculatively. This development is crucial to the interactive, open-ended nature of a poem which reveals its debt to Mallarmé in the moment that it departs from him. In presenting the Fate's confession, revelation, and despondency in terms of the three spatial dimensions conjoined by time, Valéry endows the sequence with a philosophical relativism ambient in the Parisian culture.

The horrors of World War I are the backdrop for this valiant monument of a new kind of art, also understood as a means of reclaiming the French language threatened with extinction: "Si proche de ta joue et silente la rose / Ne va pas dissiper ce délice de plis / secrètement sensible au rayon qui s'y pose."[38] In the dreamlike "La Fileuse," the rose is a figure for the divine reverie or visitation that occurs to a woman spinning thread by her window in the sun. Throughout his opus, Valéry's sensuous rose possessed a mystery that was welcomed by those for whom poetry had become a totalizing form of expression. With his *Charmes* and *Jeune parque* Valéry left poem-monuments to the twentieth century. As an essayist he also left a fuller appreciation for the accomplishments of his mentor, Mallarmé.

If the technical novelty of Mallarmé and Valéry is musical and temporal in nature, that of the most important avant-garde poet of the age, Guillaume Apollinaire (1880), was spatial and visual. In his 1913 *affiche, Antitradition futuriste,* the names of futurist and surrealist painters and poets are listed under the much larger heading "ROSE," and under a musical score headed by the playful double entendre "MER . . . . DE . . . ." ("Sea . . . of . . . ," or "Sh . . . it . . ."), as if to be sung.[39] This list of items includes all those things (museums, philologists, pedagogues, even Baudelaire and Whitman) which Apollinaire dismisses as "merde" (shit), as compared to the list of "Roses" (members of the futurist movement). Apollinaire would transform modern poetry by replacing the metrical measure with a graphic and visual one. Commenting on Apollinaire's "Zone," one critic refers to "the O of the rose window and of God's eye."[40] In his "Visée" (Aimed), an eleven-line calligram, the lines of poetry collapse along the left side, so that the final line, "Enfant aux mains coupées parmi les roses oriflammes," is disposed vertically on the page.[41]

Apollinaire's sense of humor is coupled with his amorous and geographical expansiveness in the following lyric, concerning a woman who would not accept his entreaties and fled to America. The rose mutates playfully from a literal object to a metaphor for the woman's house to a symbol of her chastity:

> Sur la côte du Texas
> Entre Mobile et Galveston il y a
> Un grand jardin tout plein de roses
> Il content aussi une villa
> Qui est une grand rose
> . . . .
> Comme cette femme est mennonite
> Ses rosiers et ses vêtements n'ont pas de bouton
> Il en manque deux à mon veston
> La dame et moi suivon presque le même rite[42]

In the 1908 serial poem "The Betrothal," love's roses are present at the birth of poetry: "Où d'ardents bouquets rouaient / Aux yeux d'une mulâtresse qui inventait la poésie / Et les roses de l'électricité s'ouvrent encore / Dans le jardin de ma mémoire."[43]

Following in the unanimistic tradition of Apollinaire's "Zone" and Walt Whitman's *Song of Myself,* Blaise Cendrars (1887) writes long poems centered on the motif of spiritual pilgrimage. His three uses of the rose in his collected poems are iconic and onomastic in nature. In homage to Apollinaire, he cites by misciting the title of a little-known obscene poem by the master, "Julie ou J'ai prêté ma rose" (Julia, or I lent my rose), writing "Julie ou J'ai perdu la rose" (Julia, or I lost the rose). The other two uses occur in poems in which the "I" character of the Swiss-born poet says he was born in Paris on the street where *Le roman de la rose* was written, and opposite a butcher shop. Revisiting this location during a German bombardment, he sees a rose tattoo (with a sword through it) on the butcher's arm, symbolizing the moment of the poet's conception at a mythic time and place now revisited during a nighttime conflagration.

> Un peu plus haut je demande du feu à un boulanger au travail.
> J'allume un nouveau cigare et nou nous regardons en souriant.
> Il a un beau tatouage, un nom, une rose et un coeur poignardé
>
> Ce nom je le connai bien: c'est celui de ma mère.[44]

The circumspect and laconic voice of Pierre Reverdy (1889) is of considerable importance to later neo-avant-garde movements that experiment with language. Reverdy is an artisan of the perceptions, and his poetry derives from a conscious attention to contingencies and mini-epiphanies. Reverdy's editors comment, "Reverdy exists in his works as a diffuse intensity by his very refusal of a perspective that would dictate the way in which the elements of the poem or painting are to be perceived."[45] Reverdy's cubist poetics rejects earlier systems of referentiality and discursive continuity. His lateral and allusive, disjointed style has strong parallels with the work of the Italian hermetics. His avoidance of proper nouns and nouns of "color" carries over to the rose, which is absent from the work.[46]

A link between the romantic tradition and the new era of cubism is provided by Saint John Perse (1887), whose long lines explore the origins of language and civilization in a series of abbreviated verse epics. *Anabase* proposes an etiological myth that traces the birth of the city back to a primeval landscape in which the rose figured greatly as a sign of the future or of the wonder confronted by primitive humans:

> ... Eh quoi! n'est-il plus grâce au monde sous la rose sauvage?
> Il vient, de ce côté du monde, un grand mal violet sur les eaux.
> . . . .
> Et l'homme enthousiasmé d'un vin, portant son coeur farouche et bourdonnant comme un gâteau de mouches noires, se prend à dire de ces choses: ". . . Roses, pourpre délice: la terre vaste à non désir, et qui en posera les limites ce soir? . . ." Et un tel, fils d'un tel, homme pauvre,
> vient au pouvoir des signes et des songes.[47]

Perse uses the "great rose" and "giant roses" in *Chronique* as signs of civilization and time: "Lève la tête, homme du soir. La grande rose des ane tourne à front serein"; a sign elusive or irrelevant to primitive humans: "Grand â, nous voici. Nous n'avions soin de roses ni d'acanthes";

LE MYSTÈRE D'UN NOM | 49

being superior, or daunting, as in the magnificent tree of old age: "cet autre [arbre], en forêt, qui s'ouvrait à la nuit, élevant à son dieu l'ample charge ouvragée de ses roses géantes"; and finally as the emblem of humanity's accomplishments and belonging in the cosmos: "O mémoire, prends souci de tes roses de sel. La grande rose du soir héberge l'étoile sur son sein comme une cétoine dorée."[48] In the ornate yet primeval world of Perse's *Amers* (Seamarks), the rose is absent; as a token element of the heraldic or encomiastic lyric, it would seem to symbolize the absence of those to whom the poet pays homage: a pagan beauty and the Virgin Mary. This spirit of renunciation is also evident in the above texts in which the rose is present, because of its grandeur, distance from our world, and its status as relic.

A comparable sense of epic grandeur and primeval mystery is present among the surrealists, especially André Breton (1896), who embraced the onrush of oneiric metaphors and lateral associations as a means of revelation: "Elle est sans fond comme le diamant et seuls les amants. . . . sauront quelles voûtes de miroir, quelle rose de lentilles de phare en une telle nuit font corbeille étincellante à leur ivresse, pourront témoigner que c'est dans une telle nuit et seulement en elle que les élans du coeur et des sens trouvent leur réponse infini."[49]

Breton credits Lautreamont, Rimbaud, and Mallarmé for a new view of human destiny, for an aesthetic no longer obeisant to the hierarchies of the past. To arrive at the "incandescent stone of the sexual unconscious," and to comprehend the All, one must renounce customary perceptual distinctions: "On a dépassé la cime des flamboyants à travers lesquels transparaît son aile pourpre et dont les mille rosaces enchevêtrées interdisent de percevoir plus longtemps la différence qui existe entre une feuille, une fleur et une flamme."[50]

What is radically different in the surrealists, aside from their abandonment of regular verse and syntax, is the obsession with the aleatory, a concern which leads them to destroy the idea of single rationalizable, mimetic or symbolic, context. For example, Robert Desnos recycles Marcel Duchamp's transvestite sobriquet Rrose Sélavy: "Dans le sommeil de Rrose Sélavy il y a un nain sorti d'un puits qui vient manger son pain la nuit."[51] A poet such as Vicente Huidobro (1893) matures the surrealist impulse into a stochastic verbal texture involving the will in its struggle for liberation. A typical image for this change in state is that of verticality and flight, and the Mallarmean theme of shipwreck.

> Il n'y a plus d'oiseaux
> > Il n'y a plus d'oiseaux
> ....
> Et la rose s'effeuillant sur l'oiseau qui chante
> A minuit quarante
>
> Oublie-moi
> > Petit astre caché
> C'est l'heure où j'embaume ma forêt[52]

The great surrealist Paul Éluard (1895) carves out his own Orphic space in love poetry and political poetry that is highly rhythmic and accessible. With the 1934 volume *La rose publique,* the full mystery and scandal of his poetry shines through. In the words of his Italian translator, *La rose publique* constitutes the arrival, after a period of "nocturnal love," into a period of "solar love," which is the becoming "public" of the "rose."[53] Here the poet describes the urban wanderings of his "best friend," André Breton:

> Il offrait à
> Toutes les femmes
> Une rose privilégiée
> Une rose de rosée
> Pareille à l'ivresse d'avoir soif
> Il les priat humblement
> D'accepter
> Ce petit myosotis
> Une rose étincelante et ridicule
> Dans une main pensante
> Dans une main en fleur[54]

Also from this volume is this poem of erotic "red roses" celebrating a love that renounces possession, as the poet sets a higher course for his "sentimental aspiration" once the "illusions of youth" are spent:

LE MYSTÈRE D'UN NOM | 51

> Puis une femme au col de roses rouges
> De roses rouges qu'on ouvre comme des coquillages
> Qu'on brise comme des oeufs
> Qu'on brûle comme de l'alcool.
> . . . .
> Ma bienfaitrice souriante
> Belle limpide sous sa cuirasse
> Ignorante du fer de l'arbre et des roses rouges
> Moulant tous mes désirs
> . . . .
> Ses mains sont vives
> . . . .
> Des mains à tenir amoureusement un bouquet de
>   roses rouges sans épines[55]

The following lines concern the bombing of Guernica during the Spanish Civil War: "Les femmes les enfants ont les mêmes roses rouges / Dans les yeux / Chacun montre son sang."[56] With the devastation of World War II, we will also see the destruction of the high and noble flower: "Dehors la terre se dégrade / Dehors la tanière des morts / S'écroule et glisse dans la boue // Une rose écorcheie bleuit."[57] Éluard will remain active politically his entire life. The following late poem marks a moment of peace in a collection entitled "Greece, My Rose of Reason," where the rose stands for a young woman's beauty: "Rose à sous les yeux / Sous l'abat-jour de ses doigts // Rose à finir sous les lèvres / En silence sous les lèvres / Du plus grand plaisir connu."[58]

A friend and associate of the major surrealists, Francis Ponge (1899) creates a road of his own and a new "poetics of things" which resembles, in its wit and scientific flair, the work of Leonardo Sinisgalli (discussed in Chapter 10). Ponge creates dense linguistic constructions that permit human qualities to emerge in objects: "rather than having the line [of poetry] depend on the mind," he writes, "I make the mind depend on the line. . . . [I]nstead of projecting the mind onto things, I try to have it so that things exist first of all, and that, only thereafter, one looks at them, but one looks at them with the intention of changing one's mind, and altering old clichés."[59]

> Le bourgeon muqueux des fraises rougeoie sous les feuilles basses.
> Collons-y les "roses" (débris cristallins) du sucre . . .
> Le trè du pédoncule tire avec lui, et sort de la fraise, un petit pain de sucre relativement insipide.
> Bêtes, allez sur la friase qui je vous ai découverte![60]

The notion of the rose as a crystalline configuration, but also as a "loaf" baked in nature's oven and discovered by the poet, has openly sexual connotations: "Les roses sont enfin comme choses au four. Le feu d'en haut les aspire, aspire la chose qui se dirige alors vers lui (voyez les soufflés) . . . veut se coller à lui; mais elle ne peut aller plus loin qu'un certain endroit: alors elle entrouvere les lèvrres et lui envoie ses parties gazeuses, qui s'enflamment."[61] By perceiving the feelings intrinsic in objects, the poet adopts a constructivist position that delights in the topology of the rose, its substance as exterior "robes" and interior marrow, the "cuisse" of the flesh, relating backwards in the tradition to the rose's personification in medieval allegories.

The surrealist René Char (1907) uses the rose in two of his earliest poems, placing it in the titles and conclusion, as he will continue to do throughout his career:

> Oeil en transe en miroir muet
> Comme je m'approche je m'éloigne
> Bouée au créneau
>
> Tête contre tête tout oublier
> Jusqu'au coup d'épaule en plein coeur
> La rose violente
> Des amants nuls et transcendants.[62]

* * *

> étoile rose et rose blanche
> ô caraesses savantes, ô lèvres inutiles![63]

Char is a poet of passion and catalysis, of "warm thinking": "La poésie est de toutes les eaux claires celle qui s'attarde le moins au reflets de

LE MYSTÈRE D'UN NOM | 53

ses ponts. / Poésie, la vie future à l'intérieur de l'homme requalifié. // Une rose pour qu'il pleuve. Au terme d'innobrables années, c'est ton souhait."[64]

In his posthumously published "In Praise of One Suspected," Char again concludes a poem with the rose: "Rose au nombre confondu où prédominaient vieillards et enfants, sur cette base incertaine la joute a pris fin. Effeuillaison de la rose. Dissipation de l'étoile."[65]

Char's use of the rose hovers around the themes of separation, death, and the "fundamental assymetry of love," in the words of Starobinski, who considers "Le bois de l'epte"—"'two wild rosebushes,' 'sprung from the corner wall of a ruin left long ago by fire'"—an allegory for the persistent risk, duality, and solitude of love. With respect to "Le jugement d'octobre," Starobinski writes, "In fact, the true couple is not the one the rose forms with her too similar sister, but the one she forms with the mortal cold and the imminent night": "Une nuit, le jour bas, tout le risque, deux roses, / Comme la flamme sous l'abri, joue contre joue avec qui la tue."[66]

Yves Bonnefoy (1923) has employed the rose only four times. As a poet of the image, he eschews all forms of litany, liturgy, and oratory; his temple is in the day-to-day, a generic yet intimate garden of the commonplace cultivated for its modest splendor: "Ici, et jusqu'au soir. La rose d'ombres / Tournera sur les murs. La rose d'heures / Défleurira sans bruit. Les dalles claires / Mèneront à leur gré ces pas épris du jour."[67] The pronounced caesuras slow the pace of lines in which the "rose of shadows" and the "rose of hours" interpenetrate. The lush alliterative texture creates an air of beauty in a poetry that comes as close as possible to being a self-regulating recursive system; in the following lines the rose flows as eddying water and is fixed as the immobile hub of the wheel. As a pure perceptual form it oscillates between the verbs of gathering and emptying: "Mais, tard, l'inespéré, soudain: que tout cela / La rose de l'eau qui passe le recueille / En se creusant ici, puis l'illumine / Au moyeu immobile de la roue."[68] One is reminded by this rose of transformations of the ascesis prominent in Claudel and his Italian translator, Piero Jahier, and of the shifting planes of reference and sudden illuminations of Pierre Reverdy, or the pure rose of the mind posited by Pound.

In general, we can conclude that French poets, particularly those born in the twentieth century, make far less use of the rose than the Italians. It is perhaps not coincidental that poets like Montale and Ungaretti, deeply involved in French culture, shy away from the rose. It must also be said that, while Italian poets have always read the French with interest, there has remained a lively and staunch resistance—from Alfieri to Leopardi to Palazzeschi to the present day—to any sort of literary colonization.

4
GOZZANO AND HIS CONTEMPORARIES
*Hay unas rosas que parecen
haberse herido con sus propias
espinas.*
Ramón Gómez de la Serna[1]

The greatest poet active in the years before World War I was the Torinese Guido Gozzano (1883). A benefactor of the lessons of Pascoli and D'Annunzio, he soon broke free of any emulation of them. His descriptive narrative poems are complemented by his restoration of traditional versification, the lack of self-pity of his characters, and the irony and wit of his adaptations of earlier forms of rhyme and meter. To better understand this early "postmodern," I will first discuss his times and the poetry of his contemporaries.[2]

Massimo Bontempelli describes the first fifteen years of the century as a time when authors shed a false and outmoded notion of the classical that lacked spirituality: "One can say that the years from the beginning of the century up to the war were used by literary Italy to disown itself of those prejudices, to cast down the dominion of classicalist literature, to rediscover its true tradition: that is, spontaneity, freedom, the interest in things, commitment."[3]

In a less optimistic light, Cristina Benussi writes, "The culture of the first fifteen years of the 20th century had been characterized by an antipositivistic wave which assumed different shadings, and thus gave rise to quite varied ideological and political positions: irrationalism, relativism, idealism, vitalism, nationalism—attitudes all given vent in the adherence to the war, which had put into circulation some highly ambiguous key-words, all open to diverse interpretations. Spirit, Soul, Life, Action, Nation."[4]

It is in reference to the poets of this era that the anti-Crocean critic G. A. Borgese in 1910 coined the term *crepuscolarismo* to describe the shared sense of living and working in a historical-biographical "twilight" by poets who struck a lugubrious chord in their attraction to the grayness of pathetic or morbid settings. A typical example is Sergio Corazzini (1886), whose use of *rosa* (the noun appears thirty-eight times in his opus, all but four in the plural) is obsessive and self-effacing in tone. His roses are figures of brevity, fleeting youth, and the futility of aspiration:

> volli portare due ceri
> nuovi, due ceri bianchi come mai
>
> e due rose—ho i miei piccoli rosai
> anch'io—due rose bianche come i ceri
> sembravano fiorite in monasteri
> chiuse, le rose, in languidi rosai.
> . . . .
> La Madonna, un po' triste fra le rose,
> disse: Che vale tua dolce esultanza
> s'io per dolore sempre mi consumo?
> . . . .
> Le rose giovinette, ne la pia
> solennità, esalarono la breve
> anima; oh gli atti e le preghiere vane![5]

Like Corazzini, Corrado Govoni (1884) was a prolific experimentalist. In his sonnet "Profane Roses," the plural noun occurs eleven times, almost as a mantra of nonmeaning:

> Eruzione di rose nei giardini,
> di rive sanguinose ed odorose,
> vive e rampanti per la mia ringhiera.

Rose e rose ne i miei vasi murrini
rose odorose, rose sanguinose
rosee bocche della primavera![6]

Govoni's work reflects the variety of his generation, born in the 1880s and destined to include *crepuscolari* and futurists, surrealists and hermetics. His tendency to construct poems from lists of nominal phrases is exemplified by "Le dolcezze," in which each line is a single sentence, as if to reflect in its syntax the pathetic sense of isolation of the poet: "I crepuscoli di sangue che muoion sulle mura. / Le rose sfogliate sul letto dei malati. / Suonare il pianoforte un giorno di festa."[7] As the era of decadentism drew to a close, elements of the new literature included oneiric and ironic approaches to the precious symbols of the past: "Sotto, il mare che sogna: un'allucinante distesa di stelle cadute, / di liquide perle malate, di pallide rose svenute. / Nello smeraldo dell'erba, come un'oscena reliquia, tutti quei rosolacci / urlano e sanguinano come risate e schiaffi di imbellettati pagliacci."[8]

Amelia Guglielminetti (1881), Gozzano's intimate friend, received critical acclaim for her second book of poems, *Vergini folli*, in 1907. She succeeded in producing a series of floral and luxurious, or "Liberty-style," works in various genres, typically involving an androgynous and willful virago figure engaged in a sensuous existence at the margins of the socially acceptable. She did so with great poetic craft: "Guglielminetti's immodesty is rigidly modest."[9] In the following vignette, from *L'insonne,* a book written in a modified sonnet form with *rimalmezzo,* the poet and a young male companion visit ruins, where he is less concerned by the fallen monuments than he is smitten by the lady: "Più che il triplice stelo di Castore e di Polluce, / ti piacque l'ardua luce de' suoi occhi dietro il suo velo. / E su le vecchie cose il giovine amore risorse, / come rinascon forse sui chiusi sepolcri le rose."[10]

In the subsequent book, *Le seduzioni,* written entirely in poems of thirteen rhymed hendecasyllables, *rosa* appears quite frequently, almost always in rhyme, as an emblem of the erotically mobile and exquisite experience of a newly cosmopolitan woman:

> Una voce nell'ombra ha qualche volta
> la morbidezza calda d'una cosa
> tangibile. Non s'ode, non s'ascolta,
> ma sul cuor che l'accoglie quasi posa
> le sue parole ad una ad una, come,
> quando langue, le sue foglie una rosa.[11]

Breaking other barriers was the futurist F. T. Marinetti (1876), whose collages of nouns on the open page were unhindered by questions of syntax. Within such a nominal clustering, the rose stands out as a trace of the lyric tradition the futurists had abandoned:

> monoplano = balcone rosa ruota tamburo
> trapano tafano > disfatta-araba bue sanguinolenza
> macello ferite rifugio oasi umidità ventaglio fre-
> schezza[12]

The Cortonese painter Gino Severini (1883), included among the futurist pantheon in Apollinaire's "Antitradition futuriste" (cited in chapter 3), writes a prose poem in French, imitating that *affiche*. In it he scorns the icons of the past, including trees, fields, animals, all paired with the term "merde," while he praises the new wonders of technology, electricity, and speed, placed under the graphic sign of "rose."[13] While generally the futurists' rose is separated from other manifestations of nature, standing as an extreme of non-naturalistic representation, in Luciano Folgore (1888), the rose intervenes in the artistic process here in a portrait of a caricaturist who is led to put down his pen when the rose leafs through his drawings:

> "Sfoglia i suoi brevi quaderni
> d'odore, la rosa.
> . . . .
> L'alba
> chiara,
> con la fontana di luce
> spruzza di rose

l'impero della porcellana.
Chiude il volume Tan-Fu:
non designa più"[14]

Futurist Ardengo Soffici (1879) addresses himself to Apollinaire by way of copying an altered citation from "Zone" ("La cétoine qui dort dans le coeur de la rose"): "Sono in un centro, come l'ape *au coeur d'une rose*."[15] Replacing the devouring cetonian beetle with a bee, Soffici erases the destructive force of the original, in comparison to whose spiritual vortex the imitation focuses on the artist's self-conception. While adopting Apollinaire's idea of spatio-temporal spontaneity, Soffici's is more blunt and telegraphic: "Tutto si paga con 24 ore di giovinezza al giorno / Atelier ateliers / Rose dei venti / Gioia bellezza miserie."[16]

Aldo Palazzeschi (1885), a friend of Soffici's, shares his sense of ironic self-complacency. Unlike the poets of *La Voce*, who also reject the sentimentalism of the *crepuscolari*, Palazzeschi makes no attempt to preserve the exquisite lyric. In "I fiori" the rose is a prostitute in a garden of pimps, incestuous families, pederasts, and masturbators: "'Ma tu chi sei? Che fai?' . . . 'Sono una rosa e faccio la prostituta.'"[17] One critic has traced the poet's numerous borrowings from D'Annunzio in his development of a "homosexual" style in which the rose is an allegory of carnal love.[18] Palazzeschi's humors are not frivolous but constitute an authentic expression of the linguistic and ontological tension extant prior to World War I, a conflict he opposed, unlike the futurists whose movement he soon left. One senses the tragedy of the war in "The Two Roses," a portrait of a sleeping soldier burning with sorrow and dread:

> Povero militare,
> che ti stringi forte alle tempie
> la rosa bianca del guanciale,
> per acchetar l'ardore
> di quella rossa,
> nascosta,
> che ti fa bruciare.
> Chi t'ha fatto male?[19]

Although the impact of surrealism on Italian poetry was limited, it did influence such figures as Massimo Bontempelli (1878) and Vincenzo Cardarelli (1887). The former, a friend of Gozzano's who founded the review *Il Novecento,* rejected decadentism and came to be identified with the emerging neoclassicism. In the volubility and uncertainty of his poetry one cannot escape the psychological impact of the war: "Verrà un'estate di rose? / Chiedi il futuro domani al cerchio lontano / delle montagne violastre che leticano di fumi ed echi tra loro."[20] The poem "Omaggio" ambiguously combines erotic and military imagery, beginning with an extended chiasmus (*divetta / rose / sibili / sibilo / rosa / divetta*) to which it returns in conclusion (*rose / divetta / sibili*), and in which machine-gun fire provides a garland of roses for the diva to cast about her bare torso, a "frenetic" emblem of the hysteria of war:

> Vengo, *divetta*—dal monte
> scendo a portarti le *rose*
> colte sui *sibili*
> che mi rasentano il collo e scivolano.
> Ogni *sibilo* di mitragliatrice
> fiorisce in cima una *rosa* per te
> *divetta.*
> . . . .
> E porto un fascio di *rose* frenetiche
> alla mia bella *divetta*
> che balla colle poppe nude
> lanciandosi intorno alla chioma
> un arabesco rapido
> di *sibili* pallidi di mitragliatrice.[21]

The merit and novelty of Cardarelli's highly wrought verse lies in his rhetorical mastery and in the "positivity of his figures of women, seasons, encounters."[22] Here the figure of a virgin, who has captivated the poet's attention, "sleeps like a rose." In her lack of consciousness she is the opposite of an angel: "Nulla d'angelico era in te che dormivi / senza sogni, senz'anima, / come dorme una rosa."[23] Cardarelli tends to describe static, atemporal relationships in vague funereal settings.

In "To Omar Khayyam," it is not man who seeks to propitiate the divinity, but a god who propitiates man, who in this deceit of roses ignores his own mortality:

Il dio che ti propiziava
questa bevanda d'inganni
faceva la tua fortuna
e il tuo canto.
E tu libavi alle rose
del tuo ridente sepolcro,
non sospettando, o impavido,
che la tua vita era già
un cimitero fiorito.[24]

In the expressionist Clemente Rebora (1885), one finds the opposite extreme from the formalism of Cardarelli, *La Ronda,* and *Il Novecento.* The Milanese poet discovers in the violence of the epoch something propitious, though what remains to be saved is a single rose:

"Èra avventizia
che strozzi il costume
. . . .
Oltre la patria e la terra
c'è da salvare qualcosa,
anche solo una rosa
da tanta guerra sbocciata."[25]

Rebora realizes, in the words of Wallace Stevens, that "The nobility of poetry is a violence from within that protects us from a violence without."[26] He rejects placid artifice and engages the rose as an emblem of vulnerability and permanence amid the upheavals of war. The poetic fragment remains for Rebora and the *vociani* the most cogent means to respond to the great ferment and turbulence of the historical period. In the following passage, which appeared in *La Voce* in 1913, Rebora employs the rose to enhance the apples on a fruit stand, whose appearance does not match their taste.

> E io mi schìccolo i raspi
> E la gola beata riceve
> Il frutto che spàppola e cola . . .
> —Pere spadone! Mele della rosa!—
> A guardare m'inganno la gioia,
> Il sapore non trova più il gusto . . .[27]

If Cardarelli reifies the rose as a reminiscence of the classical, in Rebora the disjuncture between names and things is a given. Modern custom is a fledgling "strangled" by the epoch and sold to destiny. The rose is a commonplace flower that is only made precious by the prospect of disintegration. In his "Poetry, in the lucid verse," a kind of free-verse dithyramb addressed to "poetry of dung and flowers," blasphemies and imprecations coexist with praise and wonder:

> "ma sei la certezza
> del grande destino,
> o poesia di sterco e di fiori,
> terror della vita, presenza di Dio,
> o morta e rinata
> cittadina del mondo catenata!"[28]

Cardarelli's focus on a "cosmos of extension" has switched in Rebora to a focus on the "cosmos of culture," a profound awareness of humanity's creations and its limitations when confronted by the unfathomability of the Creator. There exists in Rebora a poetic logic which designates the knowable as something circumscribed by worldly human activities and production. As in Vico, poetry is understood as a cognitive mode and path to self-knowledge. Written after his taking of vows in 1936, Rebora's final use of *rosa* was as a symbol of the resurrected Christ: "Bocciòlo di rosa reciso! / Ma ecco nell'acqua si schiude: / l'effluvio si effonde: il sorriso / dei petali casto si indora."[29]

The Giulian poet Scipio Slataper (1888) died in battle in 1915. His prose work *Il mio Carso* is an elegiac evocation of the Carso region around Trieste. Slataper understands poetry as a respite from the solitude which menaces even more acutely when one is surrounded by the fecundity of nature. We find the same sense of fatalism as in another tragic figure of the epoch, Carlo Michelstaedter (discussed in chapter 5). In the only poem of *Il mio Carso,* Slataper invokes a "beautiful" and "unknown creature" who arrives bearing erotic "roses swollen with dew":

> Cose fresche! Rose
> gonfie di rugiada
> erba su d'un rivo.
> Ah se potessi
> baciare la tua bocca![30]

Let us now return to Gozzano, whom Eugenio Montale would call "the first poet who sent off sparks by clashing the prosaic against the aulic" and "the last of our classics."[31] For Gozzano the rose is one thing in a "poetics of things"; this passion, in fact, lifts him above the status of being merely a "crepuscular" poet. Interestingly, in "The More Fit" the sickly poet's healthy brother is designated as the rightful family heir of "the roses, the goods": "A lui vada la vita! A lui le rose, i beni, / le donne ed i piaceri! Madre Natura è giusto."[32] The rose can be found as a prop in a bourgeois sitting room, as a decoration on a woman's garment, or as a sign of chivalry in the book she is reading:

> E sul divano è un guanto che rimosse
> forse da poco la Donna del Convito,
> ed un mazzo sfasciato ed avvizzito
>   di rose rosse.[33]

* * *

> (avea il volume incisioni rare
> dove il bel paggio con la mano manca
> alla donna offeria la rosa bianca
> e s'inchinava in atto d'adorare).
> . . . .
> Oh tutto ella ricorda: le turchine
> rose trapunte della bianca veste,
> la veste bianca in seta, e la celeste
> fascia che le gonfiava il crinoline.[34]

In "L'assenza," the adolescent "I" figure, whose mother is absent, finds himself "astonished." Even the flowers "seem strange" to him, yet he is consoled by the geraniums and roses: "Stupito di che? Delle cose. / I fiori mi paiono strani: / ci sono pur sempre le rose, / ci sono pur sempre i gerani . . ."[35] In "Laus Matris," the praise of the mother as rose is regal: "Eretta sullo stelo / o Rosa adamantina / invitta a la ruina, / invitta a lo sfacelo."[36] In his better-known poems ("Le due strade," "L'amica di Nonna Speranza"), Gozzano expresses nostalgia for the maternal figure: "Ha diciassett'anni la Nonna! Carlotta quasi lo stesso: / da poco hanno avuto il permesso d'aggiungere un cerchio alla gonna, / il cerchio ampissimo increspa la gonna a rose turchine."[37]

A recent critic has traced the irony of Gozzano's contemporary, Pitigrilli, to that found in "L'amica di Nonna Speranza": "Tra l'abito che m'ha un po' *bouleversée* / e l'acre odor di questa rosa *théa* / oggi mi sento un po' di cefalea; / *je crains que ce soir je ne pourrai danser.*"[38] But Gozzano is not content with the mere vignette; beneath the mise-en-scène lies a rigorous thinker, as seen in the sonnet "To a Demagogue," which seems directed against D'Annunzio's public praise of war and interventionism: "E tu non mi perdoni se m'indugio, / poiché di rose non si fanno spade / per la lotta dei tuoi sogni vermigli . . ."[39]

Norberto Bobbio has compared Gozzano to Piero Gobetti, the Turinese intellectual and martyr to fascism, because of his "aridity" and "detachment": this is a means "to raise between himself and others a barrier of protection . . . an expedient to maintain self-control despite the daily clash with a reality that rebels and will destroy us."[40] Gozzano also stood as an example of Montale's affirmation that Italian poets of his generation needed to "go through D'Annunzio."[41] That he accomplished this task is evident in the literality of the botanical-biological cornucopia he presents:

> E l'uve moscate più bionde dell'oro vecchio; le fresche
> susine claudie, le pesche fialle a metà rubiconde,
> l'enormi pere mostruose, le bianche amandorle, i fichi
> incisi dai beccafichi, le mele che sanno di rose
> emanerebbero, amici, un tale aroma che il cuore
> ricorderebbe il vigore dei nostri vent'anni felici.[42]

In Gozzano's didactic series, "Le farfalle," the rose is a figurative foil to the butterflies, here in the historical setting of a literary Arcadia in which the "shepherdess" butterfly is also an academy poetess: "L'orobia pastorella impallidiva / sotto le fresche rose del belletto / meravigliando";[43] and here as a decoration on the poet's desk: "penetrò nella mia stanza tranquilla / la Macroglossa rapida. L'illuse / questa banda di sole, questa rosa / vermiglia che rallegra le mie carte."[44] In the evident contrast to Leopardi's "sudate carte," "this vermillion rose that gladdens my papers" is an object of emotional candor and wit typical of Gozzano's "poetry of things."[45]

There is in the scientific concreteness of "Le farfalle," and in the fascination expressed for insects and butterflies, an intensive and recursive wonder that confirms Gozzano's sense of discretion and self-limitation. He stands to demonstrate the assimilation by his generation of the romanticism, the scientific growth, and the growth in technology that one philosopher has listed as the three main accomplishments of the nineteenth century.[46] What was stated above for Clemente Rebora can be repeated for the arid evasions of Gozzano. His poetry is an internal violence used against the external violence of the world: "It is the imagination pressing back against the pressure of reality."

5
THE PATHETIC AND MANNERIST ROSE

Gather ye rosebuds while ye may,
Old Time is still a-flying:
And this same flower that smiles today,
To-morrow will be dying.
ROBERT HERRICK, "TO THE VIRGINS, TO MAKE MUCH OF TIME"

Illness is a theme often accompanied in the Novecento by the theme of play. In the compresence of play and illness, or what I call the patholudic, one appreciates the perennial injunction of the Horatian carpe diem. As seen in nineteenth-century France, the poet lost his institutional approval and entered into the wretchedness of the flowers of evil. Strongly influenced by Baudelaire, Mallarmé shifted the emphasis from the pathological to the patholudic, so that his final poem, "Un coup de dés," is a meditation on the poet-helmsman's navigation in the cosmic sea of the page and of the universe, of destiny and chance. The "Mallarmé revolution," with its respect for strange and beautiful combinations of words, including the language of the chronicle, featured a cultivation of language in the directions of music and metaphysics. Rimbaud too reflects this sea-change in sensibilities. Generally speaking, the artist became a figure of the transitory and ephemeral, alienated from the immutable or eternal, as from the official life of the nation. In the Italy of the 1880s a bohemian movement had taken root:

> [T]he Milanese *scapigliatura* . . . revealed a collective condition
> of displacement and isolation from the structure of organized

society. Having traded commitment to a channel of mobility that ended in a secure (with respect to the true goals of the risorgimento) patronage for a commitment to succeed "in the real world" (i.e., to establish a genuinely active link between artistic development and social change), the intellectuals then found themselves excluded from the possibility of achieving the status they felt they deserved, as moral and spiritual guide for the nation they were working for.[1]

Such a "displacement" of poets is frequently registered in the patholudic style. As poets took greater liberties with the social content of their art, they looked back to such masters of the patholudic as Torquato Tasso, whose portrayal of the rose and parrot was an exquisite return to the Dantean lyricism of "Tre donne intorno al cor mi son venute." Tasso begins the epic octave with a reminiscence of a sonnet by Giovanni Della Casa, then places the Dantean source rose in the mouth of a parrot, next to an erotic image from Catullus:

> Così trapassa al trapassar d'un giorno
> de la vita mortale il fiore e 'l verde;
> né perché faccia indietro april ritorno,
> si rinfiora ella mai, né si rinverde.
> Cogliam la rosa in su 'l mattino adorno
> di questo dì, che tosto il seren perde;
> cogliamo d'amor la rosa: amiamo or quando
> esser si puote riamato amando.[2]

Tasso's mannerism was well suited to the climate of decadentism, which culled from it, Mario Praz comments, an "insistence on the beauty of martyrdom for the Faith, and of dark and bloody paintings looming over the altars; it is significant that Tasso's poetry touches some of its highest points in depictions where beauty and death are interwoven."[3] In many respects the decadent and crepuscular attention to illness and the carpe diem was a recognition that Italian literature itself was diseased. As Pascoli writes, "[I]n Italy pseudo-poetry is wanted, is demanded and enjoined. In Italy we are victims of literary history!"[4] Pascoli's figure of the *fanciullino,* of the child who survives in the true poet, is often tragic and pathetic, as when he lies in a funeral bed of roses:

"E per letto di morte.
che a tutti è sí grave,
che cosa ti serbo, sai tu?
Oh! rose per letto di morte,
cadute dal pruno: il soave
dolore che fu!"[5]

An early example of the patholudic rose is found in the Roman crepuscular, Fausto Maria Martini (1866), in the following portrait of a schoolgirl's anxiety when she puts on her first revealing dress, beneath which lies her "flower of evil":

La educanda ha sete
di fantasie con ombra di peccato.
Non hai paura? Avanzati! È sbocciato
un fior del male e la tua mano lambe
il morbido velluto delle gambe,

e sale tremebonda, e giunge dove
fiorirono sul petto le due nuove

rose . . . Nuove! Oh! son già tre primavere,
né sanno l'appassire delle sere
quei boccioli socchiusi: ora, li guardi . . .
Ti guardano essi! Son rose o cardi?[6]

The playfulness of this piece barely conceals the fear of sin. As Mengaldo writes on the topic, "the absolutizing of play and the sense of shame over poetry, are complementary attitudes."[7]

In 1901, Enrico Thovez (1869) publishes samples of a rose in transition between the floral abandon of symbolism and the repressed air of crepuscularism: "Cumuli d'oro, di rame, soffici moli di neve, / torri di rosa, baluardi, abissi vertiginosi!"[8] And another example: "Oh premer corpi flessuosi! cercar le forme dei seni, / lisciar carni di rosa, morder con bocche anelanti, / ghermir con avide mani, stordirsi sino alla morte!"[9] Thovez is well known as a critic, a defender of Pascoli, and a serious critic of Croce. In his poetry one sees the verbal density and allusivity of symbolism yield to more open rhythms, a freer use of rhyme, and a more concrete grounding in the immediate material culture. The pathetic dimension of the crepusculars and the ponderous ludism of the futurists derive from a common historical situation. In the saltimbanques and clowns of their melancholy fantasies one sees the accentuation of the rose's fading, its tragedy and gaiety, but also its aridity.

Futurist Paolo Buzzi forged a "symphonic" and expansive poetry in which the rose is an emblem of meditative solace and carnal excess, humor, and illness, as in "And the Convalescences":

> Il puro lavacro dei sensi,
> l'aria più tersa nel profondo, l'aurora
> d'ogni ora, il fiume delle rose
> cascante in cascata d'effluvî
> sulla novissima carne del mio andare.[10]

In "The Panic Weeping," one sees a new lexical daring, a sense of the absurd paired with grace, a sense of melody amidst disintegration, of high values amidst great loss:

> Non trovo più i miei cavoli e le rose
> di Maria, nel cosmico traslato
>
> che scorpora—le nuvola e le cose—
> in un caos disforme di vapori . . .
> E le campane piangono: e le spose . . .[11]

The trite rhyme of *rose / cose* (frequent of Gozzano) is common to Buzzi, for whom the lofty and the lowly were interdependent: "La casa è bella, piena d'alte cose. / Le memorie lucenti nei ritratti, / profumate più dell'alpestri rose."[12]

The popular Ada Negri (1870) adopted the lavish style of d'Annunzian symbolism, fusing it with a melancholy sense of foreboding: "Malinconia dei primi / solchi di ruga, oh, lievi, che al sorriso / danno una tenue grazia d'appassita / rosa, e allo sguardo il tuo mistero, o vita

...! / .... / O amore, o folle amore di giovinezza, o efèbo incoronato di rose ..."[13] Another example occurs in her "Rose rosse": "Purpuree sono, e tragiche / come divelti cuori. / .... / —O rose, tragiche come divelti cuori!"[14] Negri's rose is poised *this* side of a hoped for liberation: "her Franciscanism seems like a flower of begging." The act of supplication seems to overtake the object of the request: "Fanciulli dell'Isola, in grazia, cercate per strade, per boschi, per campi / colui che dall'alto del muro mi gettò tre rose vermiglie: / conducetelo a me, ch'io lo veda, e gli dica ch'egli è mio fratello: / e mangi con lui pane intriso di sole, e beva acqua di libertà."[15] As a fixture in this process, Negri's rose is "serial" in nature, rife with Petrarchist conventions: "i tuoi occhi hanno fra i cigli / un sogno d'alba che per vie di cielo / salga, spargendo rose senza stelo / frammiste a nivei calici di gigli."[16] It is a discursive type, as when a girl holds the "rose of her destiny" in her hand, or another brings from the garden a vermillion rose conceived to be the "rose of her destiny":

né so se sbocci dal suo cuor la rosa
o pur se dalla rosa ella fiorisca.

Da questa soglia non si partirà
la sua vibrante immagine: su questa
soglia per sempre io la vedrò, più chiara
del sole; in mano reggerà la rosa
del suo destino, rossa come il sangue[17]

This fact of "seriality" tends to "abolish relativity" (as Mengaldo has alleged for D'Annunzio).[18] After diva Eleonora Duse visited her house, Negri wrote a letter exulting in the "miracle of the roses" she had brought; Duse is endowed with prophetic powers: "Cara grande Anima, ieri avete benedetta la mia casa con la vostra presenza, e dopo di voi rimase il miracolo delle rose, che ora sono tutte sbocciate."[19] Negri's roses are always stereotypes in this sense, whether they be the "dead" roses of her native Lodi—"i tristi luoghi ruinanti in pace / ove sol parla il soffio de le cose, / dei sogni morti e de le morte rose, / e tutto il resto tace"[20]—or the sign of a mother's joy despite her child's indifference: "ed io ti direi le gioiose / parole che tutte bisbigliano / le madri ai bambini, cogliendoti // a fasci le rose. / Ma tu non volesti."[21] Here, in a moment of wordplay, the bunches, *fasci*, call to mind the baby's diapers, *fasce*. The darker side of Negri's sensibility is always implicit, as in the following setting, a sort of inverted bower of bliss:

> ove roseti carichi di thee
> bisbigliano coi pioppi de le allee,
> . . . .
> Forse . . .—ah, m'inganno. Ché un fischiar di serpi
> m'accoglierà, sol che il cancello io schiuda:
> per sùbita malia selvaggia e cruda
> vedrò le rose trasmutarsi in sterpi.[22]

Among the signs of illness (snarls, recesses of tangled brush), a wall of roses against a locked door provides an image of willful enclosure and amorous imprisonment.

> Contro la porta chiusa, grovigli di rose canine:
> . . . .
> C'è un muro di rose contro la
> porta. La chiave è perduta.
> Se quella porta s'aprisse, con la tua
> ombra là dentro sostare vorrei;
> . . . .
> barricherei la porta, col mio
> amore cangiato in rosaio, per non
> lasciarti partire.[23]

In a children's rhyme the roses are a reward given for the recovery of a child lost in the night. They mirror in microcosm the fallen stars of the Bear (Ursa Major), transformed into fishing boats and sent out to look for the child ("orsa" being an anagram of "rosa"):

> "Sette fiammelle dell'Orsa, che andate a cercare?"
> "Donna, cerchiamo un fanciullo perduto nel mare . . ."
> . . . .
> "Se quel fanciullo trovate per cale o per grotte
> vi darò tutte le rose sbocciate stanotte: . . ."

....
Sette fiammelle di barche che vanno a pescare:
l'Orsa Maggiore è caduta, è caduta nel mare.[24]

For Negri the rose can symbolize the transcendent divinity ("Scoperta arderà in mezzo al fronte l'ampia stimmate sanguinosa: / corona di re consacrato, fiamma eterna, divina rosa") or be immanent, the literal rose she holds in prayer ("né so qual sia, Signore, / il tuo più bello e raggiante volto: / se la celeste rosa, o questo fiore").[25] Negri's rose conforms to the expectations of that sentimental literature largely written by and for women. It also follows a trajectory similar to that of D'Annunzio, like her a practitioner of onomancy or word-augury. As Giulio Bollati writes, "For future literary generations D'Annunzianism will stand as the model of what *not* to be, in life and in art."[26] Just as D'Annunzio, in his aggressive "Sadian" sensuality, rapidly lost his appeal to younger poets, so too did readers drift away from Negri.[27]

If in Govoni, Gozzano, and Corazzini the "figure of the poet" was one of contradiction, a clown or a sickly observer of life, with Dino Campana (1885) one has the figure of an agitated and troubled wanderer whose writings possess an unprecedented brio and brashness. Here one reads of a walk past Florentine "Rosas" and "Gems" in shop windows (the prostitutes of the San Frediano district), who are transformed into mock talismans of Dante's "Paradise": "Me ne vado per le strade / Strette oscure e misteriose: / Vedo dietro le vetrate / Affacciarsi Gemme e Rose."[28] The ironic title "Fetid Prose" (for a poem in octonaries) expresses the low mimetic style of the parody of Dante's paradise, here once again in a Florentine brothel:

Se ne stanno Gemme e Rose
Per le scale misteriose
Verticali al Paradiso
Dei soldati e delle spose
Ingannate dal marito.
....
Il poeta se ne frega
E sta come un Pascià
Tra le Urì di miglior lega

Del paradiso di Allà
E alle rose in carta rosa
E alle labbra di carmino
Di madonna l'ulcerosa
Ha già fatto un sonettino[29]

In a poem to Sibilla Aleramo, Campana dilutes the rose by heavy iteration: "In un momento / Sono sfiorite le rose / I petali caduti / Perché io non potevo dimenticare le rose."[30] In the remaining ten lines, the rose occurs nine times! Anceschi places Campana first in his 1942 anthology, *Lirici nuovi,* as he is the first to engage the new linguistic freedom explored by the new lyricists and was a decisive link between the *"blast furnace* of crepuscolari, futuristi [and] vociani" and the poetry that followed.[31] Campana's "Orphic Songs" include vignettes, landscapes, and erotic encounters in which the "Orphic" is an equivalent for the synesthetic spell of poetry and eros, rather than a means of religious transcendence. Among his preferred images are musical instruments, prints, daguerreotypes, and paintings, frequently combined for synesthetic effects. The restless, adrenalin-like quality of Campana's verse partakes of what he calls a "double figuration"—that is, an iconic rendering of another world behind the false front of this world. In his mixture of the arcane and the novel he invokes Nietszche as an example of a positive barbarism, making frequent reference to the orders, levels, and hierarchies of Italian Gothic and primitive painting.

For the first time in Italian poetry, one gathers the exhilarating sensations and the alienation of the modern city. In the process of overturning the semantic categories of the classicalist tradition, and of loosening its syntax, Campana was rightly accused (in a 1915 review of *Canti orfici*) of writing "verses somewhat lacking in rules."[32] But it is mistaken to assert, as Cecchi did, that Campana's uniqueness has meant a lack of literary progeny: one thinks of Luzi, Bigongiari, Sanguineti, Rosselli. As Mario Luzi notes of *Canti orfici,* "it is a bridge extended as a means of exit out of the impasse in which the modern poet is involved, the poet of disillusionment and rejection. To these projections toward the world there followed a long and lasting impact."[33] Similarly the position of "irrationalism" is ill suited to the discoverer of a new phono-chromatic measure, decisive in the shift from metric verse to free verse.

A somewhat less troubled poet, also committed to the effacement of dualities (static/dynamic, sacred/profane) is Umberto Saba (1883).[34] The Triestine poet sought to locate in naturalistic and domestic situations the metaphysical sense of time passing laden with tragic and erotic sentiment. In his earliest poetry one detects the presence of crepuscular and decadent models: "Un grande abito nero / alcune rose smorte, / un prete, un cimitero / non è questa la morte?"[35] Subsequently he disavows such borrowings, rejecting the expressionism and fragmentism of the *vociani* and the vagaries of the hermetics. Saba's rose is usually a metaphor for desire and feminine beauty. In its company one finds the hand, the mannerist sign par excellence:

> Vedevi che nessuno era tra noi.
> Con un lungo sospiro,
> della tua mano mi porgevi invece
> la rosa della bocca.
> Del ben che il tuo gentile atto mi fece
> tutt'oggi il cor trabocca.[36]

Images of childhood are central to Saba, as in this recollection of his cousin Elvira:

> E' bella, ma perfida. Come
> nella sua casa signorile (un anno
> v'ero vissuto in sua custodia) odora
> di rose e mandorle amare. Se al seno,
> solo un momento, mi stringesse! O almeno
> di me tediata, mi picchiasse![37]

Saba's rose is invariably "red," an "elementary epithet" typical of the "distant yet popular language of the epic or fable"; as such it is indicative of the great distance between Saba and those moderns whose focus is on the "closure-concentration of communicating" itself.[38] Mengaldo indicates that while Saba was considered a traditionalist, his "participation in the process of metric liberation, which meant for him as well the confluence of various interweaving traditions, classical and recent, is from the start wholehearted and very effective."[39] This red rose may be the blood-rush on the cheeks of a sickly child: "le rose sulle guance affilate impallidivano."[40] Or it may reflect the masochistic interest in punishment expressed above. In his "Variations on the Rose," we read again of the rose's punishment amplified by the word "ceppo" (stem, but also "chain"): "Per te piange un fanciullo in un giardino / o forse in una favola. Punivi, / rosa inabili dita. E così vivi, / un giorno ancora, sul tuo ceppo verde."[41]

This expressive ambiguity is fully exploited in this passage concerning the blood of the innocent victim of religious sacrifice: "è bello / aver le mani nei ceppi, frustato // non piangi, anche il morir t'è meno amaro, / che ti spia fra le nubi il Dio in cui credi, / e il tuo sangue di rose il terren stampa."[42] Or in this, where it is a sign of slaughter or sacrifice, "Sul carro era una merce assai pietosa: / gli agnelli nella morte coricati, / e aveva ognuno nel collo una rosa."[43] Here and in the next two examples *rosa* appears in a facile end rhyme. In the first it is a gift not given to a woman, behind which stands the "sword" of the poet's self-destruction.

> Regalarti dovrei, Chiara, una rosa,
> ed io stesso acconciartela sul seno;
> poi tosto a me fare altro dono (cosa
> non dico io a te), ma che dà pace almeno.
>
> Oh, se il dono va bene a lei d'un fiore,
> altro a me convenire può che il ferro?[44]

In the second it stands for the supreme position among other women of Saba's wife, Lina: "Fuor'una che di te quasi è amorosa, / le amiche, fra cui t'ergi agli occhi miei / come tra i fiori minori la rosa, / dicono: 'Questa Lina è ben bizzarra, / ben superba.'"[45]

In "Interlude to Lina" *rosa* appears five times, a lofty figure for the beloved of "goodness," "purity," and "voluptuousness" set in the humblest of settings. In the envoi to the "Fugues," a set of musical meditations composed in 1929 in veiled revolt against the fascist regime, the roses are vain objects used to cover over the poet's irremediable sense of loss. They are, "in psychoanalytic terminology, sublimations": "O mio cuore dal nascere in due scisso / quante pene durai per uno farne! / Quante rose a nascondere un abisso!"[46] Here Saba expresses an internal division based on the differences in the backgrounds and characters of his parents, his mother being Jewish and his absent and "assassin" father being a Gentile. The fugue is a genre in which two themes are contrapuntally repeated, and a sublimated form of flight; it is easy to identify Saba's musical intentions and his escape in poetry from Nazi and Fascist oppression long before his actual escape from Trieste. This is an additional source of the pathos that pervades his work and his manneristic statement of the carpe diem.

A similarly wounded poet from the same region as Saba is Carlo Michelstaedter (1887), whose writings date mostly from 1909 and 1910, and whose austere symbolism derives in part from his readings of Schopenhauer, Weininger, Ibsen, and Tolstoy. Cerruti positions Michelstaedter "in the imprint of the great metaphysical poetry of Europe . . . a symbolism of a rather objective quality, meant to reveal, precisely, by means of symbols, the otherwise incommunicable cognitive-existential datum."[47] In "Marzo," the wind is construed as a capricious and marvelous demon that liberates the poet from tedium, stealing from the "stunned" and "stultified world" its "roses":

Marzo ventoso
. . . .
dài mutevol risalto
alla terra stupita

alla terra intorpidita,
mentre dal seno le strappi
e le primole e le rose.[48]

The fact that *rosa* is a hapax in Michelstaedter indicates his distrust of Italian rhetorical facility and glibness, "the sensual love of the word" seen in Negri and D'Annunzio.[49] To adopt the dichotomy of his major work, *La persuasione e la rettorica,* the man of "persuasion" knows that the wind represents rebirth and liberation, but the man of "rhetoric" would only see that as foolish. The former has incorporated recursive wonder into his epistemology and is a figure of the pathetic; the latter has not and remains "stultified," "wonder-struck." The former heeds the carpe diem; the latter does not. Michelstaedter's suicide suggests the unresolved nature of this polarity in the poet himself.

The early Salvatore Quasimodo (1901), like Saba and Michelstaedter, exalts the ancient Greeks while dodging the ornamental style of Italian classicism. The preeminent oppositions in Quasimodo—love/death, modern/ancient—stress the transitory nature of worldly phenomena and extend to the contrast between "words" and "roses":

"le tue mani . . .
sapevano di rovere e di rose;
di morte. Antico inverno.

Cercavano il miglio gli uccelli
ed erano subito di neve;

così le parole. Un po' di sole."[50]

Once again the hand is a presence. Words are sown on the page like millet, effaced by the winter snow and by the obscurity of a passion whose only equal is the rose. The analogy alludes to that earliest of Italian literary texts, the "Veronese Riddle." In Quasimodo's poem the snow-covered field indicates that the plowing season is over; the contrast of dark on light, of the rose against the hand, of seeds sown in the field, are like words on the page.[51] As Giovanni Pozzi writes, "Writing in itself does not represent that succession of sounds and concepts that is peculiar to language, that is, the linguistic reality impressed on the mind simply by the idea of motion. The act of writing reproduces that motion: the writer sees the black line of writing unfold in a manner similar to the unfolding of the voice. It is not a coincidence that writing is compared to plowing."[52]

Quasimodo seeks the poetic sublime in the mythic origins of language. The rose is never a mere object, but is a site of patholudic transformation, as here where the angel's hands form the shape of a cross: "Dorme l'angelo / su rose d'aria, candido, / sul fianco, / a bacio del grembo / le belle mani in croce."[53] In his heroic vision of "final exile" a garland of white roses is woven and placed on his head by his mother's hand, making him feel young again in a "city" suspended in the air:

> Una città a mezza'aria sospesa
> m'era ultimo esilio,
> e mi chiamavano intorno
> le soavi donne d'un tempo
> e la madre, fatta nuova dagli anni,
> la dolce mano scegliendo dalle rose
> con le più bianche mi cingeva il capo.[54]

Quasimodo's translations of ancient Greek poetry, *Lirici greci* (1940), were greeted as enthusiastically by the younger generation as Tommaseo's *Canti del popolo greco* had been a century earlier. Like the face of Quasimodo's mother, "made new by the years," the erotic roses of the ancients were newly fresh, whether scattered on tombs, used for embalming, or tossed about in the games of courtship: "Con una fronda di mirto giocava / ed una fresca rosa; / e la sua chioma / le ombrava lieve e gli omeri e le spalle."[55] In this version of a poem by Sappho, Quasimodo accentuates Atthis's memory of her beloved by means of internal rhyme (*rosa/posa*), assonance, and homophones (*rosa/rosa*):

> Ora fra le donne Lidie spicca
> come, calato il sole,
> la luna dai raggi rosa
>
> vince tutti gli astri, e la sua luce
> modula sull'acque del mare
> e i campi presi d'erba:
>
> e la rugiada illumina la rosa,
> posa sul gracile timo e il trifoglio simile a fiore.[56]

Quasimodo filters his source through echoes of other poets like Foscolo, Pascoli, and Leopardi, whose "L'infinito" is cited in this depiction of the sacred grove of Aphrodite, where Sappho's "roses" become "roseti" (rose beds): "Qui fresca l'acqua mormora tra i rami / dei meli: il luogo è all'ombra di roseti / dallo *stormire delle foglie* nasce / *profonda quiete.*"[57] Leopardi's presence is a clear sign of the pathetic in Quasimodo, as engendered by a direct supplication of nature and the indefinite. The roses of Pieria in Sappho stand for an Olympian sacrament that goes unheeded at one's peril: "Tu morta finirai lì. Né mai di te / si avrà memoria; e di te nel tempo / mai ad alcuno nascerà amore, / poi che non curi le rose della Pieria."[58]

Quasimodo succeeded in preserving the delight taken by Sappho in condemning a devious person. In doing so he "introduced to a quite vast society of readers the love for the stunned archaism, for atemporality, and for the brief texts (seemingly) charged with occult meanings."[59] This in turn led to a broad change in taste. The idea of discovering an archaic text in a fresh and contemporary language was also the aim of Ezra Pound's dictum, "Make it new!" As a young man, when he still wrote in rhyme, Pound too wrote of those who ignore the "Pierian roses," lamenting how the sacrament they represent had become a relic:

> Conduct, on the other hand, the soul
> "Which the highest cultures have nourished"
> to Fleet St. where
> Dr. Johnson flourished;
>
> Beside this thoroughfare
> The sale of half-hose has
> Long since superseded the cultivation
> Of Pierian roses.[60]

The poetry of Raffaele Carrieri (1905) has roots in his experience as a Legionnaire with D'Annunzio at Fiume, when he was only fourteen years old and where he lost the use of his left hand. This fact is eerily present in this short macabre lyric: "La morte non viene una sola volta / . . . . / Le basta che muoia una sola cosa / una sola, diversa ogni volta / e ci toglie dalle mani la rosa."[61] Carrieri was a defender of Quasimodo (against his northern Italian critics) and the author of the following epigrams: "Nella rosa come nella poesia sono nascoste parecchie varietà di parassiti"; "Le rose nell'aprirsi emettono più profumo ma entrano in agonia."[62]

Umberto Bellintani (1914), of the Florentine generation of Parronchi, Luzi, and the painter Ottone Rosai, engages the plasticity of the word in poems of great subtlety, poignancy, and erotic suggestion. In "Be Gone, Tragedy," his choral structure mimics the consciousness of his children:

> Vattene, tragedia. Non ritornar mai piú.
> Gli occhi dei miei bambini sono due gocce di lacrime.
> Gli occhi dei miei bambini sono una rosa di felicità.
> Non ritornar mai piú Non ritornar mai piú.[63]

Bellintani's mannerist style often involves hands, here in tandem with roses: "Ignaro io sono del vento che verrà / . . . . / e non conosco la rosa che fiorisce in questo palmo / illeso di terra. / Ma la mano che ha percosso il tuo volto ieri sera / è la mano dell'amore."[64] The erotic situation is a delicate matter, best if understated:

> E tratto tratto il cuore s'inteneriva delle rose
> e i sogni azzurri ronzavano nel suo capo,
> ma ricadeva in un languore di membra
> e il suo sesso sognava solitudine e sabbia
> calda del fiume.[65]

★ ★ ★

> Son belle violacciocche gli occhi tuoi,
> nere violacciocche in un'estiva
> sera morbidissima e placante.
> Son belle rose rosse le tue labbra,
> rose carnicine in una viva
> alba al mattinale verdicante.[66]

Giovanni Giudici (1924), a Ligurian transplant to Milan, embodies, according to Antonio Girardi, "that Lombard and Ligurian tradition that had known how to deepen the ethical and ontological crisis, the most disturbing of the contemporary consciousness."[67] A dominant influence on him is Pascoli, whose eighty-line poem "Casa mia," set at the family's home in Romagna, is the apparent source of Giudici's poem "Pascoli." In the original one finds climbing roses, mimosas, peonies, gladioli, clover, cedar, and bergamot. After the first quatrain (containing mimosa), the remaining nineteen are disposed symmetrically with respect to these plants, each of which is named twice by virtue of the repetition of stanzas two, four, and six in inverse order as stanzas twenty, eighteen, and sixteen. Thus the domestic gate and the rose that clings to it open and close the poem.

> M'era la casa avanti,
> tacita al vespro puro,
> tutta fiorita al muro
> di rose rampicanti.
>
> Ella non anche sazia
> di lagrime, parlò:
> —Sai, dopo la disgrazia,
> ci ristringemmo un po' . . .—[68]

Giudici's calque of "Casa mia," titled "Pascoli," is also a poem about a house, whose opening and closing quatrains contain iterations of the domestic rose. Inspired by a 1979 visit to the poet's home in Castelvecchio (Tuscany), the poem describes a house without walls, a constantly moving butterfly in the "space of the rose," a space of absolute mutability rather than permanence.

> In questa casa vagante
> In questa casa senza muri né stanze
> Casa-farfalla che si posa
> Nello spazio di una rosa
> . . . .
> Presto illegibili i segni del lapis
> E noi una i col suo punto nel folto del dizionario
> Vaghiamo nella casa di rosa
> Casa-farfalla che non si posa[69]

In his "Ode to a Mysterious Woman Named Maria," the rose is

"anything but mystical": "O germe remoto. / O frutto futuro. / O rosa tutt'altro che mistica. / O tuo nome graffito sul grigio muro."[70] And in "Neoplasias," the roses have grown into social tumors, unexcisable by "Marxian or Fanonian" remedies:

Neoplasie?

Sì, del mondo—nel quale
Io stesso una minuscola al mio centro
Neoplasia—ma a miliardi
Mentre la crisi/economia e i fiori
Che appassiscono fin la stessa rosa
Che è la rosa![71]

Giudici's rose is both figure and ground, at continuous risk of tautology: "even the rose itself / Which is the rose!" It is exasperated and playful, ironic and paradoxical, as if to demonstrate the poet's catholic understanding that neither beauty nor truth can be directly sought, but will emerge if the poetry is truly inspired. Poetic language must be like a product of nature. The attempt to realize oneself through language must not ignore the entrapments of language.

A useful means to accomplish this, as seen above, is the practice of translation and rewriting. The following poems contains an allusion to the opening of Vittorini's *Conversazioni in Sicilia*: "Io ero, *quell'inverno*, in preda ad astratti furori. . . . Da molto tempo questo, ed *ero col capo chino*."[72] The "blackness" of the factories in these lines symbolizes their control in 1958 by antilabor forces. The lyric threatens to disintegrate in the urban setting, in a bleak tonality reminiscent of Solmi and Fortini:

In *quell'inverno* m'incontrò uno sguardo
severo e cittadino:
con vergogna scoprii ch'*ero in ritardo*,
a capo chino
—e nitide tutte le cose,
nere le fabbriche, assenti
i lamenti, le rondini, le rose . . .[73]

Giudici realizes that the "roses" and sweet pastoral "laments" of a conventional lyric lexicon are "absent" and irrelevant to his current situation. A different sort of poetry is called for, as seen in the sixteen-line "Yes, Roses," which concerns the flower as amulet or symbolic marker of sacred or secular thresholds, as funeral relic or "nuptial flower," as memories "undone" in ambiguity like the petals themselves, as the markers of the author's temporal passage.

> Sì, rose—ma alla vista quasi che
> Glassate di ferrugine quali
> La rosa di Carlsbad adesso da vent'anni
> Appesa a un muro di casa—
> Rose, rappreso sangue
> Di supplicate tèche polverose
> Eppure rose da una chiesa alle cui soglie
> In bell'ordine a terra sparpagliate
> Strenue disfatte rose io vi mandavo
> A una falba penèlope remota
> Non tema—disse l'uomo che nel profluvio
> D'altri nuziali fiori discerneva
> Non tema, giungeranno
> In tutta la loro fragranza a destino:
> Intanto che il corteo di carrozze
> Lento iniziava il suo cammino[74]

Another scholar of Pascoli's work is Edoardo Sanguineti, whose patholudic lines below recall the "obscene" values which Palazzeschi had bestowed upon the rose. In the incessant wordplay one hears a verb form, "giocaste" (you played), in the name "Giocaste," the Jocastas who playfully expose their "solemnly incestuous" roses:

> le Giocaste che mettono in evidenza, senza decenza, quelle cose (quelle rose), diventano solennemente incestuose:
> . . . .
> (voterà un Sì tremundum, in occasione
> del referendum, quella poetessa caudata, che si è piuttosto spogliata,

con la sua rosa odorosa cagnazza: la Ciutazza, contessa di razza):[75]

The Ticinese Grytzko Mascioni (1936) is a poet whose mountain solitude is often shared with a convivial glass, whose ludic sensibility is apparent in the title of an early collection, *Mister Slowly e la rosa*. Conscious of the ephemeral, fleeting nature of "modern myths," Mascioni's monstrations exact a pathetic toll. As a boundary poet, he reminds one of a poet like Noventa, in search of the road back home and disillusioned by the world at large:

> a volte non trovo la strada
> che porta alla vecchia contrada
> in cui sono nato:
> è stato un altro giorno
> se c'è stato
> il giorno delle rose.[76]

Mascioni enjoys his boundary position, but there is a dark underside to his verse in which the rose stands as a poignant reminder of his solitude: "Altro nulla sapevo, ignota cosa, / altro più caldo più indifeso e chiaro / che il tuo grembo di rosa / in sé conchiuso."[77] Or there is this example: "Perché da te lo puoi vedere / quanto / possa un uomo che va / sentirsi stanco; possa uno che ha rose / nel bicchiere, / aspro bere e cicuta, / soffocare."[78]

Another poet who enjoys his boundary position and engages game-rules throughout his work is the Campanian Achille Serrao (1936), as here where the rose's petals are asked to predict the future:

> così avvilita
> la rosa, raccolti i petali nel pugno
> perché t'ami o non t'amo, durino scampo
> per noi le sonagliere nel vento,
> l'ape impazzita d'improvviso[79]

The carpe diem is also present in Serrao's later dialect works; as part of the neodialectal movement, he sees that language as a more fully expressive and authentic language of origins:

> Nun succede addu nuje ca dint'ô scuro
> pigliano suonno 'e ccose, manco 'o funno
> chiù 'nfunno 'e na rosa; 'e grisce sì, 'e grisce 'zallanute
> â saglipènnola s'addormeno 'e ll'ore
> tic tac addio gnuerno ll'uocchie e addio[80]

Finally let us examine the opening of a poem by Dario Bellezza, which is dedicated to Pier Vincenzo Tondelli, the young writer whose meteoric rise in the 1980s was ended by AIDS, as was Bellezza's life in 1996. Here too one sees the rose invoked to signal a love not ended by death, though play is terminated by disease: "Il Tevere si perde nella notte. / Il vento sforza la tua bocca / di miele; assaporo dal vivo / le rose languide della tua primavera."[81]

6
THE VOTIVE
AND HERMETIC ROSE

Rainer Maria Rilke (1875) employs the rose 162 times. High points include a monumental 24-part poem, "The Roses," and his own epitaph: "Rose, oh the pure contradiction, delight, of being no one's sleep under so many lids." As Dore Ashton writes, "Rilke set out to speak of roses; to speak, as he once said, from the experience of in-seeing which is not in-specting. Many new geometries sprang to his mind as he found in roses an incomparable source of metaphor."[1] The rose signified "innerness" in Rilke's poetic language. A thematic scansion of this lexical profusion might be presented as follows:

1. Rose as the model of exquisite or divine sensation, the source of essences: "the sweetness of your grief might be extracted, / as thousand roses yield a drop of oil."

2. Rose as icon for the Virgin, and the rose window of Notre-Dame: "That in you such roseal fenestration must be glowing?"

3. Rose as a loveliness exceeded only by that of the beloved, and as a perception accompanying the lover's growth in consciousness: "To point out a rose to you, that one, unreachably full blown upon its tree, / and give to presences long-lost a share / in your discovered sensibility."

4. Rose as the crown of Narcissus, a negative image of that same sensibility: "Now, in unfeeling water, it exposes / itself com-

pletely, and I may confer / with it for hours under my crown of Roses."

5. Rose as synonym for the ephemeral thought: "(a thought, a rose)"; "that behind-things which no name discloses / remains our real archetype and sphere."

6. Rose as metaphor for spiritual vigilance: "Have you each summer needed to recapture / the roses' scent?"

7. Rose as simile for the lover's hand, in correspondence with spiritual development: "Transform anther upon anther, / fill out your interior rose." Rilke notes, "The modern rose was developed out of the ancient eglantine by transforming the anthers into petals."[2]

In each of these cases the rose is involved in a sacrament: the immediate, knowable object has been redeemed for its spiritual value, transformed by force of desire or will. The sacramental depends on a nondistinction between the word (or sign) and that which it represents.[3] When the rose is involved in a sacrament, to adopt terms proposed by A. Korzybski, the "map" *is* the "territory": the "figure" and "figured" are assumed to be one. In this sense the votive rose will always be tautological, the product of circular and self-defining propositions. With Rilke's example in mind, I survey a host of Italian poets whose prayer, including secular prayer, engages the rose of sacrament as a votive object. As we have seen, this representation may occur at various levels of semiotic abstraction. It may limit itself to analogy and thus be an expression of extensive wonder, a static ontological model of consciousness, or it may be a figure of becoming, a vessel of spirituality emptied and replenished according to the author's understanding of eternal objects. In Girolamo Comi (1890) we see the former, the rose as a figure of Eve's passion, the pervasiveness of her "blood":

Io sono Eva sottomessa e indoma

. . . .

Dentro la sfera e nel suo arco terso

vige la tirannia misteriosa
del fiore igneo e gemmeo del mio sesso
che brulica del sangue della rosa.
Rosa universa in cui s'è inabissato
tutto il destino del mondo creato . . .[4]

* * *

Luce, memoria gaudiosa
del nostro sangue e del nostro pensare
satura di quel fuoco
che arde e squilla nella Rosa[5]

A friend of Comi's is Arturo Onofri (1885), whose Orphic and votive rose was an emblem of pulchritude and eros, and contained an element of willful imprecision reminiscent of his admired Pascoli, whom he called a "germinal poet . . . rather than a completed representative or thoroughbred poet (such as Homer, Pindar, Dante)."[6] Like Pascoli he preserved sufficient ambiguity in his imagery so that the interior dimension could prosper: "Amor mio, Zavalìh, perché non vieni? / Le rose rosse aspettano nei vasi / e le cortine nel fruscio dei rasi / sognano il tuo ritorno, Zavalìh."[7] In the dichotomy between the rose that is picked and the rose that is alive, Onofri prefers the cut rose, as it embodies the image of Christian sacrifice, but also that of an exotic amorous relation:

Io troppo a lungo avea languito; il canto
più non fluiva alla mia gola arsiccia:
e sì, la colsi, rosa primaticcia
cui l'anima, stillante, anche di pianto[8]

* * *

Il tuo vergine corpo è certo una magnolia
fiorita sulla spiaggia; la tua bocca fragrante
è una rosa del Bengala, sbocciata per me fra l'alghe . . .[9]

In his Rosicrucianism Onofri finds it natural to express faith in the rose's symbolic power. Here, in a sixteen-line section from a series titled "The Earthliness of the Sun," the scent of the rose emanates from the holy image of the cross. As if to confirm the symmetry of the two symbols, the opening and closing stanzas reflect one another.

> Un solo profumo di rosa
> in calda atmosfera veloce,
> beato di sé, si riposa
> nell'ombra che ha forma di croce.
>
> . . . .
>
> E ignara ogni vita si sposa,
> dall'ombra che ha forma di croce,
> a un cielo che odora di rosa
> in calda atmosfera veloce.[10]

The same air of naive simplicity and awe is found in Diego Valeri's madrigalesque depiction of a "Lombard Cathedral." Along the apse of the cathedral the smile of the Savior is answered by the "smile of love" of the rose window (*rosa* in rhyme with *sposa*, as in Onofri):

> E tu splendi ora tutta, o Cattedrale,
> nel chiaro viso del color di rosa,
> e mite esulti dentro un verginale
>   velo di sposa.
>
> . . . .
>
> E dalla rosa piove e si diffonde
> per l'ombra immensa un sorriso d'amore
> Dall'abside il sorriso gli risponde
>   del Redentore.[11]

Through the tracery of the rose window pours forth a rose-colored light; a nonfigurative mandala that communicates by its "smiles" with the iconic figures of Christ and the Virgin Mary. The fact that the Church is the "wife" is compatible with the derivation of "madrigale" from "madre." In Valeri's "For a rose Ofelia" there are fourteen uses of *rosa* in thirty lines; the first and sixth line of each of the poem's five sextets ends with that word (a structure also found in Baudelaire's "Réversibilité"):

> Una cosa di terra anche la rosa;
> ma la forza che al cielo la solleva
> nella corona delle verdi foglie
> e la preme dall'intimo e la scioglie
> come una fiamma di dolcezza piena,
> è il mistero di Dio dentro una rosa.[12]

To say that the rose is consubstantial with the sacredness it represents is not to eliminate ambiguities. On the contrary, in a love poet like Salvatore Di Giacomo the sacramental rose may fluctuate between the amorous and the Christian. In the following lines a monk is told to plant a rose on the burial site of a fellow monk, and always to water it so as to favor the soul's progress through purgatory: "Fratié, scavate 'o fuosso 'int' 'o ciardino, / fra Sarvatore l'atterrammo llà, / na rosa pastenatece vicino, / e maie nun ve scurdate 'e ll' adacquà."[13] The same belief in the rose's powers is humorously present when a young lad is discovered by a priest with roses he has picked for his girlfriend. "—*Che so' sti rose?* /—Io ... ll'aggio ... / còvete ... —*P' 'a Madonna?* /—Patre ... —*P' 'o mese 'e maggio?* / *Va, portancelle, va* ..."[14] In another case a young man and woman have walked to a monastery in May and had lunch; upon leaving they are invited by the prior to look around the grounds but not to pick the roses, since God would be displeased if they disturbed the tranquillity of the soul buried below. The bud of youth cannot resist, as the poem concludes: "Ncopp' a na fossa, 'a poco cummigliata, / na bella rosa gialla era schiuppatta .... / E chella, pe dispietto ... / cugliette 'a rosa e s' 'a mettette mpietto."[15]

The erotic sacrament is rendered with the same motif of the flower decorating the woman's bodice in the following double entendre, where the guitar serenader finds himself below not one but two "balconies": "Uocchie doce, lucente 'e velluto, / uocchie nire cchiù assaie d' 'o ggravone! ... / Fronne 'e rosa, che bello barcone / che v'avite saputo truvà!"[16] As with Rilke, for Di Giacomo the rose is a frequent object of contemplation and wonder, unknowable save through the decoding of a metaphor, epithet, emblem, appellative, or symbol. Here in the four-line "All is forgotten," one finds themes of eros, evanescence, and memory intertwined with the sacramental reality of Neapolitan culture:[17] "Uocchie celeste o nire, / culore 'e giglio o 'e rosa, / sempe, sempe una cosa, / semp 'e stesse suspire!"[18]

For Biagio Marin (1891), a dialect poet from Venezia-Giulia, the rose is a Marian icon, the figure of supplication and humility, of popular religious custom.

> Zogia del zorno novo
> del canto d'una gola
> che fresca intona la matina,
> fiiuri de rose sora d'ogni rovo,
> una cansona sola
> ne l'aria d'oro vespertina.
>
> * * *
>
> Semo a dissenbre e incora l'ano more;
> ma cussí lentamente
> che l'oro piove
> su le rose domente.
>
> Un dio cortese
> n'ha fato el don de rose d'ogni mese . . .[19]

The sense of divine courtesy also applies to suffering and Marin's devotion to the Virgin Mary as the maximum figure of compassion. The Madonna is figured by the rose several times in his final collection, a sequence of rhymed twelve-lined litanies: "Duta la vita xe un roser malnato, / co' le so spine ch'entra nel costato, / e fa fiurî in sima de la spina / una rosa de sangue—la Regina."[20] Of his Venetian compatriot, the Trevisan poet Andrea Zanzotto states, "What has motivated him from the beginning and ever more possessed him, as if by a courageous and seemingly solipsistic stubbornness, has been an adherence 'from below' to the environment in all its densities."[21] Zanzotto regales in the sonorous yet sibilant sounds of Marin's dialect, where alliterations and rhyme ("rose/sorose") are created that would not occur in Italian: "le rose / le gera sove e so sorose."[22] The faithfulness "from below" is evident in the following erotic-elegiac comparison of the rose, as the figure of a futile love, to the obscurity and finitude of one's own verse:

T'hè levào ogni fogia
comò a una ruosa
che se desfogia
per vêghete el boton co' l'oro.

No l'hè catao:
ma 'l to profumo m'ha 'nbriagao
e adesso moro
de tanta vogia
de quel profumo andao
disperso
comò un gno verso
desmentegao.[23]

For Giuseppe Ungaretti, the word conveys a purely interior dimension, forged in the consciousness, then sown on the terrain of the page, at the margins between the sayable and unsayable. To what extent, the avant-gardes had been asking, is poetry a rebus, a puzzle, an enigma that can only be decoded, solved, loosened by a change in consciousness, a transcendence? Ungaretti responded by casting himself as the scribe of a new age—a draftsman, a calligrapher, and a translator of an invisible and imperceptible script. He saw the poet as a marvel of nature capable of combining the violence and intensity of revelation with the refined consciousness of secular traditions. All this convened within the poetic "word," with its combined sense of alterity and emblematic truth, repression and authenticity.

Carlo Ossola has theorized on the figuration of the "invisible" that is present in a range of mystical and philosophical texts (Erasmus, Eckhardt, Loyola) and studies of rhetorical *topoi* (Curtius, Spitzer, Blumenberg). The "borderline" of spiritual signification in these texts is found, he argues, in the sign of the "repressed" that one sees in the physically encrusted imagery of the text. The practical focus for this theory is Ungaretti, whose debts to Antonin Artaud are duly noted (as they are by Zanzotto, who labels Ungaretti the first "existentialist" poet): "To look within means, at least since Poe and Baudelaire, *to look from within*: an eye watches us, spies on us, art does not reproduce but interrogates, it does not illustrate but it disturbs."[24] Though Ungaretti's versification contains various Petrarchan and baroque characteristics (antinomies, redundancy, pleonasms, pluralisms, and bi- and tri-membral correlations) they do not detract from the poet's terse language of religious aspiration.[25] Ungaretti intended his verbal frugality to reflect the "persecution of memory" of a "man of sorrow." Ungaretti's first book, *L'allegria,* contains the following lyric:

> Ho atteso che vi alzaste,
> Colori dell'amore,
> E ora svelate un'infanzia di cielo.
>
> Porge la rosa più bella sognata.[26]

In *Sentimento del tempo* one reads the 1932 "Second Song," addressed to "death," a "word" that responds to the vigilant listener with a phonic signal "reflected" in the rose: "Morte, muta parola, / Sabbia deposta come un letto / Dal sangue, / Ti odo cantare come una cicala / Nella rosa abbrunata dei riflessi."[27] As one critic has observed, "as one moves through life like a somnambulist, death's immortal image-suspensions leave deeply-felt sandy deposits in the blood, and Ungaretti believes that they provide him with his valuable atavistic perspectives."[28] The only two subsequent uses of the flower are in a death song in which "the secret rose" is intoned as a sort of dematerialized relic held in awe by the nomadic poet, and in a conversation in which the exchange of blood from a pricked finger returns to the early theme of the mystical gift:

> Rosa segreta, sbocci sugli abissi
> Solo ch'io trasalisca rammentando
> Come improvvisa odori
> Mentre si alza il lamento.[29]

* * *

> Una spina mi ha punto
> Delle tue rose rosse
> Perché succhiassi al dito,
> Come già tuo, il mio sangue.[30]

As if due to the common awareness of the fuller spiritual and formal autonomy of the artist advanced by Ungaretti, a new critical school emerged. Critics like Renato Serra and Giuseppe De Robertis stressed appreciation of technique and especially "knowing how to read" the poetic text, in contrast to the philosophical idealism of the historicist school. If Ungaretti was the partisan of artistic parsimony, others studied by these critics were determined to engage meditations on history or on the nature of the sacrament. The latter was the case for Enrico Pea (1881), seven years Ungaretti's senior. His family was also from the province of Lucca and moved to Egypt, where he became Ungaretti's friend. This lyric, which appeared in *La Voce*, employs the climbing rose as the divider between the chaste inner sanctum of worship and what lies beyond it, the torment and suffering of the flesh and the expectation of heaven:

> Spose illibate a Cristo, angeli in carne,
> o voi che state sui ginocchi prone
> senza soffrire, o voi che confinate
> vi pascete di sogni ed obliate
> i travagliati amori oltre il rosaio
> arrampicato al muro del giardino:
> Maggio rose fiorite ciel turchino
> o dormiveglia anticipazione
> di paradiso.[31]

Though Carlo Betocchi's (1899) work is commonly categorized as hermetic, its movement is toward clarity and simplicity. Debenedetti sees Betocchi as a "relational poet," like Saba, opposed to the poetry of symbolism, formalism, and linguistic contortions. In "The Rose Sold in Winter" the young poet constructs an allegory in which a rose grown in a greenhouse resents the warm unfolding enjoyed by a rose grown naturally in summer.

> Ma anzi . . . domani la rosa,
> vedrete, sarà già nulla;
> va, come una morta cosa
> sull'onda fetida e brulla;

del maggio, ch'essa ha amato tanto,
attende—ma non ode—il canto.[32]

Betocchi maintains a sacred association with the rose and, in the spirit of Ungaretti, equates it with "urges":

E allora le sùbite brame
ridesti, e lanci vorticosa
la tua insaziabile fame
di spazio, dal giglio alla rosa;
e splendi, qual sole effimero,
sui languidi color del mondo.[33]

Straining through the ephemeral for the absolute, Betocchi summons the rose as a guide to the veneration of the deity. It lives outside the world with the Virgin Mary and the persons of the Trinity:

Un dolce pomeriggio d'inverno, dolce
perché la luna non era più che una cosa
immutabile, non alba né tramonto,
i miei pensieri svanirono come molte
farfalle, nei giardini pieni di rose
che vivono di là, fuori del mondo.[34]

The rose is a "bride," mortal and passing, while the allegorical "virgin" "lass" of dawn is only "lost" until the following day, but immortal.

Misterïosa e bianca
da chius'acqua orientale
tu risali, e s'affranca
la mia pena mortale:
patisci e ti fai stanca
nel destare la rosa
che nel sole va sposa;
poi ti perdi nel ciel, virgo immortale.[35]

The aging Betocchi endured a religious crisis; here he confesses he is not the master of his life: "Fiorisce la rosa del giorno / cor, dolor del ritorno, / di mia vita non son donno. // Or s'è tinto di rosa l'oriente."[36]

Libero De Libero (1906) is a solitary poet from Ciociaria whose career was centered in Rome, although his linguistic practices and analogism place him in the milieu of the Florentine hermetics, as evident in this poem published in 1938: "La tua mano sull'erba / era una rosa / appena nata e già regina: / nella notte ero il tuo ramo, / la foglia più lontana tremava."[37] There is in De Libero a nondistinction between the poetic word and what it represents. Such a pretense is usually veiled in his rustic passion for his native landscape of Ciociaria, personified here and endowed with a "faded rose," a "putrid rose":

> Povera figlia dei monti, povera madre dei fiumi,
> il tuo passato è una rosa appassita:
> e chi vuol metterci odore
> e chi vuol metterci miele,
> chi la gonfia d'un vecchio elisire,
> e tu non rifiuti la putrida rosa.[38]

The same restive imagery of spiritual change recurs in the following images of the rose seed resting dormant in a dry clod of dirt: "E chi vuole ricercare una rosa / ancora non nata e già si riposa / dentro il seme futuro d'una zolla?";[39] "laggiù cresce la pietra come rosa, / la bella età del giorno si riposa / e in ogni zolla è un seme di furore."[40] De Libero's frequent use of negation and his dialoging with an unnamed female "tu" figure reveal the influence of Montale. The rose is an ideal of constancy that a relationship on the wane cannot live up to.

> Se primavera frizza una mattina
> sulla tua guancia illusa dalla brina,
> non dire che la rosa porporina
> ormai figura la nostra passione,
> tu non ignori il vento che la brucia,
> la livida spoglia che essa contiene.[41]

The fragility of love is again confirmed in the denial of the "seed" in the following poem to "a girl who is virtuous in the daytime": "Non ha stilla che brucia né seme che scoppia, / acerba non è la rosa che difendi / col graffio d'una livida bugia."[42]

While the term "hermeticism" often applies to a range of the New Lyricists and especially the work of Eugenio Montale and Giuseppe Ungaretti (after *L'allegria*), it refers more particularly to the group that coalesced in Florence and included Luigi Fallacara, Alfonso Gatto, Mario Luzi, and Piero Bigongiari. Mengaldo has given a succinct linguistic profile of "hermetic" practices, which I paraphrase.

1. a nominal style in which nouns become absolute due to the suspension of articles;
2. the use of plurals in the place of singulars;
3. the temporally or spatially vague and suggestive use of prepositions, especially *a*;
4. the animated and creative use of prepositions so as to defy paraphrase of a poem's literal content;
5. inversion of cause and effect;
6. abrupt use of analogies which in ordinary prose syntax or logic do not make sense;
7. Latinisms and other lexical preciosity;
8. etymological liberties taken to expand a word's semantic field;
9. transitive use of intransitive verbs;
10. synaesthesia and new, forced or improper meanings of words, or catachresis.[43]

The indeterminate nature of hermetic language is due in part to a crisis in representational language that occurred as simplex structures were replaced with duplex structures. The frequent introduction of an "io"/"tu" relation tended to problematize the psychological dimension of the lyric subject, as well as the relation between author and reader. Duplex relations presuppose a reformulation of the figure/ground relation. In votive poetry, as we have seen, this reformulation implicates a conflation, or nondistinction, between the poetic word and what it stands for. In the ambiguity and indeterminacy of duplex structures (whether thematic or linguistic-syntactical in nature) lies a new historical approach to poetic recursivity and the modeling power of language on the psyche. The interface of individual identity and collective relations could be rendered with greater complexity than was possible in a simple, easily legible, monological lyric. The use of an ambivalent and evasive syntax and lexicon tended to increase the suggestive power of the often brief and essentialist texts.

The intensely floral hermetic Luigi Fallacara (1890) was focused on being. He was an "ontological" poet for whom the rose was always a double configuration (absent/present, erotic/votive):

> Desiderosa, e il fuoco che combaci
> le rose alle spalliere agita appena
> il respiro in cui salgono le api . . .[44]

As much as any poet in this study, Fallacara privileges the melodious sounds of words as formal components of meaning, and not simply expression. The formal symmetries in Fallacara far outweigh any references to materiality, history, or proper nouns. In both "Estate" and "Rose marine" for example, the plural *rose* appears symmetrically at the beginning and end of the sonnet (lines 1 and 14, 2 and 13). In the 19-line "Etruscan garden," *rosa* occurs symmetrically in lines 1, 4, 15, and 19:

> Le bianche rose là tra gli ipogei
> svelano gli orizzonti del candore,
> come voi, tombe, quelli della tenebra.
>
> O come, per la rosa alta che irrorano
> . . . .
> ma, per la rosa al vento, ancora resta
>
> nel sonno eterno il profumo del tempo.
> Così profonda tenebra notturna,
> così decisa attesa di silenzi,
>
> o rosa, e tu . . .[45]

The phonic, lexical, and syntactic parallelisms that typify Fallacara's poems make of the rose a sort of repeatable tessera or module in the poem's constant turning about itself. There is no semantic novelty, but instead a continual return to the same aulic and chivalric motifs: the rose is "alta," "lontana" "bianca," "vertiginosa." Oreste Macrì has compared Fallacara's rose to that of Juan Ramón Jiménez, because of their "positive and affirmative conversion of the absence of Mallarmean symbolism into the Mediterranean area." Macrì cites the following examples:

> L'isola che è la rosa. . . . La rosa che non è solo la rosa. . . . E sempre esala e sempre intorno crea / lo spazio così intenso di presenza; / tra cielo e terra, d'un eterna idea, / eterno inizio, nube d'esistenza (*La rosa*), Estasi della rosa che rovescia / sé nella sua vertigine e si placa, / gaudio che dentro i petali si spande, / e diventa così suo cielo opaco (*Cielo opaco*); . . . *Più in là la rosa*.[46]

Fallacara's aspirations are situated by Macrì between the "catastrophic-nullifying skepticism" of Montale and Eliot and the persistent transcendence of Onofri and Comi: his is a "victorious poetry of mystical-Platonic stasis" situated between death and life, between oneself and the Other.[47] The rose, "autonomous and insular," is the paradigm of those objects which enable such a mediational status.

When the analogism seen in Ungaretti is treated as an abstract principle, as it is in Sergio Solmi (1899), one may speak of secular prayer or contemplation, in the manner of Leopardi. Consider "Garden," with its dramatic culmination in the "liquefaction of the roses," which ties together the lines that precede it:

> L'iridato
> getto che il vento obliqua e sfrangia, vela
> per un istante il paesaggio
> lo appanna come una memoria.
> Poi di colpo s'imprimono
> nella stillante aria il fico, il nespolo
> del Giappone, arde il chiaro
> deliquio delle rose.[48]

Unlike Fallacara, whose ontological associations emerge as so many permutations and combinations of the lyric register, Solmi's poetic concept is recursive. Thus the wonder elicted by the rose, in all its phases of being, becoming, and perishing, feeds back and has a "liquefying" effect on the poetic process. This is apparent in the title poem of *La rosa gelata* (1968), in which the rose is seen as "the perfect emblem of a day," its ruination being synonymous with its rebirth:

> La rosa
> che l'inverno dischiuse,
> svolse, innervò, arricciò,
> vetrificò
> d'incarnatini zuccheri, venò
> d'impercettibile sangue. Fissata
> nel suo gelo oltrevita, la penso
> perfetto emblema d'un giorno, a disfarsi
> non destinata foglia
> dopo foglia nel molle
> sfacelo delle stagioni, ma come
> aereo, spettrale cristallo, di colpo
> a frangersi.[49]

Solmi's historical importance is evident in this image: "The frozen rose and the last angel are no longer titles nor words, but images which remain fixed in the passage of our existence in these years. They are nocturnal figures on the verge of being swallowed up by the darkness and are immediately ready to react by redoubling the strength of their signal."[50] By not abandoning the Arcadian myth, Solmi mediates between the poetic tradition and the iconoclastic explosion of the new. Thus his "frozen rose" is party to the votive myth of the *locus amoenus* and the Feast of the Gods. Whereas in Michelstaedter the day leads inexorably to the night, to death presences and shadows, in Solmi it is the cycle and process that matter. The same could be said in a less secular form of prayer for Luzi and Betocchi. The vague diffusion of the rose's ephemeral nature comes to signify the dualities of sickness/health, plenitude/void, wholeness/fragmentation, presence/absence:

> Qui dove la sera accende
> colori d'alloro,
> sterminata bruisce in fonti e boschi

la voce senza tempo,
borbottano, ridono
gli iddii di sasso
gli iddii profondi.
Sulle loro ginocchia grige
scherza la rosa.[51]

The latter two examples conclude their respective poems, bringing the full votive weight down on the rose, whether spectral and frozen, or laughing over the kneeling, silent gods of stone.

Among the Florentine hermetics Mario Luzi (1914) is perhaps the most enduring; while melically reminscent of Fallacara, his work also evinces De Libero's sense of paradox. His opaque and highly allusive brand of symbolism finds in the rose its preferred figure of Christian charity but also the idyllic *senhal* of an absent love. An early point of reference is Luzi's "copy" of Ronsard's sonnet on the death of the French queen.[52] The poem has the form of a syllogism: just as the rose blooms splendidly in May ("Come quando di maggio sopra il ramo la rosa"), making the skies jealous of its color, and is then stricken by rain and heat and wastes away, so the beautiful young monarch is cut back by fate, a fact which leads Ronsard to implore that his tears honor the deceased whose body might remain only roses ("e il tuo corpo non sia, vivo o morto, che rose").[53]

In Luzi's early verse the contrast between rose and flower, as between member and class, recapitulates the contrast between memory and forgetfulness. The twenty-line "Passi" opens and closes symmetrically with strongly alliterative images around the rose:

Rifioriranno i tigli
e le rose serali sopra i muri
per le vie pensierose
lungo i portali calmi e le fontane?
. . . .
passano giovanette
sull'atavico ponte sconosciute

e qualcuno le chiama
più avvolgente dell'aria e delle rose
da un serico verone
ove l'altura ha senso di morire.[54]

The "atavistic bridge," the "walled streets burdened with thought," the "hesitant cities," are examples of the hermetic tendency to reverse cause-and-effect relations by means of abrupt analogies, a loosened and ambiguous syntax, and a hollowing out of the ponderous and melancholy subject. Luzi has stated that his mother was his model of a charismatic Christianity, a claim the following lines from his first book would support: "noi siamo in terra / ma ci potremo librare / esilmente piegare sul seno divino / come rose dai mure nelle strade odorose / sul bimbo che le chiede senza voce."[55]

Already the young Luzi relied on the aulic status of the rose as a gift of love. In general the liberating element of hermeticism was found in its lateral powers of association with a world in which the "gift of the rose" was at the furthest remove from any class-driven or materialistic presuppositions. The aura around the flower-gift is associated with a site in memory, and the change in life it brings. Luzi's roses reveal to the startled and bittersweet lover the transitoriness of love: "sapevi tu che vivere / dimenticanza è solo come il labbro / delle rose ai cancelli della Brenta. . . ?"[56] The inverted syntax, ambiguous use of articles and prepositions, proper name locations, and adverbs of time all lead to a highly allusive poetic message. Here, set in a "children's cemetery," where the ghostly obsession with time remains, the roses are "Florentine":

Ma le mani chimeriche e le ciglia
deserte chi solleva più al suo nome
nelle vie silenziose e l'aria come
quando la luna le celesti chiome
odorava di rose fiorentine?[57]

Luzi's analogism is fostered by a deliberately vague syntax and a lush though ambiguous adjectivization. The effect of such virtuosity is to create a metaphysical space of contact and self-validation:

> nel vento il tuo corpo raggia infingardo
> tra vetri squillanti stella solitaria
> e il tuo passo roco non è più che il ritardo
> delle rose nell'aria.[58]

As with Mallarmé, synesthesia and musicality create a sort of impressionism and willful unconcern for concrete spatial references. This is enhanced by the use of syllepsis (in which a single grammatical component possesses two semantic references), as was common among the poets of the *dolce stil nuovo*: Dante, Cavalcanti, and others. The simplest objects are surrounded by an aura, colored by rhyme, reduplication, and other phonetic figures.

> Già goccia la grigia rosa il suo fuoco
> il fuoco rapito fumido di pioggia
> sulla calce dei muri ciechi ove il fioco
> tuo bagliore s'appoggia.[59]

In Bigongiari's words, "Luzi's poetry will always be this return, this identification of a forgetfulness which touches not memory or history, but touches its own present, as a temporal continuum projected beyond itself by its own instinct."[60]

The title poem of Luzi's 1947 *Un brindisi* situates the rose at the center of this temporal continuum as a symbol of hope for a natural, undisturbed fertility and the possibility of attaining the soul's desires:

> Ma tu persa trascorri, anima mia,
> al di là dei tuoi termini sfioriti,
> brama la rosa neutra dei paesi
> dimenticati all'orlo delle strade deluse,
> di là dalle stagioni una rosa continua,
> rosa fissa nell'etere e indivisa
> pencolante tra notte e giorno, grano
> di calme primavere inattuate,
> di giardini possibili nel vento.[61]

Alessandro Parronchi (1914), a later Florentine hermetic, creates allusive and mournful landscapes in which the rose has the human qualities of a survivor or witness of destruction. The aura of the evocation dominates any emotional immediacy or sense of historical location: "Là sull'erba / è una pietra caduta. Nella tenebra al vento / un albore di rose di lontano saluta."[62] The use of exclamations actually distances one from the intensity they would denote: "Mandano le siepi / profumi intorno, volge un'ora mille / sogni, ma come povera la pietra / riflette ora il giardino ebbro di rose!"[63] In a vague theater from which the public has long departed, their faces, along with those of "lovers," will one day return "intact," like roses that reappear: "Siete state colte invano / belle rose ora scarnite! / Ma da un margine lontano / voi di nuovo trasalite . . ."[64] As with Luzi, one senses the rose has a sacral role:

> Non ancora però del bianco seme
> della luce hanno colto la nascosta
> densità, e si richiudono profonde
> nei burroni le rose e l'altre specie
> di fiori tra cui mai non è lamento
> pòrto da labbra sconsolate . . .[65]

Thus *rosa* is one of a family of sweet, melic, "Petrarchan" words intended by their very indeterminacy to evoke nature and the natural human disposition to the sacred.

The rose of Piero Bigongiari (1914) has a pathetic artificiality to it, set within a grid of copious rhymes and other figures:

> Ovunque, dove guardi, vedi,
> credi, dove ritardi,
> e qualcosa è più forte della rosa
> che ti sfiorisce accanto;
> se qualcosa sfiorisce, chi non osa
> alzare un canto?
> (Qualcosa di più completo del tuo pianto)[66]

Poetry for Bigongiari is a means of augury, as signaled by the verbs of casting (*gettare*), handling (*gestire*), and placing (*deporre*) that act on the rose:

tardi il fulmine incendia sul tuo volto
e non posa sul fiume quella rosa
baciata e data al vento dalle lacrime.
La notte canterà, l'amore scorre
lontano dalle rose che tu getti[67]

* * *

Ombra cerula apparsa dove il cuore
già piú non ti sostiene, nei giardini
solo un brando di rose vi perviene
gestito sanguinante dalla sera[68]

* * *

dove deponesti
sposa raggiunta e sola rose in cesti
destinate perché il tuo sangue varî.[69]

A strong advocate of Bigongiari's status as a pivotal figure is the critic Oreste Macrì. The following description gives an idea of the difficulty confronted by Macrì and other critics in the 1930s in naming the new poetry, which seemed a hybrid of every other known style: "On opening the book one can document the fatal chain of the abstract technical-sensorial delirium in this contemporary poetry; *classical* numerical rhythms; *baroque* metaphorism and conceits; *romantic* cosmic-mental approximation; *realistic* (but reduced and correct) physiology; the *surreal* . . ."[70]

The numerous attempts at classification point to the same kind of elusiveness that historically surrounds the hermetic. Even the older Bigongiari, who turned to long verses and the long poem, continues these deformative linguistic practices evident throughout this chapter. In the 1979 book *Moses,* based on the theme of the journey, the rose is the archaic symbol of Christ: "Prora umida di riflessi, / il fuoco ormai sia rosa sulle spine, / stilla, stigma, pupilla della fine."[71] Bigongiari's most recent work shows an even greater profusion of the lyrical-religious rose, usually enlisted for its "scent."

In a manner compatible with the rose-gift seen in this chapter, the recent work of Nella Audisio envisions an exchange and unification with another soul:

> E tu, doppio,
> che tremi
> sull'altra sponda del fosso.
> Le regalò una rosa
> per un'ora d'assenza
> perché l'unica vita
> per entrambe era una.[72]

Like Bigongiari, Alda Merini (1931) tends to conflate the roses of religious devotion and those of physical love.

> Avorio concretato fra le mani
> d'estremi Crocifissi,
> ronzio di spine ad ogni polpastrello
> delle morbide dita,
> e, dopo, rose, rose di stupore,
> placide nevicate d'innocenza,
> variare d'onde al largo dei tuoi occhi,
> fissità, di pupilla,
> vedovi cigni solitari al corso
> dei tuoi fiumi d'Amore . . .[73]

In "Per una rosa" the rose is elevated to the perfect figure of love and enduring passion that can give pause and rest to God. The poem's final line rhymes with its title: "Vorrei esser te, così violenta / così aspra d'amore, / così accesa di vene di bellezza / e così castigata."[74]

Let us now consider the Rumanian Paul Celan (1920), whose "the nothing—, the no one's rose" expresses a transformation of archaic religious objects, icons, and rituals into a form of spirituality that is negative and catastrophic.

> Praised be your name, no one.
> For your sake
> we shall flower
> Towards you.

> A nothing
> we were, are, shall
> remain, flowering;
> the nothing—, the
> no one's rose.[75]

The poem's translator writes, "The seemingly negative theology of [this] great poem, 'Psalm,' has been shown to have antecedents in both Jewish and Christian mysticism, and Celan is known to have been well versed in both." Ossola finds a "subtle consonance" between the "final epiphany of a negative mysticism" of the poetic rose of Celan (who translated Ungaretti into French) and Ungaretti's "Rosa segreta, sbocci sugli abissi," cited above.[76]

Hamburger cites the following poem as an example of the pregnant ambiguity Celan achieves, like Rilke before him, by exploiting the German language's syntactic peculiarities, such as the use of nouns to modify entire clauses, or the abundance of compound words:

> And you:
> you, you, you
> my daily true—and truer—
> worn later
> of (the) roses—:[77]

In this chapter we have seen how the "territory" and the "map" of the rose's signification may be superimposed, or identified, precisely as occurs in the formation of the sacrament. It is in the combined sense of augury and resignation that the idea of a sacramental rose persists, in the expression of wholeness and unity. Such a unity is epitomized by reversibilities and negations within the poems. The votive poet depends on equating categories which logically are to be kept distinct. The votive self divests itself in prayer and contemplation of the ways of the world. The rose is its candle and mantra.[78]

7
THE ANACREONTIC ROSE

While considerable mystery surrounds the ancient Greek poet Anacreon, for whom very few attributable texts exist, the *Anacreonta*, a series of odes written in homage to him, also help us formulate the Anacreontic. It is in fact to the *Anacreonta* that Leopardi refers when he advises that the reading of Anacreon must be done with insouciance: "The pleasure of the odes of Anacreon is so fleeting, and so resistant to any analysis, that to enjoy it one must expressly read them quickly, with little or slight attention."[1] In the few actual writings of Anacreon there is but one instance of the rose. The entire fragment is as follows:

> Each one wears three garlands,
> two of roses and one of marjoram.[2]

The festive and convivial event is transposed onto the consequent event of love. In the *Anacreonta* the rose is almost always accompanied by the figure of Bacchus; the flower is indispensable to the demigod's work of love and enchantment, and his appreciation of drink and sensual beauty. Bacchus is also a somber presence: the god of ivy, the severe object of awe and veneration whose cult seeks spiritual transformation more than delight. Despite the persistence and frankness of sexuality among the followers of Anacreon, it is always rendered gracefully. If the poets in the previous chapters seem polarized between materialism and spiritualism, mortality and transcendence, such tensions are absent from the Anacreontic and baroque poets, who delight in the *coincidentia oppositorum*.

The first Anacreontic poet in modern Italy is Ugo Foscolo, whose numerous Anacreontic imitations typically find the late-blooming rose as a mediator between the two phases of the Bacchic rite, that of the grape and that of the ivy. One of these, "The late rose," includes two vocatives to the rose, one to the image of the beloved and one to the "trophy" won in the "game" of love:

> Tu, fior splendente e semplice
> Come la mia vezzosa,
> Tu fra le spine floride
> Ancor non spunti, o Rosa.
>
> Mentre vedeati sorgere
> Il gajo Anacreonte
> Inni t'ergea cingendosi
> Di te la calva fronte.
>
> E in mezzo a danze e giubilo
> L'altrui chiamava aita
> Onde cantar tua morbida
> Foglia agli Iddii gradita.
>
> Tu sei trofeo di tenere
> Grazie, sei giuoco, o Rosa,
> D'Amor nei giorni floridi
> A Citerea scherzosa.[3]

In the following translation from the *Anacreonta* by Foscolo, the figure of the ancient poet asks Love why its "ointments" and its "roses and wine" are wasted on "monuments" and not saved for his own needy heart:

> A che pro sui monumenti
> Versi prodigo gli unguenti?
> A che pro le rose e il vin?

> Me piuttosto, fin che ancora
> Viver posso, ungi, e m'infiora
> Di corone il bianco crin.[4]

At forty-two, Foscolo writes in English from his exile in England of his sensed need to "twine" together from memory the roses and other flowers of his beloved Italy and Greece:

> I twine, far distant from my Tuscan grove,
> The lily chaste, the rose that breathes of love,
> The myrtle leaf and Laura's hallow'd bay,
> The deathless flow'rs that bloom o'er Sappho's clay . . .[5]

These lines express the spirit of the Anacreontic as a willfully vague area of poetic discourse, inclusive of sexual caprices as well as of the gnostic philosophy of its namesake. Laconic but Arcadian, the Anacreontic poet regales in the luxurious and exquisite, and possesses a heightened sense of the sensual and melic qualities of the poetic word. These ingredients are often accompanied by that brand of mimetic play that Bogue and Spariosu characterize as "'miming,' 'bringing forth,' or 'monstration,' a performative meaning that originated in archaic Greek culture. Archaic mimesis is related to the dramatic miming of the gods, to the action of manifesting and making present their power."[6]

One means of monstration that is archaic in this manner is the "onomastic" rose, Rosa. The great Venetian lyric poet, Diego Valeri, provides an example of the "onomastic" rose, which is an extension of the metaphor, rose = woman. The name Rosa, as we have seen, is a generic name for a woman of humble class. "Rosetta" in the following lines by Valeri is a young lady prematurely dead:

> Rosetta è sola nella gran chiesa,
> e il vento nuovo le giuoca attorno.
> Rosetta è ferma, distesa
> sotto le coltri nere: è una morta.[7]

Another major poet who employs the onomastic rose is Salvatore Di Giacomo (previously introduced), whose generic "Rosa" is the poet's erstwhile lover. As Pasolini writes, "In the entire body of Di Giacomo's love poetry there is never *one* woman: it is always about *woman* that he speaks, whether her name is Rosa or Nannina, names which are proper names and yet pure *flatus vocis*."[8] "Rosa," like "Maria," denotes an archetypal figure in the popular culture. In Pascoli the name is a Homeric epithet ("la Rosa / delle bianche braccia"). The Sicilian Ignazio Buttita (1899) tells the story of a Rosa whose husband disappoints her sexually, so she finds a man who gives her the baby she wants, and the husband remains happy at his new family and his "Perfect Marriage": "A Rosa, lu maritu / ci capitò mputenti; / nto lettu, a prima sira / successi n'accidenti."[9] For Giuseppe Goffredo (1956), Rosa is a long-suffering and patient woman who presides at the deathbeds of male family members:

> Rosa ha visto morire suo padre,
> Rosa ha visto morire suo fratello,
> Rosa assisteva i suoi malati.
> —Il vino!—gridavano padre e figlio,
> senza Cristo, né morti, né medici.
>
> Rosa insieme alla mamma svuota
> le bottiglie della speranza . . .[10]

In Franco Scataglini's ten-poem suite, "Rosa," the woman of that name futilely clutches a rose, finding no solace in her confrontation with death.

> —de un taciturno petto
> cosa strigne la rosa,
> Rosa: un canto, un dispetto
>
> dianzi al dorso del mare?
> Cosa pol strigne un pugno
> de fioleta che pare
> un pallidetto brugno?

> Corre ogni atto al confine
> che dà forma al suo estingue.
> *Solo el tuo sogno fine,*
> dice, *Rosa vol strigne*—[11]

As Franco Brevini writes, the suite represents "a moment of abandon to the figure of the beloved, recovered as an image of dawn, around which the negative signs of the world are arranged, by now only as possibilities and not as necessities."[12] Scataglini's *La rosa* is a "rewrite" of the opening fifth of *Le roman de la rose*. In the conclusion of this antiphonary of holy and worldly occasions, expressed in a language that radically conserves the aulic-pastoral canon of its source, one arrives at the hypostasis of the rose as beloved, a baroque profusion of namings of the rose. The pursuit of the love object is focused on the bud, on the potential bloom more than on the bloom itself; here the poet finally turns to the issue of the manuscript he is producing and the one he is translating from, both of which pale in comparison to the rose:

> irta fratta, viluchio
> che strigneva 'nt'el muchio
> de le spine gelose
> rosai carghi de rose.
> Quale smania d'approccio
> per quelle operte e in bocio
> rose me rampò via?
> Donato avría Pavia
> pure d'andà, o Parigi,
> ai fioriti fastigi.
> . . . .
> Desiai una rosa, una
> da spicà su l'impruna
> ma saría stato dolo
> pel signore del brolo.
> Soto al lume del cielo

> bocioletti col velo
> c'era 'ntra folti stoli
> de piú gonfi bocioli.
>
> Oltre le operte rose
> io li pregio, pompose
> al matino, fiorite,
> e de sera apassite.
> . . . .
> era idea ed era cosa
> quel biocolo de rosa.
>
> Simetriche, duerne
> sul calamo, ed alterne,
> otto foie guarniva
> la rosa promissiva.[13]

In this conclusion one has a mannered fusion of writing and waiting, of erotic desire and sublimation, of the rose as idea and the rose as thing. The volubility of the rhymed septenaries and the filter provided by the Ancona dialect complement this blend of passion and reflection.

The perception that the rose need not be trivialized is shared by the great love poet Jorge Guillén (1893). As Manuel Mantero demonstrates, Guillén embraced the disorder of the world, finding in poetry the means to organize its teeming chaos, to discover perfection through labor, and to be free from the sundry labels that society prepares for the "poet-professor." In Guillén's *décima* "Perfección," the hour of perfection is midday:

> Todo es cúpula. Reposa,
> Central sin querer, la rosa,
> A un sol en cenit sujeta.[14]

In "La rosa" Guillén reveals his desire to preserve the flower as something ideal and incontrovertible:

> Yo vi la rosa: clausura
> Primera de la armonía,

Tranquilamente futura.
Su perfección sin porfía
Serenaba al ruiseñor,
Cruel en el esplendor
Espiral del gorgorito.[15]

The provisional conclusion that can be drawn from the above examples concerns the continued lushness of the rose *topos* (including the onomastic rose) *because of* the secular tradition that lies behind it. It is in this spirit that Guillén satirizes Gertrude Stein's well-known line "A rose is a rose is a rose," in defense of poetry and of the density and quality of the rose *topos*: "'Es original, es nuevo.' / Lástima que a esas virtudes / Sea el snob sólo sensible. / 'A rose is a rose...,' Gertrudis. / Hacia calidad me muevo."[16]

The Anacreontic concern with common loves, labors, and aspirations gives rise to a baroque concern for the poet's craft and the awareness of the artistic practice as monstration. As we know, in the Novecento historical styles are rediscovered in hybrid form. Thus in a poet like Scataglini or the Sicilian Lucio Piccolo (1903), the sylvan pastoral coexists with the baroque. Piccolo's reverence for nature is apparent in long spiraling periods in whose images of the plow and the hawthorn one senses a debt to Pascoli.

Se la nuvola un poco si posa
sul ciglione o su la soglia
della valle, nell'ombra viva
ora vede timone d'aratro
che scuote che sfiora che sfoglia
il cespo e la rosa boschiva.[17]

* * *

Gracile Primavera cui biancospino
punge il piede errante nel cammino
èsita, implora, non osa
turbare nel sonno la rosa.[18]

The subtle elegance of this rose possesses a latent sexuality.

> Ampia conca di pietra l'errabondo
> umore accoglie—al margine vi posa
> l'anfora—e specchio fa di nubi e rami.
>
> Frangendo un giorno i labili velami
> dei muschi s'alzerà su dal profondo
> guizzo di serpe o palpito di rosa?[19]

In the posthumously published "L'anno pellegrino," the year is allegorically represented as a mendicant pilgrim winding its way through the seasons:

> Ma quando riprenderà i cammini
> verso i tersi orizzonti
> . . . .
> vuole portare a lontane motte
> erbose, nel giro dei taciti passi
> ad altri viali, ad altri giardini
> col pacato respiro
> questo tardo sentore di rose.[20]

In "Peel" Piccolo seems to evoke a Montalian "occasion," but adds to it a piercing irony and sense of uncompromised detachment:

> per chi si getta
> scabro è il tuo senso terra
> di solchi, d'erte di pietrame,
> di radure gessose ove alla stretta
> d'agosto, anche lontana da sollievo
> di fonti ancora non traspiri
> di roveti papavevi e di rose?[21]

Vittorio Bodini (1914) is a remarkable scholar and translator of Spanish poetry, a fact which colors and conditions his own poetry. The "black humor" of the Mediterranean, the "southern demon" (*il demone meridionale*) of melancholy and indolence, is alive in his verse. Bodini is a consummate stylist, a poet of fragility in the modern metropolis, in the manner of Sandro Penna and the Lorca of *Poeta en*

Nueva York. In the following passages from his early years one sees the baroque repertoire in place:

> La rosa del crepuscolo si sfoglia
> nel calice ove cede del suo verde
> lo stelo all'acqua[22]
>
> * * *
>
> Uscivano le ninfe sulle soglie:
> i girasoli e le povere rose a stampa sulle vesti
> chiudevano in un'enfatica rigidezza
> i loro fianchi smarriti.[23]

Bodini's poetry is one of struggle, an arena in which the ideal and natural strain toward union, in the perfection of love and freedom that exist despite the cynicism, betrayal, and self-sabotage that exist in the world: "Oh, a volte, chinarsi ad odorare / l'ombra trafitta d'una rosa, / tradirti."[24] His frequent use of the second-person (familiar) inflections usually concerns himself, as in the following lines, where the poet's "body of rose" houses the struggle of noonday and the baroque knowledge of its complement, the moon: "Così lotta il meriggio che ascolta / la propria morte nel tuo corpo di rosa, / ma poiché nulla è finito, ora ricordati / quale lugubre luna consumerà questi istanti."[25] In this example the poet addresses his own vanished adolescence, which he sought futilely in the "paradigm of the rose":

> Nelle sfere armillari
> nel paradigma della rosa
> ti ho cercato
> nel nome inciso
> sul banco col temperino
> e il giallo dei semafori
> sempre dove non eri.[26]

Midday is the time of greatest brightness and illusion, the time of mirages and metaphysical blindness. The rose is an ideal remembered, the womb of childhood, as well as a metaphor for the family house, understood as the dwelling place of the soul: "Noi abitammo in una rosa rossa. / Passavano treni in corsa alla periferia / —un gomito sonoro—; / e tutto il resto era un fermento di cieli."[27]

As a critic, Bodini shows how in Góngora's *Polifemo* the "renaissance rose" used for Galatea is a willful anachronism typical of the baroque style, since the banal formula for beauty contrasts effectively with the monstrosity of the cyclops. The duality found in the *Polifemo* might serve as well as a self-description by Bodini, under the surface of whose poems we find the same "astonishing aspiration toward a coexistence within a single work . . . of form and the unformed, of closed lines and open lines, of the geometrical and the grotesque."[28]

The 1936 assassination of Federico García Lorca (1898) by the Falange outraged the Italian literary community. Lorca had used the rose copiously throughout his work, including a "Casida de la rosa" and "La oración de las rosas." His exclamatory lyrics possess a choral structure and are constellated with roses alongside laurels, cypresses, carnations, and magnolias, as the flora of amorous passion. In this garland the rose is the premier figure of wonder, even when it is a "paper rose" in comparison to the soft lips of a lover. This passage from 1921 is typical of Lorca's early use of the rose as a simile of both desire and chastity:

> Junto al camino gris
>   vi una vereda en flor
> y una rosa
> llena de luz, llena de vida
> y de dolor.
> Mujer, flor que se abre en el jardín:
> las rosas son como tu carne virgen,
> con su fragrancia inefable y sutil
> y su nostalgia de lo triste.[29]

In the song "Narciso" the rose is a figure of recursive wonder; the boy Narcissus, transfixed by his image, enters into another space of consciousness. Similarly the poet is unable to articulate his absorption:

> En lo hondo hay una rosa
> y en la rosa hay otro río.
> ....
> ... y en la rosa estoy yo mismo.
> Cuando se perdió en el agua
> comprendí. Pero no explico.[30]

In the 1930s Lorca grows more expressionist and surrealistic. The rose of the "Ode to Salvador Dalí" is polymorphous in the sense of being both desired and possessed, here and elsewhere:

> Una rosa en el alto jardín que tú deseas.
> Una rueda en la pura sintaxis del acero
> ....
> Pero también la rosa del jardín donde vives.
> ¡Siempre la rosa, siempre, norte y sur de nosotros![31]

In this "Blind Panorama of New York," Lorca's refrain "no son los pájaros" (it is not the birds) constitutes a censure of civilization and a confrontation with death, which only the roses (which are not present in New York) can forget:

> No es un pájaro el que expresa la turbia fiebre de laguna,
> ....
> es una escala indefinible donde las nubes y rosas olvidan
> el griterío chino che bulle por el desembarcadero de la
> sangre.[32]

It is only upon escape from the spiritual desert of the metropolis, in those poems from his trip to Vermont, that Lorca's enumeraciones of the rose take on a "living" connotation:

> Y el caballo
> ¡qué flecha aguda exprime de la rosa!,
> ¡qué rosa gris levanta de su belfo!
> Y la rosa,
> ¡qué rebaño de luces y alaridos
> ata en el vivo azúcar de su tronco![33]

One might apply the criteria Lorca developed for evaluating Góngora's rose to his own work: "Nothing could be more ill advised than to read his madrigal to a rose with an actual rose in one's hand. Either the rose or the madrigal should be more than enough."[34] Franco Fortini rephrases this remark to insist on the importance of "objects" to Góngora, disagreeing with the notion that the fundamental difference between Góngora's poetry and that of Mallarmé is that the first is nonhermetic and capable of being glossed while the latter is hermetic and hopelessly obscure.[35] He locates the difference instead in the rose: the substantiality and presence of Góngora's *rosa* (as *cosa*) and the reified absence of Mallarmé's. If one accepts this opposition, Lorca is aligned with his fellow Spaniard.

In Alfonso Gatto (1908) the naive analogy of the rose suggests its own ostensive overdetermination or representational hollowness:

Ci furono le rose
un tempo, gli asfodeli.
Ora passa nei cieli
il cielo che rispose

alla notte degli anni,
alle paludi, ai morti.[36]

One senses a reciprocity between the illusory rose of noon and the memorial rose of night. Upon disillusionment, transformation will follow. This is also the theme of a poem about an artist's young lover who has died, leading him to speculate on what it would be like "to die in a caffè":

Direbbe "ferma" alla fioraia, "porta
le rose alla ragazza che m'è morta."
. . . .
Chi parla di noi due? Non si sente
nulla di quel che penso o forse s'ode.
Quel negozio di mode
—ricordi?—nella notte aveva il rosa
dei manichini nel ronzìo del neon.
Così il pensiero è dove si riposa.[37]

Gatto's metaphysical style is an innovation among his contemporaries, who show its influence in two seminal anthologies, *La linea lombarda* and *La quarta generazione*. Gatto wrote the above poem while in Milan, as he did the following "To the Lost Voice," during World War II, in which the rose is the flower of mourning.

> Con l'acqua morta della sera udivo
> quasi lontane rondini passare
> azzurre all'ombra del Naviglio. Intorno,
> ogni tristezza al braccio dei soldati
> era un odore povero di donna
> coi garofani scuri sopra il petto.
> Affioravano i lumi come ceri
> nelle stanze di tenebra ove a note
> basse cantava già la guerra un canto
> "Lili Marleen." Ed annottava il mondo,
> sulle donne scendevano nel pianto
> le gramaglie di rose dei cortei.[38]

The title suggests the condition of exile that pursues Gatto through his work. Many of the words used in the first half of the poem—words of darkness, and brief, plaintive suggestions of song and light—are repeated in the second half, just as the "dark carnations" of line six are echoed by the "mournings of roses" of the final line. The second half begins with a verb ("affioravano") that only receives its poetic complement in the last line ("rose"). Such a symmetry and reversibility create an ominous sense of enclosure and imprisonment. To appreciate Gatto's novelty one must recall Pascoli, whose intimism was too long allowed to obscure his technical innovations. (An accomplished poet in Latin, Pascoli in his Italian poetry overturned classicalist assumptions about linguistic propriety, regular versification, and rhyme.) In this portrait of a young woman's initiation to love, one senses the tender enclosures of Pascoli. Gatto postulates a virgin who must learn that nothing is fixed in life, that "the law must be broken for an act of life":

> A dirglielo resti la via
> e il primo oltraggio

della donna che ride
per dargli coraggio.
Racconterà che vide
la fanciulla pietosa spogliarsi come la rosa.[39]

In the following lyric, suggestive of Diego Valeri, one sees Gatto's melic and semantic simplicity, a factor which distinguishes him from the hermetics seen in Chapter 6:

La nebbia rosa
e l'aria dei freddi vapori
. . . .
Un triste davanzale, Venezia che abbruna le rose
sul grande canale.

Cadute le stelle, cadute le rose
nel vento che porta il Natale.[40]

Gatto, in the spirit of Anacreon, rises above melancholy with melody and humor. Just as these faded roses lead to an advent, a nativity, in the following lines a sunset viewed over the mountains at Trent leads the poet to a reverie in the recollection of his deceased mother.

Così la chiara spera
dei monti a lungo ammalia
nei pascoli la sera.
Odora già l'Italia
di polvere e rose.[41]

There is an eerie similarity between this poem and an elegy by Alberico Sala (1923), one that also engages "roses and dust" to remember the poet's dead mother in a work stripped of any embellishment:

Cinque colpi per un uomo;
per una donna sette:
sette colpi di campana battono
per una donna, mia madre.
Innamorata dei fiori
doveva morire d'agosto

fra rose e polvere. Domani
è dieci agosto, la porteranno via.[42]

As with Gatto, in Sala's poetry we notice a surrealistic deformation of ordinary language. Here the rose "acts" to draw blood from the poet's ear in contrast to the inaction and silence of an amorous interlocutor:

Una rosa nel mite novembre
m'ha graffiato il lobo
dell'orecchio da cui sento di più
(anche le parole che non dici).
Difendo, fra lame di cemento,
il rubino di sangue per le tue dita.[43]

The theme of the death of the mother is also present in Rocco Brindisi's (1944) powerful narrative poem "My Mother, Myshkin and the Snow," in which the oxymoronic "black rose" stands as an emblem of consciousness and eternity, a mannered and self-conscious vision of one's own death "prefigured" in the death of the mother.

le mie metafore avevano ormai consumato la sua
    coscienza di rosa rondine neve
e forse una di esse aveva prefigurato la mia morte
. . . .
mia madre sarebbe stata punta dalla nera rosa
    dell'eternità e non si sarebbe piú svegliata[44]

One of those poets anthologized in *La quarta generazione* who sense a strong affinity with Gatto is the Sicilian Bartolo Cattafi (1922), a neobaroque poet very sparse in his style. Cattafi uses *rosa* as an ordering principle, a sign of pattern and spatial orientation, and a means to contrast "map" and "territory," sign and referent:

Quelle calde compatte regioni
variegate d'odore
d'origano e di rosa
non erano regioni
il mondo è privo

d'origano e di rose
erano inchiostri sapienti
distesi su feconda cellulosa.[45]

★ ★ ★

s'uniscono i pezzi staccati
d'un disegno
. . . .
come un'onda o una rosa[46]

★ ★ ★

Dall'altra parte della mano tesa
del petalo della foglia della rosa
. . . .
tutto è pazienza e attesa
che ribalti la pietra pasquale
il lato tombale delle cose
dall'altra parte il vero disegno
il volto luminoso
il regno il regno il regno.[47]

The persistent sense of a cosmic design yet to be discovered is also manifest in the rose's being negated, decomposed, or ruined:

Becco crudele

. . . .
petalo per petalo
seccamente rimbecchi
il fioco marciume della rosa.[48]

★ ★ ★

non sono fiori
non sono rose
cani gialli usano la pianura
per camminare a sghembo

le guardie appiattite contro i muri
fanno crocchiare l'artrosi nelle mani.[49]

From an image reminiscent of Michelangelo's neoplatonic aesthetic emerges an alliterative catalogue in which the rose, like the whale and swallow, is expressed through various metonyms in order to stand finally for the larger "ungraspable something":

Da un blocco di materia
. . . .
emergono a colpi d'ala
petalo pinna piuma
il cèfalo la rondine la rosa
ti volano incontro nella mente
e quasi affiora anche l'inafferrabile qualcosa[50]

The scaling of orders and meta-orders is a typical feature of Cattafi, whose "Target Practice," written in London, describes the ruination of the genuine rose by corruption: as one arrives "at the center of the living color" of the social hierarchy, one discovers the moral emptiness of the British monarchy:

In quest'aria la rosa si rovina;
partendo dal più grande
dei cerchi concentrici,
giungendo al centro del vivo
colore trovare che di già
vi pascola la nera
la dura la vera cheratina
d'un insetto definitivo . . .

Dio vi salvi
con la vostra Regina.[51]

Cattafi relies on the rose as a figure of the multifarious, here as an envoi to a poem: "La stagione finisce in questo suono / di eriche e di vento. Va' amore, / o macchia della mente, rosa triste / desisti dal dominio."[52]

Anacreon is alive in the work of Cristina Campo (1923), here in her translation of Eduard Mörike:

> Come rapì l'inverno le rose che d'Anacreonte
> cingevano il capo al simposio, ov'egli la lira toccava,
> a lui stillò l'Afrogeneia l'essenza squisita alle chiome,
> e in ogni canto ora è fusa fragranza soave di rose.
> Ma solo se intoni un *amante* le note del vecchio sereno,
> inonda gli atrii e le sale l'antico, regale profumo.[53]

In the first poem of her own scant body of verse, "The Farewell Step," Campo writes: "E mentre indugia tiepida la rosa / l'amara bacca già stilla il sapore / dei sorridenti addii."[54] Again one sees a submerged eros in the idleness of the roses and the dripping of love's ointments. As one reads in Campo's essay "A Rose," she believed in the religious transformations that occur in fables and the liturgy. Lacking that transmission or exchange, the lover is reduced to a tumbling marble statue:[55]

> Solo la veemente
> mia ora lacerava
> sul cancello le rose . . .
> E riversa una statua
> forse mordeva—al turbine
> di quel volo—l'autunno,
> origliere di muschio[56]

The voice of Renata Giambene (1924) attests to love's consummation in "thoughts" of sexuality, conveyed by the subtle freshness of the rose's scent, the touch of its thorns, the purging force of the carnal flame:

> Rosa d'aprile lussuriosa,
> i tuoi petali spaccati di donna
> han voluttà di rugiade.
> Le foglie son come
> pensieri di carezze.
> Spine di fuoco sulle braccia nude

> di una fanciulla bionda
> che ha lo stesso profumo
> di una rosa d'aprile.[57]

In the most recent Anacreontic poets, the rose is a redemptive sign of sexual intimacy: for Giancarlo Albisola the rose petals are lips he kisses:

> Che sarà piú del biondo paglierino
> dei tuoi capelli, lisci su la nuca,
> delle tue labbra schiuse a suggellare
> il bacio, rossi petali di rosa,
> le dita esangui fatte ad evocare
> il tocco di invisibili tastiere?[58]

This tendency is also apparent in Lucio Zaniboni: "Ognuno cerca qualcuno o qualcosa / io cerco te come il giardiniere la rosa."[59] And it is evident in Luigi Tassoni (1957): "Bocca di cinque rose // smarrite nell'essere tese / sfiorite dall'ape veloce / nell'alba ch'è piena di gocce."[60]

As a footnote to this chapter concerned with artistic process, the rose of courtship, and its archaic display, let us consider Bernardo Bertolucci's (1940) use of the rose as a chaste figure of beauty that "evaporates" once a flirtation is acknowledged. Love is frustrated while the "desperate game" of amorous pursuit is fated to continue "like a vice": "Già la rosa svapora in uno screzio / caldo, ma pare / che il gioco debba ancora continuare / ingenuo e disperato, come un vizio."[61] To paraphrase from the *Anacreonta*: the poet grows old but love remains young. Foscolo and Valeri, among others, have alluded to this passage, recognizing in it the stylistic fact that in the archaic lies the key to the contemporary. Standing opposite the neoclassical, Parnassian, and symbolist roses, the archaic rose defies description. As Leopardi advised, one should not attempt to encapsulate the Anacreontic. As a mannerist, one constantly reexamines one's choices, seeking a balance between desire and renunciation, between the respect for models of the past and the drive to innovation.

8
THE IDEA OF LIGURIA
Terra dove la rosa
si dice che non alligni[1]
GIORGIO CAPRONI

The post-Risorgimento period was one of continual political crisis. This translated into a literary and artistic crisis as well, and a crisis of cultural identity. As economic divisions between North and South were exacerbated, there was growing skepticism toward the center and the status quo, which included the prevailing estheticism of the literary mainstream. Gramsci's idea of a "national-popular" literature was based on the validation of Italy's multilingual, multiregional, multi-class identity, and aimed at its deprovincialization. He illustrated his idea by citing Luigi Pirandello, an author active on the local-dialectal, national, and continental-international levels.

In this chapter I will discuss the antihegemonic and decentering force of one region long left outside the national literary life. With the Savoy monarchy to its north, Lombardy to the east, and Tuscany to the south, Liguria has long preserved its autonomy. The major authors of this boundary area typically wrote in dialect until the modern period, when many emigrated to the cultural centers of Rome, Florence, Milan, and Turin. The persistent "idea" of Liguria is one which conflates the subtle and the coarse, the genial and the ingenuous. It is also the idea of a "barbarous" periphery, in contrast to the more uniform center. Beginning with the nineteenth-century visionary and patriot Giuseppe Mazzini, this is the idea of the layman, the believer who separates his religion from the conformisms of the large institutions. In the spirit of its native son, Liguria preserved the goal of a republican Italy independent of Church and monarchy, and was not persuaded by the self-serving federalism of other regions. The idea of Liguria comports the mysteries of Genoa, a large commercial port with all the worldliness and all the secrets of Lisbon, Marseilles, or Barcelona. Viewed from without, Liguria has an exotic and romantic beauty, as in Vincenzo Cardarelli's idyllic "Liguria":

> È la Liguria una terra leggiadra.
> Il sasso ardente, l'argilla pulita,
> . . . .
> Ombra e sole s'alternano
> per quelle fonde valli
> che si celano al mare,
> per le vie lastricate
> che vanno in su, fra campi di rose,
> pozzi e terre spaccate,
> costeggiando poderi e vigne chiuse.[2]

Similarly, Gozzano, who vacationed in Liguria and published in *Riviera Ligure,* provides an intensely nostalgic vision of Ligurian eucalyptuses and roses not plucked:

> Il mio sogno è nutrito d'abbandono,
> di rimpianto. Non amo che le rose
> che non colsi. Non amo che le cose
> che potevano essere e non sono
> state . . . Vedo la casa; ecco le rose
> del bel giardino di vent'anni or sono!
>
> Oltre le sbarre il tuo giardino intatto
> fra gli eucalipti liguri si spazia. . . .[3]

Romeo Lucchese (1916), a poet from northeastern Italy, also associates the rose with the exotic lushness of the Riviera, as an extension of his own Orphic "echo":

> E la mia eco è presente ognidove:
> di fronte all'alto pettine sonoro
> delle Montagne Rocciose;
> a Tokio e, a un tempo, fra le rose di San Remo[4]

The rose of Liguria's own poets is austere and realistic. It is the actual flower that grows wildly along the rugged coastline and is known physically by the poets. As Pasolini notes, the region's dialect poets express the same "tonal" and "ingenuous realism" as do those writing in Italian.[5] An early example is Mario Novaro (1868), the editor of the important *Riviera Ligure* from 1899 to 1919. The following "fioretto" (Novaro calls his poems "little flowers") conveys in a single winding sentence a sense of wonder over the cosmos, as moon and stars gaze down on the roses and cypresses of Liguria.

> Questi pini
> questi cipressi
> e le rose come sangue rosse
> quante volte ancora
> quando io più non sia
> stupita guarderà la luna
> mute cennando guarderanno le stelle
> sul colle che solo
> restava con me
> nel silenzio notturno
> a meditare![6]

Ceccardo Ceccardi (1871), a frequent contributor to *Riviera Ligure*, draws a Ligurian landscape tinged with regret and illusion. In his poem "In a Mountain Cemetery," the spontaneous figure of the "wild rose" serves to focus the poet's meditation on life and death. Ceccardi is, in Giorgio Caproni's terms, "the precursor as well as the most tormented representative of that prestigious line of Ligurian poets ... who will know how to make of the Ligurian landscape, 'with their solemn and radical desolations and negations . . . the naked bitter emblematic country' of our disinherited contemporary soul."[7]

> Tarda il sentiero in un silenzio d'erba
> che ingialla di rammarico, e rinverde
> non mietuta, tra un vel d'aridi gambi.
> Una rosa selvatica, una stella
> di iride azzurra, affacciansi talora
> da quel deserto come un sogno. . . ; un sogno
> che intende con le pallide pupille
> a un altro sogno, lungi, interminato.[8]

Another major poet published in *Riviera Ligure* is Piero Jahier (1884). Born in Genoa, he served as an Alpinista soldier in a mountain brigade in World War I. Throughout his works one finds the austerity and zeal one might expect of the son of a Waldensian priest. His style is impetuous and ingenuous, but also subtle and brooding, a poetry of epiphany and revelation that is profoundly political, as when the poet ironically proposes the distribution of his dead body piece by piece, starting with the king of Italy. One piece is to be used as fertilizer for the "roses" and "flowers":

> E io dispongo che la mia vita
> in sei pezzi la sia taglia'
> Il primo pezzo al Re d'Italia
> che si ricordi del suo soldà . . .
> . . . .
> Il quarto pezzo alle Tofane
> che lo fiorisca di rose e fior.[9]

Jahier allows the "sweet" imagery surrounding the rose to be complemented by contradictions and antitheses, which also relate to the novel structure and new communicative context of his works. Here he anticipates World War II, desiring to fight for the protection of Italy from German nationalism; later he will renege and adopt a pacifist position. He addresses a woman he might meet en route:

> montagnola se mi vuoi bene
> come una rosa che non è sbocciata[10]

In the next poem in the sequence he writes, "Stamani ogni donna porta un seno di rose verso le tue mani che hanno accettato; il mondo è completo, istantaneo e desiderabile come la donna che si avvicina."[11] In short, one sees in Jahier the traits Pasolini labels as typically Ligurian: "the realistic force inherent in the geographical names, which in other popular lyrics have only an abstract value, as a sign of the story; the lack of idealization of the woman and the scarce and generally imported madrigalism; a dry and hurried sensuality, not of vain longings, concerning erotic events done or to be done, almost never merely imagined."[12] The devout Jahier was the translator of Paul Claudel, whom he accompanied on the French poet's first trip to Florence, and to whom he explains the wondrous beauty of the roses there quite simply: "This is Italy."

> "Certo son siepi naturali,
> siepi di campo, siepi utili, queste di rose.
> Qui è Italia."
> I campi sono tranquilli diserbati ordinati
> e intorno a questi campi le siepi sono di rose.
> —Italia—[13]

Another devout Ligurian is Giovanni Boine (1887), the author of expressionist prose poems, topical essays, and religious meditations. In his *Frantumi* (a "fragmentary" title not unlike Sbarbaro's *Trucioli* or Rebora's *Frammenti lirici*), we read of four Ligurian friends, the first of whom stands gazing at the sea from his "altar of rare roses," "rich in irony and infantileness":

> Però il primo s'è fatto un altare sopra il mare: dico davvero proprio un altare di rose rare come ceri o roghi accesi, con dei neri cipressi per candeliere;—e, come un dio, sta di lassù tutto il dì a guardare.
> . . . .
> Sempre, quando vengo via mi sceglie la sua rosa più odorosa.

Così si scaccia la malinconia: che è quasi un'allegria la vita a cosa a cosa.[14]

Boine's Christian faith was tested during years of illness before his death at age thirty. Recent scholars have corrected the earlier tendency to ignore his Ligurian nature: attached to the severe landscape, the common labors, and the past generations. In essays such as "Regional Decentralization" and "The Crisis of the Olives in Liguria," he argues the case for regional autonomy from Rome and attacks the "religion of money" that effectively dismantled the socioeconomic structures of the Ligurian agrarian culture. A tireless and spirited critic, Boine defended Mazzini against such Florentine voices as Papini and Soffici:

> And you say for example . . . that Mazzini is confusing and has unclear ideas, fished from here and there, put together who knows how, etc. But listen: Mazzini was a man and you whose ideas are so clear and pure will never, any of you, accomplish the thousandth part of the good he did for Italy; you with your pared down universals![15]

Boine defends the integral and religious man against the syllogistic *arrivisme* of the futurists and other self-promoters. His prose poem "Transfiguration" concerns his own Calvary, as he meanders lost over the Ligurian landscape, confessing his incomprehension and emptiness, citing a cherished line from the book of Job:

—Ci sono giorni di vuoto che le rose non danno profumo
né gli occhi vedono; la gente degli spettri scorre
via per strada senza rumore.
. . . .
—Sono una macerata bocca che non ha sapore; monotono
expecto donec eveniat immutatio nostra.[16]

Also for Ligurians Renato Serra (1884) and Angelo Barile, poetry is the primary vehicle of a natural religion. In each of their modest outputs, the floral *rosa* appears but once:

> Ascolto nel silenzio
> una rosa, bisbiglia:
> è lei che mi respira
> sul petto.[17]

As Barile writes, "[Serra is] a limpid voice that must be added to those of our Liguria in the broad chorus of contemporary Italian poetry"; Giorgio Petrocchi situates him in the "Ligurian Line" begun by Mario Novaro: "the suggestiveness of sonorous timbre, the melodiousness of the lyric construction, the taste for rapid breaks, have nothing impressionistic about them, even when Serra lingers lovingly over the things of nature, since the attentive and participative descriptivism is urged on by a dense reemergence of thoughts beyond the image which remains always pure."[18]

It is this purity and austerity of the image that Barile announces in a poem describing a country funeral. Poetry can approximate the "arcane language of things," only if it succeeds in being a transparent document of spiritual candor:

> Oh l'arcano linguaggio delle cose
> penetra i cuori:—"l'ala della Morte
> col suo remeggio fascia l'universo."—
> E pare che un crepuscolo sia emerso
> su da un pallido regno d'ombre smorte:
> i crisantemi nascono su le rose.[19]

Camillo Sbarbaro (1888), like his friend Montale, was a victim of fascism and was concerned throughout his work with the concept of justice. He resided in Liguria his entire life, though he did make the obligatory cultural sojourn to Florence, as is seen in the poem below. Sbarbaro was an antipositivist, and his poetry is typified by "elements of harsh stoniness, almost granularity, and of grotesque deformation."[20] His rose is a vestige of a rustic culture and a means to affirm the inherent spirituality of the creative process. In the final version of the following variant from *Trucioli*, his collected prose poems, the ceremonial "roses" are replaced by the generic "flowers," so as to echo the name of Florence's cathedral rather than one of its cafés:

> i due mignon adagiati in carrozza e coperti di *rose*
> da uomini in silenzio
> come per un rito
> mentre il cielo s'apriva su Santa Maria del Fiore.
> Firenze vuol dire
> Le sigarette Capstan
> *Je sais que tu es jolie* cantato nell'aprile 1914
> Il Bar della Rosa, il suo dolce cuore che arde
> la notte . . . [21]

The young poet declares that his love of life is not due to its placation of his "horrible sadness," or its brief fulgurations, but to the finitude of consciousness itself, as symbolized by the roses of fleeting opportunity:

> ma, Vita, per le tue rose le quali
> o non sono sbocciate ancora o già
> disfannosi, pel tuo Desiderio
> che lascia come al bimbo della favola
> nella man ratta solo delle mosche,
> per l'odio che portiamo ognuno al noi
> del giorno prima. . . . [22]

Sbarbaro's acute sense of ennui and even self-hatred is mitigated in this dialogue with "Life" by the process of observation itself, leading to what Fortini calls the "victory of form over nullism."[23]

The poet's constructivist vision of reality reinforces his scientific refinement as an expert on lichens. In the following passages *rosa* is a paper flower in one's Sunday lapel, but also a lichen:

> Tutti quel giorno avevano all'occhiello o alla cintura infilata
> una rosa di carta.
> Coi zerbinotti ci intruppammo che tra la folla indomenicata
> perseguitavano lo sciame delle fanciulle . . .

> Colorata di verde è la nostra felicità di quel giorno; di verde
> bottiglia trapunto di rose di carta.
> Ma inutilmente chiedemmo di vedere la *Rosa Fiorita,*
> promessa dall'insegna. Sfacciata doveva essere, custodita
> sotto campana di vetro, nutrita di sola rugiada.[24]

Sbarbaro sees the multifarious, polychromatic plants, including the one named "Rose in Bloom," as galaxies, tribes, little brains. The lichen represents the potential of new life forms; it lies at the boundary of the plant world, the symbiosis of an alga and a fungus (the former a plant nourished by photosynthesis, the latter nourished by absorption, especially of moisture): "E' di quegli anni l'incontro esclamativo con . . . l'*Anagallis tenella* 'per manine di foglie aggrappata all'argilla, scampanellante d'un'umile rosa.' . . . Nell'amoroso inventario d'una minima parte del mondo, quella a me congeniale, appagavo senza saperlo il 'supino amore delle cose.'"[25]

Sbarbaro is taken with the Heraclitean uniqueness of each lichen, compared to the unrepeatability of his own life, "the flower of infancy, lasted for me a moment, bloomed to my eyes but once": "Nel quaderno in cui lo riposi non fui più a cercarlo (con gli stessi occhi non si vede due volte); né in tanti a tu per tu con la terra mai più mi toccò di incontrarlo. . . ."[26] Both rose and lichen share an ethic of poverty and humility, the one as metaphor for the other, far from civilization. The humble lichen in its countless manifestations constitutes for Sbarbaro an "herbarium" or a "sample-book of the world." As such it is a figure of disillusionment, of the escape from the maelstrom.

Adriano Grande (1897) is a Genoese autodidact, journalist, and volunteer soldier in the Ethiopian war. In "Album," he lyrically compares his memories to the "pages of an album on a screen"; he equates the rose with a pain in the heart that numbs one, that inures and trains one's conscience to denounce the vanity of worldly things:

> O inutile catalogo,
> vana frondosità! Tu resti scialba,
> mia vita, resti scialba. Questa rosa
> spinosa che mi porto
> nel cuore toglie senso

alle svagate immagini. Son corti,
anche se vuoti, i giorni
che ti restano ancora, per sciuparli
in questo gioco.[27]

Against the negation and disparagement of the vain "game" of recollection, the rose stands for the self-questioning of poetry, understood as a recursive operation that "removes the sense from the unwanted images"; it thus stands for the change in the observer occasioned by one observation that is passed on to the next observation, and back again to the observer, whose awareness of this system of feedback entails a new understanding of perception and cognition.

Like his compatriots, Eugenio Montale (discussed again in chapter 9) assumes a moral position for the poet within the social fabric; but there is also a great contrast at work between the landscape and the self.[28] Montale resists abstract concepts of unity (metaphysical or poetic) in his pursuit of actuality and suchness: "To capture in words the substance of things was of course impossible, but the desire to do so persisted none the less. Montale's starting-point is with the realisation that poetry in its aspiration toward essentiality must abandon the poet's conceptualised perceptions of the world."[29] His choice to retain metric forms that others had abandoned expands the realm of possible relations with the tradition.

In "The Lemon Trees," published in 1926, one sees an opposition of the low register, of common grasses and the "lemon tree," and the high register of the poets laureate. Montale chooses the former, but in the process creates a new standard for the high lyric tradition, a new poetic language in which philosophical questions acquire the suppleness and peculiarity of natural objects. By stressing the rugged objectness of the Ligurian coastline, Montale purged unwanted ornament and tired themes and conventions—"dead" metaphors like boxwood, privet, and acanthus, but also the rose (paired with the acanthus in classical poets like Foscolo and Perse).

Giorgio Caproni (1912) is another Genoese whose ruggedness and contrastive nature instinctively reject the ills of formalism, as in this litany dedicated to the poet's native city, Genoa, and to its marketplace, in which the rose is aptly paired with garlic, popularly reputed to be the "flower of love":

> Genova nome barbaro.
> *Campana, Montale, Sbarbaro.*
> . . . .
> Genova di Soziglia.
> *Cunicolo. Pollame. Triglia.*
> Genova d'aglio e di rose,
> *di Prè, di fontane Marose.*[30]

This passage is typical of Caproni's "binarism" and "almost echolalic rhyming," and deservedly gives citizenship in the circle of Genoese poets to the Tuscan Campana.[31] In the lengthy "Litany," syntax is suspended for the sake of an avalanche of nouns and attributes set in rhyming couplets, in which the "barbarous" and the sublime freely mix. Genoa is Caproni's home city, worldly and multifarious; it is also the passageway of pilgrims, the spectacle of light and sounds evident in Campana's "Genova" and other works in which the city is an ethereal dream landscape which changes through the course of a day.

In "The Elevator," in which Caproni practically fuses the love figures of his mother and wife, he states his desire to ascend to heaven by way of the Castelletto elevator (in the Lombard Alps). The desperation over such a departure is reflected in the conversion of the rose—first stolen, then a gift—into poison. The levity of the literalization is accentuated by the sing-song rhyme of the septenaries:

> Ruberò anche una rosa
> che poi, dolce mia sposa
> ti muterò in veleno
> lasciandoti a pianterreno
> mite per dirmi: "Ciao,
> scrivimi qualche volta,"
> mentre chiusa la porta
> e allentatosi il freno
> un brivido il vetro ha scosso.[32]

Caproni described Liguria as a "land of boulders" inhabited by "a people of stone," as well as, in the epigraph to this chapter, a "land where, word has it, the rose does not stand straight" (*Res amissa*, 113). Bent by the sea wind, the Ligurians refuse to conform: "With the Ligurians Roccatagliata Ceccardi, Sbarbaro and Montale (and other poets of the Novecento who had employed analogous rhythmic techniques), Caproni shared in the tendency to emphasize the dissonance implicit in the coarser sounds of the phonic weave."[33] In the two-line "Almost aulic dedication," it is the remoteness of the picked rose, in time and space, its "mountain" origins, "as if Longobard," that give it affective density: "Ah rosa, quando ti colsi, / montana e quasi longobarda ancora. . . ."[34] Such a rose retains the symbolic potential found in sacred texts, precisely by standing for the trivial. In his final two books, Caproni continues his meditation on the word. The word is a beast, a trap, a seduction; it is the poet's "prey." As such it is both a liberation and a trace of what is lost: might this "evanescent prey," Caproni asks, be "a dungheap? a rose?":

> La preda (un letame? una rosa?)
> che tutti abbiamo in petto, e nemmeno
> le febbri di dicembre (i campi
> morti d'agosto) portano
> sotto tiro . . .
>   La preda
> evanescente . . .[35]

His final poems, short meditations on death, are conundrums. As Sereni writes, "a strategic retreat is in course in the most recent poetry, having the purpose of preserving those elements that tend to denature and overturn the poetic fact and its very presence and necessity."[36] The following poem is titled "Small Thought of the Anti-metaphysician":

> "Un'idea mi frulla,
> scema come una rosa.
> Dopo di noi non c'è nulla.
> Nemmeno il nulla,
> che già sarebbe qualcosa."[37]

The rose is "stupid," like the idea of nothing (or something) after death. As throughout Caproni, the rose evokes the *value* of poetry as the bearer of knowledge that will not be captured or rationalistically synthesized, but is ever emerging in language and resists objectification.

Carlo Bo (1911), a prodigious scholar and ally to the hermetic movement, leaves his native Liguria for Florence at age eighteen; yet he retained, in the words of Caproni, his Ligurean "refinement (*signorilità*), without ever raising his voice or seeking to turn a smile [at dinner] into noisy laughter. . . . The Ligurians are by their nature aristocrats."[38] The other essential qualities of this *licusticità* shared by Bo and Caproni are their laconism and attachment to the common world of Ligurian "things," features that tie Caproni to the Genoese dialect poets Firpo, Malinverni, and Acquarone.[39]

A key figure in contemporary Ligurian dialect poetry is Cesare Vivaldi (1925). Like Caproni, Vivaldi is a poet of "things" (including roses) more than "words": "'Cose / u vö stu ventu? A nu u cunùsciu. A porta / serrài, cu e rose / de bandùn attaccàe, d'u campusantu / mi a nu u conùsciu.'"[40] Also in his Italian verse, *rosa* is an anti-aulic fixture, a thing of compressed materiality, a figure of loss, destruction, and disillusionment:

> E tutto sembra continui come prima
> ma non è vero;
> le piazze si aprono, le strade s'ingolfano
> d'aria
> e io non cammino, non respiro, non vivo,
> perdo le mani, gli occhi,
> rotolo sul selciato come una palla di stracci
> finché tu non mi fermi,
> i pugni colmi delle rose
> fiorite sul davanzale.[41]

* * *

> Sul fiume, tra una lucertola morta,
> un sasso lucido e un bruno
> cespo di rose,
> mormora un Pan desolato e canuto.[42]

It is in this "Panic" region that one also finds the work of Giuseppe Conte (1945), about whom his fellow Ligurian Italo Calvino writes, "the 'Ligurian line' of 20th-century Italian poetry . . . has striven after starkness, aridity, attenuation, that is, qualities that are entirely opposed to [Conte's] own." And yet, Calvino argues, the regional features remain stubbornly present in Conte: "To transform a landscape into reasoning: that is certainly the real theme that Liguria has offered and continues to offer in her poets and writers."[43] Conte shows his "Ligurian" aridity in the concluding lines of his tour de force, "Elegy Written in the Gardens of Villa Hanbury": "Siamo aridi, vinti, ma nell'ora / di questo tramontare ci è possibile / un canto."[44] Against the backdrop of sea and severe slopes, Conte's rose stands as a sign of spring and self-realization, for the poet and his addressee. "Io ti ho conosciuto nel tempo / dove astri e fiori coincidono / tu stelo ellisse zoppa di luce esplosa / tra tutte le rose possibili / io anche possibile umana / rosa."[45]

Conte aligns himself with the "heretics" of the twentieth century—Antonin Artaud, Georges Bataille, Henry Miller, D. H. Lawrence—who reject the tortured Western ego and concept of a spirituality in crisis and have liberated themselves from the "great white poets" (such as Eliot) who renounced the mysteries of the "dance" by indulging in abstractionism. Conte advocates an oneiric, choral, and energic poetry free of the struggle of the will, free of the towering myths of Prometheus, Faust, and Oedipus.[46] In the playfully titled "After Marx, April," he shows this desire to lose himself, to be absorbed in the all, in a Whitmanesque liberation enabled by a "forgetting" that leads to the rediscovery of spring and the roses, as heard in the final rhyme of *rose* and *cose*:

>   l'eterno
> rinascere sterile e muto delle
> cose
> "Marzo è stato freddo e triste, ma
> poi l'Aprile, praterie, portenti
> di scarlatto lieve, ciliege, e le prime
> rose"[47]

At the limit of the transitory, as figured by the rose, lies the idea of catastrophe, of the fertile, rocky, isolated strip of land falling into the sea, its secrets intact. Here that landscape is summoned up to report on the psychic perturbations of the poet:

> Un giorno se mi leggerà il lettore del
> terzo millennio, saprà che c'erano gli
> alberi e i desideri, le palme e i pini, e gli
> eucalipti dalle foglie a quarto di luna, e le
>
> rose: chi non voleva più soffrire, e chi
> voleva amare tutto[48]

The recollection of the Etruscan presence in Liguria is in the spirit of D. H. Lawrence's *Etruscan Places,* with its notion of "phallic consciousness":

> Dicono che devastava gli orti, i
> mirteti, le lunghe siepi di rose.
>
> Ma che cosa poteva fare lui, se non
> correre, odorare, distruggere? Il sangue d'amore
> non vuole organi sottili, statici.[49]

In the following elegy, that landscape is a field of acanthus likened to the human form and specifically to classic heroes who are disarmed, transformed into lovers in the current day, before the "roses" fall at sunset:

> inarrestabile, una marea, l'inesistente
> elisse di qualunque orbita: fasciami
>
> del tuo movimento, dea della corsa e dell'arco
> nell'ora prima che cadano i raggi e le rose[50]

Conte, like his fellow Ligurian Columbus, is a cosmic navigator, as here in the voice of the Celtic god Manannan Mac Lir, whose songs are received from macrocosm and microcosm, from the moon and from the brilliance "of cherries and roses":

li porta il gemmare barbaro
dei ciliegi e delle rose
delle stelle vaganti, nuvolose
delle ragazze-cerve, dell'erica[51]

* * *

tra i fiori e gli astri, il primo sgorgare.
Neanch'io ti ricorderò più. Solo viaggiare potrò
allora, tra le madri delle rose e delle galassie.[52]

The idea of Liguria is finally a particular example of the idea of Italy, and is compatible with the "idea of Europe" proposed by Osip Mandelstam, here in terms of his own "Acmeist" revolt against the rose of symbolism:

> The [symbolist] rose is a likeness of the sun, the sun is a likeness of the rose.... Nothing is left but a terrifying quadrille of 'correspondences' nodding to one another. Eternal winking. Never a clear word, nothing but hints and resonant whispers. The rose nods to the girl, the girl to the rose. No one wants to be himself.[53]

In simple terms it is the idea of place, as opposed to the temporal and abstract symbolic regimes of the European capitals. Whether in the pathetic evocations of Ceccardi, the metaphysical questioning of Novaro, the rustic solitude of Jahier and Sbarbaro, the anti-aulic, anti-Olympian redimensionings of Boine, Caproni, and Conte (and we could add the name of the Ligurian transplant to Milan, Giovanni Giudici), it is landscape, rugged and graceful, that holds sway, a landscape pictured against the backdrop of a mythical migration, and audible, once again in Girardi's words, in "the dissonance implicit in the coarser sounds of the phonic weave."[54]

9
OF RAREFACTION AND RHETORIC
Le rose cascano, le spine rimangono.
TUSCAN PROVERB

Rhetoric, the third branch of the trivium, is based on the arts of grammar and dialectic. Traditionally paired with the erotic and celestial influences of Venus, the role of rhetoric is to persuade, to provide nuance and subtlety, coloring and conviction. But what occurs in an era when, as signaled by the work of Michelstaedter, persuasion and rhetoric can be construed as conflictive opposites? Or how, given the lexical nature of our study, does the evasion or deformation of a lexeme signal a change in literary sensibility? At root is the question of "lexical coloring," as expounded by Yuri Tynianov:

> The coloring of the word is all the more stronger when characteristic of the activity or environment which first altered and created it. Thus, *lexical coloring is realized only outside the activity and conditions for which it is characteristic.* In a strict sense, each word has its own lexical coloring (created by epoch, nationality, and environment), but this *lexical distinctiveness* is recognized only outside this epoch and nationality. In this sense, lexical coloring serves as evidence.[1]

In this chapter I examine the work of poets who manipulate lexical coloring so as to form a "theory" of the rose.[2] The theory is the product of an observer who cannot stand outside the process of observing, in this case a perceived representational dilemma concerning a certain type of poetic language. The idea of an autonomous theory, as is sought by the poets in this chapter, is that of "a theory that does not attempt to represent only the relations among the variables in reality, but also the recursiveness and changeable structure of reality."[3] Such an autonomous theory avoids the vicious circle of infinite regression by inviting recursiveness into the process. In the case of the rose *topos*, those poets sensitive to its status as a "dead" metaphor tend to treat it as a nonentity. In order to arrive at the depth and illumination that a living metaphor can provide, the dead metaphor of the rose is displaced. This is accomplished either by a rhetoric of rarefaction or by rarefaction of rhetoric. In these opposite but complementary fashions, the poet constructs an autonomous theory of the rose based on its virtuality or absence.

In the major works of Eugenio Montale—*Ossi di seppia* (Cuttlefish bones, 1925), *Le occasioni* (Occasions, 1939), *La bufera ed altro* (The storm and other things, 1956), and *Satura* (1971)—one witnesses "the wearing down of the great symbolist canon of the European bourgeois tradition, in short the exhaustion of its expressive possibilities."[4] The rose does not appear in any of these works, as if excluded by Montale's austerity and sophistication, his poetics of negation, attenuation, and memory. We remember in Montale the solitary eel and the creaking pulley above the well, the crackling of branches underfoot and the bitterness of the customs house; in short, the brief glow of the lemon trees but not the rose. In his rhetoric of lessness Montale has no use for a figure of generic beauty, theological purity, or unquestioning passion. His rhetoric tends to rarefy experiences and encounters, to pair them with emblematic objects situated on a plane of contingency. One faces the risk of being a form of human detritus in an indifferent world; his use of oxymoron illustrates the soul's options, its prescience of a general aura of metaphysical peril. The entire opus might be labeled as "enantiodromic," given its constant concern for things transformed into their opposites.

On a macro level, the Ligurian severity and harshness of Sbarbaro, "the elements of harsh stoniness, almost granularity, and of grotesque deformation," remain present throughout his younger friend's production, though sublimated in the cosmopolitan atmosphere of Florence and later Milan. With *Satura* in 1972, Montale's poetry becomes openly gnomic and propositional. By the *Diario del '71 e del '72* (1974) and the *Quaderno di quattro anni* (1977), the usually brief poems proceed by means of syllogism, enthymeme, abduction, or philosophical analogy. The recursivity of Montale's poiesis benefits from the posing of paradoxes. It is not surprising in this context that Montale shuns the rose. In fact the only two uses of the substantive *rosa* are in the late *Diari,* and they are ironic:

> Mi chiedi perché navigo
> nell'insicurezza e non tento
> un'altra rotta? Domandalo
> all'uccello che vola illeso
> perché era lungo e troppo larga
> la rosa della botta.
>
> Anche per noi non alati
> esistono rarefazioni . . .[5]

The pattern of buckshot ("la rosa della botta") is a stochastic event which stands metaphorically for the perils confronted by the modern individual.[6] One senses a kinship here with lines by fellow Ligurian Cesare Vivaldi: "mentre il piccione d'argilla / si libra in attesa della rosa di piombo."[7] In a polemical poem addressed to Marxist critic Alberto Asor Rosa, the inversion of the name of the flower to form the critic's first surname suggests the backword nature of his understanding of poetry: "Asor, nome gentile (il suo retrogrado / è il più bel fiore) / non ama il privatismo in poesia."[8] The rose is only present by periphrasis and as a dead metaphor, the irony of the term "retrograde," meaning conservative, nonprogressive.

In the *Diario del '72* the use of the rose is again second-hand, being a citation of Giuseppe Parini's famous incipit to the 1764 ode "La Educazione": "Torna a fiorir la rosa / che pur dianzi languia," where the rose stands for the blush of a boy's cheeks:

> Torna a fiorir la rosa
> che pur dianzi languia . . .
>
> Dianzi?
> Vuol dire dapprima, poco fa.
> . . . .
> E' questo il solo fiore che rimane
> con qualche merto d'un tuo Dulcamare.
> . . . .
> Basta che uno
> stupisca che il tuo fiore si rincarna
> a meraviglia[9]

By questioning the archaic language of the citation, the poet frames the "dead" rose metaphor, even as the generic "flower" metaphor is alive in the wonder expressed over the tired dancer's "reincarnation." The citation of Parini is an example of what Harold Bloom has called transumption: "Such retropings of earlier tropes could be called transumptive, or metaleptic, echoings, instances of the interpretive and revisionary power of a poetry perpetually battling its own belatedness. . . . A transumptive style is to be distinguished radically from the kind of conceited one which we usually associate with the baroque."[10]

In the case of Montale the belatedness is extreme, in comparison, for example, to Alessandro Manzoni's early ode "In morte di Carlo Imbonati," which also contains a citation of the same line of Parini, spoken by the voice of the deceased Imbonati: "E di quel, che sul plettro immacolato / Cantò per me: *Torna a fiorir la rosa.* / Cui, di maestro a me poi fatto amico, / Con reverente affetto ammirai sempre / Scola e palestra di virtù."[11] Manzoni's eulogy to his probable biological father is conducted in the high neoclassical register of Parini, whose satire of the Milanese aristocracy inspired him in his youth. Though he renounced these verses after his conversion in 1810, much of the neoclassical language remains intact in the new romantic rhetoric.

Paolo Valesio has taken the citation of Parini one step further, vulgarizing the blushing subject and overturning its theme of innocence (and echoing the *topos* of the rose and violet in the adjective applied to the term of the simile: "inviolato"). The poem's title, "To State Precisely the Infamous," points to the perceived gap between poetry's mission and the diminished conventional means of attaining it:

> Ah, grazia e consolazione della poesia:
> Quant'è mignotta la rosa
> *che pur dianzi fioria*
>   *o languìa*
> o sfiora.
> Perché la rosa, simbolo della donna
> (ah, mignona dei sogni miei)
>   e dell'amore?
> Perché la rosa somiglia un conno.
> Stretto e tepido conno dapprima, inviolato.[12]

In terms of Bloom's definition, Valesio's retroping (and re-retroping of the Montalean gloss word "dapprima") is more baroque and conceit-ridden than it is transumptive.[13] That the rose is a rhetorical sign of lessness is evident in Valesio's *La rosa verde,* a book whose only mention of the rose is in the book's title, where its "greenness" suggests the plant, not the flower. The green rose is the plant before it blooms, a state of potentiality and youth.

That this stage can be ominous is made clear in Alfonso Gatto's "The Sleeping Brakeman," a disturbing poem of nine hendecasyllables in which the greenness of youth apparently contributes to a catastrophe:

> I treni merci perdono nel cielo
> l'alba di Roma, ha il fresco d'una porta
> la campagna più verde della rosa.
> Un ragazzo annottato nel casello
> ha la lanterna morta contro il cuore
> e la bandiera al piede, sta sognando
> di chiedere per tutti il suo perdono.
>
> È strano, forse portano già al muro
> l'ombra di gioventù che gli sorrise.[14]

The syntagm "la campagna più verde della rosa" ("the countryside greener than the rose") is laden with tragedy, as suggested by the echo in line seven ("perdóno") of line one ("pérdono") and the severity of the final couplet with its image of execution by firing squad and the finality of its verb in the remote past. The linguistic coloring of the "green rose" is also found in the incipit of Joyce's *A Portrait of the Artist as a Young Man,* where the child Stephen sings an Irish song. When he sings "green wothe" it is because of a lisp. Joyce "is creating in imagination that which does not exist elsewhere."[15]

> But what kind of gift is this sun which doesn't disarm in the season long since programmed.
>   *O, the wild rose blossoms*
> *On the little green place.*
> He sang that song. That was his song.
>   *O, the green wothe botheth.*[16]

Valesio too is concerned with this vivifying of imagination. In his "Porta del sole," a "Voice" is overheard in the marketplace announcing a "living idea" that is "louder than the whispers of the flowers." At the same time the voice is an image, a Latin inscription painted on a plaque: "Rosa, servant of my heart":

> E qual è il passo prossimo?
>
> Lo indica una Voce
> che chiama un'idea viva;
> traudita nel mercato,
> più forte che i sussurri
> dei fiori, è questa una Voce
> dipinta su un cartiglio:
> "Rosa, ancilla cordis mei."[17]

The traveler finds himself in tribulation in Madrid, recording a discovered visual motif which echoes, in the name of Rose, the Annunciation by Gabriel to Mary; as he does so he is awoken by the silent "whispers" of flowers and the signals that return him to his faith. The truth of the preterition conveys the difficulty of prayer. It is a truth found in the pattern of one's errors; the difficulty of the utterance leads back to the recursive nature of poeisis itself and the invented nature of the confessor's reality. Once again an autonomous theory is formed in the encounter of effable and ineffable. The verb *traudire* (paired by Leopardi with *tradire,* to betray) has the double meaning of "overheard" and "mistaken" (Rose for Mary, visual for aural signal, whispers for silence), acknowledging as it were the smallness of the pilgrim when confronted by the gravity of his sins.

The rhetoric of rarefaction is similarly present in the neohermetic poet Silvio Ramat (1939). Here in "The Winter of Theories," the rose is subject to the figure of *adynaton,* or the positing of the impossible:

> la rosa agitata d'un sognare
> adulto, a strappi, fra i due sassi in attrito
> —il non potuto, l'impossibile—
> poi riuniti nell'unica scheggia
> che, opaca, taglia in anticipo il giorno.[18]

In the early poem "After a Garden," "the triumphant malice of the ephemeral roses" is precisely *not* a sign of the life that is present in Montale's canonical figure of "The Eel," here alluded to:

> una vita di cui non pare segno
> la malizia trionfante delle rose
> di passo, ma l'eterno sassoso della nebbia
> sulla fertilità di questo limo
> che il giardino inventato non cancella.[19]

Ramat the critic has found in "The Eel" "a self-metaphorizing which poetry itself intentionally carries out, by presupposing in such a way to mirror itself more quickly and more directly in its own possible meaning."[20] This is also a recurrent feature of Ramat's verse, as here in "Take-off," which sets out to cross an abyss to arrive at a new city built upon the ruins of the old. Life is viewed retrospectively as the concern for chance and destiny, framed by a series of rarefied images:

> Ma più fatica per te
> rimbucarti a ritroso, tentarlo carponi l'opaco

> sottocoperta ch'è stata la vita,
> la *tua* vita, ritoccarne la rosa
> dei sensi per avvertirla scheletrica oggi, chiedere
> amore ai lunghi viaggi, ai cuori più nudi del tuo:
> vita del caso anche tu, parassita fra edere,
> pronto in quel verde a sfamarti, restìo
> —cecità—a rarefarti.
> . . . .
> Disselciare, infierire
> sul tessuto d'ogni pietra. Così bene
> si umilia il disegno d'una città,
> se ne offende la rosa dei respiri
> non ancora tracciati.[21]

Rosa is at once a synesthetic figure and "the pattern of breaths not yet traced out," "the garland of the senses." In the aptly titled "Quel fiore e la sua ombra" (That flower and its shadow), Ramat presents the rose as an obsessively returning reminder of one's mortality:

> nel campo della memoria la rosa,
> l'ombra di quella sua rosa sul muro,
> col fiotto del matematico amore,
> che a un'ora della giornata—lui l'unico
> a catturarla—univa in dolci nodi
> quel fiore e la sua ombra, solo rosa
> e ombra, di tutto l'orto o giardino . . .
>
> Si ridisegna in voi come patema
> (una cosa vicina? un emblema?).[22]

A recent Ramat poem concerns a dying woman, a former rumba dancer and stenographer who, in her day, enjoyed the favor of her neighborhood, the "rose" of their applause:

> Un rione disertava
> il biliardo e le corse: per lei.
> Nella rosa dell'applauso
> la corteggiava.[23]

Another sort of theory is arrived at by Elio Filippo Accrocca (1923), who engages in verbal "graftings" (or "innestografia")—of Apollinaire, Joyce, Gadda, Pound, and here of his master, Ungaretti:

> L'HÔTEL DES CARMES *era già così nel '20*
> *e nel '13 all'epoca del suicida Sceab*
> il pugno non strangoli la rosa del simbolo
> sui muri i manifesti non lasciano dubbi
> la difesa dei prezzi è un ostacolo al dollaro[24]

Like Ungaretti, Accrocca mourned the loss of a son: "Domani è la tua festa: / diciotto rose rosse / sopra il tuo nome inciso su una pietra."[25] With his noun-centered style, Accrocca remains skeptical toward the various movements he occasionally imitates (symbolism, classicism, avant-garde). This is seen in his grafting onto Umberto Eco's rose, which concludes with a wild speculation on the possibility of a declension of the Latin noun *rosa* that is "iotic"—that is, barbaric, a solecism:

> lector/lupus
> in fabula trattata come rosa
> poi rosai rosae rosam rosa rosa
> rosae rosarum rosis rosas rosae rosis
> *semi*-sconvolta. O *iotica* per caso?[26]

An ironic "golden rose" is among the cult objects and practices eschewed by the Church in 1968, at the time of the reform of the Pontifical Court:

> cappellani segreti e custodi dei triregni
> accoliti mazzieri maestri di camera
> coppiere segretario d'ambasciata
> guardaroba sacrista foriere maggiore
> latori della rosa d'oro e scalco segreto . . .[27]

The rhetoric of rarefaction finds an extreme example in Luigi Ballerini (1940), whose elision of logical or figurative continuity results in flashing moments of sense scattered over the illusory grid of a unifying syntax. As Remo Bodei writes, "Ballerini's writing appears, thus, on the one hand, like a procedure of attenuation of the sense of reality and . . . on the other—as an induced effect—like the development of the sense of reality itself by means of the materialization, in the form of words, of possible worlds that spring forth out of ordinary living."[28] Ballerini's "navigation" around the rose cliché amounts to a theoretical reminiscence of a bygone age:

> e poi (rivolto al pubblico) mi sembra
> di morirti ogni volta tra le mani,
> di arruffare una lana ostile al tempo
> del vino e delle rose, quando emerge
> l'allarme, il messo in fila, il fiuto
> dei cani alle calcagna.[29]

In "a work of mercy," Ballerini playfully opposes the arbitrary directional "thing" that is the "compass-card" (*rosa dei venti*) to the interior and impenetrable "thing" that is the "heart," "an oily moth," a destiny subject to the winds of chance:

> Viene quindi a rimorchio
> di una borsa, di un'arpa esauriente:
> una cosa è la rosa dipinta dei venti
> e una cosa la tarma oleosa del cuore
> tirato a sorte.[30]

The neohermetic Cesare Viviani (1947) is similarly allusive and enigmatic. In "Madame" he constructs a metaphysical dialogue of absence, elegy, and error with a vaguely iconic noblewoman who resides on a coat-of-arms and banner, an ambiguous representational field that houses roses both common ("tra le rose comuni afferma / pochi passi per questo bene inutile") and lofty ("la prima ordinata affiora / altèra cima di rosa / vede spiegando il panno").[31] Viviani's texts contain allusions to Greek, Nordic, and Celtic legends, which add to the sense of extravagance and wonder at "the work [that] welcomes all these weaves into it."[32] His rhetorical distancing from the real subtends a spiritual mystery, as in the following passage in which the dead metaphor of the rose as a cliché of female beauty is retroped in order to find the live metaphor of the "work." The merit of the "double rose" is discovered in the spirituality of the flame-flower nexus:

> un angelo non aveva passato il coro
> —l'animale acquistato va in penombra
> col riso la doppia rosa che s'avvale . . .
> e assonnati investe la fiamma i calici[33]

Gaston Bachelard writes,

> Of all flowers, the rose is a veritable image-hearth for imaginary plant flames. It is the very embodiment of imagination eager to be convinced. What intensity there is in this single line by a poet who dreams of a time when
>
> > . . . the fire and the rose are one.
>
> In order to give double value to each image they must harmonize in both directions. A dreamer of roses must see an entire rosebush in his fireplace.[34]

Viviani's creation of voices and ephemeral characters continues in *Preghiera del nome* (1990), here in a lyric (recalling Leopardi's early "L'uccello") in which a bird momentarily free from its cage is recaptured and consoled:

> Mi presero. Mi riportavano a Vicenza
> perché là stavano i miei padroni, spiegarono.
> Io non capivo, supplicavo
> e loro ridevano e dicevano: "Vedrai, carino,
> che quando arriviamo e ritrovi il tuo posto
> nella voliera, accanto alla rosa,
> ricorderai ogni cosa."[35]

The same theme of an animal's orientation to its cage is present in Tiziano Rossi's (1935) "Galline," in which the boundaries of a chicken coop, as defined by habit, are compared to the memory of white roses whose images disappear at dusk:

> "Che care, che belle, le vostre gallinelle . . ."
> "Così le rose bianche sulla sera si smarrisce . . ."
> . . . .
> Nessuna mappa fino lì disegnerà
> la piccolezza di quel luogo zampettato,
> ed invisibili oramai tutte in un punto
> restano chioccianti creato logorato
> a un po' rigirarsi nella mansuetudine.[36]

In "Honey" Rossi rarefies the rose by negating it three times; the act of collecting wild chicory is set in a darkened memory:

> Questo solamente dice la compagnia,
> il vostro coro grave che
> quasi per niente si sente: "non sono rose
> non sono mica rose, non."
> S'incupisce il vocìo ma ancora non finisce
> e giù in questo oscuro, magari,
> senza parere sarà come il miele.[37]

In the following passage his rose is again concerned theoretically with the false representation, the deception, the cage:

> e perché tu conservi il tuo viso di rosa e perché
> per me buona spina rimani; e in che luogo,
> o madama odorosa, domani
> la tua pazzia delicata recherai.[38]

The Triestine dialect poet Virgilio Giotti (1885) avoids *rosa* entirely. Even in his translation of Leopardi's "Imitazione," where that poet followed the original French *rose*, Giotti uses "flower":

> 'Na roba sola so:
> che sicuro andarò do' che va tute le foie; si, tute, [s]e le xe
> bele o brute.[39]

The verse of Cesare Pavese (1908) is typified by its prosaic and tragic qualities. Reminiscent of Gatto and Michelstaedter, Pavese stretches the pseudo-Alexandrine line into free verse in which the associations customarily drawn from the rose are absent: in the pitilessly gray and complacent solitude of the aptly titled collections *Lavorare stanca* (Work is exhausting) and *Poesie del disamore* (Poems of love lost), there is no place for a canonical flower that stands for pulchritude, youth, religious devotion, or sexual passion. Instead one finds that the generic "cosa" is very frequent (as are "frutto," "foglia," "pianta," and "fiore").

In contrast to the poets seen above, who ironize with rhetorical subtlety about the ornamental stature of the classical rose, the following poets abandon that rhetoric and ignore the rose. This avoidance is seemingly undertaken for reasons of spiritual rigor and austerity, and stands in our study as a demonstration of the corollary that a scientific study must assess negative as well as positive data.

Sandro Penna (1906) is a love poet whose Catullan agape employs the rose as a metaphor for the male organ; in both of his two uses the analogy is advanced by the witty use of metonymy. In one of his typically brief, snapshot-like poems, one reads of the "swollen urinal": "La rosa al suo rigoglio / non fu mai così bella / come quando nel gonfio orinatoio / dell'alba amò l'insonne sentinella."[40] In the second, one reads of a farmhand who "felt a tuft grow in the hayloft":

> Quando discese la svelta lattaia
> un cespo sentì crescere nell'aia
> l'assonnato garzone, e in sulla cima,
> aperta come rosa mattutina,
> ma quale una rugiada assai più calda,
> il latte a lui restò, non la lattaia.[41]

In a private letter from Penna to Pasolini, written upon the latter's publication of *Poesia in forma di rosa*, one senses a conscious imitation by the laconic Roman of the effusive style of his younger compatriot:

> La rosa è la forma delle beatitudini.
> Beata l'angoscia in forma di rosa . . .
> beate le secrezioni i visceri della letteratura l'oratorio la

mistificazione
quando finalmente s'aprono in forma di rosa![42]

Bianca Maria Frabotta has expressed the need to question mainstream feminist thought's linguistic engagement with the body.[43] In her poetry she avoids any literalization or reification of corporeal notions into principles of thought:

Cantilena dolcemente
la mamma dei tassisti, meccanici sensi di rosa
seni indolenziti. Comincio a sapere cosa
s'offre la pratica dell'inconscio
radio-taxi poème:
la corsa luminosa degli scatti
e la grazia che la notte promette.[44]

Frabotta takes pleasure in onomastics and wordplay, as here in "to botanical rose": "A far calare il capo della rosa a perdere la spina / cadde infatti la esse e morte divenne la tua sorte."[45] In the title poem of her book "Flight Notes," Frabotta states that "the loudspeaker invites us,"

a permutare ciò che non è ancora stato
con ciò che non è mai stato
utopia, primizia
o rosa del deserto
questo salto nel vuoto improvviso . . .[46]

Primo Levi (1919), a survivor of Auschwitz, compiled a small but impressive body of poetry, from which the rose is absent. One possible reference to the rose is found in "Agave," a poem to the agave plant, which defends itself against extravagance and incomprehension. The plant's self-description ("Non sono utile né bella, Non ho colori lieti né profumi") and its stated ambition ("Costruirmi una casa, Forse non bella, ma conforme a un disegno") reflect the poet's desire to avoid the aggravated *vanitas* of the decorative rose.[47] One does find the flower in a translation from Heine, in which a damsel who habitually remonstrates against the "Jews" has fled her many courtly suitors, who only annoy her with their flattery. Outside the castle she finds, much to her surprise, a handsome, blue-eyed knight:

> E sommesso nelle tenebre
> Delle rose il respirare
> . . . .
> Rose rosse come il sangue
> Danno impulso al loro amore.
> "Però dimmi, cara amica,
> Perché questo tuo rossore?"
>
> "Sono state le zanzare;
> Oh, mi sono odiose, quasi
> Quanto le incresciose schiere
> Degli ebrei dai lunghi nasi."[48]

After their lovemaking, she must know his name before departing; the joyous knight reveals he is the son of a famous rabbi. The conventional use of roses suits the nature of a fable, here translated by one who was a master of tropes but for whom the word "rhetoric" always had negative associations.

The only apparent use of the rose in the work of the Lombard Luciano Erba (1922) is in his recent poem, "Autoritratto," where it symbolizes the limits of speech and the sense of wonder at being alive. Erba's pairing of "roses" and "things" contrasts the singular experiences of the "here and now," in which the rose remains a figure of wonder, and the repetitive incomprehensions of "every evening," the drab confusion of myriad objects and passing days.

> Tutto qui il tuo qui e ora?
> Interroghi l'alfabeto delle cose
> ma al tuo non capire niente di ogni sera
> sai la risposta di un mazzo di rose?[49]

In the work of Margherita Guidacci (1921) the signifying plenitude of the aulic rose collapses into nothingness. Guidacci's fourteen-line "Tu buio, buio fuoco" is a negation of such "intensities" as the sonnet, or the aulic rose. The use of *rosa* is set within a negation:

> Tu buio, buio fuoco!
> Senza scintilla né fiamma.
> Di te non diranno
> Che come rosa fiorisci
> In delicati petali,
> Non diranno che sei una stella
> Per rischiarare la notte.[50]

In "The Star-Bearer," a series of poems based on Etruscan myth, Guidacci has given extraordinary care to the flower-galaxy metaphor and its ancient rosy light:

> Tu che vedi
> una Galassia in ogni fioritura
> terrestre e un fiore in ogni stella, hai legato
> così il mio dono al più amato, per me,
> fra tutti gli astri . . .
> . . . .
> chi può, infatti, dire
> con sicurezza che sia ancora viva
> Betelgeuse? Forse noi vediamo solo
> quanto di lei ricorda il cielo, a lungo
> attraversato dall'antica luce
> rosata . . .[51]

In "Only Charity," the Christian virtue incarnate in the rose burns above hope and beyond faith:

> Arde di carità
> il tuo cuore e nel vincolo di fuoco
> adombrando la rosa, trasfigura in giardini
> tutta la tua intricata solitudine.[52]

In the first part of this chapter we saw the rose manipulated as a cliché or ironic citation. In the second part we have seen how the evasion of the rose is "a difference that makes a difference," or what Lotman calls a "minus-device." What unites the poets who rhetorize rarefaction, like Montale or Valesio or Ramat, and those who rarefy rhetoric, like Pavese, Levi, Penna, or Giotti, is their skepticism over poetry's ability to engage the real with the rote motifs of a formulary. In the former group, the "form of the expression" predominates, while in the latter it is the "form of the content." In either case one finds the implicit directive to reread *cum grano salis* the poetry of a tradition in which the troping of the rose went unquestioned.

10
THE ENCYCLOPEDIC ROSE

🌹

In his 1953 essay *Writing Degree Zero,* Roland Barthes delineated the opposition of classical and modern poetry. Classical language is "relational" and "abstract," and "form[s] a surface according to the exigencies of an elegant or decorative purpose": "the classical flow is a succession of elements whose density is even [while] classical conceits involve relations, not words." Beginning with the poetry of Rimbaud, "thanks to a kind of violent and unexpected abruptness, [words] reproduce the depth and singularity of an individual experience": "Modern poetry . . . destroys the spontaneously functional nature of language, and leaves standing only its lexical basis. It retains only the outward shape of relationships, their music, but not their reality." In modern poetry the "Word" is the "dwelling place"; the reader "receives it as an absolute"; it is "encyclopaedic" in that it "contains simultaneously all the acceptations from which a relational discourse might have required it to choose."[1]

One finds an early vision of such a voice in Guillaume Apollinaire, who, remarks the critic Giovanni Dotoli, in "[refusing] the disorder and chaos of the Italian futurists," proclaimed in 1918 the emergence of "'une liberté encyclopédique,' no less free than that of a newspaper, which on the same page treats many different subjects and simultaneously visits the most distant countries."[2] The Roman-born poet is the figure of the exile and the wandering Jew. In his first publication in 1901 we read, in "Claire de Lune":

J'ai peur du dard de feu de cette abeille Arcture
Qui posa dans mes mains des rayons décevants
Et prit son miel lunaire à la rose des vents

O rose à peine rose en des livres savants . . .[3]

The final line, added at a later date, juxtaposes sign and referent, perception and representation, in order to focus on the word and the process of learning. This line, "Oh rose barely a rose in the knowing books," echoes the previous line and adds the poetic virtue of surprise, a necessary ingredient to learning, *paideia*.

As Italo Calvino has written, "the idea of the *open* encyclopedia" is not that of the closed circle of knowledge (*enkyklo-paidéia*) of the Enlightenment, since "today we can no longer think in terms of a totality that is not potential, conjectural, and manifold."[4] Amid the considerable debate in the post–World War II period over the role of the intellectual, poets rejected the notion of "pure poetry" and sought to respond to the questions of the day. In the wake of tyranny and genocide, some even theorized the "death of poetry," or its transformation into a reactive rather than a revelatory phenomenon. It was in this climate that an encyclopedic voice emerged, to reinvest in the cognitive force of the poetic word.

In the open encyclopedia one finds a mixture of registers and discursive forms, an entry into the world of commerce and cosmopolitan culture. The word of varying densities, citizen of an expanded lexicon, advocates the democratization of knowledge in its structures and organs of distribution. The pioneers in this direction are Vittorio Sereni, Giorgio Caproni (seen above), Attilio Bertolucci, Leonardo Sinisgalli, and Andrea Zanzotto. They serve to connect the anti-aulic dialect poetry of Carlo Porta, Biagio Marin, and Giacomo Noventa to those younger voices who also resist the Pygmalion aesthetic of modernism, which seemed fixated on imagery and the oneiric world of one's phantasms. They sought to deny the canonical split between the "I" who speaks for the ethos, as an outgrowth of culture, and the natural or affective "I." In terms of Korzybski's dichotomy of "map" and "territory," a polarity which the votive poets efface under the sign of the sacrament, the encyclopedic poets depend on these terms' separation. Perception and representation are two discrete operations belonging to two distinct moments in the creative psyche. This awareness leads to a poetry of wit and circumspection, resignation and diffidence, even as it informs a lyricism rich in epiphanic fragments and agnostic glimmerings.

Largely shaped by the 1930s and 1940s, these poets achieve an aesthetic decompression and contribute to a more flexible and variable, more national tone. Shunning affiliations, they enjoy a camaraderie reminiscent of Dante's *fedeli d'amore,* who exchanged sonnets to demonstrate skill and communicate friendship, an ingredient missing among the major poets of the preceding half-generation. Though the antefact for this poetry was the experience of civil strife, the notion of "committed" literature was already passé to these writers. In response to the historical crisis of their young adulthood, they would choose to address time itself and the transitory, and find in the rose a figure at once fresh and archaic. These factors distinguish them from the post-symbolist and hermetic understanding of the "word" described by Renato Poggioli:

> With its symbolistic concept of the word as synthesis of sound and symbol, poetry re-enters, actually and potentially, with excess and defect, into a dialectic of often extreme and antithetical alternations: D'Annunzio's word-sensation and Pascoli's word-dream; Saba's word-passion and Quasimodo's word-sentiment; and, a final paradox, Montale's word-object and the word-incantation of Ungaretti. Enough to show that, in the poetics of the Word, it is not God who is made Word, but Word made God.[5]

For the encyclopedic poets there is no esoteric cult of the poet, no "Word made God," no metaphysical posturing, no horror of the void, and no abyss. As Barthes states above, the word returns to its lexical basis, a change that coincides with Contini's proposal of a "verbal criticism" of poetry. An inspiration in this regard is Pascoli, whose nominal style and highly determined lexicon offered a way out of the cul-de-sac of monolinguistic formalism.[6] Like him these poets engage a highly nominal style with an emphasis on proper nouns: names, places, myths, individuals, cultural identities. This is seen in Caproni's reference to Luzi and his "rose fiorentine" (seen above), in a poem that reveals the camaraderie I have mentioned:

> Via Guinizelli, a Monselice.
> Perduti nella mattina
> d'erba e di sole (di rose
> —nel sole—quasi fiorentine)
> io e Mario verso la stazione,
> nell'ora della separazione.[7]

Attilio Bertolucci (1911) seeks a special form of knowledge in poetry, a *paideia* by which to translate the material culture of provincial life into myth. He has the same worldliness as Sereni and the poets of the Lombard Line, yet he asserts it in a more lyrical manner, in poems saturated with light and tenderness. In one of his earliest poems, Bertolucci relates the gift of the last rose picked in the fall, overtaken by the first fogs, to "a portrait of you at thirty." The poem hinges on two verbs in the future tense, in the first and last lines, which increase the resonance of the gift:

> Coglierò per te
> L'ultima rosa del giardino,
> La rosa bianca che fiorisce
> Nelle prime nebbie.
> Le avide api l'hanno visitata
> Sino a ieri,
> Ma è ancora così dolce
> Che fa tremare.
> E' un ritratto di te a trent'anni,
> Un po' smemorata, come tu sarai allora.[8]

In "Alone" a mountain field is the site of a religious calling, where a meadow-altar is "sweetened" by "il corallo vegetale della rosa canina

/ e il ciuffo tenace che stringe la nocciola."⁹ In "The Hotel Again," a hard-working young girl is endowed with the classical image of the rose as the woman's mouth.

> non ti meravigliare
> della figlia-serva dodicenne infinitamente laboriosa—
> suo è il compito arduo di levare le macchie
>
> di trattenere il canto su la bocca bella piccola rosa.[10]

And in "A Simple Piece," the poet asks if the roses he bought for his lady were not in spirit bought for the flower vendor, a captivating seventeen-year-old "rose":

> Non vende che rose
> bruna rosa infiammata
> ragazza di calza smagliata
> che m'ha guardato negli occhi
> sino a farli abbassare.
> Diciassette anni e una sedia
> di vimini mezzo sfondata
> ora di colpo s'è alzata
> per spegnere le sue rose
> con secchi d'acqua azzurrina.
> Per chi le compro per te
> per lei che s'è illuminata
> all'improvvisa fiammata
> dell'accendino insieme
> fumando e scegliendo le rose?[11]

The same erotic potential in the day-to-day combines with a mythic dimension in the following:

> ti sei fregiata sul collo
> e lo scollo di segni vermigli
> che attendono soltanto il mite balsamo

dei baci per ardere più forte
quasi li avesse provocati
una sferza di rose . . . Tale ne usò Afrodite
a punire e gratificare Eros protervo

figlio perduto nei giardini oscuri
della nostra Parma in un eterno giugno . . .[12]

The rose is a figure of mending and regeneration that Bertolucci carries within him. Such a humble rose lends itself to prose: "as against the hermetic and symbolist tradition, I thought that one must actually fall into prose for poetry to be reborn."[13] In his research into local and family history, he consistently reconciles the demands of discourse and musicality. With respect to women, Bertolucci's rose is an emblem of interiority, as in the case of nannies who spend their most fertile years raising other people's children: "smorte rose da orto destinate / a sfogliarsi nubili, crescendo / bambini altrui, lentissime stagioni / dipanando con le dita sottili."[14]

The "epic-familial romance," *La camera da letto,* is set in and around Parma, of which it supplies ample catalogue of the material culture of the nineteenth and twentieth centuries. The "bedroom" gradually comes to symbolize the poet's family, seen over several generations. The rose appears at least forty-six times in as many "books" of the epic (the number of cantos in the *Orlando furioso*) and is a figure of great versatility. It may serve as a simile for the transitory, or be a simple printed image on a garment:

abbandonato
ora come un petalo o una foglia
di rosa alla violenza della pioggia
primaverile, che non dura, il sole
di nuovo vivo sui fiori, gli uccelli
e le palpebre di chi gli va incontro.[15]

* * *

L'incendiarsi fulmineo, il profumo
e il fumo

dello zampirone
fanno parte di una ceremonia
celebrata dalla mamma a capelli
appena sciolti sulla vestaglia
di rose rosa.[16]

The rose is found throughout the book, whether in aspects of institutional life—Church, bourgeois society, the classic literature—or in the private space in which the poet senses a "terror" that can only be "resolved" in poetry. When the rose is invoked as the flower of May, the last to bloom and the first to fade, it stands in contrast to the long work days of the poet's ancestors: "they go out so early, they return so late." Building on this pathetic image, the rose supplies the ground for that "fiction of roses" that stands for the family bond:

In questo breve
passaggio al mese delle rose facili a sfogliarsi,
in questo periodo che verrà
senza sangue abraso dalla memoria di tutti,
essi
escono così presto, tornano così tardi,
intraprendendo ognuno un viaggio diverso.
. . . .
Anche tu, riluttante, uscito
incontrerai l'avventura d'una giornata, mentre
il destino già s'accorcia e striscia
sul selciato umido di sole
dietro quelli che la notte dormono presso di te
nelle stanze comunicanti attraverso una finzione di rose?[17]

Like Bertolucci, Vittorio Sereni (1913) provides a personal, yet detached and critical, testimony, grounded in the sense of poetry as dwelling place. Sereni possesses a true *flatus vocis*, that is, the eyes and ears of a witness who endures and reports on a violent and unpredictable reality. He uses poetry to demarcate the "lost" occasion and to dialogue with the dead. This involves an opening up of poetry onto an epistemological dimension, a boundary area. The Janus-like duplicity of Sereni's historical person is related to "the theme of mirroring oneself in others or in one's double" and "the repetition of existence . . . endured as a manifestation of the viscosity of living . . . an ambiguity in which one sees, at the same time, the final shoring up and the liquidation of the twentieth-century poetics of 'memory.'"[18] Much of Sereni's free verse does indeed "mirror itself," forming strange loops of recursive inquiry, as in this early composition in which the "fields of roses" contrast with the imagery of exploding torpedoes:

> ti specchi in verde ombrato:
> siluri bianchi e rossi
> battono gli asfalti dell'Avus,
> filano treni a sud-est
> tra campi di rose.[19]

While sharing much of the "momentary" concept of the poem typical of other new lyricists, Sereni dramatizes the psychological condition of a prisoner of war held for two years in Algeria by the Allies. The rose is an image of resistance against oblivion, whose survival is threatened:

> Spesso per viottoli tortuosi
> *quelque part en Algérie*
> del luogo incerto
> che il vento morde,
> la tua pioggia il tuo sole
> tutti in un punto
> tra sterpi amari del più amaro filo
> di ferro, spina senza rosa . . .[20]

The "tu" addressed is the uncertain region of Sereni's imprisonment in Algeria, where the presence of barbed wire (*filo spinato*) is related as a "thorn without a rose" ("*filo* / di ferro, *spina* senza rosa").

Of Sereni's 1965 volume *Gli strumenti umani*, Mengaldo notes the prevalence of repetition as a stylistic marker: "Sereni's poetry fuses its three or four variable elements into recurrent units, it perpetuates within its space its three or four colors, within a continuous iterative and circular movement."[21] This iterativity takes on a musical-memorial structure in the next passage, in which the rose again resists negativity: "*Ombra verde ombra, verde*-umida e *viva*. / Per dove negli *anni* delira / di *vividi anni* mai avuti un tulipano o una rosa."[22]

Sereni's rose comments on the constructivist act of perception, on "minimal actions, and poor human tools bound to the chain of necessity, the net cast in vain into the centuries": these actions resist an undoing, a coming apart.[23] In the following lines the rose is the sign of a traitor, an embellishment which fails to cover the bitterness sensed against "a Judas" or a version of the prostitute Thais "masquerading as a forest rose":

> a risarcire vecchi danni anni
> di protrazione il bacio
> cadde sulla ferita.
>
> Presto persino a me fu chiaro
> che mi si premeva contro un giuda
> o piuttosto una taide
> travestita da boschiva rosa.[24]

The following lines from "Visit to a Factory" expose the illusory well-being of the worker's lot during Italy's economic boom, despite a more hygienic workplace:

> La potenza di che inviti si cerchia
> che lusinghe: di piste di campi di gioco
> di molli prati di stillanti aiuole
> e ersino fiorivi, cuore estivo, può superba la rosa.[25]

Sereni conceives poetry as an opening toward a sense of place, in the spirit of Apollinaire or René Char, whose works have been compared to the mortarless stone houses of his Provence: "a dwelling for both the breath and meditation."[26] The image is a powerful one for the encyclopedic poets in this chapter, given its focus on specificity, humility, the use of allegory, the Pascolian emphasis on the home, and—in the lack of "mortar"—the surpassing of outmoded means of semantic and syntactic linkage. This is the sense of the long poem "Un posto di vacanza," which deals precisely with a dwelling, and in which Sereni, Char's translator, explores the relation between intellect and affect:

> L'ombra si librava appena sotto l'onda:
> bellissima, una ràzza, viola nel turchino
> sventolante come ali.
> Traffitta boccheggiava in pallori, era esanime,
> sconciata da una piccola rosa di sangue
> dentro la cesta, fuori dal suo elemento.
> . . . .
> Amare non sempre è conoscere ("non sempre
> giovinezza è verità"), lo si impara sul tardi.
>
>   Un sasso, ci spiegano,
> non è così semplice come pare.
> Tanto meno un fiore.
> L'uno dirama in sé una cattedrale.
> L'altro un paradiso in terra.[27]

The natural imagery serves as a catalyst for a reflection on the nature of knowledge and perception. The "rose of blood" on the dying fish relates to the poet's ruminations on the "flower" that provides "a heaven on earth" and the "stone" that "branches out" into an architecture of the spirit.

Leonardo Sinisgalli (1908), who began his career as a hermetic, appreciated the anti-eloquence of a Montale, but not the obscurities of a certain neorhetorical allusiveness: "If the poets of my generation have had some merit, it is that of having considered rhetoric an unworthy operation."[28] No other poet has provided a more "mortarless" dwelling place, in the terms introduced above for Char. At once ephemeral and worldly, enigmatic and concrete, Sinisgalli's poetry is set in the "double belief (*culto*) of the Dead and of the Muses."[29] For this native of Lucania, the great importance of Leopardi was in his move toward a prose register, an insight that helps us comprehend his use of that poet's "Imitazione" (seen in chapter 1), which overturns its message of death's leveling of all things:

Naturalmente ogni cosa, anche un sasso,
Una rosa potrà bastare al mio cuore
E la musica senza posa delle striglie
Scosse nelle stalle. Questa mattina
Gli uccelli pigolano come topi, la gallina
Si spulcia a un balcone della valle.[30]

As a mathematician, Sinisgalli has a keen insight into the "irrational" knowledge of poetry, which he formulates in terms of the imaginary numbers used in calculus. As he wrote in a letter to Contini, Sinisgalli's idea of the "design" of the universe is expressed by a formula in which the multiplicand is an imaginary number, such as the square root of -1.[31] Sinisgalli is the author of a prose collection titled *La rosa di Gerico* (The resurrection plant), and his short prose works are often pithy and epigrammatic statements on the nature of poetry and the need to break rules in order to reflect on the nature of perception. His natural adversary is the Italian tradition of belletristic eloquence:

> DIRITTO E ROVESCIO.—Il diritto e il rovescio di ogni cosa, come di una calza, di una foglia, di una mano. Qual è il rovescio di una rosa?[32]

The koan-like question carries us into the realm of solid geometry and topology. As an unfolding and self-similar structure, the rose is a three-dimensional manifold that can suggest a model for the cosmos.

Similarly its odor, the intoxicant of love poets over the ages, is presented in the short dialogue "The Rose of Father Segneri" as a perceptual enigma, "form reversible and unreversible, form like a stocking." In the dialogue between a fortune teller and a king, the former cites the seventeenth-century orator Father Segneri, whose marvel at the rose is intended to prove the existence of God. The latter closes the dialogue, confirming the religous insight while converting the rare rose to a common flower, predicting a day when human awareness will have grown:

> [Fortune-teller] *"One must find who it is that inserted there so*

deeply the odor which it emits with equal sweetness on all sides; one must find who, etc. etc."

[King] Really only an ordinary flower [*une fleur quelconque*] ... But perhaps later an intelligence will come that will make a commonplace out of a phantasm, a calmer, more logical and much less excitable intelligence than ours, which will find every circumstance which seems baroque or transcendental to us no more than the link in a chain of very natural causes and effects.[33]

Whether meditating on the unchanging and impervious nature of a crystal, the metaphysical uselessness of a machine, or the organic quality of Leopardi's verse, Sinisgalli uses a "low" prose voice to reflect on the "truth of appearances" and the role of "scribe" at our historical point in evolution. In "Lucania," the ancient roses of Paestum are contrasted to the current fields of fava beans, squash, and chicory. These hungry and humble plants symbolize our present "age of the fava bean," in contrast to the proud "age of the roses," the period of fertility and classical harmony:[34]

> Di là dalla dolce provincia dell'Agri
> Siete approdati alle rive sognate,
> Oscuri morti familiari.
> Le vostre salme hanno dato salute
> Al verde degli orti.
> I campi di fave si sono allargati
> Oltre i cancelli:
> Dove arse superba l'età delle rose
> Le capre pestano la terra
> Nei giorni di siccità[35]

One critic sees this "age of the roses" as a "symbol of refoundation of a more human civilization"; he cites Sinisgalli: "Will there come an era of great exoduses, of swarms of peoples who will find, around a clump of roses, the principle of a more ardent charity?"[36] These vanished roses, at once trivial and mythic, exemplify Sinisgalli's artisanal approach to a medium he construes as personal but not confessional. As a mathematician he observes both the accuracy and the "wildness" of the world around him. In the following elegy the rose is an object of mourning, evanescence, and futility:

> Ieri il mondo era in festa
> e come in sogno
> io colgo una rosa
> nel giardino di una moschea,
> accendo un cero sulla tomba
> di Giacomo Natta, mi riempio
> le tasche di mughetti
> nei boulevards.[37]

In a poem to his daughter Sinisgalli treats the rose as a matrix of growth, life, and reawakening:

> Figlia del mio destino
> cresci come la rosa nel giardino.
> Dormi figlia mia, dormi e cresci,
> dormi come cresce il grano appena nasce.[38]

In this humorous poem Sinisgalli remembers watching his aunt change clothes, and the difference between her appearance and that of his mother.

> Non aveva le labbra strette
> di mia madre e quelle pupille
> dolorose. Zia Gerolomina era chiara
> come le rose.[39]

Sinisgalli separates the singularity of the aulic and funerary flower from the multiplicity of its "fatuous names." As he passes by a Roman flower vendor, he senses the presence of both love and death:

> Vantano i nomi fatui della rosa
> ai piedi delle statue le fioraie romane.
> Stringo le spine secche sulla proda
> ove un giorno spuntò improvviso dall'Erebo

Amore, e accolgo nel vecchio bavero
il fiato che ogni anno si fa più debole.[40]

In his book *L'età della luna,* poetry is seen as the product of a destructive instinct and a merely "ephemeral joy" that "prospers on desperation." The poet is an "inconsolable" melancholic who skeptically reevaluates certain nineteenth- and twentieth-century poets (Mallarmé, Valéry, Pound): "One can reverse Valéry's dogma and can say that the marvelous can exist only if fabricated by chance."[41] Involved in his fabrication are conventional icons, such as the rose, used to reconnect to a sense of historical place which he, as an "exile," has lost.[42] This is the sense behind the following metahistorical reflection. Standing at the tomb of the thirteenth-century emperor Frederick II, Sinisgalli invokes "a wretched rose":

Non ti negasti al gesto debole,
alle estasi vergognose, al palpito
nella gola, al tremore nel petto.
Per una misera rosa,
per una pazza zanzara.[43]

Frederick, who was also a poet, reigned with an iron hand, expelling gypseys, *jongleurs,* actors, Jews, and prostitutes from his realm. The wretched rose that resulted was conformist and unreal, earning him the irony of the iconoclast Sinisgalli, who himself frequented one prostitute in particular, whom he referred to metonymically as "la putrida rosa" (the putrid rose).

The fellow Lucanian Albino Pierro (1916), a mournful and musical dialect poet, complements Sinisgalli and reminds us of the reappraisal of the position of dialect poetry after World War II. While Sinisgalli emigrated to Milan and then Rome, Pierro never left his native Tursi. He provides a picture of the *pagus*— the social entirety and tissue of village religious culture (here in his Italian translation):

Una cosa
che dentro a un vetro raspa e chi si affoga,
e tu spaurito pensa ad una rosa

che ghiacciata sbatte sugli specchi
di una cassetta rotta e poi nel lampo
si rianima e muore.[44]

* * *

Amore,
amore forte più del vento
che sradica le piante e fa crollare
le case e che leviga le montagne,
daglielo sempre a tutte quante le cose
un poco di questo fiato di gigante
e poi una luce uguale come il lampo
che si abbraccia le spine fra le rose.[45]

In two poems in Italian dedicated to his daughter Rita, Pierro's rose is twice a figure of metamorphosis and grace. The first, constructed on the metaphor of the "swift river" of life descending to the sea, is a calque of Petrarch's sonnet "Rapido fiume che d'alpestra vena":

Pensa al rapido fiume
che qua e là s'intorbida e ingarbuglia
fra le divelte piante e le radici
terrose,
e poi, con la fragranza delle rose
sul bianco dell'altare
s'illimpidisce e placa dentro il mare.[46]

* * *

Sento le tue manine
giocherellare sul mio capo stanco
di tumulti, o mia Rita;
e penso ad uno stagno
lungo una vecchia strada
che un dolce vento sfiora
con petali di rosa.[47]

With his death approaching, the roses come to stand for a figure of redemption:

> La stanza mi sorrideva
> con la semplicità delle fanciulle
> che sbigottite guardano e ti vedono
> nell'azzurro dei campi.
> Poi le incantate cose,
> come in un dormiveglia, mi sommersero
> in un mare di rose.[48]

First published in *Linea lombarda*, Renzo Modesti (1920), sets the rose in a specific place and time—Berne on New Year's Day 1946, a localization typical of of the "Poesia *in re*" Anceschi formulated as the common trait of the Lombard line: "A poetry in which the color of the sound is born from the image, not the image from the color of the sound, a poetry which is not poetry of the idea of poetry, nor a poetry *ante rem*. Objects intense and charged so as to make of the image a symbol."[49] Modesti's rose possesses a double character: it is being and becoming, a hopeful present (the New Year) threatened by an unresolved past:

> Se s'impiglia nel cardine la rosa
> venuta sulla soglia all'anno nuovo
> (tra cenere rimena quello vecchio
> i cocci dell'indugio
> ove ritrovo
> ore stupite d'anima delusa)
> allora tornerò su quelle strade . . .[50]

The rose of Giorgio Orelli (1921) combines the sensitivity to "things" of the Lombard line with a rich Petrarchan substrate and lyricism, as exemplified by the following eight-line phonic celebration.

> La passa rosa va,
> passa tra verdi arsi,
> esita e, sfatta già,
> desidera affondare.

E c'è chi la ricorda
come da anni, e aspetta
l'Arcangelo, che suoni
dal mare la cornetta.[51]

Orelli mixes the lyrical and discursive in a manner similar to Bertolucci and Sinisgalli; his rose is at once magical and concrete, an effective prop in a believable action:

Pochi giovani sparano
a poche rose di carta. Altri ballano
nell'osteria.
Un frate dalla barba rossa s'aggira rammentando
che c'è un'altra passione per cui vende biglietti
della riffa. Nessuno grida. Nessuno pare a disagio.[52]

In the twelve-line "Country Funeral," Orelli lists a series of observations of that last sacrament, ending with the point of view of a horse, and the spontaneous rose, one of the glimmers of hope suggested by Orelli's book title *Spiracoli:* "ma sopratutto di come da un prato / ci guardava un cavallo / pensare cosa? e di come / dal suo secco rosaio una rosa . . ."[53]

One of the major forces in the encyclopedic redimensioning of the rose is Andrea Zanzotto (1922). His early works are syntactically stable and melically exquisite, and question the ability of the word to deliver accuracy and truth. The title of his first collection, *Dietro il paesaggio* (Behind the Landscape— the source of the next four citations), indicates this bracketing of the ostensive facts of nature and of the common verbal parameters assigned to "inside" and "outside." Playing on the distinction between landscape and psyche, Zanzotto pairs the rose and the sun as absent symbols of Christian prophecy:

Pasqua ventosa che sali ai crocifissi
con tutto il tuo pallore disperato,
dov'è il crudo preludio del sole?
e la rosa la vaga profezia?[54]

And again, the sun and rose as symbols of destiny, in wartime:

> Il raccolto ormai piú non sarà
> quel sole che
> custodirà domani
> l'avvento di te dai tesori
> delle rose invernali
> ma lascerà senza voce
> l'azzurro di corallo
> dei monti solitudini amorose . . .[55]

In the plaintive portrait of a girl "who has lost a hand forever in order to bid farewell to the rose," Zanzotto's sinuous line weaves around the paired sounds "abbonda" (abounds) and "abbandona" (abandons), which stand for the poles of summer and winter, love and loss.

> Là sul ponte di san Fedele
> dove la sera abbonda
> di freddo fieno
> e dove la pioggia raccoglie
> tutte le sue vele madide
> c'è da ieri una fanciulla bionda
> che ha un nome come una corona
> e che ha perduto per sempre
> una mano per salutare una rosa.[56]

The name of the bridge, "San Fedele," suggests the "fede" or wedding band on the "hand" of marriage the man has rejected, or severed, in Zanzotto's literalization of the symbol "to ask for one's hand in marriage." In the early poem "Indications and Moon," the rose is an emblem for a young girl's emotional frailty as she stares at the timeless ice of the mountains:

> quella ch'era bambina e sorella
> dalla sua casa
> comprende e vede
> l'antico gelo dei monti,
> si stringe al petto il cuore
> esile come rosa.[57]

In subsequent collections, from *Vocativo* (1957) to *Idioma* (1986), one sees the gradual suspension of logical-syntactic continuity and an increased involvement in the flux of linguistic codes—from neologisms to slang, from the specialized vocabularies of the sciences to a pregrammatical and babelic glossolalia. This experimentalism forces a contrast between the literal rose—understood as an agent of nature promoting unitive thought—and the Arcadian symbol of the rose, a verbal artifice hollow of meaning and outside of time:

> E se intorno la terra è tempestosa,
> se premono laggiù le rupi acerbe,
> oltre i secoli amica a te la rosa
> pende al lembo d'Arcadia pingue d'erbe.
> . . . .
> Quel nimbo ci dissanguerà, quel furto
> molle che tarpa con la rosa il mostro
> fossile e il marmo piega: stasi ed urto
> dove in un altro vero affonda il nostro.[58]

Quatrains two and four of this twenty-four-line "Bucolic" reveal Zanzotto's hopeful yet ironic attitude toward the pastoral.

The rose possesses a place in memory, in a peculiar and ill-defined area between the referent and the sign:

> Al di là dei pensieri distrutti
> dall'instabile acerbo me stesso
> conoscerò il rigoglio delle cose
> che s'irradiano dalla mia mano:
>
> dello scoiattolo gli stratagemmi
> o l'arguto manto del bosco
> o la nota rosa del cielo
> nel cui riflesso tu bionda a me torni?[59]

Between "the things that irradiate from [one's] hands" and "the known rose of heaven" there is a gap; thus the pairing of *cosa* and *rosa* (seen above in Pascoli, Sinisgalli, Pierro and Orelli) here stands for a radical discontinuity between the lofty "rose" and the banal "thing." Zanzotto's rose is enantiodromic. It points to its opposite; as a negative index of the ephemeral and beautiful it indicates the immutable and the ugly. Its order is an index of chaos. Yet precisely by being associated with the idea of nihilism it is an indicator of faith, consciousness, and values.

The following passage from *Vocativo* expresses a sense of stoical indifference, reminiscent of Montale, but rich in Éluardian surrealism:

> Ma non amo e non sono infelice.
> Forse verso un'altra vita
> nuota il sole,
> il sangue assassinato sulle soglie
> fa strada ad altre rose,
> in azzurro s'aggela la tosse, l'orgasmo,
> l'ormai recondito
> celestiale furore[60]

In "Little Elegy" the themes of death and fertility coincide in a darkened June. The "nuptial rose" is hollow as long as the name of love is "buried":

> Ti ridiremo, nome sepolto
> tra questi clivi dove nuziale
> s'apre la rosa ai pergolati
> e giugno appannato d'acque e funghi
> stillicidi insensibili protrae
> per la festa delle api e delle zinnie.[61]

The same mournful tone is used to refer to the disappearance of Italian dialects; the rose, like those dialects and the cultural practices they represent, is dispersed. Thus a certain chagrin is evident in Zanzotto's message of peace, unable as he is to ignore the images of darkness, indolence, and loss.

> Pace per voi per me
> buona gente senza più dialetto,
> senza pallide grandini

> da ieri, senza luce di vendemmie,
> pace propone e supremo torpore
> l'alone dei prati la cinta
> originaria dei colli la rosa
> dispersa il sole
> che morde tra le tombe.[62]

In the first eclogue of *IX Ecloghe,* lyric poetry, or "b," dialogs (mostly listening) with the lyric poet, or "a," who argues the merits of literature against science, finally concluding, in the words of Vivienne Hand, "that in spite of the greater social application of technological science, lyric poetry is still feasible and important today":[63]

> "Ma io non sono nulla
> nulla più che il tuo fragile annuire.
> Chiuso in te vivrò come la goccia
> che brilla nella rosa e si disperde
> prima che l'ombra dei giardini sfiori,
> troppo lunga, la terra."[64]

The simile establishes poetry's place in human affairs, and its vulnerability. If the rose (human affairs) is delicate and ephemeral, the droplet (poetry) is a mere visitation, pure evanescence but also pure constancy.

In the third eclogue of the same volume, Zanzotto writes of sleep as a giant rose enveloping him after the wine harvest:

> Sí, è un'ubriachezza stolta
> questa, non durerà. Col dolce
> colchico e il sonno che oltre me traspare
> come una lata ricchissima rosa
> riavrò anche il supremo il superfluo l'azzurro.[65]

Zanzotto's sense of humor emerges in headlines cited from a local journalist who invented glamorous place-names for undramatic local sites ("The Riviera of the Roses"), just to drum up interest:

"Vengono per la callaia"
"Dal Passo delle Donne, dalla
Riviera delle Rose, dall'Eremo di Giotto"
(meraviglie geografiche
vertiginosamente inidentificabili
eppure con lo stremante vellichio della presenza) . . .[66]

A compatible poet to Zanzotto is Fernando Bandini (1931), also from the Veneto, whose poetic practice is mediated through the "dead languages" of dialect and Latin. Bandini sees the latter as a "metahistorical" language capable of underscoring the most concrete and mundane issues of contemporary reality. In the concluding lines of "Two December Saints," the rose emerges as a beacon of Christian hope in the face of the universal flood and the darkness of the winter solstice:

in qua fors zephyro ramulus horreat
ac post diluvium rursus hiet rosa:
sic ad te volucris spes hiemalibus
elabens tenebris venit.[67]

The conspicuous awareness of one's locale and origins is also the focus of Umberto Piersanti (1941), a lyric poet from the Marches who has argued for the poetic identity of that region of Leopardi, Scataglini, and Volponi. Piersanti's obsessions are few: the fauna and flora of the countryside around Urbino, the mountains and valleys, the bonds and separations of familial and erotic love, and flowers, whether named with the scientific and dialectal specificity we associate with Pascoli or the genericness of Leopardi.

perso nell'appennino il più lontano
una striscia di rose e fiori bianchi
e avvampano i petali alla luce
tenera del crepuscolo che scende
profumano le rose, sono le stesse
hanno lo stesso odore, s'alzano uguali
coprono i pozzi e i muri di quegli anni[68]

A variation on the love/knowledge opposition seen above, which the encyclopedic poet feels compelled to explore dialectically, is found in the neo-avant-garde poet Alfredo Giuliani (1924), who identifies "the smell of roses" with "our errors," specifying that love is a necessary precondition to knowledge: "Non c'è rimedio a quei nostri disguidi, / al lezzo delle rose, notturne per la mente / e per l'aria gelose. Amore sempre fiorisce / prima del conoscere, in un buio tremore."[69]

Also concerned with "our errors" and the "smell of roses" is Dacia Maraini (1936), whose poetry possesses the highly nominal and discursive style we have seen in this chapter. Here she warns women against the prepackaged version of femininity that, with "wilted roses" as its garnish or prop, presents a genteel façade yet only succeeds in victimizing the women who yield to it:

> contro chi vi tradisce senza volerlo,
> contro l'idolo donna che vi guarda seducente
> da una cornice di rose sfatte ogni mattina
> e vi fa mutilate e perse prima ancora di nascere,
> scintillanti di collane, ma prive di braccia . . .[70]

In summary, the encyclopedic poets speak in the current idiom, in the spirit of the "contingency of words" and "verbal luck." In doing so they resist the symbolist elevation of the word denounced by Poggioli and satisfy the "generic" sense of what Barthes means by the "zero degree" of the poetic word, a word able to reveal "the depth and singularity of an individual experience."[71]

II
THE FEMININE VOICE, AND OTHER ALIBIS

The poet who is denied a place by the literary institutions seeks an alibi, an imposture. Such an other or "elsewhere" accompanies the development of the feminine voice in contemporary Italian letters. The feminine voice works and lives on a cultural and linguistic boundary, and is familiar with places where the creative spirit can prosper despite the experience of marginalization. Aldo Gargani provides a working definition of "feminine voice":

> One could say that the feminine voice is not even aware of the *fact* that the masculine voice strains to enunciate with a sort of inexorability, because it notices from the start the opaque background of possession for which the enunciation of a fact is only a pretext. The feminine voice pares down, so to speak, the facts, slows down and diminishes the paranoid tension with which masculine language would enforce a hard and ineluctable necessity; in the end it discovers—beyond the facts, theses, and systems erected by men—the space of contingency, intention, and sense. The feminine voice discovers the modest and uncertain form which is hidden behind the verbal armature of masculine language, which is afraid and at the same time wants to strike fear. For this reason the feminine voice extends in a long and interminable interrogation which takes place behind men's

backs, where they don't manage to see, because, naturally, they don't want to see.[1]

This definition precludes more peremptory approaches to the problem of identity, sexual coding, language, and power. By defining masculine linguistic space, one can more easily identify its opposite and antidote: a voice that emerges in "the time of decision," in "the space of contingency, intention, and sense," not as a vehicle of social rebellion but as an affirmation of memory, continuity, and social cohesion. An example of a masculine language is found in Italian futurism, with its despotic attempt to manage the feminine character and direct it away from what the fascist Ardengo Soffici called "the inverted and Jew-ified bourgeois."[2] Kenneth Burke has written of the usefulness of futurism to fascist recruitment, given the "brutality" of its Nietzschean desire to be a "yea-sayer" to the current zeitgeist and "reigning symbols of authority":

> *Apparently* active, it was in essence the most passive of frames, an elaborate method for feeling *assertive* by a resolve to drift with the current. Its incompleteness, or partiality, as a frame was drastic. A well-rounded frame of acceptance involves constant discrimination.[3]

In contrast to such a scenario of vain assertion, the feminine voice constitutes a mode of interrogation and reflection on the encoded sexual values of dominance and recession, virility and fertility. The poets of the feminine voice share a romantic, Vichian, and Leopardian view of the classics that is at times devout, at times alienated, but always aimed at creating an alibi or space apart from the coteries of the male-dominated literary world, and the "pseudo-nature" of that world. As Roland Barthes has written:

> We believe we are in a practical world of uses, of functions, of total domestication of the object, and in reality we are also, by objects, in a world of meanings, of reasons, of *alibis:* function gives birth to the sign, but this sign is reconverted into the spectacle of a function. I believe it is precisely this conversion

of culture into pseudo-nature which can define the ideology of our society.[4]

Because of her socialization, the feminine writer is aware of this cultural dualism and knows that "in emergent cultures the struggle of an individual consciousness towards affirmation and distinctness may be analogous, if not coterminous, with a collective straining towards self-definition."[5] These factors of socialization and struggle begin to explain why the feminine voice engages a "medium" style that occurs elsewhere with respect to the citadels of masculine stylistic conventions, whether rule-based or rebellion-based. Based on the primacy of experience and feeling, this poetry finds its roots in the romantics Leopardi and Foscolo, but also in Heine, Shelley, and Keats, and their "discovery of an historic and anthropological poetics."[6]

A pioneer in this space of otherness is Sibilla Aleramo (1876), the author of the first Italian feminist novel, *Una donna,* whose prodigal rose integrates love and knowledge, usually in the form of a gift or a remembrance of the beloved: "Una rosa ricordo / che il domani mi comprai. . . . Sono sola nè piango, se non forse in cuore. . . . e domani, se non io qualcuno una rosa si comprerà."[7] Aleramo's poetic rose betrays its short life as an emblem of solitude and knowing surrender to love's romantic illusion:

> Sfoglio le rose
> che m'hanno veduta piangere e sorriderti
> e poi ardere bianca,
> e metto fra i petali le mie dita
> come fra le tue mani,
> petali dolci e freschi
> che or lancerò nell'aria
> cantando sommessa, o amato,
> perché tu non ti volga.[8]

As a victim of an archaic and misogynist culture, in which her civil status as a wife determined her enslavement, Aleramo would move to the freer society of Rome, at the cost, however, of losing contact with her son. Her sorrow over that separation is apparent in the poetry, but is transmuted into an occasion to celebrate her maternal love. Aleramo's rose is subject to profuse adjectivization, being brown, full, overflowing, silent, ecstatic, meek, graceful, lofty.

> Cuor dolce d'una rosa,
> bruna,
> che non sfoglio.
> . . . .
> Crepitava arsa
> l'anima di stasera.
> Ma la rosa è molle,
> lenti i capelli,
> tanti,
> su la mia nuca dolce.[9]

Aleramo sees the rose as a recursive, self-enclosing structure. It is not an accessory to love but an animated, rhythmic participant. By minimizing rigid "masculine" protocols, Aleramo remained interrogative and dialogic in emphasis so her rose could emerge newly alive, as a gift, in the hands of other women poets.

A key Leopardian trait is that of lexical indeterminacy and "vaghezza," or genericness. Diego Valeri (1887) has written in this regard of the rose as form and gesture, as a metaphor for the woman and the gift to her: "[I]t seems that we Mediterraneans and Latins, while loving and cultivating flowers, love them generically, as 'the flower' or, even more so, as the rose, the violet, the lily."[10] In fact, Valeri stands as an example of a male poet with a feminine voice, as defined above. His *rosa* is often a rhyme-word, a generic and ambiguous metaphor for the life the senses, particularly the sense of sight. In his limpid observations of nature the rose is both erotic and metaphyiscal, as in the tradition of Petrarch, Politian, and Leopardi. In the early "Red Roses," the "three red roses" found in a lover's belt are, by poem's end, a sign of erotic fulfillment:

> tu portavi tre rose alla cintura,
> tre grandi rose, rosse come sangue.
> Io ti stringevo tutta sul mio petto,

su la nuca, tra i riccioli di seta,
e agli angoli soavi della bocca.

. . . .

E nell'ombra splendevano i tuoi occhi,
umidi, ardenti, l'anima tua stessa,

e le tre rose, le tre rose rosse.[11]

Valeri recalls how as a child his teachers discouraged students from reading Leopardi in favor of the overly composed, mechanical odes of Carducci. He himself adopts the Leopardian tendency toward a metaphyiscally inclined empiricism, often adopting the "alibi" of a religious situation. Examples are a sick patient praying to Suor Gesuina, the hermit Saint John in the desert, or the dying David who asks that his body be covered and questions the Lord about his past and his fate. In each case it is the continuity between the sensory and the sacred, the physical and the metaphysical, that stands out. In "St. John of the Hermits," the character speaks in a salvific moment from a desert oasis, even as the soft contours of the flower's "fold" suggest a woman's breast or womb:

Vedo grandi rose
sbendare il seno di pallore malnato
sopra il nitido specchio addormentato
della piscina, pigre e voluttuose.[12]

* * *

Aperti gli occhi, rividi le rose
sotto il quadro della Madonna,
e la tenda nel sole bionda,
e il cielo, e gli uomini, e le cose . . .[13]

* * *

Ma Betsabea, nella notte dolce,
splendeva nuda come la luna,
spandeva odore di rosa notturna.

> Signore, questa è la mia fine.
> La mia fine è in pensieri d'amore.[14]

The contingent dimension in Valeri's rose is comparable to that which he found in Cielo d'Alcamo's use of the superlative "aulentissima" to describe the rose as something "purely poetic" (in contrast to Saint Francis, whose use was purely conventional), a "metaphorical rose that is actually a beautiful girl who with her freshness and sweet smell causes the desirous poet to lose his senses."[15] In this way Valeri resists the rationalistic and formalistic tendencies of much twentieth-century Italian verse, leading Zanzotto to point to his creative use of conventionality as a means to attain rhythmic freedom:

> Primaluce: e tu posi quieta
> sotto le palpebre, sotto i seni.
> Nell'incerto albore ti scopri e ti celi,
> come la rosa, nuda e segreta.[16]

The *topos* of the rose as semiclad woman appears in Tasso: "la rosa / ... / che mezzo aperta e mezzo ascosa, / quanto si mostra men, tanto è più bella."[17]

A courageous anti-Fascist who never acceded to the more discursive vein of the committed writers of the *dopoguerra*, Valeri here provides a powerful reminiscence of the war:

> Io vidi già sotto un cielo d'inferno
> rotto avvampato dai fuochi di guerra
> schiudersi la corolla di una rosa
> bianca, amorosa.[18]

Rosa abounds in Valeri's verse, often in rhyme with *cosa*, as here in an allusion to the Virgilian *lacrimae rerum*: "Ho amato il giorno e la notte / .... / e il riso e il pianto delle cose di natura. / Ho amato l'erbe e i frutti della terra, / la rondine e la rosa di maggio."[19] In terms of the erotic rite, one finds the live rose surrounded by bees in the garden and the cut rose given to the lover. This latter moment, if prolonged, becomes the tragic image of roses left to fade on the vine:

> Rose di ieri, stanche nella luce,
> sfiorate appena dalle aeree dita
> del tempo, e già inclinate al sonno, al lento
> morire della terra—o rose, addio.[20]

Valeri's rose is also Leopardian in its indeterminacy, its cultivation of simple cadences and pleasing sonorities, and the sublime agony of its retrospective vision, bound to a natural human season:

> Al mio tempo fanciullo
> primavera non era
> il sole nuovo, il vento nuovo
> la nuova rosa color di rosa
> in vetta al verde spino.
> Era il lombrico biondo o bruno
> che si torceva furibondo
> tra la zolla nerastra, umida, liscia . . .[21]

Another voice that stood for the union of emotion and intellect, sensibility and perception, is Elsa Morante (1912), whose 1955 book of poems, *Alibi,* suggested the title of this chapter. In the eponymous poem she affirms, "Only those who love, know" ("Solo chi ama conosce"), and then these lines that concern the nature of contingency and the fact that the object of one's belief in love, the "rose and the bee," might be unreliable:

> Vorrei chiamarti: *Fedele;* ma non ti somiglia.
>
> La tua grazia tramuta
> in un vanto lo scandalo che ti cinge.
> Tu sei l'ape e sei la rosa.
> Tu sei la sorte che fa i colori alle ali
> e i riccioli ai capelli.
> La tua riverenza è graziosa come l'arcobaleno.[22]

In her later, more narrative, poems, Morante seeks to lose herself in the universality of need and innocence of children, and of history's victims. In this example, set in Nazi-era Berlin, she assumes the identity of a Jew: "sono uscita per le vie sfoggiando / in petto la stella gialla dei giudei / come una rosa."[23]

Antonia Pozzi (1912), who committed suicide in 1938, presents in the tragic potency of her imagery an Arcimboldi-like "re-membering" of the landscape reminiscent of Dino Campana:

> Occupano come immense donne
> la sera:
> . . . .
> Madri. E s'erigon nella fronte, scostano
> dai vasti occhi i rami delle stelle:
> se all'orlo estremo dell'attesa
> nasca un'aurora
> e al brullo ventre fiorisca rosai.[24]

A companion of Vittorio Sereni, and like him a student of philosopher Antonio Banfi, Pozzi in her *Diari* conveys the sense of a wound that the poetry is called on to remedy.

> E a noi petali freschi di rosa
> infioran la mensa e son boschi
> interi e verdi di castani smossi
> nel vento delle chiome.[25]

Her painful exploration concerns the sorrow of isolation and unreciprocated love: "la mia maternità immaginaria." Poetry provides an antidote to the vain fantasies, including the desire to give oneself when one is already rejected. This time of decision and this alibi are abruptly concluded in Pozzi's final act.

The same Arcimboldi-type landscape seen in Pozzi occurs in another student of Banfi's, Daria Menicanti (1914):

> Ho un bosco. Un grande bosco che non ho
> e le più belle aiuole
> che crescono di foglie fiori cose
> parlanti. Colori di farfalle
> vanno danzando e si posano alle rose
> con applausi. Ai piedi ho un mare bianco

di giochi e di criniere, in alto il cielo
che hanno tutti con lune e con soli
e luoghi di nuvole e tuoni
lampi socchiusi e doppi arcobaleni . . .[26]

The importance of Banfi is inestimable. One of only twelve Italian university professors to refuse to sign the Fascist loyalty oath, he addresses knowing as an intentional act that changes the known, that takes place in consciousness but also in the political reality, which one is led to out of "courage and love of the truth."[27] Such an awareness of recursivity, of the effect of the observation on the observer, is present in each of the "alibis" presented in this chapter. Since most poets were marginalized from the hegemonic culture at this time, the plight of women poets must be considered a double alienation. It is this fact that lies at the basis of their alibi.

Luigi Baldacci writes of the *"feminine* poetry" of Maria Luisa Spaziani (1924) as being a "poetry of the voice [and] the head," of "sensoriality" rather than "sensuality": "Femininity is precisely the key that allows one to enlarge and alienate the *persona,* in that the situation of isolation from the social context is typical of woman (and thus heroic)."[28] The "heroic" dimension of the feminine situation gives rise to Spaziani's refusal to opt for the informal and diaristic verse which had become the customary response to the "uncommitted" poetry of the hermetics. In her early poem "I Remember a Season," Spaziani pairs the rose with a mulberry bush. The poem is in two pentets; in the first she recollects a mulberry that "groaned so loud in the shredding wind" that at times it woke her in the night; in the second she returns years later to find that nothing has changed, a revelation symbolized by the "ancient rose" she finds "gnawed to bits" by the elements:

Ieri nel ritornarvi non sembrava
passato altro che un giorno.
La tramontana ci infuriava intorno.
Contro il cancello, intatta, era restata
una mia antica rosa morsicata.[29]

This figure of the rose is antithetical: intact but eaten away, it stands for a strength and fidelity that were preserved by good fortune. The gate stands for the poet's memory, the only force able to prevent the rose's dissolution. Spaziani's soundings of the rose rely on the idea of a golden age existing in memory, impervious to the historical devastation around her. This too is a valuable alibi, another place and name to be. It is the free will that she addressed directly in the title poem of her volume *La stella del libero arbitrio*:

> In sogno qualcuno ti scopre, sei una rosa mistica
> di forma e di odore sfumanti oltre i limiti del turchino,
> il sangue rosso di mille Tamerlani,
> l'ippogriffo che punta a sconvolgenti lune—[30]

It is apparent that the "mystic rose" of the free will stands for the interrogation of the tradition by means of a pastiche of "antique" forms, as is evident in the opening of "The Wild Mint":

> Le rose che il grigio dell'Appia un remoto gennaio ti diede.
> fra gorghi e vascelli di stelle la menta selvaggia consuma.
> Soltanto nel fuoco dipinto, deserto infinito, memoria,
> il rudere inquieto fiorisce in celesti castelli abitati.[31]

Spaziani's concern for the itinerant space of the roadside, where free will and chance might combine to create self-knowledge, carries over into her use of words like "spazio" and "sapienza" that echo her name. In "La prigione," an internal dialogue between the poet and her memory, we read:

> Come un cane ti annuso e ti raspo,
> come un guanto ti infilo e ti rovescio,
> hai spigoli aguzzi, celesti barlumi,
> sei la pioggia di rose che mi soffoca,
> l'ancora e la grisella degli *spazi*
> e museruola e zufolo e malaria.[32]

The "wisdom of the rose" ("sapienza / della rosa") in the following citation is "invented," not from books but from the world of experience and the perception of natural phenomena, as again the poet engages an unspecified "tu" figure:

> Trova quei misteriosi geroglifici
> che per me più non cantano, riscopri
> nel pentagramma dileguato i segni
> quadri del gregoriano, tu che inventi
> da suoni ancor non detti la *sapienza*
> della rosa, del vento e della rondine.[33]

In a poem to a painter friend, Spaziani again uses "sapienza" with "rosa," implying that the practice of painting a rose is one of the many "thresholds" of the "house of the prophet":

> Dipingi nel tuo orto la rosa moltifoglie
> e filtra la parola dalla sua essenza, o Dario.
> La casa del profeta, si dice, ha molte soglie
> ma tutta la *sapienza* può star nel sillabario.[34]

In the following savage lines, the "empire of the rose" is evoked not simply as a bygone era but as another space and time, or what I have delineated as the alibi of the feminine voice—that is, the pursuit of origins and purity despite the absurdity and misery that surrounds one.

> Corde spezzate, lémuri, coscienza
> vigile della notte, i cani, in orde
> fameliche vagavano nel tempo,
> signori e subalterni d'una legge
> che fu soltanto loro quando il mondo
> conobbe incontrasto sotto il sole
> l'impero della rosa.[35]

In Spaziani's "Ponte Abramo" the rose asserts itself as a multiple concept, a newly alive if "more modest" (barer and more chaste) metaphor, having survived the "tragedy of summer":

> Più alto è il sogno ora che il cielo chiude
> nel grigio le sue vaste praterie,
> sipario muto sopra la tragedia
> dell'estate. Mulinano nel vento

> degli stagni e del cuore le foglie incenerite,
> e più schiva s'inombra la rosa
> dove il muro s'aggrotta.[36]

The following quatrain *a rime baciate,* a "counter-rhyme," seems a transparent confession of helplessness, of separation between the author and her lover's face, struck by the wondrous power of the roses, though powerless against the devastation of time: "Volto stravolto di due rose gialli / fra crepe arse dal salino più amaro. / Timide lune rotte, sarete un giorno un faro / sull'onda alle mie spalle."[37] The road Spaziani takes leads away from any patriarchal concept of the national language and culture, as in the following homage to Apollinaire ("poet of the stars"), in which the subject is the River Seine: "Scorre via e ci porta tranquillamente al diavolo / fra gioie pirotecniche e nebbiosi disastri. / Una rosa di sangue fluttua sulla corrente. / Un saluto del ponte al poeta degli astri."[38] In the 1981 book *Geometria del disordine,* the contiguity of *rose* to *cose* reappears in the spirit of one who eschews preciosity for the sake of simplicity:

> L'ombra di troppi versi
> pesa, schiaccia le rose.
> Vorrei scoprirle io,
> chiamarle solo "cose,"
> come i bambini al sole
> che giocano riversi
> confusamente in cerca di parole.[39]

The interrogative mode of the feminine voice is evident in the following lines of contemplation and contingency, in which the circularity and self-enclosure of the mind is recapitulated in the rhyme:

> Mute entità di tempo, lontananze
> (ma da chi? da che cosa?).
> Fremono le penelopi, le stanze
> che intessono e poi disfano le danze
> dei raggi sopra il cuore della rosa.[40]

The last example of Spaziani's hollowing of the rose is appropriately a love poem, from her final volume. The second line, "nebulous mystery to be won in reverse," is an inadvertent description of the rose *topos* itself, which must be denied in order to be validated, and of a love which lives on though the physical bodies die and are forever separated. "Quell'uomo-stella così irraggiungibilmente vicino, / nebuloso mistero da vincersi a ritroso, / ultima fiamma di rosa ventosa di marzo, / petalo che non cade, che muore con la radice."[41]

In the Leopardian line so often adhered to by the feminine voice, one finds the distinguished translators and scholars Elena Clementelli (1923) and Giovanna Bemporad (1925). Clementelli's report message—her use of the common rose metaphor—is naive; while her command message, as clarified by the extenuating imagery, hollows out the rose of vulnerability and tenderness, confronted by the violence of our century:

> Tempo di fede e giovinezza non è più.
> Rapido corse amore alla meta bugiarda,
> il vento che ingannò le ultime rose
> svelò al traguardo il suo artiglio di fuoco.[42]

Bemporad's enamorment with the classically defined contours of the vague flower is, I believe, a form of ascetic practice, a spiritual exercise in vigilance:

> China sul margine del tuo segreto,
> o rosa in veste diafana, mollezza
> di corpo ignudo, incrollabile tempio
> che in vigilanza d'amore mi tieni,
> non so di che rilievi si componga
> la tua bellezza.[43]

Paolo Volponi (1920) participates in the "space of contingency, intention, and sense" we have been describing. Here, with characteristic simplicity, he records the occasions of family rituals over generations:

> Oh ricchezza della nostra casa

Scalcucci, Filippini, Volponi,
tutta fatta di malta e mattoni
con il pozzo, le rose, le gronde,
che passa gli anni sulla tua misura,
sui calendari d'acqua e vento
che riportano ogni evento
con il tuo copiativo commento.[44]

In "The Peasant Appennines," Volponi employs subject rhyme to unify rose, rose seed, and rosary into a single auspicious figure:

La rosa mattutina che s'impiglia ai rovi,
è l'unica notizia;
ma breve il suo splendore
dura sino al momento
che sopra il ghiaccio vola
un tordo marinaccio.
. . . .
La pioggia di primavera scopre tra i coppi
semi di geranio e di rosa,
ma inganna la terra e reca nella casa
un sottile malanno.
. . . .
Qui la tradizione nei corredi
custodisce i dolori
più che gli inganni familiari;
i santi ed i rosari
tramandano la morte.[45]

The following portrait of "The Virgin" is supple and understated:

I sassi bianchi
sono le tue spalle
gli alberi la tua statura;
è la tua gola che batte
se una rosa si muove
non vista nel giardino.[46]

Like many others in this chapter, Luciana Frezza is an experienced translator (Baudelaire, Mallarmé, Laforgue, Verlaine). The title of her 1962 book, *La farfalla e la rosa,* is derived from the following lines:

> La farfalla si stacca,
> dalla rosa invidiata
> che vive un mattino
> stretta alla sua verità . . .[47]

Ephemeral and robust, faithful and deceitful, the only stability of Frezza's rose is found in memory, as on a formal pattern in porcelain:

> Mi dicono che le rose bianche fiorirono precoci
> quando nacqui, appoggiate alla grata del giardino.
> . . . .
> A me le cose ormai dolgono
> sotto le dita, le coperte bianche e turchine
> tessute a mano, i piatti bordati d'oro
> e rose a smalto . . .[48]

* * *

> La fissità di rose la fedeltà
> del giallo cuore caduco
> la bellezza dell'incedere
> del sempre uguale
> l'accumulo
> di sfoglie luminose
> sull'insidia
> come avvisarti Adone?[49]

Another voice intent on the ineffable and the idea of rose as elusive perfection, of the transcendent and the sublime, is Gabriella Leto:

> Solo che sul divano
> cada una luce privilegiata
> che la diafana ampolla sul ripiano
> abbia una rosa ardente e atteggiata
> trema nella mia mente e si confonde

quasi in acque profonde
immagine riflessa . . .⁵⁰

In the following poem Leto names six flowers, establishing the sinuous thread of the *-osa* rhyme that concludes with the incomparable seventh flower, and fourth rhyme in a strong enjambment. One of the rose's foils in the catalogue of imperfect flowers is the anemone:

Più che non sia la mimosa
di pallido ocra, farinosa
più del giglio e del giacinto
nello stemmario accampati
più dell'anemone blu violetto
dello spirante mio gelsomino
della camelia di lei gelosa
di lei, del fiore senza difetto
che quasi come per caso spunta
dal grande vaso dalla ringhiera
la sopraggiunta, la noncurante
rosa che dicono altera.⁵¹

The odorless anemone is called a "wind rose" in Ovid, its season of blooming being closest to that of the rose present at the death of Adonis. Marcel Detienne writes, "The rose (*rhódos*) owes its name to the flood of scent (*rhûma tês odôdes*) it releases. Its perfume is so violent that it makes vultures, who hunger for the scent of rotting corpses, die. The anemone, on the other hand, is odorless."⁵²

Rosita Copioli, a reader of Detienne, is a poet and scholar of comparative mythology, who uses the rose as an evocation of a mysterial rite of passage, non-Western and chthonic in nature, combined with the deities of Greek myth. The author of a study on Helen of Troy, she presents the mother deity in a variety of traditions, including the ancient Egyptian, and stands at the littoral, at dawn, on the threshold of transformation.

Entrati, fu un'ombra, il soffice, le erbe
e gli ellebori, rose di Natale verdi
che fanno dolci i tumuli⁵³

The "Hundred-Petaled Rose" can be read horizontally or vertically:

Una rosa centifolia ovunque è il mare   Rosa centifolia nera di acciai
a fiamme, ali. Raggia   rabbrividita nella palma
le nubi come bachi. S'infusa il sole.   di latte delle mie lune, sali.
Scende   Salita
sulle sue forme di seta,   di petali contro le lance . . .[54]

The notion of "field poetry" was advanced especially after the publication in Italian in 1961 of Charles Olson's watershed essay, "Projective Verse."[55] A poet sensitive to Olson's project, and to the notion of the feminine we have been exploring, is Roberto Sanesi (1930). In the following citations the poet is seen variously explaining to a woman that the language of love and roses is as difficult as a foreign language, but is as important as one's own:

e il tuo silenzio
forse è solo disprezzo, come non è un argomento se mi parli
del tempo (il tempo che non hai, le rose . . .) . . . . .
—jeune femme en forme de fleur . . .[56]

* * *

Gli amici
hanno offerto una rosa, bruciato un incenso.
       Consentimi
per questo breve intervallo una luce,
ora e nell'ora fra le prime foglie.[57]

* * *

Cercò la pace e la trovò.
       Tralci di rose e polline, e sopra
l'anfiteatro anche la luna osserva i sorci correre: il tema
e la ripresa di un tema, esserci per ognuno, sapere
che il pensiero e il linguaggio hanno una sede occulta. [. . .]
       le rose
in tralci ormai divelti e poi sepolti.[58]

* * *

> Scoppiano rose di ghiaccio alle finestre, e una terra
> incredibile e vuota invelenisce gli alberi[59]

Sanesi objects to those who declare that poetry is empty of content; by the 1980s this objection is found in his dismissal of Weak Thought, the so-called *Pensiero debole* advanced by the latest generation of "anti-foundationalist" hermeneutic philosophers. Like the poets of the feminine voice, Sanesi trusts in sensibility and fertile ambiguity:

> An alibi as a sign of the elsewhere. The risk of non-definition of the *elsewhere* as a place where the *other place* of an event is not established. The fascination with ambiguity, with contradiction, in a device in which one finds not the dialectical clash of opposites (for example, signs, the masses, the emptinesses, the network of a writing, etc.) but rather the parts, set in relief by artifice, of a unitary body.[60]

Sanesi is an authority on contemporary English and American poetry, as seen when he writes of encounters with such figures as Conrad Aiken, Delmore Schwartz, Anne Sexton, Vernon Watkins, e. e. cummings, Cid Corman, Robert Frost, and T. S. Eliot. He is the translator of Dylan Thomas, and a sensitive interpreter of William Carlos Williams. One reads of this literary alibi throughout Sanesi's work, here in a poem referring to Ungaretti:

> Era questo il tuo regno. Lo slancio.
> L'idea di una rosa o di un ciottolo. E il tuo nessun procedere
>   dal nulla
> di una cosa che nasce da una cosa, casualmente,
> si mediava ogni volta in un anello:
> rime e rocce e creature erano la durata in questo regno.[61]

Mariella Bettarini (1942), a Pasolini scholar, tests in the following poem the measures of love in terms of the gift of a rose to a lover:

> se tanto mi dà tanto
> poco cosa darà? darà una cosa
> ingiallita tignosa
> ed una stinta rosa[62]

Patrizia Cavalli's (1947) muse, like Sandro Penna's, subtly celebrates the love of a homosexual in a heterosexually inclined society. She too works in the form of the short occasional poem, and uses the rose but once:

> Da scalfittura diventare abisso,
> da fragile membrana diventare
> la corda tesa delle vibrazioni incostanti.
>
> Comincia la stagione delle grandi cacce
> da Aquila Reale, e la rosa
> guarderà i suoi petali cadere
> ad uno ad uno.[63]

For Emanuela Fontecedro, a Leopardi scholar, the rose is a sign of wonder that alludes to female sexuality:

> Se
> via dalle foglie
> nel vento alle rose
> briciola d'aria
> se
> nel seno alle erbe muschiate
> l'umore gremito di parti boscose
> . . . .
> non misurerò brevi tenibili spazi
> a partire giù dalle stelle.[64]

The rose as sexual organ is a coarse yet "indefatigable" cliché, as here in a poem by Dania Lupi (1944):

> la mia rosa fiorita ebbe il suo spazio naturale
> sbocciata in ritardo
> rispetto alla giusta stagione
> donne con occhi diversi
> erano già a cantare della verginità
> . . . .

> e fra le nostre gambe
> la rosa si liberava
> per sempre dall'infanzia[65]

More frequently, the feminine voice addresses sexuality obliquely, as in this manneristic "Garden Party" by painter-poet Mirella Boeri (1941), which ties the phenomenon of seduction and ephemeral imagery to the bride at the altar.

> Nel fianco della rosa
> l'immagine s'incaglia
> slitta,
> s'accende,
> infiamma
> come sposa all'altare:
>
> e tramutata nutre
> la miniera profonda del suo buio,
> alza la sete della sua misura
> riconducendo nella pura maschera
> la velatura libera, creata.[66]

In "Rosalba's Diary" by Bianca Tarozzi, the first-person narrator constructs a narrative around her life before becoming a nun and her suppressed envy for her lovely sister Annarosa. Rosalba recalls from her cloister her passion for the cavalier Bonvicino, now best commemorated by roses made of plastic:

> Ho visto delle rose in un vasetto:
> rose bianche, di plastica. Chissà
> da quanto tempo sono là!
> Mi piacciono perché non sono vere:
> sono finte, diverse, indistruttibili.[67]

To summarize, the feminine voice adopts an alibi that situates it elsewhere with respect to the assertive verbal armature of the masculine voice. This results in a crossing over to another time and place, a translation to a time of decision and a place of becoming. The alibi is not the result of a flight, but of dialogue and questioning. Though the answers to the questions are often disappointing or desperate (in line with the noted Leopardism), the knowledge that is gained in the process strips away the veneer of institutional culture for writers and readers to come.

12
THE ROSE OF ADVENT

Since *Le roman de la rose*, the dream of future renewal has had an emblem in the rose. In that utopian and communitarian poem of many hypostases, the central conflict is between Love and Jealousy. Love's final victory, which anticipates the arrival of humanity to a new golden age, is crowned by the Lover's picking of the Beloved's roses. The poem is complicated by its having two authors, one more ethereal, the other more worldly in the depiction of the allegory.

The dual face of this palingenetic rose continues in the Novecento among poets of metaphysical and political advent. Mario Luzi (of the former persuasion) has stated that the idea of "revolution" so dominated literary practice and taste from the mid-eighteenth century on that the true poet was marginalized. Whatever the state regime, the poet became someone to "fear," whom it was possible to "do without": "From that point on, poetry has borne the stigmata of this experience, and has reacted in these neurotic forms, so much so that one cannot find a representation of the present that is not painful and does not carry with it accents of disapproval and condemnation."[1] It is with this sense of exclusion that the poets in this chapter undertake a retreat: to innocence, to the provinces, to childhood, to the mother language, and thus to renewal.

In Louis Aragon's 1941 poem "Les lilas et les roses," the rose stands for the values of the Resistance.

> Je n'oublierai jamais les lilas ni les roses
> Et ni les deux amours que nous avon perdus
>
> Bouquets du premier jour lilas lilas des Flandres
> Douceur de l'ombre dont la mort farde les joues
>
> Et vous bouquets de la retraite roses tendres
> Couleur de l'incendie au loin roses d'Anjou[2]

As one critic writes of these "famous" lines: "Written in the immediate emotion of the defeat [the surrender of Paris to the Germans], it calls for its memory to be prolonged, redoubled, intensified, preserved intact in a vision precipitated into verse."[3]

Aragon employs the language of surrealism to demonstrate the importance of memory in resisting those historical forces that would "gut the toys and sack the roses." Such a use of the rose is ideological, but retains the language of love and of the world, and refuses to make pronouncements:

> Laisse-les ouvrir le ventre à leurs jouets saccager les roses
> Je me souviens je me souviens de comment tout ça s'est passé.[4]

The poets of advent are distinguished by their ethical focus on matters of freedom, justice, and the religious or spiritual unification of humankind. They anticipate a liberation in a manner that recalls Mazzini's vision of the Italian people's rising up in a religious pursuit of self-education: "'Every religion holds out to men, as an end in itself, a fragment of this educative idea . . . generally first gripped by philosophy, or prepared by the progress of knowledge, or more often, by the social conditions of a people.' . . . Then strikes the hour of the new Advent. 'God puts into a people's heart or into the mind of a man strong in love and genius, a new belief, greater and more fertile than what is dying out.'"[5]

Educated to Marxism and liberalism, nihilism and idealism, these poets tend to distance themselves from the constituted powers, but also from the primary parties of opposition. The advent they foresee is expressed in terms of a "public" rose. Such an advent was augured in Pascoli's "L'Avvento," which predicts the advent of a new species of human being, *Homo humanus,* more compassionate than *Homo sapiens.* Pascoli, like Mazzini, adopted a Vichian perspective. His vision of the social-spiritual-political development of a new people was based on greater powers of charity and love, beyond the capacities of reason.

Franco Fortini has written of the poetry of the 1950s in terms of three distinct temporalities: the poets of "transition" (such as Montale and Zanzotto), those of "contradiction" (such as Jahier, Pavese, Sanguineti), and those of "advent":

> The figure of advent, of the tension toward an apocalyptic and resolutive future, is perceived in filigree in the two preceding figures; because it is alive precisely in the immobility [of contradiction] and in the change [of transition], it is a revolutionary postulation, conjugated in the future tense, it is the denial of the present, felt, in every moment, as the past and as nothingness.[6]

The antihermetic poet and essayist Giacomo Noventa (1898), who wrote in his own personalized Venetian dialect, embodies for Fortini this "nexus of prophecy and elegy." Positioning himself against the idealism and subjectivism of postsymbolist and hermetic poets (in particular the "trio" of Ungaretti, Montale, and Quasimodo), Noventa focused on poetry's link to the oral culture, and the importance of custom and faith in negotiating the imperfections of daily existence. His fellow socialist Nello Rosselli admired Noventa's ability to "pass from purely literary questions to questions of custom."[7] In him the rose is primarily a figure of value, as in this poem in which a rose dropped into the ocean is unreclaimable though he sees it in every droplet. The act is compared to the dispersal and diffusion of language, an act more worthy when done by an "ingenuous man" than by a precious "poet":

> Go' lassà cascar una rosa nel mar,
> Stravià che gèro!
> La gò cercada po' un toco e vardando

Ogni giossa portava una rosa,
Tuto el mar me se xé parfumà.

Ah el profumo del mar no' se pol
Portarselo via!
Forse più me valeva una rosa.
Forse i omeni ingenui val più
Che un poeta.
Mi son l'amigo de tuti nel mondo,
E de tuto.
De mi stesso, no.[8]

In the following poems the rose is a gift of love that requires a willing heart and an acknowledgment of sorrow and humility. These traits are the basic language of the poets of advent, often hinging on a verb in the conditional or future tense.

'Na rosa xé sbrissada
Dentro 'l to petto, Olga,
Vorìa seguir la rosa,
Ma mi no' lo so far.
No' lo so far parché
Gò anca mi i me spini,
E 'sti me spinti, Olga,
No' me li vùi cavar.[9]

* * *

O bela e bona amiga,
che ti-me-gà vardà,
Mi vogio darte una rosa,
Parchè ti-me-gà vardà.

'Na rosa, pa' i to oci,
Forse no' bastarìa:
Tuto un giardin ti-meriti,
Parchè ti-ssi-stàda mia.

> Ma mi no' gò giardini,
> 'Sto fior lo gò robà,
> El val i to basi, crèdilo,
> Parchè mi lo gò robà.[10]

Pier Paolo Pasolini (1922) contributed to the renewal of Italian dialect poetry. In his Friulian poetry he defied the linguistic politics of fascism, and in the anthology *Canzoniere italiano* (coedited with Mario dell'Arco) he added considerably to our scholarly understanding of the poetry of the Italian regions. In an early poem in Italian, *rosa* is an emblem for the bond between mother and child, as the mother gladdens the sullen boy when she places a white rose on his bedsheets. In a comparable piece written in Friulian dialect, the rose is, like the mother, forgotten by the wandering son ("Dutis dos dismintiadis / la mari e la rosa!"). In another poem from the same collection, *Poesie a Casarsa*, the twenty-year-old poet writes in dialect the following (here translated):

> Giovinetto, piove il Cielo
> sui focolari del tuo paese,
> sul tuo viso di rosa e miele,
> nuvoloso nasce il mese.[11]

Thirty years later, in 1975, Pasolini changes the above lines so that "rosa e miele" becomes "merda e mèil," (shit and honey).[12]

In the early volume *L'usignolo della chiesa cattolica*, the use of *rosa* is openly sexual in nature:

> E la gioventù insanguinata
> dal sesso puro come il sole
> guarda con dolente stupore
> la sua rosa consumata . . .[13]

Pasolini identified himself as one awash in personal contradictions. His claim also concerned a disintegration he observed in the world and among the poets. Calling himself a "beast of style," he made frequent use of pastiche and hyperbole. In his autobiographical poem

"Rage," in the 1963 volume *Poesia in forma di rosa,* the rose is repeatedly named in a kind of Freudian perseveration.

> Solo un po' di rosso, torvo e splendido,
> seminascosto, amaro, senza gioia:
> una rosa. Pende umile
> sul ramo adolescente, come a una feritoia,
> timido avanzo d'un paradiso in frantumi . . .
> . . . .
> Rinuncio ad ogni atto . . . So soltanto
> che in questa rosa resto a respirare,
> in un solo misero istante
> l'odore della mia vita: l'odore di mia madre . . .
> . . . .
> Ero chiuso nella mia vita come nel ventre
> materno, in quest'ardente
> odore di umile rosa bagnata.
> Ma lottavo per uscirne
> . . . .
>   La lotta è terminata
> con la vittoria. La mia esistenza privata
> non è più racchiusa tra i petali d'una rosa,
> —una casa, una madre, una passione affannosa.
> È pubblica.[14]

The rose, introduced with the wild endive as the sign of an archaic order of aristocracy and plebeians united, is said to lack any such unity today. Pasolini conflates this lack with his own pain as he reflects on his attachment to his mother, puts that love behind him, and finally breaks free, making this private rose into something public. The public "rose" of this book is also found in the "petals" of the title poem, "Poetry in the Shape of a Rose," which are five sorrows the poet confesses and plucks away: his "mistake" on the language question, his sense of having lost the lone occasion that life offered him, his being controlled more by obsession than by desire, his lack of love, and his delusion over history and the future:

> E' una rosa carnale di dolore,
> con cinque rose incarnate,
> cancri di rosa nella rosa
>
> prima: in principio era il Dolore.[15]

In addition to this narrative use of the flower, one finds Pasolini invoking the rose window, the omnidirectional "rosa dei venti," and the vulgar *rosa* of jargon, as in *Calderón*, the only play officially completed by the author: "Sì, quella cosa che tu credi in forma di sublime / pigna o di magnifica rosa, che si apra al mattino, / e con cui il marito ingravida la moglie. . . ."[16] The stanzas of "New Poem in the Shape of a Rose" are laid out in the shape of roses. This is a useful vehicle for versifying the "unpoetic," a graphic reminder of the Dantesque groupings in the candid rose of Paradise. As a graphic device, the drawing of the shape of the rose on the page has precedents in the 1550 *Rosarium philosophorum*. The poet deliberates on the poetic act, on his transgression or "heresy," which is also the "poet's sin" of sloth and desperation. Nevertheless, his realism is basically stoical, and his rose a vehicle for seeking knowledge in the confrontation with darkness.

For both Pasolini and Franco Fortini (1917), the rose is part of an inherited irony (in Fortini's words: "tutti i fiori non sono che scene ironiche"—all flowers are no more than ironic scenes). Though no single poet can presume to speak on behalf of the collectivity, a watershed is marked by Fortini's 1962 *La poesia delle rose* (Poem of the roses) and by the cited Pasolini volume.[17] As paradigms of recursiveness and feedback, these works assume as their antefact the sign which has endured over the centuries as an index of death and resurrection, but also as the veil of Maya, of delight and illusion. As Fortini remarks with reference to his landmark poem: "Le `rose' nascondono infatti la `valle d'abisso dolorosa' e, nel medesimo tempo, la indicano."[18] The rose proliferates in Fortini's poetry. An important early document, "The Buried Rose," establishes the flower as a symbol of repressed freedom:

> Ma il più distrutto destino è libertà.
> Odora eterna la rosa sepolta.

THE ROSE OF ADVENT | 211

> Dove splendeva la nostra fedele letizia
> Altri ritroverà le corone di fiori.[19]

Several early instances are set in an elegiac rendering of a distant and archaic Florence, as here in "Via San Marta":

> Pendeva il ramo dell'olivo asciutto,
> la mora viva oscillava di rosso
> alto al sole e la rosa dal cipresso.
> Poi la stella celeste sulla lancia
> di ferro della croce e le tre vette.
> E dove d'aria fumava la sera
> una nuvola era la città . . .[20]

In the later "The Historical Museum," the flower is seen prophetically as a relic and artifact of our prerevolutionary society:

> Vedranno con studio e pietà
> quello che ci congiunse ai nemici, nemici a noi stessi
> appariremo. Dai vetri dei musei guarderanno i giardini
> alti di luce e ai muri la nostra rosa dipinta.[21]

The rose is a symbol of the liberty/slavery polarity with which Fortini confronts Pasolini in an epigram regarding the "dead language" of poetry, as it is in *La poesia delle rose*, where he effects an evolution of the poetic sign, imagining it to be a rose "literally and in all senses." Fortini's 144-line poem is written for those in the future who will be able to decipher its contradictory sense of communication and augury: "You still sleeping: I want nothing to be lost." The poem's composite image of the rose has been seen as a "myth" pursued by Fortini through the poetic image, "in order to know and comprehend reality and to win back for this purpose the expressive force of the 'myth': the rose."[22]

As I argue elsewhere, there is a kind of magnetic charge given to the hypercoded image which occurs serially and is a caustic response to the serial poems of the neo-avant-garde on the one hand, and the negative historicism of the hermetics on the other. The word *rosa* is at the focal point of the poet's progressive exasperation with the chains of signification. In Fortini's poem the rose presides over a mutilation, a body disjointed, an anatomy without a face, an "immense inhuman mouth." Yet the possibility of redemption remains in the solution of a reader able to dwell in uncertainty, for whom the difficult job of interpreting what Fortini has called the little "morality plays" of poetry is preferable to a singular (ideological or imagistic) reading.

The rose stands for the poetic language itself; in the following lines an alliterative chiasmus stands to indicate the motion of the "breathless" poet, incessant yet stationary: "Ah contro i fiori *a*perti *a*ll'*a*fa / com'è dolce l'*a*ff*a*nno dell'*a*pe."[23] In subsequent uses Fortini seems to stress the dialectical nature of the rose's arguments, the duality of its aspect:

> perché se guardi dalla parte
> contraria se volgi le spalle
> alla preghiera del pittore al suo
> scapolare di rose
>
> . . . .
>
> tu pittore ironia scaltra austera
> della mente che s'inchina
> a cercare dove cieca
> una rosa spira e un'altra
> già ne reca la spina.[24]

* * *

>   Ma e le rose?
> Domandavo amore alle rose bianche,
> gialle e bianche.[25]

Finally, the biblical rose, like the allusion to Dante's Minos which precedes it, is but a splendid metaphor, without substance:

> Qui stiamo a udire la sentenza. E non
> ci sarà, lo sappiamo, una sentenza.
> A uno a uno siamo in noi giù volti.
>
> Quanto sei bella, rosa di Saron,
> Gerusalemme che ci avrai raccolti.
> Quanto lucente la tua inesistenza.[26]

Dense and opaque, time itself provides the limit to the logos, to the eternal "sentence" which, like the rose of Sharon and the holy city of Jerusalem, does not exist. The ones led most immediately downward "into themselves" (echoing *Inferno* V, 13–15: "dicono e odono e poi son giù volte") provide contemporary models of Minos's descent, in which certainty and ambivalence, dialectic and instinct, the ruthless chronicle and the seed of hope, coexist.

Rocco Scotellaro (1923) was mayor of his town of Tricarico in Lucania at the time of his death in 1953; the son of a cobbler, he shared the southern peasant's skeptical view of the institutions of Church and state. Falsely accused by fascists, he was briefly imprisoned. A worker toward agricultural reforms, he was a student of the anthropologist Ernesto De Martino at Bari. Scotellaro's fieldwork of interviews and his translations of Lucanian dialect poetry guide his own verse. Set within the peasant ethos, it concerns the practices of courtship and worship, of mourning and celebration, of cultivation and folklore. (Both Fortini and Amelia Rosselli were great admirers of Scotellaro.) In the post–World War II south, the agrarian bloc of monopoly-driven indentured servitude was finally ended—though with considerable counterreaction by the landed interests and the Christian Democratic Party, which had supplanted the fascist power network with its own clientelistic system.

Against this inexorable force, the painted roses on the walls represented a socialist resistance:

> Fanciulla, tenera l'erba che assaporo
> non è più tenera di te che distendi i seni.
> Di queste affogate città sei,
> è proprio vero che le rose fanno sulle murate?[27]

Above all, for Scotellaro the rose and its thorn are motifs of love and loss:

> Hai già vita abbastanza
> Tu spina e rosa:
> Si sfronda e si fidanza
> per te ogni cosa.

> . . . .
> E tu sei questo cielo
> Sempre e mai mia.²⁸

* * *

> Ora che ti ho perduta come una pietra preziosa
> so che non ti ho mai avuta né spina né rosa:
> non stavi al fondo della cassa che sarebbe bastato
> alzare panni e coperte per rivederti a posto
> con pena e occhi incerti nella massa delle cose.²⁹

In Nelo Risi (1920), a militant and diaristic poet of the Lombard Line, one finds the inclination to reminisce. Here the rose is associated with a portrait of the beloved in a distant spring (as in Sinisgalli, an "age of the roses"):

> Ho un'immagine di te tra le mie carte
> e i libri che comprammo:
>   era l'età
> felice delle rose, aprile maggio
> giugno, di là dal vetro di veranda
> i cigni popolavano il tuo lago . . .³⁰

For Risi the notion of advent as pregnant in the rose implicates its opposition to the grayness of the day-to-day, the stilling of the senses that occurs with disillusionment:

>   i giorni oscuri,
> come pioggia che lava un cimitero,
> han lasciato deserta la mia terra
> più feroce la tinta delle rose,
> in sospetto la pace³¹

The same everyday objects elicit a historical "situation" whose appearances must be validated. Thus Risi cites the political chronicle, as here the rose marks the pattern of the assassin's bullet on the face of Isaak Babel, a Soviet writer murdered in 1941:

> Giudici di tenebra: un uomo non è una dinamo
> ogni uomo brucia il suo fuoco limitato
> quando non è da voi bruciato (vedi Grimau
> azzannato alla gola o Babel
> con una rosa che gli scoppia in fronte e
> Lumumba con le ossa rotte come per un incidente
> di macchina) uomini sotto accusa
> dentro un silenzio pesante . . .[32]

In some cases the rose's nonappearance seems deliberate, as in Giovanni Raboni's "Figures in the Park," a veiled recapitulation of Fortini's *La poesia delle rose,* and thus an example of transumption.[33] The following lexemes from Raboni's thirty-three-line poem also occur in Fortini's tour de force: "polvere," "strega," "impercettibile," "curve," "lisciare," "ghiaia." Raboni's poem ostensibly records an observed murder. Almost predictably, given the proliferation of *rosa* in the source poem, here it is absent. In another bleak and unforgiving setting, an abandoned terrace in Tuscany where a now-deceased loved one had convalesced, Raboni once again finds in the caustic present a lyric motivation. It is "behind" the faded roses that one must look.

> Libero, m'affeziono allo scenario
> di prima, chaises longues scrostate, portafiori
> di terracotta rovesciati, e dove
> dietro le rose stente s'indovina
> la curva della terra,
> il celeste di Lucca o Pontedera . . .[34]

Raboni's "Anagramma" (recalling Saussure's study *Anagrammes*) regards a "mistaken" variant of a part of a prayer— "non pròbiso" for "pro nobis"—which is validated by the practice of uttering and hearing it over thirty years; the poem's incipit engages this flower which is so rare in Raboni's poetry:

> La rosa di bava che sboccia
> nel fuoco del tritume,

> metamorfosi in allume
> di un'umida, lunga agonia
> non dovrebbe sfigurare,
> penso, nella tua raccolta
> di piccole morti—stavolta
> non d'uomo, ma d'animale.[35]

Raboni also employs the rose as a figure for Italy in a ditty written on the corruption that has permeated Italian political culture since the scandal of Tangentopoli, "May 1992":

> Che male t'abbiamo fatto,
> che pena
> vuoi che scontiamo per
> appartenerti
> come cellule a un cancro,
> come inerti
> petali di rosa a una rosa piena
> di spine? Sanguinosamente,
> oscena
> mia patria, procuri indizi, reperti
> di archeologia criminale
> agli esperti
> d'altri milenni . . .[36]

The Lombard poet Giancarlo Majorino (1928), like Risi and Raboni, has a decidedly political focus. Here in "Baldorie!" the "Girl of the Roses" is the virginal girlfriend dropped off at home before the man goes shopping for a prostitute:

> 18" di tempo
> per fare l'amore con tasso
> del 7 3/4%
> lasciata la Fanciulla Delle Rose
> col bacio sulla porta
> il Fidanzato che vide
> un uomo voltare una donna

>   contro il muro di via Ostiglia
>   spalanca la portiera a 4000
>   lire di donna-nonna-feto-grisou
>   muso 'spegni la luce' . . .[37]

A more spatial poetics was initiated by members of the Gruppo 63 in their volume *I novissimi*. The awareness of cybernetics and systems theory and other scientific developments led to extensive verbal experimentation. But the flirtation with the aleatory on the part of the Italian neo-avant-garde would lapse into a specular involvement with textuality. In the words of Fortini, a leading scholar and translator of the historical avant-gardes, "the only real difference between the Neo-avant-garde and the historical avant-garde consists, when it consists, of the almost exclusively ironic and 'classicalist' use of iconographic, psychic and verbal material which in the major historical avant-garde was often still 'tragic' and of direct Romantic descent."[38]

Exceptions to this critique are the neo-experimentalists Nanni Balestrini (1935), Antonio Porta (1935), and Elio Pagliariani (1927). For Balestrini the "thing" that might resemble the rose is also the "*res pubblica*," the civic polity stripped of definitions, goals or limits. The "bunch of roses" and the "shape of the rose" here stand as projections of the present historical "situation."

>   Sul pelo dell'acqua avanzare la pinna,
>   non si dovrebbe incoraggiare la gente a farlo,
>   dopo lui giunse (osserviamoli) tutta vestita di
>   (mentre) con un mazzo di rose bianco
>   sull'arenile c'erano ancora le aste . . .[39]

* * *

>   asciúgati bene all'aria calda, e il naso finto,
>   respirabile ancora a pena fra i muri gonfi, cerca
>   la scarpa, la cosa (ma avrà una forma di rosa?)[40]

In the opinion of Antonio Porta, Balestrini's reference in the following lines is first to the "female rose," which is then transformed into the revolutionary and utopian rose:

> una rosa di una luce verde segnare un tracciato in li
> nea retta ai piedi del che sta per accasciarsi su di
> lei. . . .
> . . . .
> azioni invisibili sotto gli abiti quasi sfibrati dal so
> le come il petalo di una rosa come l'avete sempre sognata[41]

Chance plays a big part in the work of Porta and Balestrini, but, unlike most of their neo-avant-garde colleagues, they delight in the ambiguities that syntactic continuity can foster. While the early Porta opts for monotonous litanies, word-play, and asyntactic experimentation ("quando la rosa è nominare la rosa / di nome rosa nasce una rosa nuova"), in the 1970s and 1980s he adopts a more thematically coherent and epistemological poetry.[42] This change makes the later work more interesting, beginning with "La rose," a poem about the declared impossibility of making poetry. Porta says that his idea was to write a "lyric super-poem": "I began with the idea of demonstrating the impossibility of writing poetry by attempting an impossible poem. The result is disturbing because images emerged that strike very deeply":

> la rosa accoglie i propri frutti nella pace
> l'interno al riparo la bocca con foglie
> sbucciato il corpo nei giardini domenicali
> . . . .
> ai capelli arricciati cagnolini rabbiosi
> le difese ingannevoli odorano la rosa
> al giustacuore slacciato campanelli d'argento
>
> in cavità procedente inumidisce le ciglia
> l'interno della bocca nutrirà il passeggero
> statica della rosa pieno della mente
>
> la rosa maculata impensierisce i vicini
> le tettine delle amiche tremano le sue dita
> perché si è allontanata perché si è nascosta

> lei si alza dal letto a contemplare il sonno
> le amiche furenti a strappare le vesti
> si confida alla madre che approva le astinenze
> nel sogno vede un cane congiungersi con lei
> aderire alla rosa nutrirsi delle sue spine[43]

Porta's rose is an allegorization of woman laden with sexual power and mystery, but also of the unattainable virgin made legendary in the *dolce stil nuovo*: "The rose, woman and Master, with her entourage of young women: friends and *fedeli d'amore*."

Like other poets of advent, Porta assumes a prophetic and eschatological dimension in this late work in the voice of Salomé:

> il dio del vento
> il dio della montagna
> dove sono morti tutti gli dèi
> dove il sangue prende forma di rosa
> io smetto di guardare nei tuoi specchi, Madre
> io guardo le cose[44]

In 1987, shortly before his death, Porta published the lengthy ballad, "Melusina," in which the fantasy heroine is a sort of polymorphic virago who ironically recalls the D'Annunzian heroine of the same name, amid lavish scriptings of a "golden age":

> Una donna ci manda questi doni
> un bosco tappezzato di fragole e mirtilli,
> dove corrono lepri bianche
> e cantano galli cedroni
> e sostano cervi dalle carni saporite,
> e mangiano le rose.
> Questa è l'età dell'oro,
> delle piogge rotonde e dolci,
> delle donne gentili,
> dei cieli intessuti di gelsomini.[45]

Elio Pagliarini, one of the five poets of the 1963 *Novissimi* anthology, has avoided the rose in his copious narrative "recitations," coarse antilyrics that employ the daily language in collages with an ethical thrust. Pagliarani's only use of rose is not his own, being cited from Savonarola's preachings "On Ezekiel":

> Se una pianta dicesse (una rosa): "Io non voglio più stare
> sulla terra."
> (o una carota tuberosa, o la gramigna anche, erba
> infestante).[46]

At this point in Pagliarani's career, the ludic element is abandoned and the moralistic component starkly accented. As Luperini writes, "all of Pagliarani's poetic experience—and especially the most recent—is decidedly outside—and against—the tradition of symbolism."[47]

Of comparable ethical force is Gianfranco Ciabatti (1936), a voice of skepticism and reason who stands in the highest civic tradition. Ciabatti opposes the neognostic and neohermetic evasions of those contemporaries who disavow the rational in their pursuit of the "grace" of the "word enamoured."[48] It is in this context that one appreciates the lyrical beauty of the following nine-line poem, with its vigilant—one wants to say "Fortinian"—gaze to the future:

> Leva in alto il mattino lente rose,
> intricano esili peschi l'albore,
> il cerchio di ferro che schianta la fronte
> si dissolve per aria.
> La testa è una luce dispersa,
> la vista una nebbia gocciante.
> Tu mi vedessi ora,
> mentre in me sale il pianto amoroso,
> l'inseguimento della vita[49]

The figure of the sentry stands for the poet militant whose "rhythmic, amorous and political energy" gives rise to "frequent lightning bolts of the future."[50] In a poem addressed to Romano Luperini, Ciabatti's austere prose voice examines the human need, beyond the normal social functions known as "duties," to ask for "gifts" from others, so that others may realize their power of giving.

> Se è vero che siamo inumani
> non è solo perché trascurammo l'omaggio
> di un mazzo di rose,
> ma anche perché assolvendo la nostra parte d'obblighi
> non domandammo doni.[51]

As this chapter has shown, the notion of advent provides a means to recover an archaic and prophetic language that was largely avoided by the "canonical" poets of the Novecento. In its simplest form the rose of advent remains a popular means to evoke a shared socialistic struggle, as per the inspiration of Pascoli. That is the spirit of Sanguineti's homage to former Italian president Sandro Pertini:

> rosa dei rossi fuochi partigiani
> . . . .
> sbocciato è il giorno, e la notte era nera,
> ma se rigido fu l'inverno, prima,
> fiorì di rose rossa primavera,
> e la rosa risplende sulla cima:[52]

The poets of advent, irrespective of their ideological positions, draw a critical distinction between the aleatory, the chance event which cannot foresee an advent, and the stochastic, which can. In short, the lesson of surrealism was not aestheticist or formalist in nature, but concerned the altering of historical and social protocols within the praxis of social life.

13
THE OTIOSE ROSE

Throughout this study, the integration of the "form of the expression" and the "form of the content" has been sought in terms of both texts and contexts. The focus has been on the whole meaning and endogenous structuring of the poetic message. The limitations of labels and "isms" have been heeded, in recognition of the fact that the dichotomy of "structure" and "growth" is in actuality a unity of literary communication. For this purpose we have drawn on the distinction between command message and report message: "[E]very message in a communication system is both a *report* (about a situation, about another message) and a *demand* or *command* (to respond in some way, including silence), as well as a *question* (about the response)."[1] In positioning the rose in terms of its communicative features, we have been freed of the restrictive concerns of formalists and contentists alike, whose isolation of either report message or command message obscures the relation between structure and growth, thesaurus and tabula rasa, remembering and forgetting. When understood in this light, as Curtius writes, the literary tradition is bound to beauty and creativity.

By including communicative context as part of one's critical method, one can abandon the dualism of form and content (with its operant metaphors of matter and energy), and opt instead for the descriptors of information and difference. The history of a *topos* can thus represent, in the words of Anthony Wilden, a "process of dialectical change [that] corresponds to a situation where novelty at the message level in a system comes to break through the constraints of its code, restructuring the code so that previously unheard-of messages become possible."[2] In this chapter, the new messages concern the magical qualities of augury and grace occasioned by the ancient activity of *otium* or recreative leisure. Leisure was in fact a major character in the *Roman de la rose*. Paradoxically active in retreat, the otiose rose is not a hex or talisman. While these poets invoke the rose in order to distance evil and engage the votive or sacred, the semiosis involved, and the secondary (erotic, elegiac, noetic) qualities produced, differ radically from those in Chapter 6. The rose of leisure expresses the desire for a "life out of the running"; it understands that to speak of the soul in archetypal terms is to confront the dangers of habit, including the dodges of discourse. While the focus here is synchronic and descriptive, in contrast to the diachronic focus of Chapter 12, in both cases the poets are concentrated on an understanding of the ethos and radical epistemology of poetry. In either case they either inspire or typify what Luperini calls the "new rationality."[3] At the basis of this rationality is a renewed interest in the theoretical dimension of poetry.

The intriguing poems of the Sicilian Edoardo Cacciatore (1912) are born out of a studied leisure; they are often elliptical, like haiku, and contain signs of the passing season:

> È autunno e i gridi si fanno sempre più rari
> Il travertino ha una tenerezza di rosa
> Il notiziario delle morti è sempre in ordine
> La libertà è un gesto obbligatorio.[4]

The complex associations they create are the reflections of a solitary who, in his errant wandering, makes careful use of negation, that is, of the syntactic disconfirmation of certainty or identity.

> Bizzarri proprio loro i visi i luoghi soliti
> Eccomi qui è certo—e vado errando altrove
> Guastafeste la verità non dirla odi
> L'inaudito e godi in ogni addìo un inizio
> Non è cenere sparso in un campo di rose.[5]

The use of "proprio," "certo," and "Eccomi" here are emphatic, while the anacoluthon and minimal punctuation allow for a dual logic, as different sentences are formed, or associations implied, before and after the line break.

> Il viottolo di robinie e rose scempie
> Rotola verità in fondo a questo maggio
> Le tombe antiche che la nostra voce empie
> La felicità che inventò questo viaggio
> Scrutano nell'eterno le dolcezze empie
> E su in alto quei fiori aforisma ad un saggio
> Dove un calabrone porta il peso di un raggio.[6]

Cacciatore offers a uniquely cognitive and contemplative quality to his poetry, employing language to sound out rhythms that link to metaphors and allegories. He argues against any separation between form and substance, ornament and meaning. In contrast to the Arcadianism that permeates the modern canon, his work focuses on life as a continuous series of transformations. Poetry is a means to recognize, through memory and meditation, the passage from an "I" to a "we." Only through a probing exploration of the world does one defeat conformism and understand immortality as the alternation of being and not-being. In the following work the rose is "false" when compared to the swarm of insentient society, and becomes "real" in the Orphic moment or recognition:

> Ma quel racconto di vicende o gli accenti
> Le stesse fibre hanno di una finta rosa.
> Via provvisoria dai decisivi momenti
> . . . .
> Questa è la chiara prova fuggito lo sciame
> Non ti commuovi che importano i sentimenti
> Nella tua mente è fiorita una vera rosa
> Viva ancora quando ogni fibra sarà estinta.[7]

An equally difficult poet is Emilio Villa (1914), a polyglot and linguistic experimentalist, who writes not only in Italian but several other languages including Milanese dialect. For Villa language is a process and a raw material in a metaphysical and archeological investigation of the past. His hermetic and Heraclitean awareness of humanity's state of perpetual becoming, and of the incantatory power of poetic language, leads him to speak of a "pure phonetic ideology" and to stand outside the Italian national life, with its false and facile discretions: "e ma fin quando agli stradali con le pioppe nichelate / parlino l'ozono e la pioggia a fil di terra d'ideali / giubilei, di comunismo fresco 'me 'na rosa."[8]

According to one critic, Villa's "sense of catastrophe" leads him to employ "mockery" and "anticlimax" as "truly apotropaic formulas against the sacred ambiguity and thus extreme forms of defense against the anguish caused by the evocation of the sacred."[9] In this passage the poet interrogates the relation between words and things, between himself, his words, and his interlocutors, including those in prayer:

> sarà il nuovo, l'altro, peccato originale. dominus
> sit in corde, amore mio,
> meu bem. o voialtri che sapete che rosa
> che rosa ma che rosa che state aspettando[10]

As suggested by these examples, negation is a common trait of the otiose rose. In Cacciatore, we saw the the negative space of a figure-ground relationship, and in Villa we saw the paroxysms of interrogation that effectively negate the accepted rhetorical and cultural values of the flower. "What rose are you waiting for?" he asks. Negation is also a factor in Giuseppe Goffredo's (1930) poem "Condemned to Hope":

> Le rose affacciate sul parapetto
> non odorano la via involuntaria
> dove rimugino. Il nostro futuro è spento,
> le giornate trascinate a fatica,
> senza voglia poi di dormire la sera.[11]

For Giuseppe Guglielmi (1923) the rose is a spiritual challenge and the promise and pressure of impending growth:

> Batte in quel suo marmo di lettere nere
> > è solo una rosa
> è movimento ancora
> > si è creduto nell'esistenza di qualcosa
> ma una volta che ciò sia accaduto
> > il silenzio lo avvolge[12]

The Triestine Luciano Budigna (1924) writes at the winter solstice—with the snowy Appenines as his backdrop—of man's senseless hostility to man. He finds in the warmth of his hearth a rose, and a face, that work to distance evil:

> Un Natale costretto
> al fumo tra gli alari e aperto al fuoco
> insensato degli uomini nemici
> nel fango, contro il buio.
> In quella rosa
> allucinante, un viso.[13]

Amelia Rosselli (1930), the daughter and niece of Carlo and Nello Rosselli, socialist activists assassinated by Italian fascists in France in 1937, began her poetic career in a triad of languages: English, French, and Italian. Born in Paris, she found the French language capable of accessing a "surrealistic" element in the psyche.

> Les auberges ont fermé leur clefs,
> les murs internes sont roses, leurs pétales
> se répètent en se croisant les mains
> (Elle est devenue folle,
> elle ne retrouve pas son époux
> il est devenu mort)[14]

Her rose is a nexus of linguistic rupture and loss of sense, factors that remain constants in her work. It is a symbol of Eros that Rosselli potentializes in the gift of love, and a *senhal* for the absent beloved. It may also stand for the confluence of two souls, a figure of courtesy and difficulty possessing the brevity and the endurance of the buried *stornello* form that Rosselli cultivated. Her poetic language of choice was Italian, distinguished from French and English because of its high degree of musicality. Her "memorial" style creates its own "metrical spaces," which also involve, more or less allusively, the subtle presence of an argumentative structure.

In the following ten-line lyric, one of her "Bellic Variations," I have highlighted words to point to Rosselli's use of symmetry, wordplay, polysyndeton, chiasmus, duplications, and parallelisms.

> Il soggiorno in inferno era di *natura divina*
> ma le lastre della *provvidenza* ruggivano nomi
> retrogradi e le esperienze del passato si facevano
> più voraci e la luna pendeva anch'essa non più
> *melanconico* e *le rose* del *giardino sfiorivano*
> lentamente al sole dolce. Se *sfioravo* il *giardino*
> esso mi penetrava con la sua dolcezza nelle ossa
> se cantavo im*provvi*samente il sole cadeva. Non
> era dunque la *natura divina* del*le cose* che scuoteva
> il mio vigoroso animo ma la *malinconia*.[15]

The figurative premise is that hell is a city of the dead that one visits, risking in the process the fierceness of one's memories of one's deeds. Upon gaining detachment from melancholy, one returns to spring, to hope and sweetness, as a living natural force of song and light, ever subject to change. As the poet recalls this soul-journey, it was the knowledge of melancholy that shook her spirit and not the "divine nature" of what was external. In like manner there is a contrast between what first appeared in this "hell" (the "retrograde names" on the plaques) and the solar and pastoral experience of well-being (the roses fading but "no longer melancholy"). The second half of the poem begins with its second sentence, and with an irony ("sfiorivano" is echoed by "sfioravo"). The providential aura of before ("provvidenza") is altered by the suddenness ("improvvisamente") of now. Rosselli realizes finally that her "vigorous soul" is shaken like a plant, not a "thing" (even a "divine" thing). In her pursuit of compositional freedom, Rosselli commits linguistic "errors" that convey the immediacy of her passion. She even labels herself an "illiterate":

> Con tutta la candida presunzione della mia
> giovane età stabilivo inventarii. Rose coronavano
> le mie pezze e la luce brillava attraverso un
> occhio quasi crudele.
> La regola d'onore era l'inesperienza! Regolatevi
> secondo il momento giusto esclamò l'analfabeta.[16]

The poet's roses here speak of a more urgent spiritual and physical need than what language can describe. This honesty and informality persist even when Rosselli is ill with Parkinson's disease. Writing from her sickbed that the decorative rose on her garter belt represents an obstacle, she folds her hands to pray, supported in that act by her own "internal civic tension." The mixture of religious and secular is recapitulated by a switch from the second to first person of the verb:

> Ruvido il guanciale mentre non dormi, una rosetta sul porta
> calza, tiracalze; strettoie delle difficoltà. Per essere nelle
> mani di Dio giunsi le mani, le punte alleggerite da una pressione
> civica interna.[17]

The rose adorns her prayer and her memory of youth, her enigmatic uneasiness about puberty and social standing, and the looming sense of violence and ignorance in the society at large. Here the rose stands for "difficulty" and ultimately the realization in a dream that "I am among the grand and yet I hide even what is small":

> per forza v'aggiungo ch'era
> nel mio sogno una intera
> visione del vostro dipinto
> non di difficoltà di rosa
> ma come se fosse, nell'esistenza
> di qui, l'alloro che morale
> m'aveva ingiunto a dirmi
> ch'io sono tra i grandi e
> nascondo perfino il piccolo[18]

Rosselli asserts her feminine consciousness within a poetic modality of mixed registers and insistent negative litanies, in which pain, sorrow, and melancholy are funneled into an active form of resistance:

> tu fermasti gli occhi al solco della primavera
> incantando un mondo di bestie con vetrali
> lacrime che non scendevano ma s'imbrogliavano
> nel tuo sonno tutto rose.[19]

Rosselli employs "faded roses" to describe with some urgency the situation of a friend:

> Con la malattia in bocca
> spavento
> per gli spaventapasseri
> rose stinte e vi sono macchie sul muro
> piccolissime nel granaio dei tuoi pensieri:
> e con quale colore smetti di
> dipingere?[20]

By rendering the rose ostensive and transparent, she confuses the recursive and extensive wonders, as if the poem were a moebius strip. Rosselli's voyage to the underworld and plaintive indulgence in the solitude of daily rituals comprise a "growing downward" into the soul, such that she could be said to "pull epistemology down out of the realms of abstract philosophy into the much more simple domain of natural history."[21] In her rejection of simile and embrace of metaphor, Rosselli is engaged in a hollowing out or kenosis of existential dilemmas; thus I would disagree with a recent critic who attributes to her "an experimental (de)construction of the lyric voice under the pressure of a language that is always dangerously divided against itself, and close to destruction and madness."[22] Such a view ignores the effective constructivism of Rosselli's practice, in which language is a means, not an end, in a pursuit of equivalencies to musical practices learned in her early training.

For Rosselli it is the need for discovery that produces knowledge, and not vice versa. By proposing a reading under the sign of learning, I would further recommend that her aesthetic coherence is not the effect of her experimentation with language, but is its cause. Only by appropriating texts and considering the language's transparency can the reader gain a correct understanding of the temporality of Rosselli's poetic labor. This process view concerns the communicative structure and coherence of the utterances, as meaningful in context. To see how the poems produced in time, as are whole compositions strung together into a mending or suturing, is a unitive act. Thus in "Il soggiorno in inferno" above one saw the homogeneous focus on nature and natural process from within, so that the journey to the underworld was both real and imagined, positive and regressive, a recuperation of the liberating time of the decision that Giorgio Agamben refers to as "the time of history and *cairós*."[23] Thus viewed the theoretical enterprise maintains its essence as "vision." Rosselli's theoretic vision is by necessity inferential and abductive, entailing forms of the daimonic and the "bellicose" which help explain the fertile ambiguities of her mythic and heroic quest. She does not veer perilously on the abyss but confronts death in life: poetry's purpose is to distance danger, to discover transcendence in the day-to-day.

A direct link to Rosselli is found in the work of Fausta Squatriti (1941), a sculptor who is directly interrogative, dialogic, and ostensive in her poiesis: "C'erano così tante rose / e concordi nello sforzo di fiorire / che per me sola, era troppo."[24] The willfulness of these roses that overwhelm the "I" figure stands to demonstrate the poet's contemplative approach to the *topos*. Working on the basis of day-to-day crises and epiphanies, she interrogates such occasions as factors in her mental and emotional equilibrium:

> Ma che tipo di dono è
> questo sole che non disarma
> alla stagione da tempo programmata.
> Nell'aria fina
> le innumeri foglie del giardino
> cui l'ultima rosa scarlatta denuncia
> il miracolo di fede.
> Coltivo la voglia di pace
> per ritrovare l'argomento base.[25]

The rose as an emblem of purity or faith belongs to another era. But in confronting evil this constructivist poet displays, in her honesty, desire, and reason, the "candor" of that passing flower: "Essere poveri, oggi, è maleducato. / . . . . / solo la nausea mitiga il candore della rosa. / Non c'è regola cui attenersi / per fornicare senza lamenti."[26]

In Gregorio Scalise (1939) the rose is a microcosm or emblem of the life force: impenetrable, cryptic, and unknowable. Yet in this negating capacity lies an idea of potential; the prospect of not knowing a solution but of *suspecting* one exists amid a constellation of ideas and objects, and allows the matters themselves to "speak up": "gli autunni sanno / che fra le grondaie / si colgono rose e petali: / ma è inutile cercarli nella parte / razionale del mondo";[27] "parlano del centro della terra / dove gli impulsi fioriscono / mentre le rose hanno limiti assurdi."[28]

> Il cielo sferzato dalla fretta
> procede con logica rigorosa.
> Il premio, è un'anima vinta.
> Resta l'astuzia.
> Principio di sentiero
> che porta a muri di rose
> ed è così che la costanza
> diventa memoria.[29]

In the apotropaic poets' enlisting of metaphor there is a link to the primitive, archaic, or folkloric rose. In one's idleness the rose becomes an object of play and linguistic conceit. Valentino Zeichen (1938) addresses this problem of mimesis as an occasion for play:

> Come imitatore
> approffitto di una pausa e mi intrometto fra gli annusamenti
> richiedo le rose obsolete
> per donarle a MARIA
> Da una scucitura del riserbo abbiamo udito che il Duccio
> aveva portato a MARIA un affondo libertino con le rose
> succitate
> respinte al primo assalto.[30]

Zeichen uses the metaphor of woman as flower in a conceit that involves a shift in linguistic register from the voluptuary to the metalinguistic:

> esulto alla tua morte.
> Così astutamente pallida
> che la rosa probabilmente
> avvampa del tuo rossore;
> oppure essa imita in carnagione
> il belletto del tuo sangue.
> . . . .
> Durante l'agonia sento i cospiratori che
> giurano fedeltà a quel motivo floreale
> che inflaziona la metafora e si propaga
> nelle trame ornamentali; imbarazza i
> giardinieri in tempo di potatura[31]

The metatextual or self-referential rose freely appropriates fragments from or allusions to earlier texts, and draws attention to its status as command message, as in this unpresupposing poem by Pier Massimo Forni:

> Spezzare il biscotto
> di qualche parola
> tuffarlo nel latte
> vedere se cola
>
> un verso o qualcosa
> da mettere in bocca
> veder se mi tocca
> la spina o la rosa.[32]

Angelo Lumelli (1944) provides a statement on the ontology of poetry, seen as a field of experimentation which has outgrown its former boundaries of genre and mimetic projection:

> oh poemi didascalici rispettosi poemi
> dove si forma un io

che l'aria lo nasconda
. . . .
l'occhio che vola invalicabile occhio
non è il divagante sonno la rosa la sua schiuma
ciò che affievolito nella testa
così stanco, ma noi diventati maschi.[33]

In the following "Little treatise," the reader is led to consider the multiple associations of the rose in eleven invocations by Lumelli, which shoot out in trajectories of sheer verbal excess:

perché non ha scampo
se vuole essere una rosa
così non si affaccia
ma profonda nel rosso
in velluto tuffata
il suo congegno che pensa
allora diventa una rosa
oh rosa guerriera
mio rimorso di rosa
potente chi si carica un nome
mille volte sospetto dolore
inflessibilie il volto del bello
mille rose mille rose piuttosto
un buon commercio ti prego
teste più basse da scambio
caso senza prova
non prova è lo stesso
qui contrattata
rosa ottenuta
son mistica sposa
scacciato da una rosa
sfiducia di racconto
tu me mutilino
disgrazia
pregando la rosa
mia sposa

> non sfuggo abbastanza
> me rosa! sfinito
> disabitato lo strido
> guerriero di rosa!³⁴

Renzo Paris (1944) employs the rose as an allegory for a poetry that has disappeared, with its innocent "garden of roses" and "forbidden symbology." This poem is addressed to the late Adriano Spatola:

> Quella di una volta aveva un orto di rose
> e dentro una vieta simbologia ci stava bene,
> nemmeno se n'accorgeva. Quella di adesso vuole
> che stia zitto. La sento. Prendimi l'acqua, dice,
> l'acqua della cucina. A guardarla sa d'urina.³⁵

Another of the metapoets of the 1970s is Raffaele Perrotta, who here cites the oldest and most aromatic of Italian roses, Ciullo d'Alcamo's "rosa fresca aulentissima": "la terra, in un grande sole, e un fuoco / fluss)s: maschera mutevole; fluss)s / e primissimo documento, rosa fresca aulentissima . . ."³⁶ The same awareness of the hyper-codified statute of the rose, as a trial ground for imitative transgression, is manifest in Tomaso Kemeny (1939): "Andare in ossequio alla tomba della / luce perché è lì che erompe / il giorno propagando / i tuoi capelli di donna / a rimarginare in alto la bocca / dura delle rose."³⁷ Kemeny attempts to conflate metaphysics and erotics, resulting in a confusing impressionism. In each of the following passages, the rose image opens its poem but remains purely an allusion without continuation:

> tra le aiuole abbandonate la
> ghiaia s'inarca per concoscere il
> ciglio delle rose³⁸

* * *

> rimase senza rose il dito
> della forestiera ma non seppe
> impedire al lucchetto cosmico di
> chiudersi sul suo cuore³⁹

* * *

rose d'arte e di rovina
contornate da stivaletti
feretri sulle colombaie
vermi sulle rocce[40]

In short, while the Mallarmé revolution brought with it a great intricacy, and a new marriage between music and metaphysics, the abstruseness of much work that is imitative of it only diminishes poetry's capacity for combining song and thought.[41]

In contrast to the vogue in metatextual poetry, the "new rationality" (as seen in the anthology *Poesia italiana della contraddizione*), offers a stimulating mixture of orphic, narrative-historical, and epistemological styles. For example, in Maurizio Cucchi's (1945) lines "nothing was ever completed / before mind or gaze created it," we understand the constructivist perception of the rose as difference, as thought, and not as a unit of matter or energy:

nulla era già compiuto

prima che mente o sguardo lo creasse.

Penso le rose, la colonna . . .

La giusta ricompensa—sembravi chiedermi—
l'attesa quiete nel sognato illuso

dileguarsi dell'assurdo.[42]

The late Dario Villa, Cucchi's contemporary, similarly embraces a stochastic rose suspended like the poet in a startling and perilous universe: "(siamo un'ombra del caso / procediamo da cause sconosciute / precipitiamo come nebulose / in un fuoco di rose)."[43] The constellated rose is targeted to refute a false, solipsistic epistemology that would separate things ("cose") from spirit: "il cervello inclinato / a testa in giù sulle cose / le rose d'oro le rose / dello spirito incrinato / il giardino di ghiaccio, devastato."[44]

Analogous to what was said above about poetry's "alibi," its moral and aesthetic autonomy, the poets of *otium* dwell on the boundary between "I" and "we" in the communicative exchange. They share a recursive understanding of poetic language and a constructivist view of time. As R. G. H. Siu put it, rephrasing an idea from Alfred North Whitehead, "Time then is not a self-subsistent reality. It is placed *in* Nature and not, as by other metaphysicians, vice-versa."[45] In order for poetry not to lose its force and necessity, it must be temporalized, it must recognize its limits in time. As Cassirer writes, "If the lyric poet succeeds in giving 'melody and voice' to pain, by so doing, he has not only enveloped it in a new covering; he has changed its inner nature. Through the medium of the emotions he has enabled us to glimpse spiritual depths which until now were closed and inaccessible to himself as well as to us."[46]

In conclusion I would like to focus on this idea of poetry that illuminates the depths. Whether we anticipate a future Italian poetry under the sign of allegory or alibi, epistemology or ecology, the single poet will be responsible for finding a path out of the labyrinth. The orientation in the darkness may be epitomized by the figure of the "rosa dei venti," the compass-card that guides one through the array, the pure configuration of inanimate matter or *pleroma*, in order to attain, as in the celestial mythology, a value-laden symbol of the soul, of *creatura*. The lateral or spatial meaning of the rose is also a figure of structure and growth. If we recall Dante's candid rose, it was a constellation of the blessed, but also a great social and political assembly, and the culmination of a cosmic model. Curiously that model, involving curvature of space in a finite but unbounded universe, is similar to one accepted by many current experts: "we are to think of the Emyprean as somehow both surrounding the visible universe and adjacent to it. If that is the case, then the universe according to Dante would coincide exactly with the universe according to Riemann; they would differ only in the labels."[47]

Thus we can see, with Caproni, the spatial field of the rose as the site of both predator and prey: "Nel campo / d'una rosa, la vipera /—rattratta—lingueggiava / bifida."[48] Or with Accrocca, we can confront the prospect of living one's life without a compass-card: "Attraversato dalla vita e senza alcuna rosa dei venti, non inseguo altro che orme ai limiti del campo che resta."[49] In "The Excercise of Dissent," it is clear that the "limits" of Accrocca's poetic "compass" are the "thorns" of the rose:

> tra le nebbie e gl'intrichi delle voci
> anonime come lettere,
> violenze   agguati
> nelle più spinate rose dei venti[50]

In the opening of Cacciatore's "The Past," the compass-card is a metaphor for "society":

> Sfuma ma ti ama l'oggi lesto
> Vasti commenti già dirama
> La società rosa dei venti
>
> Incrocia e ingemma l'ansia irosa
> Studia ad arte ogni stratagemma
> Dà l'addìo all'odio di parte[51]

It is, in Cacciatore's words, "diligent foresight" that allows one to employ craft as a vehicle of knowledge and transport, to confront the risk of having no compass, no "rose-of-the-winds," to guide one.[52]

Our isolation in the universe, as Leopardi came to understand, obliges us to engage in cooperative labor for the public good, for the redemption of those in the future. This goal is mapped out for us in the day-to-day, if we but measure the winds. I can think of no better final signpost in this regard than Rocco Scotellaro's five-line poem "Lunedì," for it gives the breath of fresh air, of hope and risk, that greets each house on the newborn day:

> Si sveglia il lungo serpente delle strade
> per il latte e la carne, il pane e la legna.
> I treni scaricano le corse operaie e drappelli di studenti.
> Gl'impiegati tornano a toccare i tavoli nelle stanze.
> Si aprono le case alla rosa dei venti.[53]

NOTES

PREFACE

1. H. Arendt in W. Benjamin, *Illuminations*, 48.
2. C. Segre, *Introduction to the Analysis of the Literary Text*, 283.
3. J. Hillman, *Oltre l'umanismo*, 18.
4. Giovanni Pozzi, "Sul luogo comune," *Alternatim*, 449, 452.
5. E. Curtius, *European Literature and the Latin Middle Ages*, 382.
6. G. Contini, "I ferri vecchi e quelli nuovi," 225.
7. Giovanni Pozzi, "Sul luogo comune," 449, 452.

1. IN THE GARDEN OF ITALIAN LITERATURE

1. S. Pellico, *Le mie prigioni*, 153: "He took the rose and began weeping."
2. C. Ossola, *figurato e rimosso*, 11: "la più abusata metafora."
3. J. Devito, *The Communication Handbook*, 60, 266.
4. To negotiate meanings Peirce employs the term "icon" when the sign is similar by convention to the object represented, "index" when the sign "points" to the object, and "symbol" when the sign communicates the idea of the object. See Charles S. Peirce, *Letters to Lady Welby*, 12.
5. U. Eco, *Postscript to* The Name of the Rose, 3.
6. A. Crespi, *Contemporary Thought of Italy*, 35.
7. For an analysis of diffidences toward Croce, see E. Garin, *La cultura italiana tra '800 e '900*.
8. Dante Alighieri, "Tre donne . . . ," in G. Contini, in *Letteratura italiana delle origini*, 349: "Dolesi l'una con parole molto / e 'n su la man si posa / come succisa rosa: / il nudo braccio, di dolor colonna, / sente l'oraggio che cade dal volto; / l'altra man tiene ascosa / la faccia lagrimosa."

9. *Enciclopedia dantesca*, ed. U. Bosco, 1:786.

10. Curtius cites the representative list found in Homer's Hymn to Demeter, *European Literature and the Latin Middle Ages*, 186.

11. Giovanni Pozzi, *La parola dipinta*, 69, indicates Petrarch's iconicity in the verse "o fiamma, o rose sparse in dolce falda" (oh flame, oh roses spread into a soft fold) [*Rerum Vulgarium Fragmenta*, 146] in which "the expression of red + red : white (in the formula 2:1) [is] expressed by means of metaphors." In contrast, Pietro Bembo favors a "pattern on a central plan, Ariosto an alternating pattern, Marino an oppositional pattern."

12. W. Shakespeare, Sonnet 109: "For nothing this wide universe I call, / Save thou, my rose; in it thou art my all"; Sonnet 98: "Nor did I wonder at the lilies white / Nor praise the deep vermilion in the rose; / They were but sweet, but figures of delight, / Drawn after you, you pattern of all those."

13. Giovanni Pozzi, *La rosa in mano al professore*, 87. See also 12: "L'oggetto di questo esposto pur essere così definito: 1. è un tema, 2. figurale, 3. appartenente alla lingua, 4. poetico-letteraria, 5. nella forma dello stereotipo, 6. considerato in una serie di documenti, 7. delimitati cronologicamente."

14. Giovanni Pozzi, "Temi, topoi, stereotipi," 394.

15. M. Corti, *An Introduction to Literary Semiotics*, 135.

16. "Poetic function" is defined by R. Jakobson in "Linguistics and Poetics," 358: "The poetic function projects the principle of equivalence from the axis of selection into the axis of combination. . . . Measure of sequences is a device which, outside of poetic function, finds no application in language. Only in poetry with its regular iteration of equivalent units is the time of the speech flow experienced, as it is—to cite another semiotic pattern—with musical time."

17. W. V. Goethe, *Nun weiss man erst*, in F. Fortini, trans., *Il ladro di ciliege*, 57: "E che cosa è una rosa, ora si sa; / ora, passata l'età delle rose. / Sullo spino ne brilla ultima una / e tutta sola tutti i fiori ha in sé."

18. A. Manzoni, "Il nome di Maria," *Inni sacri*, 27: "Hail thee, worthy of the second name after His, oh Rose, oh Star, refuge to the troubled, illustrious as the sun, terrible as an army arrayed in the field."

19. G. Schulz, "The Stranger and the Blue Flower: Some Observations on Novalis," 34.

20. N. Tommaseo, "Fede e carità," *Opere*, 125: "As the wing of the songbird flies high over the worm which creeps up the rose, oh Faith, you stood lofty over the woeful educated ignorance of the human school."

21. G. Leopardi, "Imitazione," *Canti*, 263: "Far from your branch, poor

frail leaf, where are you going? . . . I'm going where every other thing, where naturally goes the rose leaf and the laurel leaf as well." The original poem, it should be noted, is fifteen rather than thirteen lines long.

22. This realization is borne out by his most famous idyll, "L'infinito," in which the repeated deictics "questo" and "quello" reverse their referents so that by poem's end the distant "spatial infinity" is no longer filed under "that," but is invited into the personal and recursive space of "this." See C. Segre, *Avviamento all'analisi del testo letterario*, 49.

23. G. Carducci, "Commentando il Petrarca," in F. Martini, ed., *Scelta di poesie moderne*, 84: "It is the sweet chorus of your songs, in which from a garland of roses barely trained, her golden hair descends in waves of repose down her beautiful side. Ah, the mane now shakes and the placid mouth of one of those songs now opens to the rebel cry: Italy and Rome."

24. A. Graf, "Dal libro dei ricordi," in F. Martini, ed., *Scelta di poesie moderne*, 22: "Drunk with air and sun, it silently dreams an ancient divine vision, and among the roses and the olives it hears its great—undead—ruins, tremble."

25. G. Pascoli, "Rosa di macchia," *Poesie*, 140: "Common rose, which from the lush branch laughs unseen at the mountain rose, which passes by singing refrains and calls you dog rose; if a slender hand does not gather your blossoms, do not dismay at your fortune: may the envied hundred-petaled roses be plucked one by one."

26. L. Baldacci, in M. L. Spaziani, *Poesie*, 13: "il più grande metricista della tradizione italiana." See G. Contini, "Il linguaggio di Pascoli," 231: "[Pascoli] rappresenta obbiettivamente il tipo di un autore non rinchiuso entro i confini di un genere bensì perennemente esorbitante da ogni genere."

27. G. Pascoli, "Le femminelle," *Poesie*, 51: "And the white rose says: Oh! who is uprooting me? I am sad as a meadow-saffron: so many buds sprang from my branches! They were like tender little tips of asparagus: then they made their bark: they throw them off and arm themselves with thorns. They live on my dawn-colored flowers, of pink dawn; and you do not help, oh rue. They put out a blossom: a pale crown, soon opened, soon fallen."

28. G. Pascoli, "Il mago," *Poesie*, 65: "'Roses to the garden, swallows to the terrace!' he says, and the air whistles with wings to his words, and the shaggy hedge blossoms. The wise man could do more, but doesn't want to; contented if the heaven sings to him and the earth sends him its fragrance; he sends his messengers to the native aurora, he braids their blond heads with his garlands."

29. G. Pascoli, "Psyche," *Poesie*, 1030: "Pale Psyche, place a coin be-

tween your lips which seem two faded petals of a dead rose, and hold it lightly until an old man comes and takes it. You will not even feel it, but you will close your eyes and sleep."

30. G. D'Annunzio, "Romanza," *Versi d'amore e di gloria*, 1:510: "September fills the sky with a thought-laden grief. The roses of summer languish upon his temples."

31. G. D'Annunzio, "Sonetto," ibid., 1:1047: "I—it said—am the unnatural Rose who from the breast of Beauty grows. It is I who infuse the highest ecstasy. I am the one who exalts and gives repose." Ezra Pound, whose reading of D'Annunzio, it would seem, was cursory at best, displays an inverse pattern in the *Cantos*: singular: 14; plural: 3.

32. G. D'Annunzio, "Il censore," ibid., 1:243: "My rosebeds are all stripped. No more garlands! And my cup is empty."

33. G. D'Annunzio, "Assisi," ibid., 2:386: "I also saw Francis's flesh, enflamed by the carnal demon, bleeding onto the thorns of the rose."

34. G. D'Annunzio, "Sonetto all'antica," ibid., 1:1047–48: "Mona Francesca carried in her dress as many roses to her meadow-guest to twine about her head as ever had Heaven white angels. / . . . . / A verse of Petrarch rose in the air: 'Thus he separated the words and the roses.'" See D. Alonso, *Pluralità e correlazione in poesia* 79, for a discussion of the Petrarchan text "Due rose fresche, e còlte in paradiso." The sonnet is found in the appendix of *Il piacere* (1889), the first of D'Annunzio's passionate "Novels of the Rose." The others are *L'innocente* (1892) and *Trionfo della morte* (1894).

35. G. D'Annunzio, "Le armonie," *Maia*, 101: "Bellosguardo, certainly tomorrow I shall come to your rose-bushes which you bear laden with still unopened roses. // I know well that the blossoms will be like the swollen nipples of a pubescent lass. But maybe the first-blossomed rose up on the grate where the loquacious pail hangs in the well, will be white. Oh hill that is our Meeting place, through the window I see you all pink, not like the roses but like the flowers of the heath . . ."

36. G. D'Annunzio, "L'oleandro," *Versi d'amore e di gloria*, 2:520: "And thus that Florentine Arethusa spoke of the rose and laurel, a mutable wave with a face of gold. Her voice was like silvery water smelling of lavender or even mint or sage or other fresh morning herb. Ruled entirely by my sincere disposition, I said, 'I wish to be crowned only with oleander.' And Arethusa was happy; and she clipped two more branches for me and did me the honor of twining them at my temples, saying to me: 'For your new poems! May you always have the blue and tawny Summer in your heart and may your poems be born as are its simple roses!'" As Enrico

Thovez had done, Mario Praz documents D'Annunzio's heavy reliance on literary models, to the point of plagiarism (in this case the lines are a calque of Régnier); see *La carne, la morte e il diavolo nella letteratura romantica,* 408–9.

37. G. P. Lucini, "La danza d'amore," in R. Jacobbi, *L'avventura del Novecento,* 289: "The Lady and Gentleman go far away, far beneath the green vault of the laurels: and in the gentle splendors of serene nights the sonorous dance and rhythm are lost, on the roses, of love, bloomed among bushes and faded among breasts white and hard: My note is dying."

38. R. Jacobbi, *L'avventura del Novecento,* 287: "l'inquieto europeismo socialista, esoterico, estetizzante di Lucini." A source for Lucini's "rose" is Saint-Pol-Roux (1861), author of *La rose, et les épines du chemin.*

39. R. M. Rilke, "The First Elegy," *The Duino Elegies,* trans. J. Leishman and S. Spender, 25.

40. B. Brecht, "Ach wie sollen wir die kleine Rose buchen?" *Poems 1913–1956,* trans. J. Willet, 447.

41. E. Pound, "Envoi (1919)," *Personae,* 27.

42. E. Pound, Canto LXXIV, *Cantos,* 449. This passage has been seen by G. Singh, "Dante and Pound," 323, as a "recollection reminiscent of Dante's sense of relief as he moves from Hell to Purgatory," although Lethe, and the river Eunoe, are actually crossed after the Purgatorial climb, upon entering the Earthly Paradise.

43. H. Kenner, *The Pound Era,* 146. Kenner finds here the idea of an integrated pattern or force field that is the major organizational principle of vorticism.

44. M. L. Spaziani, "Colle oppio," *Utilità della memoria,* 52: "The Colosseum, tonight, is a rose in pieces and life breaks apart with it under the moon. I am looking for the single verse, the stem, the magic spell to reconstitute every fractured image into one."

45. P. V. Mengaldo, *Poeti italiani del Novecento,* xx; hereafter abbreviated *PIN.* See also *Leopardi e il Novecento;* G. Lonardi, *Leopardismo;* C. Rebora, *Per un Leopardi mal noto.*

46. F. Fortini, "Un dialogo su Leopardi," in V. Abati et al., eds., *"Uomini usciti di pianto in ragione,"* 18–81.

47. See E. Curtius, *European Literature and the Latin Middle Ages,* 396.

48. N. Brown, *Love's Body,* 262.

49. J. Kristeva, "The System and the Speaking Subject," 50. Kristeva continues, "[S]ince it is itself a metalanguage, semiotics can do no more than postulate this heterogeneity: as soon as it speaks about it, it homogenizes the phenomenon, links it with a system, loses hold of it. Its speci-

ficity can be preserved only in the signifying practices which set off the heterogenity at issue: thus poetic language making free with the language code; music, dancing, painting, re-ordering the psychic drives which have not been harnessed by the dominant symbolization systems and thus renewing their own tradition."

50. Ibid., 52, 54.

51. I draw here on the valuable introduction to *A General Rhetoric* by the Group μ.

2. ROSES AND VIOLETS, OR THE PROBLEM OF WONDER

1. D. De Robertis, "Le violette sul seno della fanciulla," 76.

2. Dante, *Purgatorio* xxxii, 58, trans. Allen Mandelbaum: "the tree . . . was now renewed, showing a tint that was less than the rose, more than the violet."

3. D. De Robertis, "Le violette sul seno della fanciulla," 98–99.

4. U. Foscolo, "Le grazie," *Tutte le poesie*, 39: "an unknown violet sprouted at the base of the cypresses; and suddenly several scarlet roses joyously turned to white. It then became religious custom to make libations with milk wrapped in white roses, and to sing hymns under the cypresses, and to offer to the altar pearls and the first flower announcing April."

5. V. Di Benedetto, "Le 'bianche rose' e la forma depurata," 334–35.

6. F. Petrarca, *Canzoniere*, CCVII, 266: "thus spring has roses and violets, and winter has snow and ice."

7. G. Leopardi, "Il sabato del villaggio," *Canti*, 193–94: "The girl returns from the fields at sunset, with her bundle of grass; and in her hand she carries a bunch of roses and violets, that tomorrow, the feast day, she will use, as is usual, to adorn her breast and hair."

8. G. Pascoli, *Prose*, 1:58: "Rose e viole nello stesso mazzolino campestre d'una villanella, mi pare che il Leopardi non le abbia potute vedere. A questa, viole di marzo, a quella, rose di maggio, sì poteva . . ."

9. C. Varese, "Pascoli e Leopardi," in *Leopardi e il Novecento*, 70.

10. G. Carducci, "Tedio invernale," *Poesie*, 291: "But was there ever a day / Of sunshine on this earth? / Were there roses and violets, / Light, smiles, warmth?" Notably, *rosa* appears in a variant of Carducci's "Alla stazione in una mattina d'autunno."

11. G. Carducci, "Ballata dolorosa," *Poesie*, 300: "And the violets breathe a sweet desire and in the roses a sweet ardor is burning."

12. G. Pascoli, "Digitale purpurea," *Poesie*, 222–23: "They see; and their

thought is scented with the odor of roses and violets in bunches, of a scent of innocence and mystery.... I was alone with the green rose beetles. The wind carried the smell of roses and violets in bunches."

13. G. Pascoli, "I filugelli," in G. Almansi and R. Barbolini, eds., *La passion predominante*, 365: "But you unlace your white corset, oh blond Rosa. Outside the sun shines clear, and two doves coo upon the roof. You undo your bra. The odor of white violets fills the garden. Oh! leave it like before. It's beautiful the way it is. No other flower is needed. There are two blossoms red at the top. // Do not entrap in your white breast, oh Rosa, the flower of sleep. Does it not have vigil there and never rest, day and night?"

14. Anonymous (fifteenth century), "Strambotti," in M. Santagostini, *Il manuale del poeta*, 85: "Come now, undo that lace upon your chest and let me see those violets: let heaven remain open, where the sun and moon do rise! The sun rises and the moon rests, say goodnight to that fine rose."

15. A. Fogazzaro, "LXVII," *Miranda*, 196–97: "Yet the air was changing, up along the mountain slopes the snow recedes, one sees in the blackening clouds, and in the warm rain one hears the new season. Rose's little boy brought me violets."

16. A. Onofri, *Poesie edite e inedite (1900–1914)*, 109: "May those of us who know of love have our florid temples wrapped in roses, lilies, and violets. And from all around, let songs of desire erupt like winged outrootings to the fresh winds of dawn."

17. E. Thovez, "Inverno," *Il poema dell'adolescenza*, 17: "A rose-hued gleaming of violet, soft, tender, like a warm breath from a wet mouth, enflamed over the dark green, it burns in the forest, while here it shatters against the intact whiteness, in shadows of rose."

18. G. D'Annunzio, "Rosa," *Versi d'amore e di gloria*, 1:47: "Pale rose, who from the green hedge laugh with placid desire // Lo there, your stem trembles at the languid kiss of a dragonfly lover, and the violets look on with envy at your divine merriments."

19. G. D'Annunzio, "Tristezza," ibid., 2:599: "You seem to be alone Hermione, like her who in the silence comes toward you alone carrying her white hem like a wing. Yes, you resemble her so that I would be deceived if I did not see a clump of violet on her cheek still wet with the cloud. She has so many roses in her lap."

20. G. D'Annunzio, "L'Alfeo," *Maia*, 68: "A pious pilgrim, I gathered the roses of the laurel-like oleander and the violet flower of the verbena among the ruins."

21. G. D'Annunzio, "Rondò," *Versi d'amore e di gloria*, 1:534: "Like har-

monious bees coming out into the new sun through the glad flower-beds of lilies and roses, . . . on the odorous locks which Love is wont to twine with dreams and violets may sweet things be inspired like harmonious bees."

22. G. Gozzano, "Paolo e Virginia," *Opere*, 184: "I reclined mute over that face where already the violets of death blended with the roses of modesty . . . Desperate sorrow! Pain without voice and without tears!" As the editor of this volume notes, Gozzano borrows from Bernardin de Saint-Pierre's *Paul et Virginie*.

23. M. Bontempelli, "Vetrate," *Il purosangue*, 15: "Little birds of the West / pushed by the smoking of the roses / within a dense rain of petals, / beyond the rain they are veils of sun. // A feather fell onto a barge / another one rests upon the pink smoke / one is sailing amid the violets / but the last feather is winding among the first veils of the sun."

24. G. Gerbino, "La gabbia del popolo," in V. Scheiwiller, ed., *Poeti del secondo futurismo italiano*, 90: "The square? An enchanted cage, where, in the evening, roses and violets, red carnations, tulips, spit every bitterness to the earth."

25. B. Corra, "La morte dei fiori," ibid., 22: "But certainly for many nights we will suffocate with brutality this new horrible modern soul of ours, and shall greedily spread over ancient alcoves some drops of the essences of roses and violets."

26. B. Barbarani, "A spasso co le rose," *Tutte le poesie*, 144: "—Rosa rosana, listen to me: you are a queen in springtime, but the chatterbox violets gossip about you morning and night . . . You were born with them, in the grasses, and yet, they say, you are haughty.—Rosa rosana answered thus: so often do appearances deceive!"

27. C. Segre, in F. Scataglini, *La rosa*, vii: "la storia di un innamoramento."

28. F. Scataglini, *La rosa*, 50: "no periwinkles or violets, no graceful stems of fragrant broom. On the right were the roses. Vast, grand petals, as if multiplying."

29. L. Fallacara, "Estate," *Poesie*, 122: "The roses will gasp and one summer, lightning, flashing between your dampened lashes, will sweetly burn the ambered rocks, a sea of white flowers insensate. // They will have evenings of slow violets mythical in the taciturn pallor, wet breasts overflowing from the sidereal urns that are emptied of wind."

30. L. Sinisgalli, "Pasqua 1952," *The Ellipse*, 98, 100: "I had been waiting thirty years for an Easter among the ditches, the moss over the stones,

violets among the roof tiles. But the dead sleep in chestnut coffins, . . . All that I know cannot help me erase all that I have seen. The children blow on coal so that the simulacrum of the rose will bloom out of lead."

31. L. Sinisgalli, "Le sorelle," *L'età della luna,* 43: "The rarest rose in the family was Nuccia the rose, the proudest among the roses was Anna. Enza and Angela grew in the wild garden, violets upon the wall."

32. L. Anceschi, *Linea lombarda,* 8.

33. A. Gatto, "La rosa," *Poesie,* 126: "If blue colors the rose with itself red in the green raises up the rose, wild rose red rose brilliant with blue, violet from the black water."

34. M. Luzi, "(se musica è la donna amata)," *Tutte le poesie,* 52: "from the sea (a breathless violet in the white memory of vestige) a desolate wind leaned against your windows with a gray feather // and if you wanted to gather from it a brown offended solitude your hand was pressing in its sweet-smelling limbos against roses unrealized, in the distance."

35. L. De Libero, "Sono uno di voi," *Poesie,* 122: "We will live in yet another realm and we say a prayer, to the rose born this morning, and we tear away the violet of evening that betrays with its scent, the certainty of being what we want changes nothing of the fact that decides."

36. L. De Libero, "Il mio amico C. piange la madre," *Di brace in brace,* 95: "Your presence was a flame . . . a perennial event of the rose, to be eternal, the eternal illusion. . . . where March curled up blue leaves on the almond tree and verses of violets, the meadow that yesterday was victorious will tomorrow be a livid desert."

37. M. L. Spaziani, "Convento nel '45," *Utilità della memoria,* 37–38: "Time of white violets, arduous ascent of youth to the crossings of the instant. You dazzle me still, diamond fragment, undisputed empire of the rose over the slope of fresh clover."

38. G. Bassani, "Dove sei?" *L'alba ai vetri,* 64: "Where are you? Where are you calling from? Are you present only in things, only to the vanquished, the surrendered? And for whom do the roses from human gardens have human words? Do the faded and distant violets laugh only to the dead?"

39. A. Bertolucci, *La camera da letto,* 316: "Who down here in the plains can remember such a winter so mild as to reblossom roses up until Christmas, to bud violets at the tearful and laughing end of short February? Very little flu and sickness, the healthy effect of a poor, wartime diet."

40. G. Raboni, *Poesia degli anni sessanta,* 232: "poeta antinarrativo, eppure sempre cosí denso di 'materia' narrativa."

41. P. P. Pasolini, *La religione del mio tempo*, 72, 74: "everything happens as if in some past hour of my existence: mysterious mornings of Bologna or Casarsa, sorrowful and perfect as roses. . . . As a child I would dream of these breezes, already fresh and warmed by the sun, fragments of forests, Celtic oaks, among undergrowth and blackberry bushes stripped bare in the reddish glow, as if uprooted by sunny autumn—and inlets of blindly deserted northern rivers where the odor of lichens pierced the air, fresh and nude, like violets at Easter time . . . The flesh then was without limits."

42. G. Testori, *Diadèmata*, 85: "gathering between his fingers the putrid rose of his sister's panties."

43. G. Testori, "Nella landa ingrigita," in E. Krumm and T. Rossi, eds., *Poesia italiana del Novecento*, 963: "Worms cry out; livid they grab on to the moribund relic; in the background, among nodes of medusas there rush by rotting roses, soffocated lights, narcisuses."

44. C. Della Corte, "Amore, rosa rossa, lento fiume," in A. Manuali and B. Sablone, eds., *Poesie d'amore del '900 italiano*, 153: "Much wind and now the violets are budding; winter has consumed its colors old and new; leaves clot up in the knots; Love, red rose, slow river, I foretell your flesh, your silence, the water heavy with leaves at your shores."

45. R. Modesti, in L. Anceschi, ed., *Linea lombarda*, 109: "and already life seems to be purple pink."

46. L. Erba, "In Romagna," *Il cerchio aperto*, 49: "in a pink painted country house. . . . A baby came out of a long or low house, shouting, 'I see purple!' 'It must be Violani,' 'No!, it's the calomel' all night the neighbours argued."

47. M. Luzi, "Avorio," in P. V. Mengaldo, ed., *PIN*, 655: "Roses were violating the horizon, hesitant cities resided in the sky."

48. D. Bellezza, "La mia casa, l'entrata," *Libro di poesia*, 19–20: of the senses; "may there remain on the threshold inviolate only fear, searched for like a perfumed rose."

49. M. Coviello, "Marabella," in A. Porta, ed., *Poesia degli anni settanta*, 567–69: "The rose is the scented violet / pay no mind if I am nervous / the thing pays no mind to the thing / thus I am nothing I'm sorry / . . . . / the thing pays no mind to the thing / pay no mind if I am nervous / the rose is the scented violet / thus I am nothing I'm sorry."

3. Le Mystère d'un Nom

1. P. Valéry, "La ceinture," *Selected Writings*, 70–71: "Time plays among the roses."

2. G. de Nerval, "Artèmis," *The Chimeras*, trans. P. Jay, 24: "Love who loved you from the cradle to the hearse. Alone my love still loves me tenderly, She is Death—or the dead one . . . Torment! Joy! The rose she carries is the *Mallow* rose. Neapolitan Saint with your hands full of fire, Rose with the violet heart, Saint Gudula's flower, In heaven's desert have you found your cross? White roses, fall! You insult our gods: Fall, white phantoms, from your burning skies:—The saint of the pit is holier in my eyes!"

3. G. de Nerval, "El desdichado," ibid., 14–15: "You who consoled me, in the tombstone night, Bring back my Posilipo, the Italian sea, The flower that so pleased my wasted heart, And the arbour where the vine and rose agree."

4. G. de Nerval, "Chanson gothique," *Poésies*, 81: "Beautiful bride I love your tears! It is the rosebush that sits among the flowers. // The beautiful things / Have but one springtime, / Let us sow roses / The steps of time! // Are you brunette or blonde / Must one choose? / The God of the world / is Pleasure."

5. T. Adorno, *Aesthetic Theory*, 73–74.

6. C. Baudelaire, "Le soleil," *Flowers of Evil*, trans. David Paul: "The all satisfying sun, anaemia's enemy, Gives life to the worm and the rose impartially." The term "zero degree" is coined by Roland Barthes in his 1953 *Le degré zéro de l'écriture*, referred to in Chapter 10.

7. C. Baudelaire, "Spleen," *Les fleurs du mal*, 80: "I am an old boudoir full of withered roses Wherein lie a whole confusion of antiquated styles."

8. C. Baudelaire, "Femmes damnées: Delphine et Hippolyte," ibid., 177: "'Hippolyte, dear heart, what are you saying? Do you now understand it is not necessary to offer the holy sacrifice of your first roses to the violent blowings which could fade them?"

9. C. Baudelaire, "Un voyage a Cythère," ibid., 136: "Beautiful island green with myrtle, full of open flowers, Ever honored by every nation, Where sighs of hearts in adoration Roll like incense over a garden of roses."

10. P. Verlaine, "Spleen," *Oeuvres poétiques*, 162: "The roses were entirely red, And the ivy entirely black. My dear, if you but move slightly, all my despairs are reborn."

11. P. Verlaine, "Pénitence," *Sagesse: Liturgies intimes*, 191: "Yes, you dictate and make us complete excellent Acts due to the excellence of the causes, Blooming, on the thorns, of the roses Which the Father then comes with slow steps to pluck: Penitence."

12. S. Mallarmé, "Crise de vers," *The Poems*, 46–47, trans. K. Bosley: "I

say: a flower! and, out of the oblivion to which my voice consigns any outline, being something other than known petal-cups, musically rises, an actual and sweet idea, the one absent from all bouquets."

13. S. Mallarmé, "Toast funèbre," *Collected Poems*, trans. H. Weinfield, 38, 45: "The Master's piercing eye, wherever he would go, Has calmed the unquiet marvels of Eden's wild delights, Of which the final spasm, in his lone voice, excites For the Lily and the Rose the mystery of a name."

14. S. Mallarmé, "L'après-midi d'un faune," *Collected Poems*, trans. H. Weinfield, 38: "Did I love a dream? / My doubt, night's ancient hoard, pursues its theme / in branching labyrinths, which, being still / The veritable woods themselves, alas, reveal / My triumph as the ideal fault of roses."

15. S. Mallarmé, "L'après-midi d'un faune," *The Poems*, trans. K. Bosley, 122–23: "I snatch them, still entwined, and fly to that clump of roses the flighty shadows hate, which shrivels every perfume in the sun."

16. M. Luzi, in S. Mallarmé, *Il pomeriggio d'un fauno*, 53.

17. G. Mazzotta, "The Theology of Mario Luzi's Poetry," 196.

18. A. Rimbaud, "Ce qu'on dit au poète à propos de fleurs," *Complete Works*, trans. W. Fowlie, 104: "O Poets, if you had Roses, blown Roses, Red on laurel stems, And swollen with a thousand octaves!"

19. A. Rimbaud, "Mémoire," *Complete Works*, trans. W. Fowlie, 124: "Ah! dust of the willows shaken by a wing! The roses of the reeds devoured long ago!"

20. L. Bersani, *A Future for Astyanax*, 252.

21. A. Rimbaud, "Un coeur sous une soutane: Intimités d'un séminariste" (A heart under a cassock), *Complete Works*, trans. Wallace Fowlie, 261–83: "I plucked the petals of this poetic rose! I took my cithara. . . . He debased my poetry! He spat on my rose! . . . but my heart understood: it was the Rose of David, the Rose of Jesse, the mystic Rose of Scripture, it was Love! . . . Thimothina {Vas devotionis, Rosa mystica. . . . The sacristan's wife, . . . her hollow chest leaning forward, . . . was amorously pulling the petals from a rose."

22. J. Laforgue, "Complainte des formalités nuptiales," *Poems of Jules Laforgue*, trans. P. Dale, 94, 98: "[He]: Yes, but the Law Unique requires the oath we say / Be baptised with the roses of your new cross here; / Your eyes turn mortal but your destiny calls me clear. . . . [He]: O universal decline! // My one and only's to be born of mutual sowing, mine! / For love's strong roses, she, / My nubile lily, will forsake / Her shadows so remote, and take / Her turn to be / Woman in finery / Of Maya. // Alleluia."

23. J. Laforgue, "Dialogue avant le lever de la lune," ibid., 226–27: "—And to be with it's the equivalent, / Isn't it of matching to a thing? /—

It follows, as the rose in flowering / is necessary to its needful bent. / —A way of singing quite a common tune: / That vicious circles only make the whole! /—Vicious, but the whole!"

24. J. Laforgue, "III dimanches," ibid., 376–77: "(My Self, it's Galatea blinding Pygmalion's stares. / Impossible to modify this state of affairs.) / So then, poor and pale and pitifully unsublime, / Who only trusts his Self in his spare time, / I watched my fiancée detaching, / Carried off by the way it goes, / Just like the thorn catching / The fall, the pretext evening, of its loveliest rose."

25. J. Laforgue, "Esthétique," ibid., 336–37: "Without a hope or scene let's pick. / After the rose, flesh withers too. / Let's run through all the scales, and quick, / For there is nothing else to do."

26. P. Claudel, "Le quinze aout," *Bréviaire poétique*, 158: "*You shall lead them to water*, says the psalm, *at the torrent of the voluptuous!* A crumbling of all kinds of benedictions upon us pell mell, and our arms will not be enough for this armful! But the rose has become the rosary, this handful of agglomerated grain that calls the finger: *I hail you Mary full of grace!* from the middle of the hand that prays."

27. P. Claudel, "Le mois de Marie," ibid., 125–26: "Roses of Jericho! . . . The double uncertain rose that feathers out against the wax, the flame like a breath. . . . Accept this I pray, oh Mary!"

28. See N. Hellerstein, *Mythe et structure dans les cinq grandes odes de Paul Claudel*, 40: "On remarquera d'abord ici que le poète prononce directement le nom 'Rose,' le vrai nom de la femme aimée, mais que cette présence du nom est compensée par l'absence de l'être qu'il désigne. La 'rose' humaine achève donc l'évolution du thème de la rose, cet échange graduel entre la réalité physique et la réalité linguistique qui marque le parcours spirituel sacrificiel de l'Ode."; 282: "La valeur totalisatrice, suggérée par la forme circulaire de la fleur, dominait au début; à la fin domine sa fragilité, sa tragique insaisissabilité." See also Jacqueline de Labriolle, "Le thème de la rose dans l'oeuvre de Paul Claudel."

29. P. Claudel, *A Hundred Movements for a Fan*, trans. A. Harvey and I. Watson, 1: "You / call me the Rose / says the Rose / but if you knew / my real name / I would / shrivel / at once."

30. G. Caproni, "Concessione," *L'opera in versi*, 805: "Feel free to discard / any work of poetry or prose. / None has ever managed to define, / in its essence, a rose."

31. P. Claudel, "Cette nuit . . . ," *A Hundred Movements for a Fan*, 14–15: "To / night / it rained / wine / I know there was no / way to stop the / roses from talking."

32. A. Artaud, "Soir," *Oeuvres complètes,* 184: "Some ships on the sea stretch out their pink sails, The rose-window loses its leaves in the shadow of the steeple, And one sees the errant petals of the celestial rose disperse in the evening sky."

33. A. Artaud, "Allégorie," *Oeuvres complètes,* 176: "I dream one evening of calyxes laden with birds Where the myrrh burning at the breast of the blue baths Sparks like a ruby; and the horses Compass-cards are mixed in the mane of the reeds."

34. J. Cocteau, "Crucifixion, ou la douleur petrifiée," *Poèmes 1916–1955,* 149–50; trans. M. Crosland, *Cocteau's World,* 210: "There were thuds. Thuds of iron on iron. Old rose of the winds. Thuds. Rust of thuds on the outspread fan of foot-bones. On the mat of toe-bones. On planks."

35. The emphatic quality of Spanish song is seen in Jiménez's dilatation of the rose. Juan Ramón Jiménez, "¡Amor!" *Poesía (en verso) (1917–1923),* 84: "Todas las rosas son la misma rosa, / ¡amor!, la única rosa" (All roses are the same rose, Love! the only rose).

36. See H. Weinfield in S. Mallarmé, *Collected Poems,* 51.

37. P. Valéry, "La jeune parque," *Paul Valéry: An Anthology,* trans. D. Paul, 213, 209, 213, 215, 223: "Between the rose and me I see it lurking; Over the dancing dust it glides"; "Death seeks to inhale this priceless rose Whose sweetness matters to its dark purpose!" "And, roses! the sigh I heave lifts you, vanquishing Alas, the arms so soft folded about your cradle . . ."; "Hail! Deities in virtue of the rose and salt, And earliest playthings of the infant light, Islands!"

38. P. Valéry, "Au bois dormant," *Selected Writings,* trans. J. Kirkup, 64–65: "The slow petaled rose that hangs so close to your cheek Will never squander those unfolded treasuries That blush in secret when the sun's rays on them break." See "Narcisse," 30, 36: "O douceur de survivre à la force du jour, Quand elle se retire, enfin rose d'amour, . . . Dites qu'une lueur de rose ou d'émeraudes."

39. G. Apollinaire, in P. A. Jannini, *Le avanguardie letterarie nell'idea critica di Apollinaire,* 11.

40. T. Conley, "1913—Lyrical Ideograms," 845.

41. G. Apollinaire, "Visée," *Selected Writings,* trans. R. Shattuck, 172–73: "A child with its hands cut off among roses like flags."

42. G. Apollinaire, "Annie," *Selected Poems,* trans. Oliver Bernard, 58–59: "On the coast of Texas / Between Mobile and Galveston there is / A great big garden overgrown with roses / It also contains a villa / Which is one great rose. . . . // Since this woman belongs to the Mennonite sect /

Her rose trees have no buds and her clothes no buttons / There are two missing from my jacket / This lady and I are almost of the same religion."

43. G. Apollinaire, "Les fiançailles," *Alcools*, trans. A. H. Greet, 172–73: "Where blazing bouquets crumbled Before the eyes of a mulatto girl who invented poetry And the roses of electricity still unfold In the garden of my memory."

44. B. Cendrars, "Soudain les sirènes mugissent," *Complete Poems*, trans. Ron Padgett, 351, 222: "A little further up I go in and ask a butcher for a light. I light up a new cigar and we exchange a smile. He has a nice tattoo, a name, a rose, and a heart with a dagger through it. It's a name I know well: it's my mother's."

45. M. A. Caws and P. Terry, "Introduction," *Roof Slates and Other Poems of Pierre Reverdy*, xvi.

46. See L. Erba, "Une poésie du vertige cosmique," *Huysmans e la liturgia*, 61–62. "On trouve, dans le meilleur Reverdy, un refus superbe du nom propre, ou, tout au moins, du nom destiné à faire tache de couleur; ce qui revient à a dire que Reverdy a aboli le *nom* déjà du temps où d'autres se considéraient à l'avant-garde pour avoir eu l'audace d'abolir l'*adjectif*."

47. Saint John Perse, *Anabasis*, trans. T. S. Eliot, n.p.: "How, under the wild rose is there no more grace to the world? Comes from this side of the world a great purple doom on the waters. . . . And man inspired by wine, who wears his heart savage and buzzing like a swarm of black flies, begins to say such words as these: '. . . Roses, purple delight; the earth stretched forth to my desire—and who shall set bounds thereunto, this evening? . . .' and upon such an one, son of such an one, a poor man, devolves the power of signs and visions."

48. Saint John Perse, *Chronique*, 4, 8, 17, 21; trans. R. Fitzgerald, 28, 32, 41, 45: "Raise your head, man of evening. The great rose of the years turns round your serene brow"; "Great age behold us. We cherished neither rose nor acanthus"; "that [tree] spread itself open to the night, raising to its god the ample and finely wrought burden of its giant roses"; "O memory, take thought for your roses of salt. The great rose of evening lodges a star on its breast like a golden beetle."

49. A. Breton, *Arcane 17*, 77: "It is as bottomless as the diamond and only lovers . . . will know which mirrored vaults, which rose of a beacon's lenses in such a night, will make a sparkling garden to their drunkenness, and be able to testify that the impulses of the heart and of the senses do find their infinite response."

50. A. Breton, *Oeuvres complètes*, 737. *Mad Love*, trans. M. A. Caws, 69:

"We have gone past the peak of the coral trees through which its scarlet wing appears and whose thousand intertwined rose grills forbid anyone's perceiving the difference between a leaf, a flower, and a flame."

51. A. Breton, "Manifest du surréalisme," *Oeuvres complètes*, 1: 339: "As Rrose Selavy sleeps, a dwarf, arisen from a well, comes in the night to eat her bread."

52. V. Huidobro, "Automne regulier," *Relativity of Spring*, trans. M. Palmer and G. Young, 2–3: "There are no more birds / There are no more birds / . . . . / And the rose shedding petals on the bird that sings / At forty past midnight // Forget about me / Little star / this is the hour I perfume my forest."

53. F. Fortini, in P. Éluard, *Poesie*, 50.

54. P. Éluard, "Une personnalité toujours nouvelle . . . ," *Poesie*, 218: "He offered each woman a privileged rose, A rose of dew Similar to the drunkenness of being thirsty Praying them humbly to accept This little forget-me-not A resplendent and ridiculous rose In a heavy hand In a hand in bloom."

55. P. Éluard, "La lumière éteinte . . . ," *Oeuvres Complètes*, 1:426: "Then a woman with red roses at her neck Red roses that open like shells Which break like eggs Which burn like alcohol. . . . My smiling benefactrice Beautiful limpid under her armor Ignorant of iron of the tree and of the red roses Molding all my desires. . . . Her hands are alive. . . . Hands to lovingly hold a bouquet of red roses without thorns."

56. P. Éluard, "La victoire de Guernica," *Poesie*, 294: "Women, children have the same red roses / In their eyes / Each one shows their own blood."

57. P. Éluard, "Du dehors," *Poésie et vérité*, 62: "Outside, the earth is degraded Outside, the den of the dead A bruised petal-less rose crumbles and slides in the mud."

58. P. Éluard, "Repos d'été," *Oeuvres complètes*, 1: 1219: "Rose that ends up under her eyes Under the dressing-screen of her fingers Rose to end up beneath the lips In silence under the lips Of the greatest known pleasure."

59. F. Ponge, "Interview with Serge Gavronsky," *The Sun Placed in the Abyss*, 97.

60. F. Ponge, "Particularité des fraises," *Selected Poems*, trans. J. Montague, 119: "The mucous burgeoning of strawberries reddens under the lower leaves. Let's add 'the roses' (the crystalline debris) of sugar. . . . the clover stalk brings with it, out of the strawberry, a little sugar loaf, relatively insipid. Beasts, glut yourselves on the strawberry I have discovered for you."

61. F. Ponge, "La parole étouffée sous les roses," *Le grand recueil*, 144–45: "Roses are like something in the oven. The flame overhead breathes them in, breathes in what moves towards it (like a soufflé) . . . The flame wants to embrace the rose, but she can only go so far and no further: she parts her lips and sends up her gassey parts to the flame, who ignites them . . ."

62. R. Char, "La rose violente," *Oeuvres complètes*, 12: "Eye in a trance silent mirror / As I approach I grow distant / Buoy in crenelations // Head against head to forget everything / Until the blow of the shoulder to the heart / The violent rose / of the worthless and transcendent lovers."

63. R. Char, "Voici," ibid., 12: "Pink star and white rose // Oh knowing caresses, oh useless lips."

64. R. Char, "A la santé du serpent," in P. Auster, ed., *Random House Book of Twentieth-Century French Poetry*, trans. J. Matthews, 398–99: "Poetry is of all clear streams the one that lingers least about its reflected bridges. Poetry: life's future held in requalified man. // A rose that it may rain. At the end of innumerable years, that is your wish."

65. R. Char, "É d'une soupçonnée," *Selected Poems*, trans. Cid Corman, 138–39: "Rose indistinguishable in number where old folk and children predominated, on this uncertain base has the contest ended. Shedding of the rose. Dissipation of the star."

66. J. Starobinski, "René Char and the Definition of the Poem," 122–23. R. Char, "Le jugement d'octobre," *Oeuvres complètes*, 434: "A night, day having set, the entire risk, two roses, / Like the flame under shelter, cheek against cheek with the one that kills it."

67. Y. Bonnefoy, "Ici, toujours ici," *Early Poems*, 282–83, trans. G. Kinnell and R. Pevear: "Here, until nightfall. The rose of shadows Like a dial, on the walls. The rose of hours, Silent, will lose its color. The marble floor will guide our steps towards the light they love."

68. Y. Bonnefoy, "Deux barques," *Poems 1959–1975*, 98–99: "But suddenly, late, the unexpected: that all Should gather into the rose of flowing water As it hollows out here, and be made light And the steel hub of the wheel."

4. Gozzano and His Contemporaries

1. R. Gómez de la Serna, *Aphorisms*, 60: "There are some roses that seem to have wounded themselves with their own thorns."

2. G. Baldissone, in G. Gozzano, *Opere*, 29: "Gozzano è un post-mo-

derno.... è quello che alla fine di un movimento poetico, concluso e senza seguito di novità, scopre il metalinguaggio come unica autentica novità, come filo di ricerca verso approdi ancora lontani."

3. M. Bontempelli, *L'avventura novecentista*, 156.

4. C. Benussi, *L'età del fascismo*, 58.

5. S. Corazzini, "Cappella in campagna," *Poesie edite e inedite*, 71–72: "I wanted to get two new candles, two of the whitest candles and two roses—I too have my little gardens—two roses white as candles; they seemed to have blossomed, closed, in monasteries, the roses, in languid gardens. ...The Madonna, a bit sad among the roses, said: What good is your sweet exultance if I forever consume myself in sorrow? ... The young roses, in pious solemnity, exhaled their brief soul; oh the vain actions and prayers!"

6. C. Govoni, "Rose profane," in M. Santagostini, *Il manuale del poeta*, 66: "Eruption of roses in the gardens, of bloody and odorous shores, live and climbing up my railing. Roses and roses in my precious vases odorous roses, bloody roses pinkish mouths of spring!" See the exhaustive chapter on Govoni by F. J. Jones, "Govoni and the Development of a Modern Baroque Outlook," *The Modern Italian Lyric*, 226–58.

7. C. Govoni, "Le dolcezze," in A. Gentili and C. O'Brien, eds., *The Green Flame*, 56: "Twilights of blood which die on the walls. Roses disheveled on the sickbeds."

8. C. Govoni, "Il mare di Sanremo e i rosolacci," in P. Gelli and G. Lagorio, eds., *Poesia italiana del Novecento*, 83: "Below, the dreaming sea: a spellbinding expanse of fallen stars, of sickened liquid pearls, of pale roses that had fainted. In the emerald of the grass, like an obscene relic, all those poppies cry out and bleed like laughter and slaps of clowns in greasepaint."

9. G. A. Borgese, in A. Guglielminetti, *Le seduzioni*, xiv: "l'impudicizia della G. è rigidamente vereconda."

10. A. Guglielminetti, "Le rovine, "*L'insonne*, 69: "More than the triple stem of Castor and Pollux, you enjoyed the burning light of her eyes behind her veil. And young love rose up over the things of old, as perhaps roses are born on the closed tombs."

11. A. Guglielminetti, "Una voce," *Le seduzioni*, 53: "A voice in the shadows sometimes has the warm softness of a tangible thing. One does not hear or listen to it, but, on the heart that welcomes it, it almost lays down its words, one by one, like a languishing rose its petals."

12. F. T. Marinetti, "Battaglia," *I poeti futuristi*: "monoplane = balcony—rose—wheel—drum—drill—horse-fly > Arab—defeat ox bloodiness slaughter wounds refuge oasis humidity fan freshness."

13. See G. Severini, "Art du fantastique dans le sacré," in P. A. Jannini, *Le avanguardie letterarie nell'idea critica di Apollinaire*, 31: "Nous avons donc un profond dégout pour les spectacles immobiles de la nature agreste et panoramique. / *Merde*, n'est-ce pas, Apollinaire? pour les montagnes, la mer, les rivières, les paysans, les arbres, les champs, les porcs, les boeufs, etc . . . ainsi que pour le nu dans l'atelier ou ailleurs, pour la mélancolie contemplative, et le sérieux tragique. / *Rose*, pour les forêts de cheminées, pour les Grands Boulevards, pour la poudre de riz-rouge aux lèvres, la lumière électrique, les transatlantiques, les aéros, les autors, les cinémas, les express internationaux, ainsi que pour le champagne, le rire, la danse, la blague, qui engendrent les grandes idées et les grandes oeuvres. / *Rose*, à notre merveilleuse vie moderne et à la Place Pigalle à Minuit, le plus beau paysage du monde."

14. L. Fulgore, "Il cinese caricaturista," in E. Krumm and T. Rossi, eds., *Poesia italiana del Novecento*, 115: "The rose glances through his short, odorous notebooks. // The bright dawn, with its fountain of light, sprays the empire of porcelain with roses."

15. A. Soffici, "Correnti," in M. Giacon, "Simbolismo e plurilinguismo in Soffici," 115: "I am in a center, like the bee in the heart of a rose."

16. A. Soffici, "Atelier," in P. V. Mengaldo, ed., *PIN*, 345: "Everything is paid for with 24 hours a day of youth / *Atelier ateliers* / Compass-cards / Joy Beauty Miseries."

17. A. Palazzeschi, "I fiori," in G. Spagnoletti, ed., *Antologia della poesia italiana contemporanea*, 1:389: "'But who are you? What do you do?' . . . 'I'm a rose and I'm a prostitute.'"

18. See G. Marcon and D. Trento, *Allegoria e varianti in* riflessi *di Aldo Palazzeschi*, 44: "in *riflessi* la metafora stellare delle rose fa risuonare un'iterazione pressoché ininterrotta, dominata da una lunga unità melodica; ma il fatto più sostanziale è costituito dal radicale rovesciamento semantico delle rose-stelle, con l'eliminazione, in *Allegoria di novembre*, della connotazione 'pornografica' delle stesse."; 5: "Perciò già nella scrittura dannunziana il dato naturalistico diventa segno allegorico. Ad esempio un'onda 'ilare, flebile, umile, ironica, lusinghevole, disperata, crudele' può diventare, come le rose di Palazzeschi diventeranno labbra, vergini, fanciulli, pensieri, sorrisi."

19. A. Palazzeschi, "Le due rose," *Poesie*, 130: "Poor soldier who hugs the white rose of the pillow so tight against your temples, to quiet the burning of that other red one, hidden, which makes you burn. Who has hurt you so?"

20. M. Bontempelli, "Paesaggio," in P. V. Mengaldo, ed., *PIN*, 426:

"Will a summer of roses ever come? Ask for the future tomorrow from the distant circle of purplish mountains which now argue among themselves in smokes and echoes."

21. M. Bontempelli, "Omaggio," *Il purosangue*, 112: "I'm coming, little diva—I'm coming down the mountain to bring you the roses gathered upon the hisses which graze and slide over my neck. Every machine gun's hissing blooms at its tip a rose for you little diva. . . . And I'm carrying a bunch of frenetic roses to my beautiful diva who is dancing with her breasts bare casting about her tresses a rapid arabesque of pale hisses of machine guns." Emphasis mine.

22. F. Fortini, *I poeti del Novecento*, 84.

23. V. Cardarelli, "Il sonno della vergine," *Opere*, 77: "There was nothing angelic in you who slept dreamless, soulless, like a rose sleeps."

24. V. Cardarelli, "A Omar Kayyâm," ibid., 22: "The god that propitiated you so you would drink up these lies made your fortune and your song. And you sipped at the roses of your laughing tomb not suspecting, oh fearless one, that your life was already a cemetery in bloom."

25. C. Rebora, "Fantasia di carnevale (variazioni italiane)," *Le poesie*, 176–77: "Adventitious epoch which strangles custom. . . . Beyond one's country and the earth there is something worth saving, if only a rose blooming after so much war."

26. W. Stevens, cited by S. Heaney, *The Redress of Poetry*, 1.

27. C. Rebora, "Il ritmo della campagna in città," in G. Papini and P. Pancrazi, eds., *Poeti d'oggi*, 565: "I glut myself on grapes And my glad throat receives the fruit as it comes apart and is sticky—Great sword pears! Apples of the rose!—Looking at the joy I deceive myself, the taste no longer finds the flavor. . . ."

28. C. Rebora, "Poesia nel lucido verso," *Le poesie*, 85–86: "but you are the certainty of the great destiny, oh poetry of dung and flowers, terror of life, presence of God, oh enchained citizen of the world dead and reborn!"

29. C. Rebora, "Bocciòlo di rosa reciso!" ibid., 395: "Severed bud of the rose! But here in the water it opens: its exhalation is shed: the chaste smile of the petals is gilded."

30. S. Slataper, *Il mio carso*, 131: "Fresh things! Roses swollen with dew, grass on a riverbank. Oh if I could kiss your lips!" In 1909 Slataper published a fable titled "Il petalo della rosa" in Trieste's *Giornalino della domenica*.

31. E. Montale, in G. Gozzano, *Le poesie*, 7, 9.

32. G. Gozzano, "Il più atto," *Opere*, 174: "May life go to him! To him the

roses, the property, the women and pleasures! Mother Nature is just." In an earlier variant the "rose" were instead "case."

33. G. Gozzano, "Suprema quies," *Opere*, 258: "And on the sofa a glove which the Woman of the Banquet has perhaps just taken off, and a bouquet of red roses unbound and withered."

34. G. Gozzano, "Primavere romantiche," *Opere*, 379: "(the volume had rare etchings where the handsome page offered to the lady a white rose with his left hand and knelt down in the act of adoration).... O she remembers everything: the deep blue roses embroidered on the white dress, the white silk dress, and the sky blue band that puffed out her crinoline."

35. G. Gozzano, "L'assenza," *Opere*, 167: "Astonished by what? By things. / The flowers seem strange to me: / yet there are still the roses, / there are still the geraniums...."

36. G. Gozzano, "Laus Matris," *Opere*, 260: "Erect on your stem / oh adamantine Rose / invincible against ruin / invincible against corruption."

37. G. Gozzano, "L'amica di Nonna Speranza," *Opere*, 209: "Grandma is seventeen! Carlotta almost the same: they've just gotten permission to add a ring to their skirts, the sweeping band waves the skirt with turquoise roses."

38. Pitigrilli, "Rime aristocratiche," in G. Zaccaria, *Il Novecento letterario in Italia*, 93: "Between the dress which has me a bit upset and the acrid odor of this tea-rose, today I have a bit of a headache; I fear that tonight I shan't be able to dance."

39. G. Gozzano, "A un demagogo," *Opere*, 340: "And you do not forgive me if I tarry, since swords for your struggle of vermillion dreams are not made from roses."

40. N. Bobbio, *Italia fedele*, 84. As Bobbio notes, Croce centered his essay on Gozzano on his quality of "aridità."

41. E. Montale, in G. Gozzano, *Poesie*, 14.

42. G. Gozzano, "L'ipotesi," *Opere*, 308: "And the muscat grapes whiter than old gold; the fresh claudian plums, the philic peaches half rubicond, the enormous monstrous pears, the white almonds, the figs carved up by the fig-peckers, the apples that smell like roses, would emanate, friends, such an aroma that the heart would recall the vigor of our twenty happy years." Gozzano notes, 302, "*L'Ipotesi* è cosa della mia prima maniera, scritta poco più che ventenne, in quei polimetri che oggi—affinato ad una metrica più severa—mi riescono intollerabili."

43. G. Gozzano, "Storia di cinquecento vanesse," *Opere*, 419: "The

orobia shepherdess grew pale under the fresh roses of her makeup, astonished."

44. G. Gozzano, "Macroglossa stellatarum," ibid., 451: "The speedy Macroglossa came into my quiet room. It was enticed by this ray of sunlight, this vermillion rose that gladdens my papers."

45. G. Leopardi, "A Silvia," *Canti*, 167: "the sweat-stained papers."

46. A. N. Whitehead, *Science and the Modern World*, 95.

5. The Pathetic and Mannerist Rose

1. R. Dombroski, *The Properties of Writing*, 66.

2. T. Tasso, *Gerusalemme liberata*, xvi, 15, 438: "Thus the flower and the green of mortal life pass by like the passing of a day; not so that April may ever return, or could reflower or be green again. Let us pick the rose in the splendid morning of this day, for soon the calm sky is gone; let us pluck the rose of love: let us love now when by loving we may be loved in return."

3. M. Praz, *La carne, la morte e il diavolo nella letteratura romantica*, 32.

4. G. Pascoli, *Il fanciullino*, 52: "Ma in Italia la pseudopoesia si desidera, si domanda, s'ingiunge. In Italia noi siamo vittime della storia letteraria!"

5. G. Pascoli, ibid., 40: "And for a death bed, which for all is so hard and grave, what do I save for you, do you know? Oh! roses for your death bed, fallen from the brambles: soft sorrow that was!"

6. F. M. Martini, "Elegia del primo abito 'décolleté,'" in G. Almansi and R. Barbolino, eds., *La passion dominante*, 378: "The schoolgirl is thirsty for fantasies with the shadow of sin. Aren't you afraid? Move ahead! A flower of evil // has bloomed and your hand grazes the soft velvet of the legs, // and rises trembling, and arrives where on the breast two new roses were // budding . . . New? Ah! it's been three years and those buds haven't seen the fading light of evening: now, you look at them . . . They're looking at you! Are they roses or thistles?"

7. P. V. Mengaldo, "Grande stile e lirica moderna," *La tradizione del Novecento: Terza serie*, 14.

8. E. Thovez, "Nuvole," *Il poema dell'adolescenza*, 25: "Cumuluses of gold, of brass, soft moorings of snow, towers of rose, bulwarks, vertiginous abysses."

9. E. Thovez, "Dissolvimento," *Il poema dell'adolescenza*, 97: "Oh to press upon supple skin! to seek out the forms of the breasts and folds, to smooth out the flesh of the rose, to bite with desiring mouths, to clutch with avid hands, to distract oneself until the point of death."

10. P. Buzzi, "E le convalescenze," *Poesie scelte*, 166: "The pure cleansing of the senses, the crisper air in the depths, the dawn of every hour, the river of roses cascading in waterfalls of effluvia upon the remarkable flesh of my passing."

11. P. Buzzi, "Il pianto panico," *Poesie scelte*, 267: "I can't find my cabbages anymore and the roses of Mary, in the cosmic metaphor that is disembodied—the clouds and things—in a different chaos of vapors... And the bells are weeping: and the brides...."

12. P. Buzzi, "La casa," *Poesie scelte*, 234: "The house is beautiful, full of lofty things. The shining memories in portraits, sweeter smelling than mountain roses."

13. A. Negri, "Malinconia," *Poesie*, 398: "Melancholy of the first furrowed wrinkles, oh, so slight, that give the smile the tenuous grace of a faded rose, and give, oh life, your mystery to her gaze!... Oh love, oh mad love of youth, oh adolescent crowned with roses...."

14. A. Negri, "Rose rosse," *Dal profondo*, 148: "They are purple, and tragic as hearts rent open....—Oh roses, tragic as hearts torn apart!"

15. S. Comes, *Ada Negri: Da un tempo all'altro*, 51: "il suo francescanesimo sembra un fiore d'accatto." A. Negri, "L'offerta delle rose," *Poesie*, 630: "Children of the Island, in grace, look in the streets, the forests, the fields for the man who threw me three vermilion roses from atop the wall: lead him to me, that I might see, and tell him he is my brother: and eat bread with him soaked with sun, and drink the water of freedom."

16. A. Negri, "La pietà," *Opere scelte*, 99: "your closed eyes have between the eyelashes a dream of dawn which climbs up the stairs of the sky, spreading about stemless roses mixed with snow-white calyxes of lilies."

17. A. Negri, "Bimba con rosa in mano," ibid., 229: "nor do I know if the rose is blooming from her heart or if she rather is blooming from the rose. Her vibrant image will not depart from this threshold: I shall always see her on this threshold, brighter than the sun; she will hold the rose of her destiny, red as blood."

18. F. Fortini, "Prima delle 'Laudi,'" *Nuovi saggi italiani*, 97, cites Mengaldo's statement that D'Annunzio's "serialità" is "la causa più profonda della fluenza o affanno o tumescenza che non sono solo della 'strofe lunga' delle 'Laudi' ma di quasi tutta la sua poesia e di gran parte della prosa. 'Ogni relatività del linguaggio è in lui abolita.'"

19. A. Negri, "Chiesa di Sant'Anna," *Prose*, 1006: "My dear great Soul, yesterday you blessed my house with your presence, and after you left there remained the miracle of the roses, which now have all bloomed."

20. A. Negri, "Piazza di San Francesco in Lodi," *Opere scelte*, 88: "the

sad places collapsing in peace where only the breath of things, of dead dreams and dead roses, speaks and all else is quiet."

21. A. Negri, "In memoria," ibid., 86: "and I would tell you the joyous words which all mothers whisper to their children, gathering up bunches of roses for you. // But you did not want it."

22. A. Negri, "Il recesso," ibid., 113: "where beds laden with rosehips for tea whisper to the poplars of the avenues. . . . Maybe . . .—but I deceive myself. Because a hissing of snakes shall envelop me, as soon as I open the gate: through sudden sorcery wild and crude I shall see the roses be transmuted into tangled brush."

23. A. Negri, "Rifugio fiorito," ibid., 187: "Against the closed door, snarls of dog roses: . . . There is a wall of roses against the door. The key is lost. If that door were to open, I would want to pause inside with your shadow. . . . I would barricade the door, with my love become a rosebush, so as to not let you go."

24. A. Negri, "Filastrocca," ibid., 187–88: "'Seven lights of the Bear, what are you looking for?' 'Lady, we are looking for a boy lost in the sea. . . .' 'If you find that boy along the streets or caves I shall give you all the roses that bloom tonight: . . .' Seven lights of boats which are going out to fish: the Ursa Major has fallen, it has fallen in the sea."

25. A. Negri, "Ritorno per il dolce natale," ibid., 192: "Uncovered there will burn upon his forehead the broad bloody stigmata: the crown of the consacrated king, eternal flame, divine rose"; and "Ti vedo in un fiore," ibid., 230: "nor do I know which is your most lovely and illumined face, oh Lord, the celestial rose or this humble flower of the field."

26. G. Bollati, *L'italiano*, 173, emphasis mine.

27. C. Salinari, cited in M. David, *Letteratura e psicanalisi*, 160.

28. D. Campana, "La petite promenade du poète," *Canti orfici e altri scritti*, 22: "I pass through dark, narrow mysterious streets. I see Gems and Roses peer out from behind shop windows." Giovanni Pozzi, *La parola dipinta*, 52–53, has constructed "diagrams" from this poem "formed by the regular positions of the phoneme-graphemes . . . all formed by regular alternations of the vowels in the stressed syllables"; the text is not transcribable by simply separating lines of text by slashes, because a new factor, the "indivisible unity of the phoneme-grapheme," has emerged.

29. D. Campana, "Fetida prosa," *Canti orfici e altri scritti*, 96: "There are Gemmas and Rosas / Up the mysterious vertical / Steps to the Paradise / Of solders and wives deceived / By their husbands. / . . . . / The poet doesn't care / And stands there like a Pasha / Among the Yuris of a higher

alloy / Of the paradise of Allah / And he's made a little song / To the pink paper roses / And the ruby-red lips / Of the ulcerous madonna."

30. D. Campana, "In un momento," *Canti orfici e altri scritti*, 132: "In a moment / The roses faded / The petals fallen / Because I could not forget the roses."

31. L. Anceschi, *Lirici nuovi*, 17, ix, xx. The goal of the volume was to present the period "from 1919 to 1945, from *La Ronda* to hermeticism."

32. G. De Robertis, "Canti orfici," in G. Ferrata, ed., *La voce*, 551.

33. M. Luzi, in P. Gelli and G. Lagorio, *Poesia italiana del Novecento*, 1:105.

34. See T. Adorno, *Aesthetic Theory*, 318–19: "For the longest time art had expected the homeostasis of universal and particular to spring from the dynamic principle. This expectation has been invalidated. Since Baudelaire, the sense of form has demystified the dynamic principle as well, exposing its weaknesses."

35. U. Saba, "Un pensiero," *Tutte le poesie*, 883: "A large black cape / a few ashen roses, / a priest, a cemetery / is this not death?"

36. U. Saba, "L'amorosa spina," *Canzoniere*, 196: "You saw that no one was with us. With a deep sigh, instead of your hand you offered me the rose of your mouth. Still today my heart overflows with the goodness of that kind act of yours."

37. U. Saba, "Vacanze," ibid., 400–401: "She's beautiful but perfidious. She smells of roses and bitter almonds, as in her aristocratic home (where I stayed a year in her care). If only she would hug me to her breast for just a moment! Or at least, weary of me, she would hit me!"

38. G. L. Beccaria, *Le forme della lontananza*, 60, 35: "il lontano e pur popolare linguaggio dell'epica o della fiaba"; "la chiusura-concentrazione del comunicare."

39. P. V. Mengaldo, *La tradizione del Novecento: Terza serie*, 63.

40. U. Saba, "Per un fanciullo ammalato," *Canzoniere*, 464: "the roses on the tapering cheeks were growing pale."

41. U. Saba, "Variazioni sulla rosa," ibid., 530: "A boy is crying for you in the garden or perhaps in a fable. Rose, clumsy fingers, you were punishing him. And thus you live another day on your green stem."

42. U. Saba, "La vittima," *Tutte le poesie*, 285: "it is beautiful to have one's hands in chains, whipped // you do not cry, for death is less bitter for you, the God you believe in looks down on you and your blood of roses imprints the ground."

43. U. Saba, "Nel chiasso," *Canzoniere*, 152: "On the wagon was a

piteous freight indeed: / lambs gone to sleep in death, / and each one had a rose on its neck."

44. U. Saba, "Lascia che m'inginocchi a te adorata," ibid., 202: "I ought to give you a rose, Chiara, / and pin it on your breast myself; / then quickly give another gift to myself (what, I will not tell you), which at least can give some peace. // Oh, if the gift of a flower suits her, / is there something for me more suitable than the sword?"

45. U. Saba, "L'ultima tenerezza," ibid., 129: "Other than one of them who is almost in love with you, the girlfriends, among whom you stand out before my eyes like the rose amid lesser flowers, say: 'This Lina is quite queer, and a snob to boot.'"

46. R. Luperini et al., eds., *Poeti italiani: Il Novecento*, 194. U. Saba, "Fughe," *Canzoniere*, 384: "Oh my heart, split in two since birth, how much suffering I endured to make you one! So many roses to hide an abyss!"

47. M. Cerruti, *Carlo Michelstaedter*, 106.

48. C. Michelstaedter, "Marzo," *Poesie*, 61: "Windy March. . . . you give a changing relief to the stunned earth to the stultified earth, while you tear from her breast the buds and the roses." See M. Cerruti, 110: "La 'ventata' di marzo è 'folle' (si pensi alle meditazioni di M. sul fatto che l'esperienza rinnovatrice e liberatrice di chi persegue la 'persuasione' appare un caso appunto di 'follia' all'uomo della rettorica)."

49. M. Praz's chapter, "D'Annunzio e 'l'amor sensuale della parola,'" concerns that poet's word-worship and takes its title from D'Annunzio's words on Petrarch in *Il venturiero senza ventura*, 424: "[Al Petrarca] mancava l'amor sensuale della parola" (Petrarch lacked the sensual love of the word).

50. S. Quasimodo, "Antico inverno," *Tutte le poesie*, 34: "your hands . . . smelled like oak and roses; like death. Ancient winter. The birds looked for millet and were immediately of snow; so the words. A bit of sun . . ."

51. The vitality of this archaic metaphor is evident in two poems by Pier Paolo Pasolini and Andrea Zanzotto, which, like Quasimodo's poem, use snow-covered fields to show that the time of fertility is over. See Pasolini, "La Guinea," *Poesia in forma di rosa*, 17, and Zanzotto's obituary poem to Pasolini in *Idioma*, 67.

52. G. Pozzi, *La parola dipinta*, 35.

53. S. Quasimodo, "L'angelo," cited in F. J. Jones, *The Modern Italian Lyric*, 515: "The angel sleeps on roses of air, pure, on its side, its fine hands in the shape of a cross, over its breast."

54. S. Quasimodo, "Di fresca donna riversa in mezzo ai fiori," *Tutte le*

poesie, 60: "A city suspended in mid-air was my final exile, and they called all around me the sweet women of days gone by and the mother, made new by the years, choosing the whitest of the roses to bind about my temple."

55. S. Quasimodo, "Con una fronda di mirto," from Archilochus, *Lirici greci*, 113: "She was playing with a frond of myrtle and a fresh rose; and her tresses cast a light shadow on her shoulders and back."

56. S. Quasimodo, *Lirici greci,* from Sappho, "Ad attide ricordando l'amica lontana," 69–70. See *Sappho: Poems and Fragments,* trans. J. Balmer, 47: "now she surpasses all the women / of Lydia, like the moon, / rose-fingered, after the sun has set, // shining brighter than all the stars; its light / stretches out over the salt-/ filled sea and the fields brimming with flowers: // the beautiful dew falls and the roses / and the delicate chervil / and many-flowered honey-clover bloom."

57. The observation is found in G. Hays, "*Le morte stagioni:* Intertextuality in Quasimodo's *Lirici greci,*" 39. Emphasis mine. See *Sappho: Poems and Fragments,* trans. J. Balmer, 67: "there, far away beyond the apple branches, cold streams / murmur, roses shade every corner / and, when the leaves rustle, you are seized / by a strange drowsiness."

58. S. Quasimodo, "E di te nel tempo," from Sappho, *Lirici greci,* 65: "You will end up dying there. Nor shall any memory of you remain; and no love shall be born in anyone for you in time, since you have chosen not to care for the roses of Pieria." Mary Barnard's translation reads, 82, "Death will finish you: afterwards no one will remember or want you: you had no share in the Pierian roses."

59. F. Fortini, *I poeti del Novecento,* 91.

60. E. Pound, "XII," *Personae,* 26.

61. R. Carrieri, "Non una sola volta," in V. Masselli and G. A. Gibotto, eds., *Antologia popolare di poeti del Novecento,* 201: "Death does not come just once.... It is sufficient for one thing alone to die / one alone, different every time / for it to steal from our hands the rose."

62. R. Carrieri, *Il grano non muore,* 78, 257: "In the rose as in poetry several varieties of parasites are hidden"; "Roses in opening emit more perfume but they are entering into agony."

63. U. Bellintani, "Vattene tragedia," *E tu che m'ascolti,* 56–57: "Be gone, tragedy. Never return. / My children's eyes are two teardrops. / My children's eyes are a rose of happiness. / Never return. Never return."

64. U. Bellintani, "Ignaro io sono . . . ," ibid., 91–92: "I am ignorant of what wind might come.... and I don't know the rose that is blooming in this unharmed stretch of earth. But the hand that shook your face last night is the hand of love."

65. U. Bellintani, "Antonia," ibid., 91–92: "And little by little her heart grew tender over the roses and blue dreams buzzed about her head, but she lapsed into drowsiness, her limbs grew tired, and her sex dreamed of solitude and warm river sand."

66. U. Bellintani, "Ai tuoi occhi," *Forse un viso tra mille*, 61: "Your eyes are lovely stock-flowers, black stock-flowers in a most soft and peaceful summer night. Your lips are beautiful red roses, fresh pink in a bright dawn before morning growing green."

67. See A. Girardi, *Cinque storie stilistiche*, 127.

68. G. Pascoli, "Casa mia," *Poesie*, 672, 675: "The house was before me still in the pure vespers, the wall abloom with climbing roses. She not sated yet with her tears, spoke: 'You know, after the tragedy, we had to cut down quite a bit. . . .'"

69. G. Giudici, "Pascoli," *Poesie 1953–1990*, 2:101–2: "In this wandering house In this house without walls or rooms A butterfly-house that alights In the space of a rose. . . . And now the signs of the pencil illegible And now we are an "i" with its point in the thickness of the dictionary We wander in the house of a rose A butterfly-house which never stops its flight."

70. G. Giudici, "Ode a una misteriosa dama di nome Maria," ibid., 1:278: "Oh distant seed Oh future fruit. Oh anything but mystical rose. Oh your name scratched into the grey wall."

71. G. Giudici, "Neoplasie," ibid., 1:335: "Neoplasias? Yes, of the world—in which I too a minuscule tumor at my center Neoplasia—but billions of them While the economy/crisis and flowers Which fade even the rose itself Which is the rose!"

72. E. Vittorini, *Conversazioni in Sicilia*, 5: "I was in that winter chased by abstract furies. . . . This had gone on for a long time, and I had my head bowed." Emphasis mine.

73. G. Giudici, "Inverno a Torino," *Poesie 1953–1990*, 2:457: "I encountered in that winter a severe city-dweller's gaze: I shamefully discovered I was behind the times, my head bowed over—and all things neat and trim, the factories black, absent all laments, swallows, roses. . . ." Emphasis mine.

74. G. Giudici, "Rose," ibid., 2:319: "Yes, roses—but in their viewing almost Glassy with rust like the Rose of Carlsbad now twenty years past Hanging on a wall in the house—Roses, clotted blood Of dusty reliquaries supplicated And yet roses from a church at whose Threshold strewn in fine order upon the ground Strenuous roses undone I sent to you To a distant tawny Penelope Do not fear—said the man who was Discerning in

the flood of other nuptial flowers Do not fear, they will arrive at their Destiny in all their fragrance: While meanwhile the line of carriages Slowly began its journey."

75. E. Sanguineti, "Postkarten" (April 1974), *Segnalibro*, 193: "the Jocastas who display, without decency, those things (those roses), become solemnly incestuous: . . . (she will vote a giant YES, that tailed poetess who has disrobed, on the occasion of the referendum, with her odorous bitch's rose: Ciutazza, a purebred countess): . . ."

76. G. Mascioni, "Se piove senza posa," *Poesia 1952–1982*, 210: "at times I can't find the road to the old town I was born in: if the day of the roses existed it was another day than this."

77. G. Mascioni, "1970: 'Chez Dupont,' Restaurant (Cointrin)," ibid., 304: "I knew nothing else, anonymous thing, nothing more warm more defenseless and clear than your rose-like womb, self-enclosed."

78. G. Mascioni, "Uno che ha rose," ibid., 108: "Because you can see on your own how much a man on his way can feel tired; how one who has roses in his glass, bitter drink and hemlock, can suffocate."

79. A. Serrao, "Divagazioni su acque d'agosto," in A. Manuali, B. Sablone, eds., *Poesie d'amore del '900 italiano*, 173: "thus degraded / the rose, petals grasped in the fist that I might love you or not love you, let the bridle-bells endure as our escape in the wind, the bee suddenly crazed."

80. A. Serrao, "'E ccose" (The things), "From Language to Dialect," trans. T. Peterson, 276: "Among us it does not happen that / things fall asleep in the dark, nor does / the most hidden depth of a rose; gray things / yes, the infantilized gray things fall asleep / in the see-saw of the hours."

81. D. Bellezza, "Il tevere si perde nella notte . . . ," *Serpenta*, 46.

6. The Votive and Hermetic Rose

1. D. Ashton, *A Fable of Modern Art*, 65.
2. R. M. Rilke, *Poems 1906 to 1926*, trans. J. B. Leishman, 355, 64, 95, 124, 146, 152, 275, 276, 295, 300.
3. G. Bateson, *Mind and Nature*, 12.
4. G. Comi, "Primo canto di Eva," *Sonetti e poesie*, 57: "I am Eve, subjected and untamed. . . . Within the sphere, in its terse arc prevails the mysterious tyranny of the inflamed gemmed flower of my sex which swarms with the blood of the rose. Whole rose in which the entire destiny of the created world has sunken."

5. G. Comi, "Cantico della luce," ibid., 43: "Light, joyous memory of our blood and our thought saturated with that flame that burns and chimes in the rose."

6. A. Onofri, *Giovanni Pascoli,* 13: "un poeta germinale. . . . piuttosto che un compiuto poeta rappresentativo o di razza (tipo Omero, Pindaro, Dante)."

7. A. Onofri, "Per un'araba," *Poesie edite e inedite,* 367: "My love, Zavilìh, why don't you come? The red roses are waiting in the vases, and the curtains in the rustling of satin dream of your return, Zavilìh."

8. A. Onofri, "Storia d'amore," ibid., 351: "For too long had I languished; the song no longer flowed in my parched throat: / and yes, I plucked it, the early rose, whose soul dripping wet, also with tears. . . ."

9. A. Onofri, "Lacustri," ibid., 201–2: "Your virgin body is surely a magnolia / blooming on the beach; your fragrant mouth / is a rose of Bengal, blossoming for me amid the algae . . ."

10. A. Onofri, "Terrestrità del sole," ibid., 160: "A lone scent of rose swift in a hot clime happy in itself, rests within the cross-shaped shadow. . . . And every life, unknowing, is wed, from the cross-shaped shadow, to a heaven scenting of rose in a swift hot clime."

11. D. Valeri, "Cattedrale lombarda," *Poesie piccole,* 48: "And you are all aglow, oh Cathedral, in the bright rose colored face, and meek you exult within the veil of a virginal wife. . . . And from the rose window there rains and spreads through the immense shadows a smile of love. From the apse the smile of the Redeemer answers it."

12. D. Valeri, "Per una rosa Ofelia," *Poesie scelte,* 44: "The rose is an earthy thing; but the force that carries it skyward in the wreath of green leaves and presses it from deep within and melts it like a flame aburst with sweetness, is the mystery of God within a rose."

13. S. Di Giacomo, "'O munasterio' XXXV," *Poesie e prose,* 115: "Brother, dig a ditch in the garden, we are burying Brother Salvatore there, plant a rose nearby, and never forget to water it."

14. S. Di Giacomo, "IV," ibid., 80: "'What are these roses?' 'I . . . picked them . . .' 'For the Madonna?' 'Father . . .' 'For the month of May? Go on now, take them to her, go. . . .'"

15. S. Di Giacomo, "'O munasterio' XXXVI," ibid., 117: "Over a grave, just recently put in order, a beautiful rose had bloomed . . . And she, in spite . . . picked the rose and put it on her breast. . . ."

16. S. Di Giacomo, "'A chitarra," ibid., 205: "Sweet eyes, soft and shining, eyes far blacker than coal! . . . Petals of the rose, what a beautiful balcony you were able to find!"

17. Examples of Di Giacomo's rose (in *Poesie e prose*) include metaphor, 213: "'A vi' llà; vestuta rosa / e assettata a nu sedile, / risciatanno st' addurosa / e liggiera aria d' abbrile"; appellatives, 10: "Aggio appurato ca se chiamma Rosa, / essa ha saputo ca me chiammo Ndrea . . . / Che faccio mo? Lle dico o no quaccosa?"; emblem, 30: "Abbrile, abbrile! Mmiez' 'e ffronne 'e rosa / vaco vennenno 'o frutto 'e chisto mese"; epithet, 21: "Ah, fronn' 'e rosa mia, frunnella 'e rosa! / E' muorto 'e na ventina 'e malatie, / e ogne tanto 'o risusceta quaccosa, / cierti penziere, cierti ffantasie . . . "; and narrative symbol, 29: "Lettera amirosa": "Dinto ce voglio mettere tre cose, / nu suspiro, na lacrema e na rosa, / e attuorno attuorno a ll'ammilocca nchiusa / ce voglio da' na sissantina 'e vase."

18. S. Di Giacomo, "Tutto se scorda," *The Hidden Italy*, trans. H. Haller, 145: "All is Forgotten": "Blue eyes or black, skin the color of the lily or the rose, is the same, it's always the same, always the same sighs!"

19. B. Marin, "Alessandra," in H. Haller, *The Hidden Italy*, 254–55: "Joy of the new day, of the song of a throat that freshly intones the morning, the blossoming of roses above every bramble, a single song in the golden air of evening."; and, "Semo a dissenbre e incora l'ano more," in F. Brevini, ed., *Poeti dialettali del Novecento*, 125: "We are in December and the year still dying, but so slowly that the gold rains upon sleeping roses. A courteous god has given us the gift of roses of every month . . ."

20. B. Marin: "Regina sacratissimi rosarii," *Le litànie de la madona*, 20: "All of life is an illborn rose-bush, with its thorns which pierce the ribs, and cause to flower at the thorn's tip a rose of blood—the Regina."

21. A. Zanzotto, "La poesia di Marin," *Fantasie di avvicinamento*, 279: "Ciò che lo ha spinto fin dall'inizio e sempre più invasato, come per una coraggiosa caparbietà apparentemente solipsistica, è stata un'adesione 'dal basso' all'ambiente in tutti i suoi spessori."

22. B. Marin, cited by A. Zanzotto in "La poesia di Marin," ibid., 281: Italian translation: "le rose / erano sue e sue sorelle"; "the roses were hers and were her sisters."

23. B. Marin, "T'hè levào ogni fogia," in *La passion predominante*, ed. G. Almansi, 427: "I tore every petal off you, like a rose that loses its petals, just so I could see your golden button. // I didn't find it: but I got drunk on your perfume and now I'm dying from the desire of that perfume that is now dispersed like one of my forgotten lines of verse."

24. A. Zanzotto, *Fantasie di avvicinamento*, 81: "Da Ungaretti tra il '16 e il '19 venne proposta per la prima volta in Italia forse la tematica più caratteristica di quello che poi doveva precisarsi come 'esistenzialismo.'" C. Ossola, *figurato e rimosso: Icone e interni del testo*, 9: "Guardare all'interno

significa, almeno da Poe e da Baudelaire, *guardare dall'interno:* un occhio ci guarda, ci spia, l'arte non riproduce, ma interroga, non illustra ma inquieta."

25. The early Ungaretti retained much of D'Annunzio's thematic and linguistic apparatus. For a discussion of stylistic debts to D'Annunzio, see P. V. Mengaldo, *La tradizione del Novecento.*

26. G. Ungaretti, "Rosso e azzurro," *Vita d'un uomo,* 147: "I waited for you to get up, Colors of love, And now you unveil a heavenly infancy. // It hands over the most beautiful rose dreamed of."

27. G. Ungaretti, "Canto secondo," ibid., 182: "Death, silent word, Sand deposited like a bed By the blood, I hear you singing like a cicada in the Black-draped rose of reflections."

28. F. J. Jones, *The Modern Italian Lyric,* 27.

29. G. Ungaretti, "Ultimi cori per la terra promessa," *Vita d'un uomo,* 277: "Secret rose, you bloom over the abyss Only that I might be startled to recall How suddenly your scent unfolds As lamentations are sounded."

30. G. Ungaretti, "12 settembre 1966," ibid., 299: "A thorn from your red roses has pricked me, so that I might suck my blood, as I already have yours, from my finger." This last poem, published on Ungaretti's eightieth birthday, is responded to in the same chapbook, *Dialogo,* by the young poet Bruna Bianchi.

31. E. Pea, "I," in G. Ferrata, ed., *La voce,* 642: "Chaste brides to Christ, angels in the flesh, oh you who kneel there without suffering, oh you who stand at the limit who graze on dreams and ignore the tormented loves beyond the rose bush climbing on the garden wall: May, bloomed roses, turquoise sky, oh anticipation of heaven in the moment of waking."

32. C. Betocchi, "La rosa venduta d'inverno," *Tutte le poesie,* 50: "But instead ... tomorrow the rose, / you'll see, will already be nothing; / go, like something dead / over the fetid and bare wave; it awaits—but does not hear— / the song of May, month it had loved so much."

33. C. Betocchi, "Alla danza, alla luce, ode," *Poems,* 40: "And so you gave back the sudden urges, and twisting you cast your insatiable hunger for space, from the lily to the rose; and you shine, as a sun which is passing, upon the languid colors of the world."

34. C. Betocchi, "Un dolce pomeriggio d'inverno," ibid., 114: "One soft winter afternoon, sweet / because the moon was no longer but / an immutable thing, not dawn nor sunset, my thoughts vanished like many butterflies, / in the gardens full of roses / that live on the other side, outside the world."

35. C. Betocchi, "Canto per l'alba imminente," *Tutte le poesie,* 40: "White and mysterious you rise up out of the enclosed eastern waters and my mortal pain is reconciled and freed; you suffer and grow weary in waking the rose who in the sun is wed then you are lost, immortal virgin, in the heavens."

36. C. Betocchi, "Strada mattutina," *Tutte le poesie,* 479: "The rose of the day is blooming / my heart, sorrow of return, / I am not the master of my life. // Now the east is tinged with pink."

37. L. De Libero, "VII," *Poesie,* 80: "Your hand on the grass was a rose barely born and already queen: in the night I was your branch, the most distant leaf was trembling."

38. L. De Libero, "O mia patria in tutti i pensieri," ibid., 109: "Poor daughter of the mountains, poor mother of the rivers, your past is a faded rose: and those would make it smell sweet, and those who would add honey, those who would inflate it with an old elixir, and you do not refuse the putrid rose."

39. L. De Libero, "Per una rosa di Gaeta," ibid., 119: "And who wants to look for a rose still unborn and already resting inside the future seed of a clod of earth?"

40. L. De Libero, "Lettera d'estate," ibid., 126: "down there the stone grows like a rose, the beautiful age of the day is relaxing and in every clod of earth is a seed of fury."

41. L. De Libero, "Scempio e lusinga," ibid., 122: "If Spring's chill bites your cheeks and you are fooled by the late frost, do not say that the scarlet rose is now a figure of our passion, you're not unaware of the wind that sets it ablaze, and the livid spoils it contains."

42. L. De Libero, "Per una ragazza virtuosa di giorno," *Di brace in brace,* 13: "The rose you defend with the scratching of a livid lie is not unripe, it has no drips that burn or seeds that explode."

43. P. V. Mengaldo, "Il linguaggio della poesia ermetica," *La tradizione del Novecento: Terza serie,* 131–57. Mengaldo's examples are taken from the works of De Libero, Bigongiari, Luzi, and Gatto.

44. L. Fallacara, "Notturno," in G. Gramigna, *Le forme del desiderio,* 68: "Desirous one, you the flame who joins the roses to the trellis, barely stir your breath in which bees are alighting. . . ." The passage is cited as an example of "procedimento anagrammatico o se si preferisce usare i termini saussuriani, ipogrammatico o paragrammatico: costituendosi un reticolo entro il quale una cellula verbale funziona come generatrice del testo."

45. L. Fallacara, "Giardino etrusco," *Poesie,* 148–49: "The white roses

there among the hypogeums unveil the horizons of candor, just as you tombs unveil those of darkness. Or just as the high rose, sprinkled on . . . but for the rose in the wind there still remains the perfume of time in eternal sleep. So profound the nocturnal darkness, such a resigned waiting in silence, oh rose, and you . . ."

46. O. Macrì, in L. Fallacara, *Poesie*, 46: "The island which is the rose. . . . The rose which is not only the rose. . . . And ever it exhales and ever it creates around it / the space so intense with presence; / between heaven and earth, beginning of an / eternal idea, cloud of existence (*The rose*), Ecstasy of the rose which turns over in its dizziness and is calmed, / mirth that expands within the petals, / and thus becomes its opaque sky (*Cielo opaco*); . . . *The rose is ever beyond*."

47. Ibid., xx.

48. S. Solmi, "Giardino," *Poesie, meditazioni e ricordi*, 1:45: "The rainbowed spray which the wind shears oblique and ragged, veils for an instant the landscape, it fogs over like a memory. Then suddenly the fig tree, the Japanese medlar, are impressed on the prickly air, and the clear fainting of the roses is set to burning."

49. S. Solmi, "La rosa gelata," ibid., 99: "The rose which winter opened, unfolded, enervated, wrinkled, made into glass of blush-pink sugars, veined with imperceptible blood, I consider a perfect emblem for a day, undone not as leaf after destined leaf in the soft ruination of the seasons, but like an airplane, spectral crystal, shattered in an instant."

50. See A. Porta, ed., *Poesia degli anni settanta*, 55.

51. S. Solmi, "Villa gregoriana," *Poesie, meditazioni e ricordi*, 117–18: "Here where evening lights up the colors of laurel, the voice of no time is rustling in fountains and forests, the gods of stone, the profound gods are murmuring, they are laughing. On their gray knees the rose is jesting."

52. See P. V. Mengaldo, *La tradizione del Novecento* (1991), 154: "la prova maggiore del giovane Luzi è certamente la mirabile versione o 'copia' del sonetto della rosa di Ronsard."

53. M. Luzi, "Copia da Ronsard (Per la morte di Maria)," *Tutte le poesie*, 42: "As when in May the rose upon the branch / . . . . / and that your body, alive or dead, be no more than roses."

54. M. Luzi, "Passi" (1937), ibid., 48: "Will the lindens and evening roses rebloom over the walled streets burdened with thought, by the calm portals and fountains? . . . young girls are passing unknown over the atavistic bridge and someone more enveloping than the air and the roses

calls them from a terrace of silk where the heights have a sense of death.

55. M. Luzi, "Alla vita," in A. Gentili and C. O'Brien, eds., *The Green Flame,* 148: "we are on earth but we could soar away / faintly rest upon the divine breast / like roses from the walls of scented streets / over the infant who silently asks for them."

56. M. Luzi, "Allure," in L. Anceschi, ed., *Lirici nuovi,* 559: "did you know that living forgetfulness is no more than being the lip of a rose tumbling over the gates of the Brenta . . . ?"

57. M. Luzi, "Cimitero delle fanciulle" (1936), *Tutte le poesie,* 68: "But who raises anymore their chimaerical hands and blank brows to her name in the silent streets and the air as when the moon and the heavenly hair smelled of Florentine roses?"

58. M. Luzi, "Già colgono i neri fiori dell'Ade," ibid., 73: "Your lazy body radiates in the wind a solitary star between clanging windows and your raucous step is by now no more than the slowing down of roses in the air."

59. M. Luzi, "Già goccia la grigia rosa il suo fuoco," ibid., 90: "The gray rose already drips its flame the stolen flame smoking with rain on the blind slaked lime wall where your tired gleaming is resting."

60. P. Bigongiari, *Poesia italiana del Novecento,* 2:514.

61. M. Luzi, "Un brindisi," in L. R. Lind, ed. and trans., *Twentieth-Century Italian Poetry,* 324: "But you, my soul being forgotten, hurry beyond your faded borders, desire the neutral rose of countries forgotten on the brink of regretful streets, beyond the seasons a rose persists, a rose fixed in space and undivided wavering between night and day, grain of calm unconsummated Springs, of gardens possible within the wind."

62. A. Parronchi, "Notte di marzo," *Per strade di bosco e città,* 79: "There on the grass is a fallen stone. In the darkness a distant dawn of roses greets the wind."

63. A. Parronchi, "Ora un anno tramonta," ibid., 58: "The hedges send out their odors, an hour contains a thousand dreams, but oh how poor the stone now reflects the garden drunken with roses!"

64. A. Parronchi, "Coretto dei visi," ibid., 58: "You were picked in vain, beautiful roses now stripped bare! But from a distant border you once give a start. . . ."

65. A. Parronchi, "Boschiva," ibid., 38: "As soon as the roses and the other species of flowers from whom no cries ever issue from disconsolate lips have culled the hidden density from the white seed of light, and enclosed themselves deeply in ditches . . ."

66. P. Bigongiari, "Lettera d'amore," *Stato di cose*, 158: "Wherever, where you look, you see, where you linger, you believe, and something is stronger than the rose fading by your side; if something fades, then who can not raise up a song? (Something more complete than your weeping)."

67. P. Bigongiari, "La notte canterà," ibid., 40–41: "late the lightning burns upon your face and that rose kissed and given to the wind by tears does not rest upon the river. Night shall sing, love flows distant from the roses you cast out."

68. P. Bigongiari, "Duello," ibid., 76: "Sky blue shadow appeared where your heart no longer supports you, only a sword of roses reaches you, in the gardens, wielded bleeding by the evening."

69. P. Bigongiari, "Evidenza e oblio," ibid., 85: "where you, become a bride and all alone, placed roses in baskets in order to change your blood."

70. O. Macrì, *Studi sull'ermetismo*, 89; emphasis mine.

71. P. Bigongiari, "Fuoco equoreo," *Moses*, 95: "Bow wet with reflections, may the flame now be the rose on its thorns, a droplet, stigma, the pupil of the end."

72. N. Audisio, "Dietro la furia, dietro il polverone," in E. Faccioli et al., eds., *Nuovi poeti italiani 1*, 60: "And you, my double, who tremble on the other side of the ditch. She gave her a rose for an hour of absence because the only life for both of them was one."

73. A. Merini, "Santa Teresa del bambino Gesù," in P. Chiara and L. Erba, eds., *Quarta generazione*, 166: "Ivory made concrete between the hands of Crucifixes *in extremis*, the buzzing of thorns on every fingertip of the soft fingers, and, afterwards, roses, roses of wonder, placid snowfalls of innocence, a variation of waves in the depths of your eyes, the fixity of the pupil, I see there solitary swans gliding down your rivers of Love. . . ."

74. A. Merini, "Per una rosa," *La presenza di Orfeo*, 108: "I'd like to be you, so violent so rude in love, your veins of beauty so ignited and so punished."

75. P. Celan, "Psalm," *Poems*, 143, trans. M. Hamburger.

76. C. Ossola, "La rosa profunda," 479. He also cites in this regard Jorge Luis Borges, "The Unending Rose," *Obra poética*, 459: "Rosa profunda, ilimitada, íntima, / Que el Señor mostrará a mis ojos muertos" (Profound, unlimited, intimate rose, / that the Lord will unveil to my dead eyes).

77. P. Celan, "Engführung" (The straitening), *Poems*, trans. M. Hamburger, 18–19: "Und du: / du, du, du, / mein täglich wahr—und wahrer—

/ geschundenes Später / der Rosen—." I have cited Hamburger's "faithful rendering" of the problematic passage instead of his poetic translation.

78. See G. Bachelard, *The Flame of a Candle*.

7. THE ANACREONTIC ROSE

1. G. Leopardi, "Zibaldone" [4177], April 22, 1826, *Tutte le opere*, 2:1099: "Il piacere delle odi di Anacreonte è tanto fuggitivo, e così ribelle ad ogni analisi, che per gustarlo, bisogna espressamente leggerle con una certà rapidità, e con poca o ben leggera attenzione."

2. *Anacreon*, 162, trans. B. Gentili: "ognuno aveva tre ghirlande / una di maggiorana (?) due di rose."

3. U. Foscolo, "La rosa tarda," *Tutte le poesie*, 170: "You, resplendent and simple Flower, like my fetching one, You amidst the breasty thorns Still do not bloom, oh Rose. While gay Anacreon watched you rise, he mounted hymns to you, wrapping you about his bald forehead. And amid the dances and celebration the other one called for help whence came songs of your soft leaf welcome to the Gods. You are a trophy of tender Graces, you are a game, oh Rose, Of Love with playful Cythaera In the lusty days."

4. U. Foscolo, trans. of Anacreon, "Ode IV," in G. Contini, *Letteratura italiana del Risorgimento*, 165: "Why do you bother pouring your love oils in great quantities onto monuments? What good are the roses and wine? Why not anoint me instead, as long as I am alive, why not crown my white forehead with flowers?"

5. U. Foscolo, "To Callirhoe" (April 26, 1820), *Tutte le poesie*, 103.

6. R. Bogue and M. Spariosu, *The Play of the Self*, vii.

7. D. Valeri, "Rosetta," *Poesie scelte*, 37: "Rosetta is alone in the large church, the wind playing over her head. Rosetta doesn't move, laid under black blankets: she's dead."

8. P. P. Pasolini, *Passione e ideologia*, 13: "In tutto il canzoniere d'amore digiacomiano non si trova *una* donna: è sempre *della* donna che egli parla, si chiami Rosa o Nannina, nomi che sono puri *flatus vocis* benchè propri. . . ."

9. I. Buttita, "Matrimoniu pirfettu," *The Hidden Italy*, 524–25, ed. and trans. H. Haller: "Rosa found herself / with an impotent husband: / in the bed, the first night, / an accident happened."

10. G. Goffredo, "Rosa Calella," in A. Berardinelli, ed., *Nuovi poeti italiani 2*, 57: "Rosa saw her father die, Rosa saw her brother die, Rosa

tended her sick ones.—The wine!—father and son did cry, without Christ, neither dead nor doctors. Rosa together with her mother emptied the bottles of hope."

11. F. Scataglini, "Rosa," *Rimario agontano,* 207: "What can poor Rosa hug to her taciturn breast but a rose, a corner, a trifle, in comparison to the vast sea. What can be squeezed in the fist of a little girl that seems no more than a shriveled prune? Everything rushes toward its end, and this limit gives form to its death. 'All that Rosa wants to hug,' he says 'is your fine and trifling dream.'"

12. F. Brevini, *Poeti dialettali del Novecento,* 491.

13. F. Scataglini, *La rosa,* 92–94: "the bind-weed crowding out the clusters of jealous thorns and rosebeds overflowing with roses. What urge to draw near those open roses in bloom pushed me away? I would have given all of Pavia or Paris to be able to attend the flowery celebrations. . . . I desired a rose, one to pluck up above the thorns, but it would have distressed the gardener. Beneath the light of heaven small buds were hidden among the thick fogliage of stems of swollen buds ready to bloom. // I praise them more than the open roses, so pompous in the morning in bloom, then faded by evening. . . . that bud of the rose was both the idea and the thing. // Symmetrical, signatures on the quill, and alternate pages, eight sheets provided by the promissory rose."

14. J. Guillén, "Perfección," in Mantero, ed., *Antología,* 26–27. Mantero glosses: "High above, at the highest verticality, the sun, from which the rose hangs in its south, passed through by the radius (radius, ray) at the zenith. At the base of the hemisphere, a foot which walks feeling the totality of the world, material and affective totality: incorporation of the human element . . . in the normal ecstasy of Nature."

15. J. Guillén, "La rosa," *Aire nuestro,* 252: "I saw the rose: premier / enclosure of harmony / Tranquilly future, / perfect, without envy, / appeasing the nightingale / Too cruel in the spiral / splendor of its trills."

16. J. Guillén, "Una rosa es una rosa," *Aire nuestro,* 1588: "'It's original, it's new.' Too bad that only the snobs are aware of such virtues. 'A rose is a rose,' Gertrudis. I myself move toward quality."

17. L. Piccolo, "Veneris Venefica Agrestis," *Collected Poems,* 142: "If the cloud rests for a while on the ridge or entrance to the valley, she now sees in the living shade the shaft of the plough that shakes skims strips the tuft and the sylvan rose."

18. L. Piccolo, "Oratorio di Valverde," *Collected Poems,* 82–83: "Graceful Spring whose hawthorn pricks the foot wandering on its way hesitates, implores, does not dare disturb the sleeping rose."

19. L. Piccolo, "Dove più folto è il mirto," *La seta,* 37: "A broad stone indentation collects the water—at the edge there sits a jug—it mirrors clouds and branches. Will there rise out of the depths, one day, tearing apart the labile veils of moss, the flash of a snake or a rose's palpitation?"

20. L. Piccolo, "L'anno pellegrino," ibid., 75–76: "But when he sets out again toward terse horizons. . . . he wants to carry, his breath calm, this late odor of roses to distant grassy crevices, as silent footsteps journey onto other roads, toward other gardens."

21. L. Piccolo, "Buccia," in E. Krumm and T. Rossi, eds., *Poesia italiana del Novecento,* 802: "for one who throws it away, is your feeling harsh, earth, is it full of furrows, of inclines of scattered stones, of exposed limestone where the squeeze of August, still far from the solace of soothing springs, does not yet breathe of brambles poppies and roses?"

22. V. Bodini, "La rosa del crepuscolo si sfoglia," *Tutte le poesie,* 161: "The rose of twilight drops its petals in the calyx where it yields the stem of its greenery to the water."

23. V. Bodini, "Pioggia minore," ibid., 156: "The nymphs came out into the doorways: the sunflowers and poor roses printed on their dresses enclosed their lost thighs in an emphatic rigidity."

24. V. Bodini, "Cosa dire al tuo pianto," ibid., 163: "Oh, at times, to bend over to smell the pierced shadow of a rose, to betray you."

25. V. Bodini, "Il cerchio azzurro, le alghe trasparenti," ibid., 79: "Thus struggles the noontime that listens to its own death in your body of a rose, but since nothing is finite, remember now what lugubrious moon will consume these instants."

26. V. Bodini, "Nelle sfere armillari," ibid., 76: "In the armillary spheres, in the paradigm of the rose, I sought you, in the name carved with penknife on the desk and the yellow of stoplights always looking where you weren't."

27. V. Bodini, "Tanti anni," in R. Aymone, ed., *L'età delle rose,* 174: "We lived inside a red rose. Trains used to race by on their way out of the city—a sonorous jolt—; and everything else was a ferment of skies."

28. V. Bodini, *Studi sul barocco di Góngora,* 73: "quella stupefacente aspirazione a una coesistenza all'interno d'una stessa opera . . . di forma e di informe, di linee chiuse e linee aperte, di geometrico e di grottesco."

29. F. García Lorca, "Con la frente en el suelo," *Obras completas,* 588: "Next to the gray road I saw a flowery path and a rose full of light, full of life, and sorrow. Woman, flower that opens in the garden: the roses are like your virgin flesh, with its ineffable and subtle fragrance and its nostalgia for sadness."

30. F. García Lorca, "Narciso," ibid., 386: "In the depths there is a rose and in the rose there is another river. . . . and in the rose I find my very self. // When the boy was lost in the water I understood. But I won't explain."

31. F. García Lorca, "Oda a Salvador Dalí," ibid., 618, 621: "A rose in the high garden you desire. A wheel in the pure syntax of steel. . . . But also the rose in the garden where you live. Ever the rose, forever our North and South!"

32. F. García Lorca, "Panorama ciego de Nueva York," ibid., 494–96: "It is not a bird which expresses the stormy fever of the lagoon, . . . it is an undefinable stair where roses and clouds forget the Chinamen's cries boiling along the dockside of blood."

33. F. García Lorca, "Muerte," ibid., 506: "And the horse, what a sharp arrow it squeezes from the rose, what a gray rose its raises with its snout! And the rose what a herd of lights and lowings it ties to the living sugar of its stem."

34. F. García Lorca, "La imagen poética de Góngora," ibid., 73–74.

35. F. Fortini, in Luis de Góngora, *Sonetti*, vi: "Per dirla con un epigramma: García Lorca ricorreva a uno dei bambini terribili delle Avanguardie storiche (afflitti dal bisogno di lavare la macchia indelebile delle proprie origini romantiche) quando, a proposito di Góngora, proclamava che 'è il madrigale che interessa e non la rosa'. Credo invece, con Solmi, che il precipitato della grande chimica gongorina sia di 'oggetti,' nomi-cose, e quindi anche di 'rose'; laddove in Mallarmé una chimica solo apparentemente analoga perviene sì ad una 'rosa' ma *dans les tènèbres*, al Fiore Assente, quindi a tutt'altra immagine del mondo e della mente."

36. A. Gatto, "Novembre a Pesto," *Osteria flegrea (1954–1961)*, 142: "Once there were roses, asphodels. Now the sky which answered the night of the years, the swamps, the dead, passes through the heavens."

37. A. Gatto: "Se morissi in un caffè . . . ," *La storia delle vittime*, 161–62: "He would say 'stop' to the flower-vendor, 'take some roses to the girl who died on me.' . . . Which of the two of us is speaking? No one hears what I'm thinking . . . or perhaps they do. The fashion boutique—do you remember?—had in the night the pink of the mannequins in the buzzing neon. Thus thought is where one rests."

38. A. Gatto, "Alla voce perduta," ibid., 66–67: "With the dead water of the evening I heard swallows passing, as if far away, blue in the shadows of the Naviglio. All about on the arms of soldiers every sadness was a poor odor of woman with dark carnations on her chest. Lamps blossomed in the darkened rooms like great candles where the war already sang a song

in low notes, 'Lili Marleen.' And night came over the world, the mournings of roses in courtyards descended on the women in their weeping."

39. A. Gatto, "Ragazzo a sera," in R. Aymone, ed., *L'età delle rose*, 55–56: "Let the road be the one to tell her and may the first insult from the mocking woman give her courage. She will later tell the story of having seen the pious lass pull off her clothes, like the petals of the rose."

40. A. Gatto, "Natale al caffè Florian," *Poesie (1929–1969)*, 101: "Pinkish fog and air of cold mists. . . . A sad window ledge, Venice which is fading all the roses along the Grand Canal. The stars fallen, the roses fallen in the wind bringing Christmas."

41. A. Gatto, "Ai monti di Trento," in A. Gentili and C. O'Brien, eds., *The Green Flame*, 142–43: "And so the clear circle of the mountain charms at length the evening in the fields. Italy already smells of dust and roses."

42. A. Sala, "Sette colpi," *Epigrafi e canti*, 51: "Five chimes for a man; for a woman seven: they ring the bell seven times for a woman, my mother. Enamored of flowers she had to die in August amidst roses of dust. Tomorrow is August 10, they will take her away."

43. A. Sala, "Il rubino," *La prova del nuovo*, 19: "A rose in mild November scratched the lobe of the ear I hear better in (your unspoken words included). I am defending, among blades of cement, the ruby of blood through your fingers."

44. R. Brindisi, "Mia madre, Miskin e la neve," in W. Siti, ed., *Nuovi poeti italiani 3*, 190, 192: "my metaphors had by then consumed her conscience of rose of swallow of snow / and perhaps one of them had prefigured my death. . . . my mother would have been pricked by the black rose / of eternity and would not have woken up again"

45. B. Cattafi, "Regioni," *Poesie 1943–1979*, 224: "Those warm dense regions variegated by the smell of oregano and roses were not regions the world has no oregano and roses they were learned inks spread upon fecund cellulose."

46. B. Cattafi, "S'uniscono i pezzi," ibid., 211: "the scattered pieces of a design are unified. . . . like a wave or a rose"

47. B. Cattafi, "Dall'altra parte," ibid., 179: "On the other side of the outstretched hand of the petal, the leaf of the rose. . . . all is patience and expectation which overturn the Easter stone the sepulchral side of things on the other side the true design the luminous face the kingdom the kingdom the kingdom."

48. B. Cattafi, "Strelitzia," ibid., 177: "Cruel beak. . . . you dryly peck petal by petal the weary rot of the rose."

49. B. Cattafi, "Un tempo," ibid., 157: "they are not flowers they are not roses yellow dogs use the plains to walk crooked the guards flattened against the walls make the arthritis creak in their hands."

50. B. Cattafi, "L'ultimo velo," ibid., 136: "From a block of matter. . . . emerge in a fluttering of wings petal fin feather the whale the swallow the rose fly into you in your mind and even the ungraspable something almost blooms."

51. B. Cattafi, "Tiro a segno," ibid., 24: "The rose is ruined in this air; starting out from the largest of the concentric circles, arriving at the center of living color, only to find the black hard true keratin of a definitive insect already feeding there. // May God save you with your Queen."

52. B. Cattafi, "Brughiera," ibid., 20: "The season ends in this sound of heathers and wind. Go now love, oh thicket of the mind, sad rose desist from the dominion."

53. C. Campo, "Con una testa di Anacreonte e una fiala d'olio di rose," translation of E. Mörike, *La tigre assenza,* 74: "As winter stole away the roses that bound / Anacreon's head at the symposium, where he was playing / the lyre, Afrogeneia dripped exquisite essences / on his hair, and now the soft fragrances of / roses are fused in every song. / If but a *lover* intone the notes of the old serene one, / the atriums and the halls will fill with the ancient, regal perfume."

54. C. Campo, "Passo d'addio," ibid., 19: "And while the warm rose lingers / the bitter berry is already dripping with the taste / of the smiling farewells."

55. See C. Campo, *Gli imperdonabili,* 9–11.

56. C. Campo, "Canzoncina interrotta," *La tigre assenza,* 35: "Only my hour of vehemence lacerated the roses on the gate . . . And an overturned statue perhaps was biting—in the spinning of that flight—in autumn, at a pillow of moss."

57. R. Giambene, "Prima rosa," in A. Manuali and B. Sablone, eds., *Poesie d'amore del '900 italiano,* 139: "Lustful rose of April your cracked petals of woman have the voluptuousness of the dew. The leaves are like thoughts of caresses. Thorns of fire on the naked arms of a blond woman who has the same scent as an April rose."

58. G. Albisola, "Imago (Elegia)," in E. Faccioli et al., eds., *Nuovi poeti italiani 1,* 23: "What more shall there be of the blond straw of your hair, smooth against the nape, of your lips opened to seal the kiss, red rose petals, your pale fingers made to evoke the touch of invisible keyboards?"

59. L. Zaniboni, "Dicotomia," in G. Dego and L. Zaniboni, eds., *La*

svolta narrativa della poesia italiana, 88: "Everybody is looking for someone or something / I'm looking for you like a gardener the rose."

60. L. Tassoni, "Bocca di cinque rose," in S. Meccati, ed., *La poesia in mostra,* 79: "A mouth of five roses / lost in their being extended / faded by the swift bee / in the dawn moist with dew."

61. B. Bertolucci, "Dietro a una ragazza," *In cerca di mistero,* 45: "Already the rose evaporates in a hot marbling, but it seems that the game must still go on ingenuous and desperate, like a vice."

8. The Idea of Liguria

1. G. Caproni, *Res amissa,* 113: "A land where, word has it, / the rose does not stand straight."

2. V. Cardarelli, "Liguria," *Opere,* 72: "Liguria is a gay land. Burning stone, clean-washed clay.... Shadow and sunlight alternate through deep valleys hidden from the sea, along stone-paved streets climbing skyward among fields of roses, wells and broken lands, hugging next to small farms and closed vineyards."

3. G. Gozzano, "Cocotte," *Opere,* 219–20: "My dream is fed with abandon and regret. I love only the roses I did not pluck. I love only the things which could have been and weren't . . . I see the house; there are the roses of the beautiful garden of twenty years ago! // Beyond the bars lies your intact garden, it wanders out into the Ligurian eucalyptus. . . ."

4. R. Lucchese, "Canto di Orfeo," in P. Chiara and L. Erba, eds., *Quarta generazione,* 263: "And my echo is everywhere present before the high sonorous comb of the Rocky Mountains; in Tokyo and, at once, among the roses of San Remo."

5. P. P. Pasolini, *Canzoniere italiano,* 51.

6. M. Novaro, "Quante volte ancora," in P. Gelli and G. Lagorio, eds., *Poesia italiana del Novecento,* 1:20: "These pines these cypresses and roses red like blood how many more times when I am gone shall the moon wonderstruck gaze, the mute stars watch pointing to the hill which alone remained with me in the nighttime silence to meditate!"

7. G. Caproni (paraphrasing in part Luciano Anceschi), in ibid., 1:24.

8. C. R. Ceccardi, "In un cimitero di monti," in ibid., 1:29: "The path lingers in a grassy silence which fades with regret, and grows back unharvested, amid a veil of arid stalks. A wild rose, a star of blue iris, sometimes emerge from that desert like a dream . . . ; a dream that implicates with its pale pupils another dream, far off, not yet over."

9. P. Jahier, *Con me e con gli alpini*, 127–28: "I will arrange to have my life / cut into six pieces / The first piece to the King of Italy / so that he may remember his soldier. . . . The fourth piece to the Tofane mountains / so that it may bloom into roses and flowers."

10. P. Jahier, "Con me (V)," *Poesie in versi e in prosa*, 74: "mountain girl, if you should love me / like a rose not yet in bloom."

11. P. Jahier, "Con me (VI)," ibid., 77: "This morning every woman carries a rose on her breast toward your accepting hands; the world is complete, instantaneous and desirable like the woman who is approaching."

12. P. P. Pasolini, *Canzoniere italiano*, 51.

13. P. Jahier, "Con me," *Poesie in versi e in prosa*, 65: "'Certainly these rose hedges are natural hedges, / field hedges, useful hedges. / This is Italy.' / The fields are calm weeded and in order / and around these fields the hedges are made of roses. /—Italy—."

14. G. Boine, "I miei amici di qui," *Il peccato e altre opere*, 153–54: "However, the first one made himself an altar over the sea: I mean a real altar of roses, as rare as large candles or bonfires alight, with black cypresses for candlesticks;—and, like a god, he stands there all day long gazing out. . . . Whenever I prepare to depart, he chooses for me the most odorous rose. Thus melancholy is abandoned: and life is, as such, almost a joy." The Milanese Clemente Rebora (discussed in Chapter 4) was also of Ligurian heritage and had published in *Riviera Ligure*.

15. G. Boine, "Epistola al 'Tribunale,'" ibid., 370.

16. G. Boine, "Trasfigurazione," ibid., 122: "There are days of emptiness in which the roses give off no smell nor do eyes see; the people of ghosts runs along streets with no sound. . . . I am a remorseful mouth with no taste; monotonous I will wait until my change comes."

17. R. Serra, "Ascolto nel silenzio," *Piccolo canzoniere*, 37: "I listen to a rose in the silence, it whispers: it is she who is breathing upon my chest."

18. A. Barile and G. Petrocchi, in R. Serra, ibid., 215, 10.

19. A. Barile, "Funerale," *Poesie*, 161: "Oh the arcane language of things penetrates hearts: 'the wing of Death with its flapping encloses the universe.' And it seems that a sunset has emerged from a pale kingdom of faded shadows: chrysanthemums are born upon the roses."

20. P. V. Mengaldo, *La tradizione del Novecento: Terza serie*, 128. See P. P. Pasolini, *Passione e ideologia*, 374–75: "forse la poesia di Sbarbaro è il prodotto più perfetto uscito dalla rivoluzione linguistica vociana o genericamente del primo Novecento"; Sbarbaro possesses "la furia pascoliana . . . per giungere il più dentro possibile nei 'particolari,' negli oggetti o nei

gesti quotidiani: determinati fino all'eccesso di evidenza, ma (come osserva Contini per il Pascoli) contro un fondo *sempre indeterminato*."

21. C. Sbarbaro, *L'opera in versi e in prosa*, 1:145: "the two darlings in the carriage, well-to-do and covered with roses by silent men as if in a rite while the sky expanded over Santa Maria del Fiore. Florence means Capstan cigarettes 'I know you are pretty' sung in April, 1914, the Bar of the Rose, its tender heart which burns the night. . . ."

22. C. Sbarbaro, "Non, Vita, perché tu sei nella notte," *Poesia e prosa*, 7: "but, Life, for your roses which either haven't yet bloomed or are already falling apart, for your Desire which leaves only flies in the rapt hand of the child, as in the fable for the hate which each of us feels for the us of the day before. . . ."

23. F. Fortini, *I poeti del Novecento*, 20.

24. C. Sbarbaro, "Coronata," *Poesia e prosa*, 58: "Everyone that day had a paper rose stuck in his lapel or belt. We filed along with the dandies who, in Sunday best, pursued the swarm of girls. . . . Our happiness from that day is colored green; that of a green bottle stuck with paper roses. We uselessly asked to see the *Rose in Bloom*, promised by the sign. It must have been fetching, kept under a bell jar, nourished by the dew alone."

25. C. Sbarbaro, "Licheni," *Poesia e prosa*, 81: "The exclamatory encounter with the *Anagallis tenella*, 'gripped onto the clay by its little leafy hands, chiming with a humble rose' . . . is from those years. . . . In the amorous inventory of a tiny part of the world, the one congenial to me, I satisfied without knowing it the 'supine love of things.'"

26. C. Sbarbaro, "Montegrosso," *L'opera in versi e in prosa*, 412–13: "I would not go back to look for it in the notebook where I placed it; nor in so many encounters with the earth was I to find it again." The "idea of Liguria" also emerges in Sbarbaro's numerous references to Genoa in his prose poetry.

27. A. Grande, "Album," in L. Anceschi, ed., *Lirici nuovi*, 268: "Oh useless catalogue, vain leafiness! You remain pale, life of mine, you are faded. This thorny rose I carry in my heart removes the sense from the unwanted images. The days are short, if empty, which are remaining to you, to waste them in this game."

28. See S. Romagnoli, "Spazio pittorico e spazio letterario da Parini a Gadda," 548–49: "The harsh, narrow, luminous coast of Liguria, the brief spaces of the gardens, the fruit orchards extending upwards or outwards in the limited tracts of land overlooking the sea, these are the real places that are contrasted and interpenetrate and are measured with the nullifying fragility of man in so much of Montale's poetry, especially in *Ossi di*

seppia. ... Montale's novelty rests in the symbolic value assigned to the landscape (almost without residue) as a verbal representation of the existential incommunicability to which modern man (and the man of the civic chronicle forced to traverse the dark times of dictatorship) is condemned and the proud solitude he places his trust in."

29. R. Dombroski, in P. Brand and L. Pertile, eds., *The Cambridge History of Italian Literature*, 506.

30. G. Caproni, "Litania," *Tutte le poesie*, 183: "Genoa a barbarous name. *Campana, Montale, Sbarbaro.* /.... / Genoa of the Soziglia quarter. *Rabbit meat. Poultry. fish.* Genoa of garlic and roses, *of the quarters of Prè and Fontane Marose.*"

31. See P. V. Mengaldo, "Questioni metriche novecentesche," 583.

32. G. Caproni, "L'ascensore," *Tutte le poesie*, 177: "I shall also steal a rose which then, my sweet wife, I shall convert for you into poison leaving you meek on the ground floor to tell me: 'Ciao, write me sometime,' as the door had closed and the brake released a shudder shook the window."

33. A. Girardi, *Cinque storie stilistiche*, 107.

34. G. Caproni, "Quasi ad aulica dedica," *Tutte le poesie*, 293: "Oh when I picked you! A mountain rose, and almost Longobardian to boot."

35. G. Caproni, "La preda," *Il Conte di Kevenhüller*, 30: "The prey (a dungheap? a rose?) which we all have in our breast, and which not even the fevers of December (the dead fields of August) can shoot down ... The evanescent prey."

36. V. Sereni, in P. Gelli and G. Lagorio, *Poesia italiana del Novecento*, 2:611.

37. G. Caproni, "Pensatina dell'antimetafisicante," *Il Conte di Kevenhüller*, 153: "'An idea stirs in me, stupid as a rose. After us there is nothing. Not even nothing, which would already be something.'"

38. G. Caproni, cited in G. Tabanelli, *Carlo Bo: Il tempo dell'ermetismo*, 217–18.

39. P. P. Pasolini, "Caproni," *Passione e ideologia*, 422.

40. C. Vivaldi, "Partendo da Imperia," in G. Spagnoletti and C. Vivaldi, eds., *Poesia dialettale dal Rinascimento a oggi*, 542: "'What does this wind want? I don't know. Shut the gate, with the tin roses attached, of the graveyard. I don't know.'"

41. C. Vivaldi, "La ferita," *Poesie scelte* (1952/1992), 88: "And everything seems to continue as before / but it is not true; / the piazzas open up, the streets are flooded / with air / and I do not walk, or breathe or live / I lose my hands, my eyes, / I roll on the pavement like a ball of rags / until you

stop me, / your fists overflowing with the roses / blooming on the window ledge."

42. C. Vivaldi, "Fiume e bambù," *Poesie scelte*, 28: "By the river, between a dead lizard, a shiny stone and a brown clump of roses, a desolate gray-haired Pan is mumbling."

43. I. Calvino, in G. Conte, *The Ocean and the Boy*, trans. L. Stortoni, xx.

44. G. Conte, ibid., 71: "We are arid, vanquished, but in the hour / of this sunset a song is still / possible.

45. G. Conte, "Bellatrix," *L'oceano e il ragazzo*, 150: "I met you in the time when planets and flowers coincide, you a stem an ellipse crippled with exploded light among all the possible roses I too a possible human rose."

46. G. Conte, in T. Kemeny and C. Viviani, eds., *Il movimento della poesia italiana negli anni settanta*, 105–9.

47. G. Conte, "Dopo Marx, Aprile," *L'ultimo aprile bianco*, 91: "the eternal sterile and mute rebirthing of things 'March was cold and sad, but then April, jaunts on the meadow, portents of glad scarlet, cherries and the first roses.'"

48. G. Conte, "Decorazioni e estasi," *L'oceano e il ragazzo*, 44: "One day if the reader of the third millennium should read me, he will know that here there were trees and desires, palms and pine trees, and eucalyptus with quarter-moon shaped leaves, and roses: there were those tired of suffering and those who wanted to love too much."

49. G. Conte, "Animali etruschi," in G. Pontiggia, ed., *La parola innamorata*, 51: "They say that it would devastate gardens, beds of myrtle, long rows of roses. But what else could it do, if not run, sniff wildly, and destroy? The blood of love does not want subtle or static organs."

50. G. Conte, "Elegia scritta nei giardini di Villa Hanbury," *The Ocean and the Boy*, trans. L. Stortoni, 64: "a tide enters me, the nonexistent ellipse of any orbit: bind me up with your movement, goddess of the footrace and of the bow, in the hour before rays and roses set."

51. G. Conte, "Frammenti dalla voce di Manannan Mac Lir," ibid., 80: "the barbarous budding of / cherry trees and roses brings them, / the wandering cloudy stars of / doelike girls, of heather." With reference to this poem, Calvino writes, xx: "At the wellspring of the West, Hercules and Prometheus are linked to a Celtic god Manannan Mac Lir; to make this connection, the poet changes meter: after a cadence sounding almost like hexameters, he adopts the rhythm of the Nordic rhymed ballad, pursuing a cosmic identification of everything with everything."

52. G. Conte, "Natura morta con clessidre (II)," ibid., 104–5: "between the flowers and the stars, the first gush. Nor will I remember you any longer. Only then can I travel, among the mothers of roses and galaxies."

53. O. Mandelstam, "On the Nature of the Word" (1922), cited in S. Heaney, *The Government of the Tongue*, 78.

54. See G. Ficara on Conte's overdetermined notion of Liguria, in G. Conte, *L'oceano e il ragazzo*, 13–14.

9. OF RAREFACTION AND RHETORIC

1. Y. Tynianov, *The Problem of Verse Language*, 71.

2. I cite a useful definition of theory by V. E. Cronen and W. B. Pearce, *Communication, Action, and Meaning*, 104–5: "A theory is a formal device for chunking information, allowing the theorist to lift him/herself from the morass of data by his/her own brain cells. But the problem—like that of Archimedes who would move the world with his lever and fulcrum—is that of finding a place to stand. If there is no limit to recursiveness, then at whatever level N the theory is written, the theorist must be thinking and communicating at level N + 1, and the very existence of the theory is sufficient evidence to show it incapable of accounting for the level of activity necessary to produce it."

3. Ibid., 111.

4. R. Luperini, P. Cataldi, F. D'Amely, *Poeti italiani: Il Novecento*, 243.

5. E. Montale, "Il tiro a volo," *Tutte le poesie*, 435: "You ask me why I navigate / in insecurity and do not try / another route? Ask / the bird who is flying unharmed / because it was far off and the spray of buckshot / too wide. // Rarefactions also exist for those of us / without wings."

6. See G. Bateson, *Mind and Nature*, 253: "If a sequence of events combines a random component with a selective process so that only certain outcomes of the random are allowed to endure, that sequence is said to be *stochastic*."

7. C. Vivaldi, *Poesie scelte*, 50: "while the clay pigeon is freed in expectation of the scatter of buckshot." One also hears again the surprise sound of gunshots in three of Montale's earlier poems: "Falsetto," "Mia vita, a te non chiedo lineamenti," and "Il gallo cedrone."

8. E. Montale, "Asor," *Tutte le poesie*, 554: "Asor, gentle name (its letters inverted are the loveliest flower), does not love privatism in poetry."

9. E. Montale, "La danzatrice stanca," ibid., 578: "The rose blush returns which 'ere was yet languishing . . . 'Ere? It means just a while ago, before.

". . . This is the only flower left with something of the merit of your woody nightshade. . . . Suffice that one be amazed that your flower is wondrously reincarnate."

10. H. Bloom, *The Breaking of the Vessels*, 74.

11. A. Manzoni, "In morte di Carlo Imbonati," *Poesie prima della conversione*, 195: "And of he, who on the immaculate plectrum / Sang for me: *The rose blush returns*. / First my teacher then my friend, whose / School and palaestra of virtue I always / Admired with reverent affection."

12. P. Valesio, "Effare l'in-fame," *Prose in poesia*, 17: "Ah, grace and consolation of poetry: How whorelike the rose who just before was blooming or languishing or is just touching. Why the rose, symbol of woman (ah, strumpet of my dreams) and of love? Because the rose resembles a vagina. A tight and warm vagina at first, inviolate."

13. We might recall in this light that G. Parini also used *rosa* to impugn the sybaritic habits and presumptuousness of men of commerce, who complain if the rose petals on their couches are wrinkled ("Il Mezzogiorno" ll. 690–700, *Il giorno*, 177).

14. A. Gatto, "Il frenatore addormentato," in P. Gelli and G. Lagorio, eds., *Poesia italiana del Novecento*, 2:586. "The freight trains lose the Roman dawn in the sky, the countryside greener than the rose has the freshness of a door. A boy stationed overnight in the signal-house has the dead lantern against his heart and the flag at his feet, he is dreaming of asking everyone to forgive him. It is strange, perhaps they are already leading to the firing squad the shadow of youth that smiled on him."

15. B. Seward, "The Artist and the Rose," 69. She continues: "As a flower whose colour is that of Ireland and whose creation is dependent upon Stephen's imagination, the green rose of the child's initial artistic effort acts as a symbolic foreshadowing of the young man's final determination 'to forge in the smithy of my soul the uncreated conscience of my race.'"

16. J. Joyce, *A Portrait of the Artist as a Young Man*, 7.

17. P. Valesio, "Porta del sole," *La rosa verde*, 49–50: "And what is the next step? A Voice which calls out a living idea points the way; overheard in the market, louder than the whispers of flowers, it is a Voice painted on a sign: 'Rosa, servant of my heart.'"

18. S. Ramat, "VIII," *L'inverno delle teorie*, 19: "the agitated rose of an adult dreaming, torn in pieces, in attrition between two stones—the unable, the impossible—later reunited in the single fragment which, in advance, opaque, severs the day."

19. S. Ramat, "Dopo un giardino," *Corpo e cosmo,* 17: "a life for which the triumphant malice of the ephemeral roses is not a sign, but the eternal stoniness of the fog on the fertility of this slime that the invented garden does not erase."

20. S. Ramat, *Storia della poesia italiana del Novecento,* 640.

21. S. Ramat, "Take-off," *Orto e nido,* 22, 27: "But harder for you to crawl back to your hideout, to reach out on hands and knees to the opaque under-cover that was life, *your* life, to touch once again the range (*rosa*) of the senses, to find it today a skeleton, to ask for love from the long trips, from hearts more naked than your own: you too a life of chance, a parasite among the ivy, ready to gorge yourself in that green, reluctant—blindness—to rarefy yourself. . . . To rip up the pavement, to rage upon the texture of every stone. So well is the design of a city humiliated that the pattern (*rosa*) of breaths not yet traced out is offended by it."

22. S. Ramat, "(quel fiore e la sua ombra)," *Pomerania,* 58: "in the field of memory the rose, the shadow of that rose of his on the wall, with the rushing forth of a mathematical love that at one precise moment of the day—he is the only one to grasp it—united in sweet knots that flower and its shadow, just the rose and the shadow, of the whole flowerpatch or garden . . . It is redrawn in you as grief (something near? an emblem?)."

23. S. Ramat, "Fastidiosa fa velo . . . ," *Numeri primi,* 38: "A neighborhood gave up on pool parlors and the races: for her. By the rose of their applause, they courted her."

24. E. F. Accrocca, "I binari di Apollinaire," *Poesie,* 161: "the Hotel of the Carmelites was already that way in 1920 / and in 1913 at the time of Sceab's suicide // let the fist not strangle the rose of the symbol / on the walls the posters leave no doubts / the defense of prices is an obstacle to the dollar."

25. E. F. Accrocca, "L'onomastico," ibid., 14: "Tomorrow is your birthday: / eighteen red roses / over your name carved into a stone. . . ."

26. E. F. Accrocca, "Eco di rosa," ibid., 142–43: "A Reader-Wolf / *in fabula* treated like a rose / then *rosai rosae rosam rosa rosa / rosae rosarum rosis rosas rosae rosis* / half-deranged. Or perhaps *iotic?*"

27. E. F. Accrocca, "Notizia di Romadesso," ibid., 81: "secret chaplains and custodians of the papal tiaras / acolytes in charge of maces masters of the chamber / cup-bearer secretary of an embassy / wardrobe sacristan major scout / couriers of the golden rose and secret steward. . . ."

28. R. Bodei, in L. Ballerini, *Il terzo gode,* 10–11.

29. L. Ballerini, "Archeologia," *Che figurato muore,* trans. T. Harrison, 144–45: "and then (addressing the audience) I seem / each time to die in your hands, / to ruffle a wool that is hostile to times / of wine and roses,

when the alarm / arises, and the line-up, and the flair / of hounds at one's heels."

30. L. Ballerini, "opera di misericordia," *Il terzo gode,* 96: "He then comes to tow away a handbag, an exhausting harp: a painted compass-card is one thing and another is the oily moth of the heart thrown to chance."

31. C. Viviani, "Signora," *L'amore delle parti,* 62–63: "among the common roses she affirms a few steps for this useless good"; "the prime ordinal is blooming / the lofty peak of a rose / she sees the cloth unfolding."

32. C. Viviani, ibid., 63: "accoglie tutte queste maglie l'opera...."

33. C. Viviani, "L'amore delle parti," ibid., 110: "an angel had not passed the chorus—the purchased animal goes into the shadows with its laughter the double rose one makes use of . . . and the sleepy calyxes are stricken by the flame."

34. G. Bachelard, *The Flame of a Candle,* 57, citing T. S. Eliot, *Four Quartets.*

35. C. Viviani, "XXII," *Preghiera del nome,* 101: "They captured me. They were taking me back to Vicenza, they explained, because my masters were there. I didn't understand, I begged and they laughed and said: 'You will see, my dear, when we get there and you are back in your bird-cage, next to the rose, you will remember everything.'"

36. T. Rossi, "Galline," *Miele e no,* 52: "'How sweet, how pretty your little hens. . . .' 'Just so one loses sight of the white roses at dusk . . .' / . . . . / No fine map there will draw the smallness of that claw-scratched place, by now they are invisible staying in one clucking place created by them, of worn earth, huddling, as it were, in their gentleness."

37. T. Rossi, "Miele," *Miele e no,* 45: "This alone says your company, your grave chorus that is barely audible: 'they are not roses, they're not roses at all, they're not'. The low voice grows glum but doesn't stop and down into this darkness, perhaps, without seeming so, it will be like honey."

38. T. Rossi, "L'incantesimo," *Il cominciamondo,* 19: "and because you keep your rose-like face and because you are still a good thorn for me; to what place, oh odorous madame, will you carry your delicate madness tomorrow."

39. V. Giotti, "La canzon de la foia portada dal vento (*Imitazione da Leopardi*)" (1906), *Opere,* 325: "I know one thing: that I shall surely go where all leaves go; yes, all of them, whether beautiful or ugly."

40. S. Penna, *Poesie,* 221: "The rose in its luxuriance was never so beautiful as when in the swollen *pissoir* of dawn it loved the sleepless sentry."

41. S. Penna, "Quando discese la svelta lattaia," *Confuso sogno*, 77: "When the svelte milkmaid descended the drowsy farm-hand felt a tuft grow in the hayloft, and at its top, open like a morning rose, but like a much warmer dew, the milk was left to him, not the milkmaid." P. Bigongiari, in G. Pozzi, *La poesia italiana del Novecento*, 321, has called Penna's poetry "a flower without a visible stem."

42. S. Penna, "A Pier Paolo," in N. Naldini, *Pasolini: Una vita*, 277: "The rose is the form of blessings Happy anguish in the shape of the rose . . . blessed secretions the guts of literature oratory mystification when finally they open in the form of the rose."

43. Cited by A. Porta in his preface to B. M. Frabotta, *Il rumore bianco*, 10: "Feminism, especially that most consonant with French psychoanalytic thought, has contributed to the construction of the current myth of the body, but has also exposed the risks of a pacific continuity between language of the body and that of thought. I share the latter fears more than the former enthusiasms."

44. B. M. Frabotta, "Il serpe si morde la coda," *Il rumore bianco*, 37: "Big momma of taxi drivers, her mechanical senses of rose, her breasts in pain, hums a sweet song. I begin to understand what the practice of the unconscious radio-taxi poem offers: the luminous ride of the meter clicks and the grace the night promises."

45. B. M. Frabotta, "a rosa botanica," ibid., 51: "Lowering the head of the rose to rid of the thorn what fell off was the 's' and your destiny became death."

46. B. M. Frabotta, "Appunti di volo," *Appunti di volo: E altre poesie*, 11: "to permute what has yet to be, with that which has never been, utopia, early fruit, or desert rose this sudden leap into the void."

47. P. Levi, "Agave," *Ad ora incerta*, 51: "I'm neither useful nor beautiful, I have neither joyful colors nor perfumes"; "To build myself a house, Maybe not beautiful but meeting a design."

48. H. Heine, "Donna Clara," *Ad ora incerta*, trans. P. Levi, 91: "Holding his breath / Amidst the dark shadows of the roses/ . . . . / Roses red as blood / Give impulse to their love. / 'But tell me, dear friend, / Why are you so flushed?' // 'It was the mosquitoes; / Oh, I hate them, almost / As much as the unpleasant crowds / Of long-nosed Jews.'"

49. L. Erba, *Il tranviere metafisico*, 67: "All here your here-and-now? You interrogate the alphabet of things but do you know the answer of a bouquet of roses to your every night's non-understanding?"

50. M. Guidacci, "Tu buio, buio fuoco," *Paglia e polvere*, 47: "Darkness, you dark fire! / Without sparks or flame. / They will not say of you / That

like a rose you bloom / Into delicate petals, / They won't say that you are a star / To light up the night."

51. M. Guidacci, "Il porgitore di stelle," *Il buio e lo splendore,* 59: "You who see a Galaxy in every earthly flowering and a flower in every star, have thus tied my gift to what is my most beloved star. . . . in fact, who can say with certainty that Betelgeuse is still alive? Maybe we are only seeing what the sky remembers of her, long traversed by the ancient pinkish light."

52. M. Guidacci, "La carità soltanto," in G. Davico Bonino and P. Mastrocola, *Antologia delle poetesse del '900,* 303: "Your heart burns with charity and in the bond of fire hiding the rose, it transfigures your entire intricate solitude into gardens."

10. THE ENCYCLOPEDIC ROSE

1. R. Barthes, *Writing Degree Zero,* 45–46, 48, 44.
2. G. Dotoli, citing Apollinaire, *Nascita della modernità,* 64.
3. G. Apollinaire, "Claire de lune," *Alcools,* 180, 278: "I am afraid of the flaming arrow of this bee Arcturus / Who has cast a deceptive light into my hands, / And has gathered his lunar honey from the rose compass-card of the winds // Oh rose barely a rose in the knowing books. . . ."
4. I. Calvino, *Six Memos for the Next Millennium,* 116.
5. R. Poggioli, *The Theory of the Avant-Garde,* 199.
6. Among Pascolian stylemes Pasolini lists, in *Canzoniere italiano,* 89: "solecismi, elissi deliziose, fresche coordinazioni per asindeto, ingenue inversioni ('*carne de Rosa mia nu' ne tuccate*'), infantili raffigurazioni espressionistiche da iconografia magica."
7. G. Caproni, "Via Guinizelli," *Res amissa,* 116: "Via Guinizelli, in Monselice. Lost in the morning of grass and sun (of roses—in the sun—almost Florentine) Mario and I towards the station, in the hour of separation."
8. A. Bertolucci, "La rosa bianca" in P. V. Mengaldo, ed., *PIN,* 573: "For you I will pick the last rose in the garden, the white rose that blooms in the earliest fog. The avid bees visited it until yesterday, but it is still so sweet it makes you tremble. It is a portrait of you at thirty, a bit forgetful, as you will then be."
9. A. Bertolucci, "Solo," in A. Porta, ed., *Poesia degli anni settanta,* 193: "the vegetal coral of the dog rose and the tenacious thicket that grips the hazelnut."
10. A. Bertolucci, "Ancora l'albergo," in A. Porta, ed., *Poesia degli anni settanta,* 193: "do not be amazed by the infinitely hard-working twelve-

year-old daughter-servant—hers is the difficult job of removing spots, of keeping the song upon her mouth, lovely little rose."

11. A. Bertolucci, "Pezzo semplice," *Verso le sorgenti del Cinghio*, 31: "She sells only roses / brunette rose aflame / girl with a run in her stockings / who looked me in the eyes / so long I had to lower them. // Seventeen years old and a cane chair half broken-through / now suddenly she's on her feet to quench her roses' thirst / with pails of pale blue water. // Who am I buying them for? for you / for her who shone so suddenly / in the flame of her cigarette lighter while, / smoking, she picked out the roses?" Bertolucci's poetry is discussed by Pasolini in his review of *Viaggio d'inverno*, 15: "Attilio ha fatto di tutto perché non si piangesse, di lui, e di ciò su cui lui piange, e l'ha fatto perfettamente, ogni sua poesia è un sorriso, egli si è premunito con suprema abilità poetica e con tutto un sistema ideologico non detto."

12. A. Bertolucci, "N. di giugno," 4: "you scratched yourself on the neck / and neckline with vermilion signs / which now wait only for the mild balsam / of kisses to outburn them / as if provoked by a lashing of roses . . . Such did Aphrodite / use to punish and gratify insolent Eros // a lost child in the dark gardens / of our Parma in an eternal June . . . "

13. A. Bertolucci, *Europeo*, February 4, 1984, 93.

14. A. Bertolucci, *La camera da letto*, 16: "pale roses from the garden destined to fall apart while still nubile, as they raise other peoples' children, winding their seasons so slow into a skein with her thin fingers."

15. A. Bertolucci, ibid., 92–93: "abandoned now like a rose petal or leaf to the violence of the spring rain, which doesn't last, the sun again alive on the flowers, the birds and eyelids of those who go to meet them."

16. A. Bertolucci, ibid., 106: "The sudden burning, the smell and smoke of mosquito-repellent are part of a ceremony celebrated by the mother her hair just untied over her robe of pink roses."

17. A. Bertolucci, ibid., 160–61: "In this brief passage to the month of easily plucked roses, in this period which will be razed bloodless from everyone's memory, they go out so early, they return so late, each one undertaking a different journey. . . . Will you too, reluctant, having gone out meet the adventure of a day, while destiny already grows short striping the pavement wet with sun behind those who sleep near you in the night in the adjoining rooms through a fiction of roses?"

18. P. V. Mengaldo, *PIN*, 750.

19. V. Sereni, "Concerto in giardino," *Tutte le poesie*, 5: "you mirror yourself in shadowy green: white and red torpedoes strike the asphalt of the Avus, trains wind to the southeast through fields of roses."

20. V. Sereni, *Tutte le poesie*, 87: "Often along twisting paths someplace in Algeria the location uncertain which the wind bites, your rain your sunshine all in one point between bitter brambles of the bitterest iron wire, thorn without a rose . . ."

21. See P. V. Mengaldo, "Ricorrenze e dominanti stilistiche," in P. Bertinotto and C. Ossola, eds., *La pratica della scrittura*, 133.

22. V. Sereni "Giardini," *Tutte le poesie*, 130: "Shadow, green shadow, wet-green and alive. There in the years where a tulip or a rose grows delirious over the vivid years never had." Emphasis mine.

23. V. Sereni, "Ancora sulla strada di Zenna," in P. Gelli and G. Lagorio, eds. *Poesia italiana del Novecento*, 2: 652: "minimi atti, i poveri / strumenti umani avvinti alla catena / della necessità, la lenza / buttata a vuoto nei secoli."

24. V. Sereni, "Traducevo Char," *Tutte le poesie*, 259: "the kiss fell upon the wound to redeem old injuries, years of prolonging. Soon it was clear, even to me, that a Judas was pressing against me or rather a whoring Thais masquerading as a forest rose."

25. V. Sereni, "Una visita in fabbrica," *Poesie*, 126: "The power which surrounds one with invitations, with blandishments: of playing fields, running tracks rolling lawns dripping flowerbeds and even the rose, summer heart, can proudly bloom there."

26. R. Char, cited by M. A. Caws, *Selected Poems*, xvi.

27. V. Sereni, "Un posto di vacanza," *Poesie*, 231, 233: "The shadow barely loosed itself beneath the wave: beautiful, a rocket, purple in the dark blue waving lobes like wings. Once pierced it overbrimmed in pallors, it was bleached white, disturbed by a small rose of blood inside the fisherman's basket, outside its element. . . . Loving is not always knowing ('youth is not always truth'), one finds this out late in life. A stone, they explain to us, is not as simple as it seems. A flower even less. The one branches out into a cathedral. The other a heaven on earth."

28. L. Sinisgalli, in V. Masselli and G. A. Cibotto, eds., *Antologia popolare di poeti del Novecento*, 220.

29. S. Ramat, *La poesia italiana 1903–1943*, 398.

30. L. Sinisgalli, "Naturalmente ogni cosa," *Vidi le muse*, 207: "Naturally every thing, even a stone, a rose, will suffice for my heart and the unceasing music of the horse-brushes jangled together in the stalls. This afternoon the birds are chirping like mice, the hen is picking off fleas on the balcony facing the valley."

31. G. Contini, "Ricordo lucano di Sinisgalli," *Ultimi elzeviri*, 402: "si rappresentava la poesia come a + bj, cioè la somma d'un numero reale e

d'un numero immaginario (j, l'unità immaginaria, è la radice quadrata di −1), un entità 'silvestre.'"

32. L. Sinisgalli, *Horror vacui,* 47: "FRONT AND BACK.— The front and back, the inside and out, of anything, like a stocking, a leaf, a hand. What is the back side of a rose?"

33. L. Sinisgalli, "La rosa di Padre Segneri," *L'indovino,* 27.

34. L. Sinisgalli, in R. Aymone, ed., *L'età delle rose,* 84: "questa magnifica flora mangereccia. Sono i fiori delle fave e delle zucche disseminate al posto delle antiche rose perfino nei cimiteri."

35. L. Sinisgalli, "Lucania," ibid.: "Beyond the sweet province of the Agri / You set out for the dreamed shores, / The obscure dead of one's family. / Your corpses have brought health / To the green of the gardens. / Fields of fava beans have spilled out / Over the fences: / Where the proud age of roses burned / Now goats pound the earth / In the days of drought."

36. L. Sinisgalli, *Vidi le muse,* 149.

37. L. Sinisgalli, "Ieri il mondo," in R. Aymone, ed., *L'età delle rose,* 208: "Yesterday the world was in celebration and as in a dream I pick a rose in the garden of a mosque, I light a large candle on the tomb of Giacomo Natta, I fill my pockets along the boulevards with lilies of the valley."

38. L. Sinisgalli, "Nenia," ibid., 114: "Daughter of my destiny grow like the rose in the garden. Sleep my daughter, sleep and grow, sleep like the wheat grows as soon as it is born."

39. L. Sinisgalli, "Zia Gerolomina," ibid., 139: "She didn't have my mother's tight lips or those sorrowful pupils. Aunt Gerolomina was fair as the roses."

40. L. Sinisgalli, "Santo Stefano 1946," *I nuovi campi elisi,* 109: "The Roman florists flaunt at the feet of statues the fatuous names of the rose. I grasp dry thorns upon the shore where once Love suddenly bloomed from Erebus, and I collect under my lapel the breath which each year grows weaker."

41. L. Sinisgalli, *L'età della luna,* 159: "un effimero gaudio"; 219: "La poesia prospera sulla disperazione"; 146: "Si può rovesciare il dogma di Valéry, si può dire che non possono esistere meraviglie se non fabbricate a caso."

42. As G. Steiner writes with reference to Valéry (*In Bluebeard's Castle,* 130): "[T]hat 'poetry of facts' and realization of the miraculous delicacies of perception in contemporary science already informs literature at those nerve-points where it is both disciplined and under the stress of the future."

43. L. Sinisgalli, "Davanti al sepolcro di Federico II nel Duomo di Palermo," *L'età della luna,* 16: "You didn't deny yourself the weak gesture, the shameful ecstasies, the throbbing in your throat, the tremor in your chest. For a wretched rose, for a crazed mosquito."

44. A. Pierro, "Curtelle a lu sóue," *Un pianto nascosto,* xx: "Something is scraping and drowned inside a glass, and you, frightened, think of a frozen rose struck against the mirrors of a broken drawer which is then reanimated in the lightning and dies."

45. A. Pierro, "Amore," ibid., 37: "Love, love stronger than the wind that uproots plants and makes the houses crumble and smooths out the mountains, give to all things a bit of this breath of the giant and then a light, even like the lightning that embraces the thorns among the roses."

46. A. Pierro, "A Rita," *Appuntamento,* 183: "Think of a swift river that here and there grows murky and entangled among uprooted plants and muddy roots, and then, with the fragrance of roses on the white of the altar grows clear, calm, and clean in the sea."

47. A. Pierro, "A mia figlia Rita," ibid., 26: "I feel your little hands play over my head weary with troubles, oh my Rita; and I think of a pond along an old road that a sweet wind has glanced with a shower of rose petals."

48. A. Pierro, "Ritorno dalla clinica," ibid., 189: "The hospital room smiled on me with the simplicity of young girls who, amazed, watch and see you in the blue of fields. Then the enchanted things, as in a waking sleep, submerged me in a sea of roses."

49. L. Anceschi, *Linea lombarda,* 22: "Una poesia, dunque, in cui il colore del suono nasce come dall'immagine, non l'immagine dal colore del suono, una poesia che non sia poesia dell'idea di poesia, e neppure una poesia *ante rem.* Oggetti intensi e carichi fino a fare dell'immagine simbolo."

50. R. Modesti, "Memoria di Berna," in L. Anceschi, ed., *Linea lombarda,* 97: "If the rose, reaching the threshold of the new year, gets caught up in the hinges (the old year stirs in its ashes the broken pots of indecisiveness where again I find the astonished hours of a disappointed soul) then I shall return to those streets."

51. G. Orelli, "Torcello," *L'ora del tempo,* 46: "The faded rose moves on, it is passing among burnt greens, it hesitates and, now undone, wants to drown. // There is one who has remembered it, as if for years, and waits for the Archangel to blow his cornet from the sea."

52. G. Orelli, "Di passaggio a Villa Bedretto," *Sinopie,* 19–20: "Some youths are shooting at paper roses. Others are dancing in the tavern. A

friar with a red beard wanders about, reminding those running numbers that another passion exists. Nobody is shouting. No one appears to be hurting."

53. G. Orelli, "Funerale in campagna," *Spiracoli,* 72: "but especially of how from a pasture a horse was watching us / thinking what? and of how from its dry rosebed a rose."

54. A. Zanzotto, "Elegia pasquale," in P. Gelli and G. Lagorio, eds., *Poesia italiana del Novecento,* 2: 815: "Windy Easter climbing up the crucifixes with all your desperate pallor, where is the crude prelude of the sun? and the rose the vague prophecy?"

55. A. Zanzotto, "Notte di guerra, a tramontana," *Selected Poetry,* 37: "From now on the harvest will not be / that sun which / tomorrow will safeguard / your advent from the treasures / of the winter roses / but it will leave voiceless the blue coral of the mountains, the amorous solitudes."

56. A. Zanzotto, "Là sul ponte," *Poesie (1938–1986),* 63: "There on the bridge of San Fedele where the evening abounds in cold oats and where the rain gathers all its soaked veils a blond girl has been standing since yesterday whose name is like a garland and who has lost a hand forever in order to greet a rose."

57. A. Zanzotto, "Indizi e luna," *Selected Poetry,* 6–7: "she who was child and sister from her house understands and sees the mountains' ancient ice, hugs to her breast the heart, frail as a rose."

58. A. Zanzotto, "Bucolica," *Vocativo,* 80–81: "And if the earth around you is stormy, if bitter peaks press down upon you, the rose, your friend beyond the centuries hangs upon the edge of grass-plump Arcadia. . . . That storm-cloud will bleed us, that damp thievery that paralyzes the fossil monster with the rose and bends marble: stasis and shock where our truth sinks into another."

59. A. Zanzotto, "Nuovi autunni," ibid., 43: "Beyond the thoughts destroyed by me, by my unstable and unformed self, shall I know the exuberance of the things that irradiate from my hands: the strategies of the squirrel or the crisp mantle of the woods or the known rose of heaven in whose reflection you, blond, return to me?"

60. A. Zanzotto, "Amo e sono infelice?" ibid., 89: "But I do not love and am not unhappy. Perhaps the sun swims towards another life, the blood murdered upon the thresholds opens the way to other roses, the cough, the spasm, the by now hidden celestial fury, is hidden in the blue."

61. A. Zanzotto, "Piccola elegia," ibid., 15: "We will say your buried name again on these slopes where the nuptial rose blooms in sheltered

glades, darkened by waters and mushrooms, insensible drippings, and June prolongs the celebration of the bees and zinnias."

62. A. Zanzotto, "Fuisse," ibid., 82: "Peace to you, peace to me good folks now without a dialect, without the pale hail of days gone by, without the light of the grape harvests, peace is extended to you along with a supreme torpor, the glow of meadows, the original ring of hills, the rose dispersed, the sun that bites between the tombs."

63. V. Hand, *Zanzotto*, 93.

64. A. Zanzotto, "Ecloga I: I lamenti dei poeti lirici," *IX Ecloghe*, 11: "But I am nothing, nothing more than your fragile nod of assent. Enclosed in you I will live like the droplet that shines in the rose and is dispersed before the shadow of the gardens, too long, grazes the earth."

65. A. Zanzotto, "Ecloga III," *IX Ecloghe*, 19: "Yes, this one is a stupid drunkenness, but it won't last. With the sweet saffron and sleep which appears beyond me like a wide fecund rose, I will soon regain the supreme the superfluous the blue sky."

66. A. Zanzotto, "Gli articoli di G.M.O.," *Idioma*, 13: "'They're coming through the gap' 'From the Women's Pass, from the Riviera of Roses, from Giotto's Hermitage' (geographical wonders dizzily unidentifiable and yet with the exhausting titillation of presence)."

67. F. Bandini, "Due santi di Dicembre," in E. Krupp and T. Rossi, eds., *Poesia italiana del Novecento*, 911: "where perhaps there is a branch that shudders in the zephyr / and after the flood the rose once again is in bloom: / thus winged hope comes toward you / in flight from the winter darkness."

68. U. Piersanti, "In tempi diversi sull'Appennino," *I luoghi persi*, 25: "lost in the most distant Appennines / a patch of roses and white flowers / and the petals are enflamed in the tender / light of the twilight descending // the roses exude their scent, they are the same / they have the same smell, they stand up the same / they cover the wells and walls of those years."

69. A. Giuliani, "Predelizioni," *I novissimi*, 82: "There is no remedy to our errors, to the smell of roses, nocturnal to the mind and to the air jealous. Love always blooms before knowledge, in a dark tremor."

70. D. Maraini, "Donne mie," in A. Porta, ed., *Poesia degli anni settanta*, 269: "against the one who betrays you without wanting to, against the woman idol who watches you seductive from a frame of wilted roses every morning and who makes you lost and mutilated even before you are born, scintillating with necklaces, but without any arms."

71. R. Barthes, *Writing Degree Zero*, 43.

11. The Feminine Voice, and Other Alibis

1. A. Gargani, *Lo stupore e il caso*, 40–41.
2. A. Soffici, cited by C. Benussi, *L'età del fascismo*, 84.
3. K. Burke, *Attitudes Toward History*, 30–33.
4. R. Barthes, "Semantics of the Object," *The Semiotic Challenge*, 188; emphasis mine.
5. S. Heaney, *The Redress of Poetry*, 6.
6. A. Battistini and E. Raimondi, "Retoriche e poetiche dominanti," 93.
7. S. Aleramo, "Rosa dell'anno," *Selva d'amore*, 82–83: "I recall a rose you bought me the next day.... I am alone but do not cry, save perhaps in my heart.... and tomorrow, somebody, if not I, shall buy themselves a rose."
8. S. Aleramo, "Sfoglio le rose," ibid., 58: "I pluck the roses which saw me weep and smile at you and then burn white, and I place my fingers between the petals as between your hands, sweet fresh petals I shall cast into the air singing quietly, my beloved, so you will not turn back...."
9. S. Aleramo, "Ricchezza," ibid., 28: "The tender heart of a rose, brownish, which I do not pluck.... The soul of the evening was crackling burnt. But the rose is soft, the hair, so much of it, loose on my tender neck."
10. D. Valeri, *Giardinetto*, 13.
11. D. Valeri, "Rose rosse," *Umana*, 105–6: "you were wearing three roses in your belt, three large roses, red as blood. I hugged you tight against my chest, the nape of your neck, the silken curls, the soft corners of your mouth.... And glowing in the shadows were your eyes, moist and burning, your very soul, and the three roses, the three red roses."
12. D. Valeri, "San Giovanni degli Eremiti," *Poesie scelte*, 23: "I see large roses, lazy and voluptuous, unclothe their folds of ill-born pallor, over the concise mirror of the pool, asleep."
13. D. Valeri, "Suor Gesuina," ibid., 26: "Having opened my eyes, I again saw the roses under the picture of the Madonna, and the curtain white with sun, and the sky, and the men, and the things...."
14. D. Valeri, "Davìd morente," ibid., 76: "But Bathsheba in the sweet night, shone naked as the moon, the odor of a nocturnal rose spread forth. // Lord, this is my end. My end is in thoughts of love."
15. D. Valeri, "Difficoltà del superlativo assoluto in poesia," 898: "la quale metaforica rosa è in realtà una bella figliola che con la sua freschezza e col suo buon odore fa perdere i sentimenti al voglioso poeta."
16. D. Valeri, "A Doride," *Poesie scelte*, 92: "First light: and you quietly

rest under your eyelids, under your breasts. In the uncertain dawn you uncover yourself and hide yourself, like the rose, naked and secret."

17. T. Tasso, *Gerusalemme liberata*, xvi, 14: "the rose . . . that half open and half closed, / the less it shows, the more beautiful it is."

18. D. Valeri, from *Calle del vento, Poesie scelte*, 59: "I just saw under a hellish sky burnt and broken by the flames of war a white, amorous rose open its corolla."

19. D. Valeri, "'Petit testament,'" *Poesie scelte*, 85–86: "I loved the day and night / . . . / the laughter and weeping of the things of nature. / I loved the grasses and the fruits of the earth, / the swallow and the rose of May."

20. D. Valeri, *Poesie vecchie e nuove* (1930): "Yesterday's roses, tired in the light, barely grazed by the airy fingers of time, and already bent over in sleep, the slow death of the earth—oh roses, farewell."

21. D. Valeri, "Al mio tempo fanciullo," from *Calle del vento, Poesie scelte*, 31: "In my boyhood spring was not the new sun, the new wind the new pink rose above the green thorn. It was the light or dark earth-worm which twisted itself furiously through the blackish, wet, smooth clod. . . ."

22. E. Morante, "Alibi," *Alibi*, 53: "I'd like to call you *Faithful*; but it doesn't suit you. Your grace changes the scandal which envelops you into a boast. You are the bee and you are the rose. You are the fortune which gives wings their colors and hair its curls. Your reverence is gracious as the rainbow."

23. E. Morante, "Canzone finale della stella gialla detta pure La Carlottina," in M. Cucchi and S. Giovanardi, eds., *Poeti italiani del secondo Novecento. 1945–1995*, 749: "I went out through the streets showing off / the yellow star of the Jews on my chest / like a rose."

24. A. Pozzi, "Le montagne," *Parole*, 331–32: "Like immense women they occupy the evening: . . . Mothers. And branches of stars stand up on their foreheads, move away from their vast eyes: at the extreme limit of waiting, the dawn is born and rosebeds bloom out of barren wombs."

25. A. Pozzi, "Pan," ibid., 319: "And fresh rose petals make a garland for our table and they are whole forests green with chestnuts blown in the wind of their locks."

26. D. Menicanti, "Fancy," in E. Krumm and T. Rossi, eds., *Poesia italiana del Novecento*, 945–46: "I own a woods. A grand woods I do not own / and the most beautiful flowerbeds / that grow with talking leaves flowers / things. Colors of butterflies / go dancing and at the roses they stop / and entertain applause. At my feet I have a white sea / full of games and manes, up above the sky / which everybody owns with moons and suns / and sites of clouds and thunder / lightning opened up and double rainbows."

27. C. Benussi, *L'età del fascismo*, 95. Also, 95: "[W]hile adhering to the theoretic lines of a Marxist research, especially attentive to the problems of praxis, [Banfi] had for some time approached the phenomenology of Edmund Husserl."

28. L. Baldacci, in M. L. Spaziani, *Poesie*, 14.

29. M. L. Spaziani, "Ricordo una stagione," *Poesie*, 113: "Yesterday upon returning there no more / than a day seemed to have passed. / The north wind thrashed furiously around us. / Against the gate, intact, there remained / one of my ancient roses, gnawed to bits."

30. M. L. Spaziani, "La stella del libero arbitrio," in A. Gentili and C. O'Brien, eds., *The Green Flame*, 218: "In a dream someone discovers you, you are a mystic rose shaded in form and scent beyond the limits of turquoise, the red blood of a thousand Tamerlaines, the Hippogriff who points to disturbing moons."

31. M. L. Spaziani, *Poesie*, 91: "The roses which the gray of the Appian Way gave you one distant January, amid whirlpools and starships, are now consumed by the wild mint. Only in the painted flame, infinite desert, memory, the restless ruin blooms with flowers in inhabited heavenly castles."

32. M. L. Spaziani, "La prigione," ibid., 54: "Like a dog I nuzzle you and paw you, I put you on like a glove and turn you inside out, you have sharp edges, heavenly glows, you are the rain of roses which suffocates me, the anchor and rope-ladder of spaces and a muzzle and a whistle, and malaria." Emphasis mine.

33. M. L. Spaziani, "Il fumo che saliva dalle nostre," ibid., 99–100: "Find those mysterious hieroglyphs which no longer sing for me, rediscover in the vanished pentagram the square signs of the Gregorian, you who invent the knowledge of the rose, the swallow, the wind from sounds not yet uttered." Emphasis mine.

34. M. L. Spaziani, "Per un catalogo di un amico," ibid., 56: "Paint the multi-petaled rose in your garden and filter the word out of its essence, oh Dario. The house of the prophet, it is said, has many thresholds while all of knowledge fits within the Syllabary." Emphasis mine.

35. M. L. Spaziani, "La landa silenziosa dove il rantolo," ibid., 97: "Snapped ropes, lemurs, the wakeful conscience of the night, dogs in starving hordes were roving through time, the masters and servants of a law which was theirs alone when the world first knew the empire of the rose undisputed under the sun."

36. M. L. Spaziani, "Ponte Abramo," ibid., 116: "The dream is higher now that its vast meadows are enclosed in the gray of the sky, a silent

curtain over the tragedy of summer. The ashen leaves turn the mill in the wind of the ponds and the rose more modest is enveloped in shadows where the wall is shored up."

37. M. L. Spaziani, "Contrerime," ibid., 162: "Face overwhelmed by two yellow roses amid cracks burned by the bitterest of brine. Timid broken moons, one day you shall be a beacon, shining upon the waves at my back."

38. M. L. Spaziani, "Dopo la tempesta," ibid., 146: "It flows away and carries us calmly to hell among pyrotechnic joys and foggy disasters. A rose of blood floats in the current. A bridge sends a greeting to the poet of the stars."

39. M. L. Spaziani, "Frammenti negli anni," *Geometria del disordine*, 84: "The shadow of too many verses / is heavy, it crushes the roses. / I would like to discover them myself, / call them only 'things,' / like babies in the sunshine / who play turned over on their backs / confusedly in search of words."

40. M. L. Spaziani, "IV," *Geometria del disordine*, 92: "Mute entities of time, distances / (but from whom? from what?). The turlews tremble, as do the rooms / woven together and then pulled / apart by the dances of / rays over the heart of the rose."

41. M. L. Spaziani, "Quell'uomo-stella . . . ," in F. Pansa and M. Bucchich, eds., *Poesie d'amore*, 60: "That man-star so unreachably close, nebulous mystery to be won in reverse, final flame of a windy rose of March, petal that doesn't fall, that dies with the root."

42. E. Clementelli, "La breve luce," in P. Gelli and G. Lagorio, eds., *Poesia italiana del Novecento*, 2: 897: "The time of faith and youth is over. Love sped quickly to its lying end, the wind which deceived the last roses revealed in the gun-site its fiery claws."

43. G. Bemporad, "A una rosa," in P. Gelli and G. Lagorio, eds., *Poesia italiana del Novecento*, 2: 981: "Bend over the edge of your secret, oh rose in diaphanous dress, insurmountable temple which in vigilance of love keep me, I know not of what reliefs is composed your beauty."

44. P. Volponi, "Le catene d'oro," *Poesie e poemetti*, 92: "Oh wealth of our home / the Scalcucci's Filippini's Volponi's / all made of malt and bricks / with the well, the roses, the gutters, / that passes the years at your scale, / on the calendars of water and wind / that bring each event back / with your comment as copyist."

45. P. Volponi, "L'Appennino contadino," *Poesie e poemetti*, 125: "The morning rose that is caught in the briars is the only notice, but its splendor is brief, it lasts until the moment when a sea thrush flies over the ice. . . .

The spring rain uncovers among the clay planters seeds of geranium and rose, but it deceives the earth and carries into the house a subtle malady. . . . Here the tradition of trousseaus is for the safekeeping of family sorrows more than of family deceits; the saints and rosaries pass on death."

46. P. Volponi, "La vergine," ibid., 65: "The white stones are your shoulders the trees your stature; it is your throat that beats if a rose moves unseen in the garden."

47. L. Frezza, "La farfalla si stacca," *La farfalla e la rosa*, 72: "The butterfly parts from the envied rose that lives a morning wrapped in its truth."

48. L. Frezza, "La casa," ibid., 118, 123: "They tell me that the white roses bloomed early when I was born, leaned against the garden grate. . . . By now things hurt below my touch, the white and dark blue handwoven blankets, the plates with the borders of gold and enamel roses."

49. L. Frezza, "Venere," in F. Pansa and M. Bucchich, eds., *Poesie d'amore*, 132: "The fixity of roses the faithfulness of the yellow fragile heart the beauty of the solemn pace of the never changing the accumulation of luminous layers over deceit oh how to warn you Adonis?"

50. G. Leto, "Solo che sul divano," in E. Faccioli, ed., *Nuovi poeti italiani 1*, 163: "That a privileged light fall alone upon the sofa, that the diaphanous flask on the shelf have a burning rose and, posed, it trembles in my mind and is confused like a reflected image in deep waters . . ."

51. G. Leto, "Più che non sia la mimosa," in ibid., 183: "A paler ochre than the mimosa, more powdery than the lily and the hyacinth perched on the coat-of-arms, more purple-blue than the anemone, than my aspiring jasmine than the camellia jealous of her, of the flawless flower which almost by chance is budding from the large pot, arriving at the railing, the carefree rose reputed to be haughty."

52. M. Detienne, *Dionysos Slain*, 50, citing Ovid, *Metamorphoses*, ll. 731–39.

53. R. Copioli, "L'albero di Giuda, al puntone," *Il furore delle rose*, 104: "Having entered, it was a shade, the softness, the grasses and the hellebores, green Christmas roses that sweeten the tombs."

54. R. Copioli, "Rosa centifolia," ibid., 38–39: "A hundred-petaled rose wherever the sea is / in flames, wings. Irradiates / the clouds like berries. Infused in it the sun. / Descending / on its silken forms"; "Hundred-petaled rose of black steel / trembled in the milky / palm of my moons, rise up. / Ascent of petals against lances."

55. C. Olson, "Projective Verse," *Il Verri* 1 (1961): 9–23. For Olson, writes Eniko Bollobás (*Charles Olson*, 59–60), "The poem is a field where

intensive events may occur without redundancy; but 'abundance' (R. Duncan) and 'generosity' (Whitehead) can only characterize space that is open, kinetic (it derives its energy from the tension of aperiodic rhythm (Shrödinger), and composed of material that—as medium—strives not toward completeness but toward wholeness."

56. R. Sanesi, "Rapporto informativo," *Rapporto informativo,* 29: "your silence / perhaps is only scorn, as if it were no topic if you speak to me / of time (time you do not have, the roses . . .) . . . . /—jeune femme en forme de fleur . . ."

57. R. Sanesi, "Pavane per una gatta defunta," *La differenza,* 30: "Friends offered a rose, burnt an incense. Allow me in this brief interval a light, now and in the hours between the first leaves."

58. R. Sanesi, "Busto di Giano in un anfiteatro," *Rapporto informativo,* 110: "Vines of roses and pollen, and over / the amphitheater the moon too watches the mice as they scurry: the theme / and the reprise of a theme, to be there for everyone, to know / that thought and language have a hidden center. [. . .] the roses / in buds by now ripped apart and buried."

59. R. Sanesi, "Capricornio," ibid., 109: "Roses of ice explode at the windows, and an incredible / and empty earth poisons the trees . . . "

60. R. Sanesi, *Carte di transito,* 118.

61. R. Sanesi, "Falsamente dedicata," *Rapporto informativo,* 75: "This was your realm: the impulse. / The idea of a rose or a pebble. And your non-proceeding from the nothingness / of a thing that is born of a thing, by chance, / was mediated each time in a ring: / rhymes and rocks and creatures were the duration in this realm."

62. M. Bettarini, "Scherzose / con spine," in F. Pansa and M. Bucchich, eds., *Poesie d'amore,* 90: "if by giving a lot I receive a lot, what will I get from a little? it will give something faded and worm-eaten, it will give a discolored rose."

63. P. Cavalli, "Da scalfittura diventare abisso," *Poesie,* 16: "From a scratch to become an abyss, from a fragile membrane to become the tight cord of inconstant vibrations. The season of the great hunts, as for noble birds of prey, is beginning, and the rose will watch its petals fall one by one."

64. E. A. Fontecedro, "Desiderio," in F. Pansa and M. Bucchich, eds., *Poesie d'amore,* 189: "If away from the leaves in the wind on the roses a smattering of air if in the breast of the mossy grasses the humour wet with foresty parts. . . . I shall not measure brief defendable spaces starting from the stars down."

65. D. Lupi, "Cantando l'incontro," in L. Di Nola, ed., *Poesia femmin-*

ista italiana, 136: "my budding rose had its natural space a late bloomer with respect to the right season women with different eyes were already singing of virginity . . . . and between our legs the rose was freed of its infancy forever."

66. M. Boeri, "Festa in giardino," in M. L. Spaziani, ed., *Sette poeti del Premio Montale*, 15: "In the side of the rose the image is run aground, it slips, it ignites in flames like a bride at the altar: and transmuted it nourishes the deep mine of its darkness, it raises up the thirst of its measure by reconducting the free, created veil back into the pure mask."

67. B. Tarozzi, *La buranella*, 100: "I saw some roses in a vase: white roses, plastic roses. Who knows how long they've been there! I like them because they are not real: they are imagined, different, indestructible."

12. The Rose of Advent

1. M. Luzi, *Discorso naturale*, 16.

2. L. Aragon, in P. Auster, ed., *The Random House Book of Twentieth-Century French Poetry*, 248: "I shall never forget the lilacs or the roses nor those two loves whose loss we have incurred: bouquets of the first day, lilacs, Flanders lilacs, soft cheeks of shadow rouged by death—and you, bouquets of the retreat, delicate roses, tinted like far-off conflagrations: roses of Anjou."

3. J. Roubaud, "Lire *Le Crè-Coeur* en 1997," 74.

4. L. Aragon, in J. Cortázar, *Around the Day in Eighty Worlds*, 210: "Let them disembowel their toys and sack the roses / I remember I remember how everything took place."

5. G. Salvemini, citing G. Mazzini, *Mazzini*, 23.

6. F. Fortini, "Poesie degli anni cinquanta," 8045.

7. E. Raimondi, *Le poetiche della modernità italiana*, 69.

8. G. Noventa, "Gò lassà cascar," in P. V. Mengaldo, ed., *PIN*, 638–39: "I dropped a rose in the sea, so distracted was I! Then I looked for it a while, and, as I watched, every drop carried a rose, the whole sea was perfumed. // Oh, one cannot carry away the perfume of the sea! Perhaps a rose was worth more to me. Maybe ingenuous men are worth more than a poet. I am a friend of everyone, And everything. But not of myself."

9. G. Noventa, "'Na rosa xé sbrissada," *Opere complete*, 2:70: "A rose bloomed in your chest, Olga, I would like to pursue that rose, but I don't know how. // I don't know how because I already have my own thorns, and, Olga, these thorns of mine, you don't want to pull them out."

10. G. Noventa, "O bela e bona amiga . . . ," ibid., 2:78: "Oh lovely and

good friend, who have set your eyes on me, I want to give you a rose, Because you have set your eyes on me. // One rose, for your eyes, might not be enough. You deserve a whole garden, Because you have given yourself to me. // But since I have no gardens, I have stolen this flower, It is worth your kisses, believe it, Because I have stolen it."

11. P. P. Pasolini, "Ploja tai cunfìs," *Bestemmia*, 1:15: "Lad, the Heavens rain upon / the hearthstones of your town, / on your face of rose and honey, / the cloudy month is born."

12. P. P. Pasolini, "Ploja fòur di dut," ibid., 1083: "Spirit of a lad, the Heavens rain down on the hearths of a dead town: in your face of shit and honey, a rainy month is born." The contrast could not be greater with the hope of his early days, when Pasolini taught the *rosa rosae* of Latin grammar by showing the students the plants themselves. See A. Zanzotto, cited in L. Betti, *Pasolini: Cronaca giudiziaria, persecuzione, morte*, 47: "Stringimento di cuore al pensiero degli entusiasmi di quei tempi, col motto 'educazione e democrazia,' che tanti giovani insegnanti (bicicletta, un solo pasto al giorno, stanza non riscaldata) condividevano. Attivizzare perfino l'intirizzata grammatichetta latina, far diventare rose vere il *rosa rosae*, così ingenuo, di quelle grammatiche. Lui faceva il giardinetto nel cortile della scuola e insegnava il nome latino delle piante."

13. P. P. Pasolini, "Lettera ai corinti," *L'usignolo della Chiesa Cattolica*, 107: "And bloodied youth, their sex pure as the sun watches with painful wonder its rose consumed . . ."

14. P. P. Pasolini, "La rabbia," *Le poesie*, 306–8: "Just a bit of red, splendid and grim, half-hidden, bitter, with no joy: a rose. Humbly hanging from the adolescent branch, as if on a gun sight, the timid remainder of a shattered paradise. . . . I give up all action . . . I only know that in this rose I stop to breathe, in a single wretched instant, the odor of my life, of my mother. . . . I was imprisoned in my life, as in the mother's womb, in this burning odor of a humble dew-dropped rose. But I was struggling to escape. . . . The struggle ended with victory. My private existence is no longer trapped between the petals of a rose,—a house, a mother, a breathless passion. It is public."

15. P. P. Pasolini, "Poesia in forma di rosa," *Poesia in forma di rosa*, 51: "It is a carnal rose of pain, with five roses incarnate, cancers of rose in the first rose: in the beginning there was Pain."

16. P. P. Pasolini, *Calderón*, 67: "Yes, that thing you believe to be in the sublime form of a pine cone or a magnificent rose, which opens in the morning, and with which the husband impregnates his wife. . . ." Rosaura and Anna Rosa, protagonists in *Calderón*, are, like Pascoli's "Rosa," a

"paradigm of lyrical narration" (Varese) and probable homage to Leopardi.

17. P. P. Pasolini, *Poesia in forma di rosa*; Franco Fortini, *La poesia delle rose* in *Una volta per sempre*, 263–69. See U. Eco, "Postille a *Il nome della rosa*," on the proliferation of symbolic associations for the rose.

18. F. Fortini, *Memorie per dopo domani*, 27: "The 'roses' in fact hide the 'woeful valley of the abyss' and, at the same time, they point to it."

19. F. Fortini, "La rosa sepolta," *Una volta per sempre*, 41: "But the most destroyed of destinies is freedom the buried rose's fragrance eternal. Where our faithful joy shone, someone else will again find the wreaths of flowers."

20. F. Fortini, "Via Santa Marta," *Una volta per sempre*, 111: "The branch of dry olive was hanging the live blackberry shimmered with red high in the sun and the rose by the cypress. Then the heavenly star over the iron lance of the cross and the three peaks. And where evening breathed out its air the city was a cloud. . . ." Other examples are "In lingua mortua," 73: "in the city of Florence and I cannot forget the green of San Miniato or the olive mornings, the bitter roses, the washed stone pavement, the veins of cypress on the Mensola . . ."; "In una strada di Firenze," 118: "On a street in Florence is a door facing a stone courtyard. Ancient graffiti are on the walls: Hercules and Hydra, Love, crowns of leaves carved laurels and rose-beds. . . . Surely those clouds pass within me as well, those walls stand inside me. And so I look and look at that silence, the crowns of ancient ivy, and I believe a rose is pausing within the stone"; "Ai poeti giovani," 141: "We know then that the rose is a rose the word a thing, pain a discourse: that the voice most alone harmonizes many cries, that each heart recalls how many souls it has penetrated"; "Prologo ai vicini," 148: "So here I stand and from here I bitterly speak. What does it matter if they do not like me what does it matter if I do not like them either. Some of the mind's roses dare to smile at the snow."

21. F. Fortini, "Il museo storico," *Una volta per sempre*, 236: "They will see with pity and study what joined us to our enemies, we will seem enemies to ourselves. They will look out of museum windows to high gardens and our painted rose upon the walls."

22. C. De Michelis, "Il coraggio di parlare delle rose," 74, refers to the rose in Fortini's poetry as a "simbolo radioso e felice, ostinatamente contrapposto, nel suo estivo sapore, alla desolata solitudine di un inverno dei sentimenti e degli umani valori." A. Berardinelli, *Franco Fortini*, 105, calls the poem "una perfetta figura di antitesi inconciliata, un'immagine di

negazione irriducibile e di violenta proiezione utopica." See also R. Luperini, *La lotta mentale,* 23: "La rosa è la rivoluzione e il desiderio inconscio."

23. F. Fortini, *Una volta per sempre,* 263: "Oh against the flowers open to the mist how sweet the struggle of the bee!"

24. F. Fortini, "From Wall to Wall," *Paesaggio con serpente,* 16–17: "because if you look from the opposite side if you turn your back on the prayer of the painter to his scapular of roses.... you a painter, austere clever irony of the mind that kneels down to look where blindly a rose is breathing and another already bears the thorn."

25. F. Fortini, "27 aprile 1935," ibid., 20: "But what of the roses? I was asking the white roses, the yellow and white roses, for love."

26. F. Fortini, "Per l'ultimo dell'anno 1975 ad Andrea Zanzotto," ibid., 39: "Here we stand to hear sentence. And we know there will be no sentence. We are swept downwards, into ourselves, one by one. How beautiful you are, oh rose of Sharon! Jerusalem who will have gathered us up. Oh how brilliant your nonexistence." See, also in *Paesaggio,* "Then I Shall Begin...," 102: "And yet: the clamourous speech, the sonorous language of the Italians will not be able to help me. Have we not known this for many years? that a rose is not a rose, that water is not water, that words lead to other words and every thing to some other thing, equally estranged from the true?"

27. R. Scotellaro, "Invito," *Marherite e rosolacci,* 100: "Girl, the tender grass I taste in my mouth is no softer than you who let down your breasts. You come from these drowned cities, is it really true that they make roses on the walls?"

28. R. Scotellaro, "Scherzetti per M.," ibid., 115–16: "You already have sufficient life / You the thorn and the rose / Every thing for you sheds its leaves / And vows to you its love. // ... // And you are this sky / Always and never mine."

29. R. Scotellaro, "Ora che ti ho perduta," *È fatto giorno,* 143: "Now that I have lost you like a precious stone / I know I never had you neither thorn nor rose: / You weren't standing at the base of the box that would have been enough / to hang out clothes and blankets to air, to see you back in your place again / with pain and your eyes uncertain in the mass of things." This poem is dated June 17, 1953, just before Scotellaro's death.

30. N. Risi, "Lettera," in L. Anceschi, ed., *Linea lombarda,* 92: "I have a picture of you among my papers and the books we bought: it was the happy time of the roses, April May June, beyond the veranda window swans were inhabiting your lake"

31. N. Risi, "Situazione," in ibid., 93: "the dark days, like rain that washes a cemetery, have left my land deserted, more fierce the tint of the roses, the peace not to be trusted."

32. N. Risi, "La colonna infame," *Poesie scelte*, 73: "Judges of gloom: a man is not a dynamo every man burns his limited flame when he is not burned by you (look at Grimau, his throat slit, or Babel with a rose exploding on his forehead and Lumumba with his bones broken as from an automobile accident) men who stand accused within a heavy silence."

33. Fortini's notes to his poem (*Una volta per sempre*, 368) begin, "In a park of roses and couples one attends and participates in the repetition of a rite. A figure of askesis and negation is changed into a young witch for a bloody rite." Thus we have the "figures in the park."

34. G. Raboni, "Celeste," *Nel grave sogno*, 13: "Free, I grow fond of the former scenery, peeling chaise lounges, clay flowerpots overturned, and where behind the sickly roses one divines the curve of the earth, the sky-blue of Lucca or Pontedera . . . "

35. G. Raboni, "Anagramma," *A tanto caro sangue*, 130: "Rose of slobber that blooms in the flame of trifles, metamorphosis in alum of a long, wet agony, it should not I think put on a bad face among your collection of little deaths—animal this time, not human."

36. G. Raboni, "Maggio 1992," *Corriere della sera*, February 3, 1993, 6: "What harm have we done you, what contrition must we pay in order to belong to you like cells to a cancer, like inert rose petals upon a rose full of thorns? Bloodily, my obscene country, you procure evidence, the relics of criminal archeology for the experts of other millennia . . . "

37. G. Majorino, "Baldorie!" in G. Luzzi, *Poeti della linea lombarda*, 145: "18 minutes / to make love at a rate / of 7 3/4% / after leaving the Girl of the Roses / with a kiss at her door the Fiancé who saw / a man turn a woman / against the wall of via Ostiglia / the woman doorkeeper opens it up for just 4000 / lire, woman-grandma-fetus-hot thing / with a snout that reads 'turn out the light.'"

38. F. Fortini, *Il movimento surrealista*, 99.

39. N. Balestrini, "Il sasso appeso," in A. Giuliani, ed., *I novissimi*, 159: "Passing the fin over the water's surface people shouldn't be encouraged to do it after she arrived (let's watch them) all dressed in (while) with a white bunch of roses there were still masts upon the beach . . ."

40. N. Balestrini, "Osservazioni sul volo degli uccelli," ibid., 143: "dry off well in the warm air, and your fake nose, still barely breathable between swollen walls, he looks for the shoe, the thing (but will it have the shape of the rose?) . . ."

41. N. Balestrini, "Non smettete," in A. Porta, ed., *Poesia degli anni settanta*, 128–29: "a rose out of a green light to mark a profile in a straight line at the feet of which it is about to grow disheartened over her / . . . . / invisible actions under the clothes almost unravelled by the sun like the petal of a rose as you have always dreamed it to be."

42. A. Porta, "Balene delfini bambini," in T. Harrison, ed., *The Favorite Malice*, 290: "when the rose is the naming of the rose / a new rose is born from the name rose."

43. A. Porta, "La rose," in A. Porta, ed., *Poesia degli anni settanta*, 44, 178–79: "the rose gathers its own fruits in peace / within in safety the mouth with leaves / the body shed its skin in the Sunday gardens / . . . . / to the curled hair rabid puppies / the deceitful defenses sniff the rose / unfastened vestment silver bells / the inside of the mouth full of the mind / the splotched rose causes the neighbors to worry / the small breasts of her girlfriends cause her fingers to tremble / because she's gone away because she has hidden / she gets out of bed to contemplate sleep / her girlfriends furious to strip her naked / she confides in her mother that she approves of the abstinences / she sees a dog in the dream coupling with her sticking to the rose feeding on its thorns."

44. A. Porta, "Salomé, le ultime parole," in L. Ballerini, ed., *Shearsmen of Sorts*, 598: "god of wind / god of the mountain / where all the gods died / where blood takes the shape of the rose / I shall quit looking into your mirrors, Mother / I shall look at things."

45. A. Porta, *Melusina*, 19: "A woman sends us these gifts a forest carpeted with strawberries and blueberries where rabbits run and roosters crow and deer of delicious meat stop to eat the roses. This is the Age of Gold, of gentle sweet rains, of skys woven with jasmine."

46. E. Pagliarani, "VI," *Epigrammi ferraresi*, 23: "What if a plant (a rose) were to say: 'I no longer want to remain on earth' (or a tuberous carrot, or even the couch grass, an infesting weed)."

47. R. Luperini, ibid, 8.

48. See G. Pontiggia and E. Di Mauro, eds. *La parola innamorata: I poeti nuovi 1976–1978*.

49. G. Ciabatti, "Sentinella con l'elmo stretto," *Preavvisi al reo*, 48: "The morning lifts up slow roses, slender peach trees tangle in the glow, the circle of iron that splits the forehead is dissolved in the air. The head is a light dispersed, sight is a dripping fog. If only you could see me now, as the cry of love rises within me, the pursuit of life."

50. F. Fortini, in G. Ciabatti, *Niente di personale*, xi.

51. G. Ciabatti, "Autodifesa," *Preavvisi al reo*, 60: "If it is true that we are

inhuman it is not simply because we ignored the tribute of a bunch of roses, but also because by completing our share of the obligations we did not ask for gifts."

52. E. Sanguineti, "Per una rosa," *Senzatitolo,* 135: "rose of the red Partisan flames. . . . the day has blossomed, and the night was dark, but if winter was icy cold, before, spring then bloomed with red roses, and the rose shines at the top."

13. THE OTIOSE ROSE

1. A. Wilden, *The Rules Are No Game,* 256.
2. A. Wilden, ibid., 259.
3. R. Luperini, "Una nuova razionalità?" in F. Cavallo and M. Lunetta, eds., *Poesia italiana della contraddizione.,* 297–302.
4. E. Cacciatore, "XLI," *Graduali,* 69: "It is autumn and the shouts grow fewer and fewer / The travertine marble has the softness of a rose / The death notices are kept in good order / Freedom is an obligatory gesture."
5. E. Cacciatore, "VI," ibid., 84: "They themselves bizarre their faces the usual locations / Here I am that's for sure—and I keep wandering elsewhere / Party-pooper the truth don't tell it listen / To the unheard and enjoy in every farewell a beginning / It is not a scattering of ashes over a field of roses."
6. E. Cacciatore, "VI," ibid., 114: "Path of acacias and shriveled roses / A rolling truth in the depths of this May / Ancient tombs our voice fills up / The happiness that invented this journey / They search in eternity for the impious delights / And high above, those flowers, aphorism to a sage / Where a wasp bears the weight of a ray of light."
7. E. Cacciatore, "IV," *La restituzione,* 81–82: "But that tale of situations or accents / They have the same fibres as a fake rose. / The provisional manner of decisive moments / . . . . / This is the clear proof once one has fled the swarm / You are not moved, but what matter feelings? / In your mind a true rose has bloomed // Let it still be alive when every fibre is extinguished."
8. E. Villa, "Pezzo 1941," *Opere poetiche,* 50: "and but as long as the ozone and rain at the edge of earth may speak to the roads with nickel-plated poplars about ideal jubilees, about communism fresh as a rose."
9. A. Tagliaferri, in E. Villa, ibid., 17.
10. E. Villa, "Sì, ma lentamente," ibid., 150: "it is probably the new, the

other original sin. god, remain in my heart, my love, my goodness. or the rest of you who know what rose what rose but what rose are you waiting for?"

11. G. Goffredo, "Dannati a sperare," in A. Berardinelli, ed., *Nuovi poeti italiani 2*, 47: "The roses which hang from the balcony give no scent to the involuntary road where I ponder. Our future is over, the days wearily dragged along, with no desire then in the evening to sleep."

12. G. Guglielmi, "Découplage II," in F. Cavallo and M. Lunetta, eds., *Poesia italiana della contraddizione*, 127–28: "He types into his marble of black letters / it is only a rose / it is still movement / one believed in the existence of something / but once that has happened / the silence envelops him."

13. L. Budigna, "Episodio," in P. Chiara and L. Erba, eds., *Quarta generazione*, 150: "A Christmas constrained to the smoke between the andirons and open to the senseless flame of men who are enemies in the mud, against the darkness. In that amazing rose, a face."

14. A. Rosselli, "Les auberges ont fermé leur clefs," *Primi scritti 1952–1963*, 36: "The hotels have locked their keys, the internal walls are roses, their petals are repeated as they cross their hands (She went mad, she couldn't find her husband, he became dead)."

15. A. Rosselli, "Il soggiorno in inferno," *Antologia poetica*, 42: "The sojourn in Hell was divine in nature but the plaques of providence roared out retrograde names and the experiences of the past grew more voracious and the hanging moon too no longer melancholy and the roses of the garden were slowly fading in the sweet sun. If I passed quickly by the garden it penetrated me to my bones with its sweetness, if I sang suddenly the sun would sink. Thus it wasn't the divine nature of things that shook my vigorous soul but it was melancholy."

16. A. Rosselli, "Con tutta la candida presunzione," *Antologia poetica*, 69: "With all the candid presumption of my young age I established inventories. Roses crowned my togs and light shone through an almost cruel eye. // The rule of honor was inexperience! Adjust yourself according to the right moment exclaimed the illiterate one!"

17. A. Rosselli, "Risposta," *Antologia poetica*, 87: "The pillow rough when you don't sleep, a rosette on the garter-belt; the straits of difficulty. To be in God's hands I put my hands together, the tips lightened by an internal civic pressure."

18. A. Rosselli, "Impromptu," in S. Meccati, ed., *La poesia in mostra*, 22–23: "I add by necessity that in my dream it was a whole vision of your

painting, not of a rose's difficulty but as if it were, in the existence of here, the laurel which, being moral, had enjoined me to tell myself that I am among the grand and yet I hide even what is small."

19. A. Rosselli, "Cercare nel rompersi della sera un nascondiglio," *Antologia poetica*, 106: "you set your eyes on the furrow of spring / bewitching a world of beasts with tears / of glass which did not fall but grew entangled / in your sleep entirely of roses."

20. A. Rosselli in T. Kemeny and C. Viviani, eds., *I percorsi della nuova poesia italiana*, 85: "With the disease in your mouth a fright for the scarecrows faded roses and there are tiny splotches on the wall in the hayloft of your thoughts: and with what color do you make your final brushstroke?"

21. G. Bateson, "Afterword," in J. Brockman, ed., *About Bateson*, 237.

22. L. Re, "Variazioni su Amelia Rosselli," 135. The citation continues: "The stubborn persistence of this personal voice, this lyric 'I' that wants to be listened to and especially to be loved (thus placing herself provocatively on the wake of a masculine tradition of the love lyric that includes Petrarch's *Rime* and Shakespeare's *Sonnets*—both extremely important for the formation of Rosselli's lyric) is the apparently regressive element that leaves the critics perplexed."

23. G. Agamben, *Infancy and History*, 104. In contrast, Re's erudite approach—she enlists Lacan, Foucault, Kristeva, Culler, Felman, De Certeau, Benveniste, Frye—loses sight of the author by reifying the smallest, atomized units of texts. Thus Rosselli is compared, because of her use of figures of doubling and repetition, to Gertrude Stein. Moreover the critic posits the Italian language's nonmystical quality in parallel with Rosselli's pursuit of her Italian "secular" father and, conversely, the mystical engagement of recovering her English heritage, language, and mother.

24. F. Squatriti, "Quarta categoria," *La natura del desiderio*, 26: "Thus there were so many roses all unified in the effort to bloom that it overwhelmed me."

25. F. Squatriti, "Canto sinistro," *La natura del desiderio*, 30: "But what type of gift is this sun that does not disarm in the season programmed now for some time? In the fine air the innumerable leaves of the garden to whom the last scarlet rose denounces the miracle of faith. I cultivate the desire for peace in order to find again the root argument."

26. F. Squatriti, "Cerimoniale," *La natura del desiderio*, 51: "Nowadays it is considered rude to be poor. . . . only nausea mitigates the pure white-

ness of the rose. There is no rule you can cling to fornicate without complaint."

27. G. Scalise, "Il sole carica le nuvole su un fianco," in T. Broggiato, ed., *Canti dell'universo,* 130: "the autumns know that roses and petals are gathered unto drainpipes and ditches: it is useless to look for them in the rational part of the world."

28. G. Scalise, "se iniziasse un tempo," in T. Broggiato, ed., *Canti dell'universo,* 134: "they speak of the center of the earth where impulses flourish whereas roses have absurd limitations."

29. G. Scalise, "I segni," in A. Berardinelli and F. Cordelli, eds., *Il pubblico della poesia,* 265: "The heavens whipped by hurry proceed with rigorous logic. The prize is a vanquished soul. Astuteness alone remains. The beginning of the path which leads to walls of roses, and it is thus that constancy becomes memory."

30. V. Zeichen, "Un giorno di rosso trionfo," *Il pubblico della poesia,* 182: "As imitator I take advantage of a pause and I insert myself into the probings, I request obsolete roses in order to give them to MARY. From an unraveling of reserve we heard that Duccio had brought MARY a libertine donation with the above-mentioned roses rejected on the first assault."

31. V. Zeichen, "Il sogno d'una agonia," *Museo interiore,* 48: "I exult in your death. So astutely pale that the rose is probably ablaze with your blush; or it imitates in complexion the rouge of your blood.... As you lay dying I hear the conspirators who swear loyalty to that floral motif which inflates the metaphor and propagates itself on the decorative trellises; it embarrasses the gardeners at pruning-time."

32. P. M. Forni, "IX," *Stemmi,* 23: "To break the cookie / of some word / dip it in milk / see if it drips / a verse or something, / in the mouth it goes / to see if what touches me / is the thorn or the rose."

33. A. Lumelli, "Felicità obbligata," in T. Harrison, ed., *The Favorite Malice,* 186–87: "oh didactic poems respectful poems where an I is formed may the air hide it away.... the eye that flies unbridgeable eye that which has grown faint in the head, so tired, is not wandering sleep the rose its foam, but is us made men."

34. A. Lumelli, "Trattatello incostante," in R. Perrotta, *Altro Polo,* 178–79: "because it has no excape / if it wants to be a rose / thus it does not show itself / but deep in the red / plunged into velvet / its thinking gadget / then becomes a rose / oh warring rose / my rose remorse / powerful he who takes on a name / thousandfold suspect pain / inflexible the face of the

beautiful / a thousand roses a thousand roses rather / a good deal I pray you / even lower exchangeable heads / proofless case / doesn't prove it's the same / here contracted / rose obtained / not mystical bride / expelled by a rose / distrust of narration / you me little dumb one / misfortune / praying the rose / my bride / I don't flee enough / me rose! exhausted / uninhabited the shriek / rose warrior!"

35. R. Paris, "Per Adriano," in A. Berardinelli and F. Cordelli, eds., *Il pubblico della poesia,* 169: "The one of days gone by had a rose garden and within it a forbidden symbology thrived, she didn't even notice it. The one these days wants me to be quiet. I hear her. Get the water, she says, the water from the kitchen. To look at it, it seems like urine."

36. R. Perrotta, "Esiodo Caos," in L. Ballerini, ed., *Chelsea,* 206–7, trans. D. Scanlon: "the earth, in a great sun, is a fire flux)s: a mutable mask: flux)s and the earliest proof, though sweetly smelling fresh red rose."

37. T. Kemeny, "Qualità di tempo," in S. Meccati, ed., *La poesia in mostra,* 48: "Go in homage to the tomb of / light, for it is there that day / erupts by spreading out your womanly hair / to seal the high wound / the hard mouth of the roses."

38. T. Kemeny, "ri-cor-da-te," *The Hired Killer's Glove,* 68–69: "among the deserted flower-beds the / gravel arches its back to meet the / brow of the roses."

39. T. Kemeny, "graduale," ibid., 70–71: "the stranger's finger ran out of / roses but she didn't succeed in / keeping the cosmic padlock from / closing on her heart."

40. T. Kemeny, "il carnevale d'arlecchino," ibid., 96–97: "roses of art and ruin / surrounded with bootees / coffins on the dove-cots / worms on the rocks."

41. The insistence of the ontological perspective is evident in such recent anthologies as *Il pubblico della poesia* (ed. Berardinelli and Cordelli) and *La parola innamorata* (ed. Pontiggia and Di Mauro), which represent a neoconservative retreat from ethics and history.

42. M. Cucchi, "Ogni stagione ha le sue morte . . . ," in G. Ridinger, ed., *Italian Poetry 1950–1990,* 380: "nothing was ever realized // before mind or gaze created it. / I am thinking of roses, of the column . . . / You seemed to be asking me for your just deserts, / the quiet wait within the illusory dream // where absurdity disappears."

43. D. Villa, "lassù l'assurda," *Lapsus in fabula,* 91: "(we are a shadow of chance / we proceed from unknown causes / we crash down like nebulas in a fire of roses)."

44. D. Villa, "il cervello inclinato," ibid., 104: "the brain inclined / with

head bent over upon things / the golden roses the roses / of the cracked spirit / the garden of ice, devastated."

45. R. G. H. Siu, *Ch'i: A Neo-Taoist Approach to Life*, 92.

46. E. Cassirer, *The Logic of the Humanities*, 84.

47. See R. Osserman, *Poetry of the Universe*, 89–91.

48. G. Caproni, "Pasqua di Resurrezione," *Il Conte di Kevenhüller*, 89: "In the field of a rose, the snake—contracted—flashed its forked tongue."

49. E. F. Accrocca, "La distanza," *Poesie*, 174: "Crossed through by life and having no compass-card, I now follow nothing but the footprints at the limits of the field of what remains."

50. E. F. Accrocca, "Esercizio del dissenso," *Esercizi radicali*, 111: "amidst the fog and the tangles of voices anonymous as letters, / assaults ambushes / in the thorniest of the roses of the wind."

51. E. Cacciatore, "Il passato," *Lo specchio e la trottola*, 125: "The quickness of today is smoking, but it loves you / Already society, rose of the winds, / Branches outward vast commentaries // It engems and hybridizes the irate anxiety / It studies artistically every strategy / It bids adieu to the hatred between parties."

52. E. Cacciatore, "Intorno alla poesia e all'uomo moderno," *Lo specchio e la trottola*, 26: "Di qui il danno nella poesia moderna: in quella autentica che *non si è lasciato adescare il potere visionario da tale solerte previdenza che ha pure un suo vitale diritto.*"

53. R. Scotellaro, "Lunedì," *È fatto giorno*, 141: "The long snake of the streets wakes up for milk and meat, bread and firewood. Trains unload their Corsican laborers and platoons of students. Bureaucrats return to touching tables in their rooms. Houses open to the compass-card."

BIBLIOGRAPHY

Primary Sources

Accrocca, Elio Filippo. *Esercizi radicali*. Foggia: Bastogi, 1984.

———. *Poesie: La distanza degli anni 1942–1987*. Rome: Newton Compton, 1988.

Aleramo, Sibilla. *Selva d'amore*. Rome: Newton Compton, 1980.

Almansi, Guido, and Roberto Barbolini, eds. *La passion predominante: Antologia della poesia erotica italiana*. Intro. G. Almansi. Parma: Guanda, 1988.

Anacreon. Ed. Bruno Gentili. Rome: Edizioni dell'Ateneo, 1958.

"Anakreon, The Complete Writings." Trans. Guy Davenport. *Conjunctions* 6 (1984): 44–82.

Anceschi, Luciano, ed. *Linea lombarda*. Varese: Editrice Magenta, 1952.

———, ed. *Lirici nuovi*. Milan: Mursia, 1964.

Anceschi, Luciano, and Sergio Antonelli. *Lirica del Novecento: Antologia di poesia italiana*. Florence: Vallecchi, 1961.

Apollinaire, Guillaume. *Alcools*. Trans. Anne H. Greet. Foreword by Warren Ramsey. Berkeley: University of California Press, 1965.

———. *Calligrams*. Trans. Anne H. Greet. Santa Barbara, Calif.: Unicorn, 1970.

———. *Poesie*. Ed. Renzo Paris. Rome: Newton Compton, 1971.

———. *Selected Poems*. Trans. with intro. by Oliver Bernard. London: Anvil Press, 1986.

———. *Selected Writings*. Trans. with intro. by Roger Shattuck. New York: New Directions, 1971.

Artaud, Antonin. *Oeuvres complètes,* vol. 1 (of 9). Paris: Gallimard, 1976.

Artioli, Mario, ed. *Lettere inedite di Gian Pietro Lucini ad Aldo Palazzeschi*. Bologna: Massimiliano Boni, 1975.

Auster, Paul, ed. *The Random House Book of Twentieth-Century French Poetry.* New York: Random House, 1982.

Balestrini, Nanni. *Osservazioni sul volo degli uccelli.* Milan: Scheiwiller, 1988.

Ballerini, Luigi. *Che figurato muore.* Trans. Thomas J. Harrison. Milan: All'Insegna del Pesce d'Oro, 1988.

———. *Il terzo gode.* Venice: Marsilio, 1994.

———, ed. *Chelsea 37: The Waters of Casablanca, Analogic and Ablative Poiesis towards Ontologic Writing in Italy.* New York: Chelsea Foundation, 1978.

———, ed. *Shearsmen of sorts: Italian poetry 1975–1993.* Stony Brook, N.Y.: Forum Italicum, 1992.

Barbarani, Berto. *Tutte le poesie.* Ed. Giuseppe Silvestri. Milan: Mondadori, 1984.

Barile, Angelo. *Poesie: Primasera; Quasi sereno; A sole breve. 1930–1963.* Milan: All'Insegna del Pesce d'Oro.

Bassani, Giorgio. *L'alba ai vetri: Poesie 1942–50.* Turin: Einaudi, 1963.

Baudelaire, Charles. *Les fleurs du mal.* Paris: Éditions Garnier Frères, 1961.

———. *Flowers of Evil.* Ed. Marthiel and Jackson Mathews. New York: New Directions, 1955.

Bellezza, Dario. *Libro di poesia.* Milan: Garzanti, 1990.

———. *Serpenta.* Milan: Mondadori, 1987.

Bellintani, Umberto. *E tu che m'ascolti.* Milan: Mondadori, 1963.

———. *Forse un viso tra mille.* Florence: Vallecchi, 1953.

Berardinelli, Alfonso, ed. *Nuovi poeti italiani 2.* Turin: Einaudi, 1982.

Berardinelli, Alfonso, and Franco Cordelli, eds. *Il pubblico della poesia.* Cosenza: Lerici, 1975.

Bertolucci, Attilio. *Al fuoco calmo dei giorni.* Ed. Paolo Lagazzi. Milan: Rizzoli, 1991.

———. *La camera da letto.* Milan: Garzanti, 1988.

———. "N. di Giugno." *Paragone* 348 (1979): 4.

———. *Verso le sorgenti del Cinghio.* Milan: Garzanti, 1993.

Bertolucci, Bernardo. *In cerca del mistero.* Rome: Gremese, 1988.

Betocchi, Carlo. *Poems.* Trans. I. L. Salomon. New York: Clarke and Way, 1964.

———. *Tutte le poesie.* Ed. Luigina Stefani. Milan: Garzanti, 1996.

Bigongiari, Piero. *Moses.* Milan: Mondadori, 1979.

———. *Poesia italiana del Novecento.* 2 vols. Milan: Il Saggiatore, 1980.

———. *Stato di cose.* Milan: Mondadori, 1968.

Blake, William. *The Portable Blake.* Ed. Alfred Kazin. New York: Viking, 1946.

Bodini, Vittorio. *Metamor.* Milan: All'Insegna del Pesce d'Oro, 1967.

———. *Tutte le poesie.* Ed. Oreste Macrí. Lecce: BESA, 1997.

Boine, Giovanni. *Il peccato e altre opere.* Ed. Giancarlo Vigorelli. Parma: Guanda, 1971.

Bonnefoy, Yves. *Early Poems, 1947–1959*. Trans. Galway Kinnell and Richard Pevear. Athens: Ohio University Press, 1990.

———. *In the Shadow's Light*. Trans. J. Naughton with an interview with Yves Bonnefoy. Chicago: University of Chicago Press, 1991.

———. *Poems 1959–1975: Being a Translation of* Pierre ecrite *and* Dans le leurre du seuil. Trans. Richard Pevear. New York: Random House, 1985.

Bontempelli, Massimo. *Il purosangue*. Ed. Vanni Scheiwiller. Milan: Scheiwiller, 1987.

Borges, Jorge Luis. *Obra poética, 1923–1976*. Buenos Aires: Emecé Editores, 1977.

Brecht, Bertolt. *Poems 1913–1956*. Ed. John Willet, Ralph Manheim, and Erich Fried. London: Methuen, 1976.

Breton, André. *Arcane 17*. Paris: Jean-Jacques Pauvert, 1971.

———. *Mad Love (L'Amour fou)*. Trans. Mary Ann Caws. Lincoln: University of Nebraska Press, 1987.

———. *Oeuvres complètes*. Ed. Marguerite Bonnet. 2 vols. Paris: Gallimard, 1992.

Brevini, Franco, ed. *Poeti dialettali del Novecento*. Turin: Einaudi, 1987.

Broggiato, Tiziano, ed. *Canti dall'universo: Dieci poeti italiani degli anni '80*. Milan: Marcos y Marcos, 1987.

Buzzi, Paolo. *Poesie scelte*. Ed. Emilio Mariano. Milan: Ceschina, 1961.

Cacciatore, Edoardo. *Graduali*. Lecce: Piero Manni, 1986.

———. *La restituzione*. Florence: Vallecchi, 1955.

———. *Lo specchio e la trottola*. Florence: Vallecchi, 1960.

Campana, Dino. *Canti orfici e altri scritti*. Florence: Vallecchi, 1952.

Campo, Cristina. *Gli imperdonabili*. Milan: Adelphi, 1987.

———. *La tigre assenza*. Ed. Margherita Pieracci Harwell. Milan: Adelphi, 1991.

Caproni, Giorgio. *Il Conte di Kevenhüller*. Milan: Garzanti, 1986.

———. *L'opera in versi*. Ed. Luca Zuliani. Milan: Mondadori, 1998.

———. *Res amissa*. Ed. Giorgio Agamben. Milan: Garzanti, 1991.

———. *Tutte le poesie*. Milan: Garzanti, 1983.

Cardarelli, Vincenzo. *Opere*. Ed. Clelia Martignoni. Milan: Mondadori, 1981

Carducci, Giosue. *Poesie*. Milan: Garzanti, 1978.

Carrieri, Raffaele. *Il grano non muore (I brogliacci) 1930–1980*. Milan: Mondadori, 1983.

Cattafi, Bartolo. *Poesie 1943–1979*. Ed. Vincenzo Leotta and Giovanni Raboni. Milan: Mondadori, 1990.

Catalano, Ettore, ed. *Le rose e i terremoti: La poesia in Basilicata da Scottellaro a Nigro*. Venosa: Osanna, 1986.

Cavalli, Patrizia. *Poesie*. Turin: Einaudi, 1992.

Cavallo, Franco, and Mario Lunetta, eds. *Poesia italiana della contraddizione.* Rome: Newton Compton, 1989.
Cendrars, Blaise. *Complete Poems.* Trans. Ron Padgett. Intro. Jay Bochner. Berkeley: University of California Press, 1992.
Ceserano, Giorgio. *L'erba bianca.* Milan: Schwarz, 1959.
Char, René. *Oeuvres complètes.* Paris: Gallimard, 1983.
———. *Selected Poems of René Char.* Ed. Mary Ann Caws and Tina Jolas. New York: New Directions, 1992.
Chiara, Piero, and Luciano Erba, eds. *Quarta generazione: La giovane poesia (1945–1954).* Varese: Magenta, 1954.
Ciabatti, Gianfranco. *Niente di personale.* Florence: Sansoni, 1989.
———. *Preavvisi al reo.* Lecce: Piero Manni, 1985.
Cicala, Roberto, ed. *"Con la violenza la pietà": Poesia e resistenza.* Novara: Interlinea Srl Edizioni, 1995.
Claudel, Paul. *Bréviaire poétique.* Paris: Gallimard, 1962.
———. *A Hundred Movements for a Fan.* Trans. with intro. by Andrew Harvey and Iain Watson. London: Quartet Books, 1992.
Cocteau, Jean. *Poèmes 1916–1955.* Paris: Gallimard, 1956.
Comi, Girolamo. *Sonetti e poesie.* Milan: Ceschina, 1960.
The Complete Works of William Shakespeare. New York: Avenel, 1975.
Conte, Giuseppe. *The Ocean and the Boy.* Ed. and trans. Laura Stortoni. Berkeley: Hesperia Press, 1997.
———. *L'oceano e il ragazzo.* Milan: Rizzoli, 1983.
———. *L'ultimo aprile bianco.* Milan: Guanda, 1979.
Contini, Gianfranco, ed. *Letteratura italiana delle origini.* Florence: Sansoni, 1971.
———. *Letteratura italiana del Risorgimento.* Florence: Sansoni, 1986.
Copioli, Rosita. *Furore delle rose.* Parma: Guanda, 1989.
Corazzini, Sergio. *Poesie edite e inedite.* Ed. Stefano Jacomuzzi. Turin: Einaudi, 1968.
Cortázar, Julio. *Around the Day in Eighty Worlds.* Trans. Thomas Christensen. San Francisco: North Point Press, 1984.
Crovi, Raffaele. *Elogio del disertore.* Milan: Mondadori, 1973.
Cucchi, Maurizio, and Stefano Giovanardi, eds. *Poeti italiani de secondo novecento, 1945–1995.* Milan: Mondadori, 1996.
D'Annunzio, Gabriele. *Maia.* Milan: Mondadori, 1956.
———. *Versi d'amore e di gloria.* 2 vols. Ed. Luciano Anceschi, Annamaria Andreoli, Niva Lorenzini. Milan: Mondadori, 1982 (vol. 1), 1984 (vol. 2).
———. *Versi d'amore e di gloria: Tutte le opere di Gabriele D'Annunzio.* Ed. Egidio Bianchetti. Vols. 1 and 2 (of 9). Verona: Mondadori, 1958–1964.

Dego, Giuliano, and Lucio Zaniboni, eds. *La svolta narrativa della poesia italiana*. Lecco: Agielle, 1984.
De Libero, Libero. *Di brace in brace. 1956–1970*. Milan: Mondadori, 1971.
———. *Poesie*. Ed. Alvaro Valentini. Intro. Carlo Bo. Milan: Mondadori, 1980.
Di Giacomo, Salvatore. *Poesie e prose*. Ed. Elena Croce and Lanfranco Orsini. Milan: Mondadori, 1977.
Di Nola, Laura, ed. *Poesia femminista italiana*. Savelli, 1975.
Éluard, Paul. *Oeuvres complètes*. 2 vols. Paris: Gallimard, 1968.
———. *Poesie*. Trans. and intro. Franco Fortini. Milan: Mondadori, 1985.
———. *Poésie et vérité*. Neuchâtel: Editions de la Baconniere, 1943.
———. *La vie immédiate*. Paris: Gallimard, 1973.
Erba, Luciano. *Il cerchio aperto*. Milan: All'Insegna del Pesce d'Oro, 1983.
———. *Il tranviere metafisico*. Milan: Scheiwiller, 1987.
Faccioli, Emilio, Franco Fortini, Paolo Fossati, Natalia Ginzburg, Camillo Pennati, and Marco Vallore, eds. *Nuovi poeti italiani 1*. Turin: Einaudi, 1980.
Fallacara, Luigi. *Poesie (1914–1963)*. Ed. Oreste Macrì. Ravenna: Longo, 1986.
Ferrata, Giansiro, ed. *La Voce: 1908–1918*. Rome: Landi, 1961.
Finzi, Gilberto. *Tre formule di desiderio: Poesie 1975–1980*. Milan: Spirali, 1981.
Fogazzaro, Antonio. *Miranda*. Milan: Galli, 1896.
Forni, Pier Massimo. *Stemmi*. Milan: Scheiwiller, 1977.
Fortini, Franco. *Il ladro di ciliege e altre versioni di poesia*. Turin: Einaudi, 1982.
———. *Memorie per dopo domani: Tre scritti 1945, 1967 e 1980*. Ed. Carlo Fini. Siena: Quaderni di Barbablu, 1984.
———. *Paesaggio con serpente*. Turin: Einaudi, 1984.
———. *Una volta per sempre*. Turin: Einaudi, 1978.
Foscolo, Ugo. *Tutte le poesie*. Milan: Rizzoli, 1952.
Frabotta, Biancamaria. *Appunti di volo: E altre poesie, 1982–1984*. Rome: Edizioni della Cometa, 1985.
———. *Il rumore bianco*. Milan: Feltrinelli, 1982.
Frezza, Luciana. *La farfalla e la rosa*. Milan: Feltrinelli, 1962.
Gatto, Alfonso. *Osteria flegrea (1954–1961)*. Verona: Mondadori, 1962.
———. *Poesie (1929–1969)*. Milan: Mondadori, 1972.
———. *La storia delle vittime: Poesie della resistenza (1943–47, 1963–65)*. Milan: Mondadori, 1966.
Gelli, Piero, and Gina Lagorio, eds. *Poesia italiana del Novecento*. 2 vols. Milan: Garzanti, 1980.
Gentili, Alessandro, and Catherine O'Brien, eds. *The Green Flame: Contemporary Italian Poetry with English Translations*. Dublin: Irish Academic Press, 1987.

Giotti, Virgilio. *Opere*. Ed. R. Derossi, E. Guagnini, B. Maier. Trieste: Edizioni LINT, 1986.
Giudici, Giovanni. *Poesie (1953–1990)*. 2 vols. Milan: Garzanti, 1991.
Giuliani, Alfredo, ed. *I novissimi: Poesie per gli anni sessanta*. Turin: Einaudi, (1965) 1977.
Gómez de la Serna, Ramón. *Aphorisms*. Ed. and trans. Miguel González-Gerth. Pittsburgh: Latin American Literary Review Press, 1989.
Gozzano, Guido. *Opere*. Ed. Giusi Baldissone. Turin: UTET, 1983.
———. *Le poesie*. Milan: Garzanti, 1960.
Guglielminetti, Amelia. *L'insonne*. Milan: Fratelli Trevis, 1918.
———. *Le seduzioni*. Turin: Lattes, 1921.
Guidacci, Margherita. *Il buio e lo splendore*. Milan: Garzanti, 1989.
———. *Paglia e polvere*. Cittadella veneta: Rebellato, 1961.
Guillén, Jorge. *Aire nuestro: Cantico, clamor, homenaje*. Milan: All'Insegna del Pesce d'Oro, 1968.
———. *Antología: Aire nuestro*. Ed. Manuel Mantero. Barcelona: Plaza and Janés, 1980.
Haller, Hermann W., ed. and trans. *The Hidden Italy*. Detroit: Wayne State University Press, 1986.
Harrison, Thomas J., ed. and trans. *The Favorite Malice*. New York: Out of London Press, 1983.
Huidobro, Vicente. *Relativity of Spring*. Trans. Michael Palmer and Geoffrey Young. Berkeley: Sand Dollar, 1976.
Jahier, Piero. *Con me e con gli alpini*. Rome: "La Voce," 1920.
———. *Poesie in versi e in prosa*. Ed. Paolo Briganti. Turin: Einaudi, 1981.
Jiménez, Juan Ramón. *Poesía (en verso) (1917–1923)*. Madrid: Taurus, 1981.
Joyce, James. *A Portrait of the Artist as a Young Man*. New York: Viking Press, 1964.
Kemeny, Tomaso. *The Hired Killer's Glove: Il guanto del sicario*. Milan: Out of London Press, 1976.
Kemeny, Tomaso, and Cesare Viviani, eds. *Il movimento della poesia italiana negli anni settanta*. Bari: Deadalo, 1979.
———, eds. *I percorsi della nuova poesia italiana*. Naples: Guida, 1980.
Krumm, Ermanno, and Tiziano Rossi, eds. *Poesia italiana del Novecento*. Milan: Skira, 1995.
Leonetti, Francesco. *Le scritte sconfinate*. Milan: Scheiwiller, 1994.
Leopardi, Giacomo. *Canti*. Turin: Loescher, 1964.
———. *Tutte le opere*. 2 vols. Ed. Walter Binni. Florence: Sansoni, 1969.
Levi, Primo. *Ad ora incerta*. Milan: Garzanti, 1984.

Lind, L. R., ed. and trans. *Twentieth-Century Italian Poetry: A Bilingual Anthology*. Indianapolis: Bobbs-Merrill, 1974.
Lorca, Federico García. *Obras completas*. Madrid: Aguilar, 1967.
Lotman, Yury. *Analysis of the Poetic Text*. Ed. and trans. D. Barton Johnson. Ann Arbor: Ardis, 1976.
Lucini, Gian Pietro. *Marinetti Futurismo Futuristi: Saggi e interventi*. Ed. Mario Artioli. Bologna: Massimiliano Boni, 1975.
Luzi, Mario. *Tutte le poesie*. Milan: Garzanti, 1988.
Majorino, Giancarlo. *Cangiante*. Milan: Scheiwiller, 1991.
Mallarmé, Stephane. *Collected Poems*. Trans. with commentary by Henry Weinfield. Berkeley: University of California Press, 1994.
———. *The Poems*. Trans. and intro. Keith Bosley. Harmondsworth, England: Penguin, 1977.
———. *Il pomeriggio d'un fauno*. Ed. Paolo Manetti. Turin: Einaudi, 1976.
Manuali, Angelo, and Benito Sablone, eds. *Poesie d'amore del '900 italiano*. Foggia: Edizioni Bastogi, 1981.
Manzoni, Alessandro. *Inni sacri: Tragedie*. Intro. and notes by Vittorio Spinazzola. Milan: Garzanti, 1974.
———. *Poesie prima della conversione*. Ed. Franco Gavazzeni. Turin: Einaudi, 1992.
Maraini, Dacia. *Donne mie*. Turin: Einaudi, 1974.
Marin, Biagio. *Le litànie de la madona*. Intro. and trans. Edda Serra. Padua: Edizioni Carroccio, 1988.
Marinetti, Filippo Tommaso, and Paolo Buzzi, eds. *I poeti futuristi*. Milan: Edizioni Futuriste di "Poesia," 1912.
Mascioni, Grytzko. *Poesia (1952–1982)*. Milan: Rusconi, 1984.
Masselli, Vittorio, and Gian Antonio Gibotto, eds. *Antologia popolare di poeti del Novecento*. Florence: Vallecchi, 1973.
Mecatti, Stefano, ed. *La poesia in mostra*. Florence: Le Lettere, 1982.
Merini, Alda. *La presenza di Orfeo*. Milan: Scheiwiller, 1993.
Michelstaedter, Carlo. *Poesie*. Milan: Adelphi, 1987.
Montale, Eugenio. *Tutte le poesie*. Milan: Mondadori, 1977.
Morante, Elsa. *Alibi*. Milan: Garzanti, 1988.
Negri, Ada. *Dal profondo*. Milan: Treves, 1926.
———. *Opere scelte*. Ed. Elena Cazzulani. Lodi: Lodigraf, 1984.
———. *Poesie*. Milan: Mondadori, 1966.
———. *Prose*. Milan: Mondadori, 1966.
Nerval, Gérard de. *The Chimeras*. Trans. Peter Jay. Redding Ridge, Conn.: Black Swan, 1984.

———. *Poésies*. Geneva: Mermod, 1947.
Novaro, Mario. *Mumuri ed echi*. Ed. G. Cassinelli. Milan: Scheiwiller, 1994.
Noventa, Giacomo. *Opere complete*. 2 vols. Venezia: Marsilio, 1987.
The Odes of Anacreon. Trans. T. Moore. London: Gibbings, 1901.
Onofri, Arturo. *Poesie edite e inedite (1900–1914)*. Ed. Anna Dolfi. Ravenna: Longo, 1982.
Orelli, Giorgio. *L'ora del tempo*. Milan: Mondadori, 1962.
———. *Sinopie*. Milan: Mondadori, 1977.
———. *Spiracoli*. Milan: Mondadori, 1989.
Pagliarani, Elio. *Epigrammi ferraresi*. Lecce: Piero Manni, 1987.
Palazzeschi, Aldo. *Poesie*. Ed. Sergio Antonelli. Milan: Mondadori, 1971.
Pansa, Francesca, ed. *Poesie d'amore: I più importanti poeti italiani presentati da cinquanta scrittrici*. Rome: Newton Compton, 1987.
Pansa, Francesca, and Marianna Bucchich, eds. *Poesie d'amore: L'assenza, il desiderio*. Rome: Newton Compton, 1986.
Papini, Giovanni, and Pietro Pancrazi, eds. *Poeti d'oggi (1900–1925)*. Florence: Vallecchi, 1925.
Parini, Giuseppe. *Il giorno*. Ed. Ettore Bonora. Milan: Rusconi, 1984.
Parronchi, Alessandro. *Per strade di bosco e città: Poesie dal 1937 al 1955*. Florence: Polistampa, 1994.
Pascoli, Giovanni. *Il fanciullino*. Milan: Feltrinelli, 1982.
———. *Poesie*. Milan: Mondadori, 1939.
———. *Prose*. Vol. 1. Milan: Mondadori, 1956.
Pasolini, Pier Paolo. *Bestemmia: Tutte le poesie*. 2 vols. Ed. Graziella Chiarcossi and Walter Siti. Milan: Garzanti, 1993.
———. *Calderón*. Milan: Garzanti, 1973.
———. *La meglio gioventù*. Florence: Sansoni, 1954.
———. *Poesia in forma di rosa*. Milan: Garzanti, 1964.
———. *Le poesie*. Milan: Garzanti, 1975.
———. *La religione del mio tempo*. Milan: Garzanti, 1961.
———. *L'usignolo della Chiesa Cattolica*. Milan: Longanesi, 1958.
———, ed. *Canzoniere italiano: Antologia della poesia popolare*. Parma: Guanda, 1955.
Paul Celan: Poems. A Bilingual Edition. Trans. Michael Hamburger. New York: Persea Books, 1980.
Pavese, Cesare. *Poesie edite e inedite*. Ed. Italo Calvino. Turin: Einaudi, 1962.
Pellico, Silvio. *Le mie prigioni*. Milan: Mursia, 1983.
Penna, Sandro. *Confuso sogno*. Ed. Elio Pecora. Milan: Garzanti, 1980.
———. *Poesie*. Milan: Garzanti, 1989.

———. *This Strange Joy: Selected Poems of Sandro Penna.* Trans. W. S. Di Piero. Columbus: Ohio State University Press, 1982.
Perrotta, Raffaele, ed. "Italian Poetry Today: A Critical Anthology." *Altro polo* 3 (1980). University of Sydney, Frederick May Foundation for Italian Studies.
Perse, Saint John. *Anabasis.* Trans. T. S. Eliot. New York: Harcourt and Brace, 1949.
———. *Chronique.* Trans. R. Fitzgerald. New York: Pantheon, 1961.
———. *Seamarks.* Trans. Wallace Fowlie. New York: Harper, 1958.
Petrarca, Francesco. *Canzoniere.* Intro. Roberto Antonelli. Essay by Gianfranco Contini. Notes by Daniele Ponchiroli. Turin: Einaudi, 1964.
Piccolo, Lucio. *Collected Poems.* Trans. and ed. Brian Swann and Ruth Feldman. Princeton, N.J.: Princeton University Press, 1972.
———. *La seta e altre poesie inedite e sparse.* Ed. Giovanna Musolino and Giovanni Gaglio. Milan: All'Insegna del Pesce d'Oro, 1984.
Pierro, Albino. *Appuntamento (1946–1967).* Bari: Laterza, 1967.
———. *Metaponto.* Milan: Garzanti, 1982.
———. *Un pianto nascosto.* Ed. Francesco Zambon. Turin: Einaudi, 1986.
Piersanti, Umberto. *I luoghi persi.* Turin: Einaudi, 1994.
Poe, Edgar Allan. *The Selected Poetry and Prose.* New York: Random House, 1951.
Poems of Jules Laforgue. Trans. and intro. Peter Dale. London: Anvil Press, 1986.
Ponge, Francis. *Le grand recueil: Pièces.* Paris: Gallimard, 1961.
———. *Selected Poems.* Trans. C. K. Williams, John Montague, and Margaret Guiton. Ed. Margaret Guiton. Winston-Salem, N.C.: Wake Forest University Press, 1994.
———. *The Sun Placed in the Abyss and Other Texts.* Interview, essay, and translations by Serge Gavronsky. New York: Sun, 1977.
Pontiggia, Giancarlo, and Enzo Di Mauro, eds. *La parola innamorata: I poeti nuovi 1976–1978.* Milan: Feltrinelli, 1978.
Porta, Antonio. *Melusina: Una ballata e un diario.* Essay by Niva Lorenzini. Milan: Crocetti, 1987.
———. *Nel fare poesia (1958–1985).* Florence: Sansoni, 1985.
———, ed. *Poesia degli anni settanta.* Milan: Feltrinelli, 1979.
Pound, Ezra. *The Cantos.* New York: New Directions, 1981.
———. *Personae.* New York: Liveright, 1926.
Pozzi, Antonia. *Parole.* Rome: Mondadori, 1939, 1964.
———. *La vita sognata e altre poesie inedite.* Milan: Scheiwiller, 1986.
Quasimodo, Salvatore. *Tutte le poesie.* Milan: Mondadori, 1960.
———, trans. *Lirici greci: Dall'Odissea, Dall'Iliade.* Milan: Mondadori, 1979.

Raboni, Giovanni. *A tanto caro sangue: Tutte le poesie 1953–1987*. Milan: Mondadori, 1988.
———. *Cadenza d'inganno*. Milan: Mondadori, 1975.
———. *La casa della Vetra*. Milan: Mondadori, 1966.
———. *Nel grave sogno*. Milan: Mondadori, 1982.
Ramat, Silvio. *Corpo e cosmo (1964–1972)*. Milan: All'Insegna del Pesce d'Oro, 1973.
———. *L'inverno delle teorie*. Milan: Mondadori, 1980.
———. *Numeri primi*. Venice: Marsilio, 1996.
———. *Orto e nido*. Milan: Garzanti, 1987.
———. *La poesia italiana: 1903–1943: Quarantun titoli esemplari*. Venice: Marsilio, 1997.
———. *Pomerania*. Milan: Crocetti, 1993.
Rebora, Clemente. *Le poesie (1913–1957)*. Milan: Garzanti, 1988.
Reverdy, Pierre. *Roof Slates and Other Poems of Pierre Reverdy*. Trans. with prefaces by Mary Ann Caws and Patricia Terry. Boston: Northeastern University Press, 1981.
Ridinger, Gayle, ed. and trans. Co-edited by Gian Paolo Renello. *Italian Poetry 1950–1990*. Boston: Dante University Press, 1996.
Rilke, Rainer Maria. *Duino Elegies*. Trans. J. B. Leishman and Stephen Spender. New York: Norton, 1939.
———. *Poems 1906 to 1926*. Trans. with intro. by J. B. Leishman. London: The Hogarth Press, 1968.
Rimbaud, Arthur. *Rimbaud: Complete Works, Selected Letters*. Trans. with intro. by Wallace Fowlie. Chicago: University of Chicago Press, 1966.
Risi, Nelo. *Poesie scelte (1943–1975)*. Ed. Giovanni Raboni. Milan: Mondadori, 1977.
Rosselli, Amelia. *Antologia poetica*. Ed. Giacinto Spagnoletti. Milan: Garzanti, 1987.
———. *Primi scritti 1952–1963*. Milan: Guanda, 1980.
Rossi, Tiziano. *Il cominciamondo*. Urbino: Argalia, 1963.
———. *Miele e no*. Milan: Garzanti, 1988.
Saba, Umberto. *Canzoniere*. Turin: Einaudi, 1948.
———. *Tutte le poesie*. Ed. Arrigo Stara. Milan: Mondadori, 1988.
Saint-Pol-Roux. *La rose, et les épines du chemin*. Mortemart Mezieres-sur-issoire: Rougerie, 1980.
Sala, Alberico. *Epigrafi e canti*. Florence: Vallecchi, 1957.
———. *La prova del nuovo*. Milan: Garzanti, 1988.
Sanesi, Roberto. *Carte di transito*. Treviso: Amadeus, 1989.
———. *La differenza*. Milan: Garzanti, 1988.
———. *Information Report*. Trans. William Alexander. London: Cape Goliard Press, 1970.
———. *Rapporto informativo*. Milan: Feltrinelli, 1966.

Sanguineti, Edoardo. *Segnalibro: Poesie 1951–1981*. Milan: Feltrinelli, 1989.
———. *Senzatitolo*. Milan: Feltrinelli, 1992.
Sappho. Trans. Mary Barnard. Berkeley: University of California Press, 1958.
Sappho: Poems and Fragments. Trans. with intro. by Josephine Balmer. Newcastle upon Tyne: Bloodaxe Books, 1992.
Sbarbaro, Camillo. *L'opera in versi e in prosa*. Ed. Gina Lagorio and Vanni Scheiwiller. Milan: Garzanti, 1985.
———. *Poesia e prosa*. Ed. Vanni Scheiwiller. Milan: Mondadori, 1979.
———. *Trucioli (1920)*. Ed. Giampiero Costa. Milan: Scheiwiller, 1990.
Scataglini, Franco. *Rimario agontano (1968–1986)*. Ed. Franco Brevini. Milan: Scheiwiller, 1987.
———. *La rosa*. Turin: Einaudi, 1992.
Scheiwiller, Vanni, ed. *Poeti del secondo futurismo italiano*. Milan: All'Insegna del Pesce d'Oro, 1973.
Scotellaro, Rocco. *È fatto giorno*. Ed. Franco Vitelli. Milan: Mondadori, 1954.
———. *Margherite e rosolacci*. Ed. Franco Vitelli. Milan: Mondadori, 1978.
———. *L'uva puttanella: Contadini del sud*. Rome: Laterza, 1986.
Sereni, Vittorio. *IX Ecloghe*. Milan: Mondadori, 1962.
———. *Poesie*. Ed. Dante Isella. Milan: Mondadori, 1995.
———. *Poesie scelte*. Milan: Mondadori, 1973.
———. *Tutte le poesie*. Ed. Maria Teresa Sereni. Milan: Mondadori, 1986.
Serra, Renato. *Piccolo canzoniere*. Turin: Albert Meynier, 1987.
Severini, Gino. "Art du fantastique dans le sacré: Peinture de la lumière, de la profondeur, du dynamisme: Manifeste futuriste," in *Témoignages 50 ans de réflexion*, 31. Rome: Edizioni Artistiche Moderne, 1963.
Sinisgalli, Leonardi. *The Ellipse*. Trans. W. S. Di Piero. Princeton, N.J.: Princeton University Press, 1982.
———. *L'ellisse*. Ed. Giuseppe Pontiggia. Milan: Mondadori, 1974.
———. *L'età della luna*. Milan: Mondadori, 1962.
———. *Horror vacui*. Ed. with essay by Renato Aymone. Cava dei Tirreni: Avagliano, 1995.
———. *L'indovino*. Intro. and notes by Renato Aymone. Cava dei Tirreni: Avagliano, 1994.
———. *I nuovi campi elisi: Poesie (1942–1946)*. Milan: Mondadori, 1947.
———. *Vidi le muse*. Ed. Renato Aymone. Cava dei Tirreni: Avagliano, 1997.
Siti, Walter, ed. *Nuovi poeti italiani 3*. Turin: Einaudi, 1984.
Slataper, Scipio. *Il mio carso*. Milan: Rizzoli, 1989.
Solmi, Sergio. *Poesie, meditazioni e ricordi*. Vol. 1 (of 2). Milan: Adelphi, 1983.
Spagnoletti, Giacinto, ed. *Antologia della poesia italiana contemporanea*. 2 vols. Florence: Vallecchi, 1946.

Spagnoletti, Giacinto, and Cesare Vivaldi, eds. *Poesia dialettale dal Rinascimento a oggi*. Milan: Garzanti, 1991.
Spaziani, Maria Luisa. *Geometria del disordine*. Milan: Mondadori, 1981.
———. *Poesie*. Intro. Luigi Baldacci. Milan: Mondadori, 1979.
———. *La stella del libero arbitrio*. Milan: Mondadori, 1986.
———. *Utilità della memoria*. Milan: Mondadori, 1966.
———, ed. *Sei poeti del Premio Montale*. Rome: Centro Internazionale Eugenio Montale, 1985.
———, ed. *Sette poeti del Premio Montale*. Milan: Scheiwiller, 1992.
Squatriti, Fausta. *La natura del desiderio: Poesie 1977–1987*. Pref. Francesco Leonetti. Milan: All'Insegna del Pesce d'Oro, 1987.
Tarozzi, Bianca. *La buranella*. Venice: Marsilio, 1996.
Tasso, Torquato. *Gerusalemme liberata*. Ed. Claudio Varese and Guido Arbizzoni. Milan: Mursia, 1972.
Testori, Giovanni. *Diadèmata*. Turin: Garzanti, 1986.
Thovez, Enrico. *Il poema dell'adolescenza*. Ed. Stefano Jacomuzzi. Turin: Einaudi, 1979.
Tommaseo, Niccolo. *Opere*. Ed. Aldo Borlenghi. Naples: Ricciardi, 1958.
Ungaretti, Giuseppe. *Vita d'un uomo: Tutte le poesie*. Ed. Leone Piccioni. Milan: Mondadori, 1970.
Valeri, Diego. *Calle del vento*. Milan: Mondadori, 1975.
———. *Giardinetto*. Milan: Mondadori, 1974.
———. *Poesie*. Pref. and note by Giuseppe Raimondi. Milan: Mondadori, 1967.
———. *Poesie piccole*. With a letter by Gianfranco Folena. Milan: All'Insegna del Pesce d'Oro, 1969.
———. *Poesie scelte*. Ed. Carlo della Corte. Milan: Mondadori, 1977.
———. *Poesie vecchie e nuove*. Verona: Mondadori, 1952.
———. *Umana*. Ferrara: Taddei, 1916.
Valéry, Paul. *Paul Valéry: An Anthology*. Selected with intro. by James R. Lawler. Princeton, N.J.: Princeton University Press, 1977.
———. *Selected Writings of Paul Valéry*. New York: New Directions, 1964.
Valesio, Paolo. *Prose in poesia*. Milan: Guanda, 1979.
———. *La rosa verde*. Padua: Editoriale Clessidra, 1987.
Verlaine, Paul. *Oeuvres poétiques*. Paris: Editions Garnier Frères, 1969.
———. *Sagesse: Liturgies intimes*. Paris: Colin, 1958.
Villa, Dario. *Lapsus in fabula*. Milan: Nigri, 1984.
Villa, Emilio. *Opere poetiche*. Ed. Aldo Tagliaferri. Milan: Coliseum, 1989.
Vivaldi, Cesare. *Poesie scelte (1952/1992)*. Rome: Newton Compton, 1993.
Viviani, Cesare. *L'amore delle parti*. Milan: Mondadori, 1981.
———. *Preghiera del nome*. Milan: Mondadori, 1990.

Volponi, Paolo. *Poesie e poemetti 1946–66*. Ed. Gualtiero De Santi. Turin: Einaudi, 1980.
Zanzotto, Andrea. *Idioma*. Milan: Mondadori, 1980.
———. *IX Ecloghe*. Milan: Mondadori, 1962.
———. *Poesie (1938–1986)*. Ed. Giorgio Luzzi. Turin: L'Arzanà, 1987.
———. *Selected Poetry of Andrea Zanzotto*. Ed. and trans. Ruth Feldman and Brian Swann. Princeton, N.J.: Princeton University Press, 1975.
———. *Vocativo*. Milan: Mondadori, 1957.
Zeichen, Valentino. *Museo interiore*. Parma: Guanda, 1987.

SECONDARY SOURCES

Adorno, T. W. *Aesthetic Theory*. Ed. Gretel Adorno and Rolf Tiedemann. Trans. C. Lenhardt. London: Routledge and Kegan Paul, 1984.
Agamben, Giorgio. *Infancy and History: The Destruction of Experience*. Trans. Liz Heron. London: Verso, 1993.
Allen, Beverly. *Andrea Zanzotto: The Language of Beauty's Apprentice*. Berkeley: University of California Press, 1988.
Alonso, Damaso. *Pluralità e correlazione in poesia*. Bari: Adriatica, 1971.
Anceschi, Luciano. *Autonomia ed eteronomia dell'arte*. Milan: Garzanti, 1976.
———. *Barocco e Novecento*. Milan: Rusconi e Paolazzi, 1960.
———. *Le poetiche del Novecento in Italia*. Venice: Marsilio, 1990.
Ashton, Dore. *A Fable of Modern Art*. Berkeley: University of California Press, 1991.
Asor Rosa, Alberto. "La poesia di Franco Fortini." In *Poesia oggi*, ed. Massimiliano Mancini, Mirella Marchi, and Dora Marinari, 110–21. Milan: Franco Angeli, 1986.
Avalle, d'Arco Silvio. "Poesia." In *Enciclopedia Garzanti*, 408–22. Milan: Garzanti, 1963.
Aymone, Renato. *L'età delle rose: Note e letture di poesia: Quasimodo, Gatto, Sinisgalli, Bodini, de Libero*. Naples: Edizioni Scientifiche Italiane, 1982.
Bachelard, Gaston. *The Flame of a Candle*. Trans. Joni Caldwell. Dallas: Dallas Institute of Humanities and Culture, 1988.
Barthes, Roland. *The Semiotic Challenge*. Trans. Richard Howard. New York: Hill and Wang, 1988.
———. *Writing Degree Zero*. Trans. Annette Lavers and Colin Smith. New York: Hill and Wang, 1968.
Bateson, Gregory, and Jurgen Ruesch. *Communication: The Social Matrix of Psychiatry*. New York: Norton, 1951.
———. *Mind and Nature*. Toronto: Bantam, 1980.

Battistini, Andrea, and Ezio Raimondi. "Retoriche e poetiche dominanti." In *Letteratura italiana,* vol. 3,I (of 9), 5–339. Turin: Einaudi, 1984.

Beccaria, Gian Luigi. *Le forme della lontananza.* Milan: Garzanti, 1985.

Benjamin, Walter. *Illuminations.* Ed. Hannah Arendt. Trans. Harry Zohn. New York: Schocken, 1969.

Benussi, Cristina. *L'età del fascismo.* Palermo: Palumbo, 1978.

Berardinelli, Alfonso. *Franco Fortini.* Florence: Castoro, 1973.

Bersani, Leo. *A Future for Astyanax.* Boston: Little Brown, 1976.

Bertinetto, Pier Marco, and Carlo Ossola, eds. *La pratica della scrittura.* Turin: Paravia, 1976.

Betti, Laura, ed. *Pasolini: Cronaca giudiziaria, persecuzione, morte.* Milan: Garzanti, 1977.

Bigongiari, Piero. *Poesia italiana del Novecento.* 2 vols. Milan: Il Saggiatore, 1978 (vol. 1), 1980 (vol. 2).

Bloom, Harold. *The Breaking of the Vessels.* Chicago: University of Chicago Press, 1982.

Blumenberg, Hans. *Work on Myth.* Trans. R. M. Wallace. Cambridge: MIT Press, 1985.

Bo, Carlo. *Letteratura come vita.* Ed. Sergio Pautasso. Turin: Milan, 1994.

Bobbio, Norberto. *Italia fedele: Il mondo di Gobetti.* Florence: Passigli, 1986.

Bodini, Vittorio. *Studi sul barocco di Góngora.* Rome: Edizioni dell'Ateneo, 1964.

Bogue, Ron, and Mihai Spariosu, eds. *The Play of the Self.* Albany: State University of New York Press, 1994.

Bollati, Giulio. *L'italiano.* Turin: Einaudi, 1983.

Bollobás, Eniko. *Charles Olson.* New York: Twayne, 1992.

Bontempelli, Massimo. *L'avventura novecentista.* Florence: Vallecchi, 1974.

Bosco, Umberto, ed. *Enciclopedia dantesca.* Rome: Istituto dell'Enciclopedia Italiana, 1976.

Brand, Peter, and Lino Pertile, eds. *The Cambridge History of Italian Literature.* Cambridge: Cambridge University Press, 1996.

Brockman, John, ed. *About Bateson.* London: Wildwood House, 1978.

Bronzini, Giovanni Battista. *L'universo contadino e l'immaginario poetico di Rocco Scotellaro.* Bari: Edizioni Dedalo, 1987.

Brown, Norman. *Love's Body.* New York: Random House, 1966.

Burke, Kenneth. *Attitudes Toward History.* Berkeley: University of California Press, 1984.

Calvino, Italo. *Six Memos for the Next Millennium.* Trans. Patrick Creagh. Cambridge, Mass.: Harvard University Press, 1988.

Carnasciali, Franca. "Didascalismo e poesia nel poemetto gozzaniano sulle farfalle." In *Letteratura e scienza nella storia della cultura italiana,* ed. V.

Branca, P. Mazzamuto, G. Petronio, M. Sacco Messineo, G. Santangelo, A. Sole, C. Spalanca, N. Tedesco, 824–30. Palermo: Manfredi, 1976.

Cassirer, Ernst. *The Logic of the Humanities*. New Haven: Yale University Press, 1960.

Cerruti, Marco. *Carlo Michelstaedter*. 1967. Milan: Mursia, 1987.

Cicala, Roberto, ed. *"Con la violenza la pietà": Poesia e resistenza*. Rome: Interlinea, 1995.

Cocteau, Jean. *Cocteau's World: An Anthology of Writings*. Ed. and trans. Margaret Crosland. New York: Dodd, Mead, 1972.

Comes, Salvatore. *Ada Negri: Da un tempo all'altro*. Milan: Mondadori, 1970.

Conley, Tom. "1913—Lyrical Ideograms." In *A New History of French Literature*, ed. Denis Hollier. Cambridge, Mass.: Harvard University Press, 1989.

Contini, Gianfranco. *La parte di Benedetto Croce nella cultura italiana*. Turin: Einaudi, 1989.

———. "I ferri vecchi e quelli nuovi." In *L'analisi letteraria in Italia*, ed. D. S. Avalle, 216–28. Milan: Ricciardi, 1970.

———. "Il linguaggio di Pascoli." In *Varianti e altra linguistica: Una raccolta di saggi (1938–1968)*, 219–45. Turin: Einaudi, 1970.

———. *Ultimi esercizî ed elzeviri*. Turin: Einaudi, 1988.

Corti, Maria. "Il genere *disputatio* e la transcodificazione in dolore di Bonvesin da la Riva." *Il viaggio testuale*. Turin: Einaudi, 1978.

———. *An Introduction to Literary Semiotics*. Trans. Margherita Bogat and Allen Mandelbaum. Bloomington: Indiana University Press, 1978.

Crespi, Angelo. *Contemporary Thought of Italy*. New York: Knopf, 1926.

Cronen, Vernon E., and W. Barnett Pearce. *Communication, Action, and Meaning*. New York: Praeger, 1980.

Cucchi, Maurizio. *Dizionario della poesia italiana*. Milan: Mondadori, 1983.

Curtius, Ernst Robert. *European Literature and the Latin Middle Ages*. Trans. Willard Trask. Princeton: Princeton University Press, 1953.

Davico Bonino, Guido, and Paola Mastrocola, eds. *Antologia delle poetesse del '900*. Milan: Mondadori, 1996.

David, Michel. *Letteratura e psicanalisi*. Milan: Mursia, 1967.

Debenedetti, Giacomo. *Poesia italiana del novecento*. Milan: Garzanti, 1974.

De Michelis, Cesare. "Il coraggio di parlare delle rose." *Angelus novus* 1, no. 1 (1964): 72–81.

Detienne, Marcel. *Dionysos Slain*. Trans. Mireille Muellner and Leonard Muellner. Baltimore, Md.: Johns Hopkins University Press, 1979.

Devito, Joseph A. *The Communication Handbook*. New York: Harper and Row, 1986.

Di Benedetto, Vincenzo. "Le 'bianche rose' e la forma depurata." *Lo scrittoio di Ugo Foscolo*, 332–47. Turin: Einaudi, 1990.

Dombroski, Robert S. *Properties of Writing: Ideological Discourse in Modern Italian fiction*. Baltimore: Johns Hopkins University Press, 1994.

Dotoli, Giovanni. *Nascita della modernità: Baudelaire, Apollinaire, Canudo, il viaggio dell'arte*. Fasano: Schena, 1995.

Eco, Umberto. *Postscript to* The Name of the Rose. Trans. William Weaver. San Diego: Harcourt Brace Jovanovich, 1984.

Erba, Luciano. *Huysmans e la liturgia*. Bari: Adriatica, 1971.

Fortini, Franco. "Che cos'è stato il 'Politecnico.'" *Nuovi argomenti* 1 (1953): 181–200.

———. "Dialogo su Leopardi." In *"Uomini usciti di pianto in ragione,"* Ed. Velio Abati et al., 179–86. Rome: Manifesto libri, 1996.

———. *I poeti del Novecento*. Rome-Bari: Laterza, 1975.

———. "Poesia degli anni cinquanta." In *Novecento*, ed. Gianni Grana, 8039–46. Milan: Marzorati, 1982.

———. *Nuovi saggi italiani*. Milan: Garzanti, 1987.

———, ed., with Lanfranco Binni. *Il movimento surrealista*. Milan: Garzanti, 1959.

Fowlie, Wallace. *Mallarmé*. Chicago: University of Chicago Press, 1953.

Gargani, Aldo. *Lo stupore e il caso*. Bari: Laterza, 1985.

Garin, Eugenio. *La cultura italiana tra '800 e '900*. Bari: Laterza, 1963.

———. *Intellettuali italiani del XX secolo*. Rome: Riuniti, 1974, 1987.

Giacon, Mariarosa. "Simbolismo e plurilinguismo in Soffici." In *Poetica e stile: Saggi su opsis e lexis, Raimbaut d'Aurenga, Tasso, Leopardi, Palazzeschi, Soffici, Montale, Lingua poetica di consumo*, ed. Lorenzo Renzi, 105–49. Padua: Liviana, 1976.

Girardi, Antonio. *Cinque storie stilistiche: Saba, Penna, Bertolucci, Caproni, Sereni*. Genoa: Marietti, 1987.

Giuliani, Alfredo. *Immagini e maniere*. Naples: Edizioni Scientifiche Italiane, 1996.

Góngora, Luis de. *Sonetti*. Selected and trans. C. Greppi. Milan: Mondadori, 1985.

Gramigna, Giuliano. *Le forme del desiderio*. Milan: Garzanti, 1986.

Group μ (Jacques Dubois, Francis Edeline, Jean-Marie Klinkenberg, Philippe Minguet, François Pire, Hadelin Trinon). *A General Rhetoric*. Trans. Paul B. Burrell and Edgar M. Slotkin. Baltimore, Md.: Johns Hopkins University Press, 1981.

Hand, Vivienne. *Zanzotto*. Edinburgh: Edinburgh University Press, 1994.

Hays, Gregory. "*Le morte stagioni*: Intertextuality in Quasimodo's *Lirici greci*." *Forum Italicum* 29, no. 1 (1995): 26–43.

Heaney, Seamus. *The Government of the Tongue*. New York: Noonday, 1988.

———. *The Redress of Poetry*. New York: Farrar, Straus and Giroux, 1995.

Hellerstein, Nina. *Mythe et structure dans les cinq grandes odes de Paul Claudel.* Paris: Annales Littéraires de l'Université de Besançon, v. 414, 1990.
Hillman, James. *Oltre l'umanismo.* Ed. Francesco Donfrancesco. Bergamo: Moretti and Vitali, 1996.
Jacobbi, Ruggero. *L'avventura del Novecento.* Ed. Anna Dolfi. Milan: Garzanti, 1984.
Jakobson, Roman. "Linguistics and Poetics." In *Style in Language,* ed. T. A. Sebeok, 350–77. Cambridge, Mass.: MIT Press, 1960.
Jannini, P. A. *Le avanguardie letterarie nell'idea critica di Apollinaire.* Rome: Bulzoni, 1979.
Jones, F. J. *The Modern Italian Lyric.* Cardiff: University of Wales Press, 1986.
Kenner, Hugh. *The Pound Era.* Berkeley: University of California Press, 1971.
Kristeva, Julia. "The System and the Speaking Subject." In *The Tell-Tale Sign: A Survey of Semiotics,* ed. T. A. Sebeok, 47–55. Lisse, Netherlands: De Ridder, 1975.
Labriolle, Jacqueline de. "Le thème de la rose dans l'oeuvre de Paul Claudel." *La Revue des Lettres Modernes* 134–136 (1966): 65–103.
Leopardi e il Novecento: Atti del III convegno internazionale di studi leopardiani. Florence: Olschki, 1974.
Lonardi, Gilberto. *Leopardismo.* Florence: Sansoni, 1974.
Luperini, Romano. *La lotta mentale: Per un profilo di Franco Fortini.* Rome: Editori Riuniti, 1986.
Luperini, Romano, Pietro Cataldi, and Floriana D'Amely, eds. *Poeti italiani: Il Novecento.* Palermo: Palumbo, 1994.
Luzi, Mario. *Discorso naturale.* Milan: Garzanti, 1984.
Luzzi, Giorgio. *Poeti della linea lombarda.* Milan: CENS, 1987.
Macrì, Oreste. *Studi sull'ermetismo: L'enigma della poesia di Bigongiari.* Lecce: Milella, 1988.
Manacorda, Giuliano. "Una rivista 'equivoca' degli anni trenta: *La riforma letteraria.*" In *La cultura italiana negli anni '30–'45,* 1:129–42. Naples: Edizioni Scientifiche Italiane, 1984.
Marchese, Angelo. *L'officina della poesia.* Milan: Mondadori, 1985.
Marcon, Giorgio, and Dario Trento. *Allegorie e varianti in riflessi di Aldo Palazzeschi.* Bologna: Il Cassero, 1988.
Martini, Ferdinando, ed. *Scelta di poesie moderne.* Florence: Sansoni, 1917.
Mazzotta, Giuseppe. "The Theology of Mario Luzi's Poetry." In *Play, Literature, Religion: Essays in Cultural Intertextuality,* ed. Virgil Nemoianu and Robert Royal. Albany: State University of New York Press, 1992.
Mengaldo, Pier Vincenzo. "Iterazione e specularità in Sereni." *Strumenti critici* 17 (1972): 19–46.

———. "Questioni metriche novecentesche." In *Forme e vicende per Giovanni Pozzi*, ed. Ottavio Besomi, Giulia Gianella, Alessandro Martini, and Guido Pedrojetta, 555–98. Padua: Antenore, 1988.
———. *La tradizione del Novecento*. Milan: Feltrinelli, 1975.
———. *La tradizione del Novecento: Terza serie*. Turin: Einaudi, 1991.
———, ed. with intro. *Poeti italiani del Novecento*. Milan: Mondadori, 1978.
Mincu, Marin, ed. *La semiotica letteraria italiana*. Milan: Feltrinelli, 1982.
Moriarty, Sandra E. "Abduction: A Theory of Visual Interpretation." *Communication Theory* 6, no. 2 (1996): 167–87.
Naldini, Nico. *Pasolini: Una vita*. Turin: Einaudi, 1989.
Olson, Charles. "Projective Verse," *Il Verri* 1 (1961): 9–23.
Onofri, Arturo. *Pascoli: Scritti editi ed inediti*. Ed. Franco Lanza. Bologna: Massimiliano Boni, 1990.
Osserman, Robert. *Poetry of the Universe*. New York: Anchor, 1995.
Ossola, Carlo. *figurato e rimosso: Icone e interni del testo*. Bologna: Il Mulino, 1988.
———. "La rosa profunda." *Lettere italiane* 34, no. 4 (1982): 461–83.
Pasolini, Pier Paolo. *Passione e ideologia*. Milan: Garzanti, 1960.
———. Review of Attilio Bertolucci, *Viaggio d'inverno*. *Nuovi argomenti* 22 (1971): 15.
Payen, J. C. *La rose et l'utopie*. Paris: Éditions Sociales, 1976.
Peirce, Charles S. *Letters to Lady Welby*. Ed. I. C. Lieb. New Haven: Whitlock, 1953.
Peterson, Thomas E. *The Ethical Muse of Franco Fortini*. Gainesville: University Press of Florida, 1997.
Pieri, Marzio. "La rosa tradita." *Nuovi argomenti* 65–66 (1980): 267–72.
Poe, Edgar Allan. "Philosophy of Composition." *Poems and Essays*. New York: Dutton, 1972.
Poggioli, Renato. *The Theory of the Avant-Garde*. Cambridge, Mass.: Harvard University Press, 1968.
Pozzi, Gianni. *La poesia italiana del Novecento. Da Gozzano agli ermetici*. Turin: Einaudi, 1965.
Pozzi, Giovanni. *Alternatim*. Milan: Adelphi, 1996.
———. *La parola dipinta*. Milan: Adelphi, 1981.
———. *La rosa in mano al professore*. Fribourg: Edizioni Universitarie, 1974.
———. "Temi, topoi, stereotopi." In *Letteratura italiana*, vol. 3,I, ed. Alberto Asor Rosa, 391–436. Turin: Einaudi, 1984.
Praz, Mario. "D'Annunzio e 'l'amor sensuale della parola.'" *La carne, la morte e il diavolo nella letturatura romantica*, 401–56. Florence: Sansoni, 1966.
Raboni, Giovanni. *Poesia degli anni sessanta*. Rome: Editori Riuniti, 1976.

Raimondi, Ezio. *Le poetiche della modernità italiana*. Milan: Garzanti, 1990.
Ramat, Silvio. *Storia della poesia italiana del Novecento*. Milan: Mursia, 1982.
Re, Lucia. "Variazioni su Amelia Rosselli." *Il Verri* 3–4 (1993): 131–50.
Rebay, Luciano. *Le origini della poesia di Giuseppe Ungaretti*. Rome: Edizioni di Storia e Letteratura, 1962.
Rebora, Clemente. *Per un Leopardi mal noto*. Ed. Laura Barile. Milan: Scheiwiller, 1992.
Rella, Franco. *L'estetica del romanticismo*. Rome: Donzelli, 1997.
Rilke, Rainer Maria. *A Verse Concordance to His Complete Lyrical Poetry*. Leeds: W. S. Maney, 1980.
Robertis, Domenico De. "Le violette sul seno della fanciulla." *Forme e vicende: Per Giovanni Pozzi (Medioevo e umanesimo 72)*, 75–99. Padua: Antenore, 1989.
Romagnoli, Sergio. "Spazio pittorico e spazio letterario da Parini a Gadda." In *Storia d'Italia: Annali 5: Il paesaggio*, ed. Cesare De Seta, 429–559. Turin: Einaudi, 1982.
Roubaud, Jacques. "Lire *Le Crè-Coeur* en 1997." In *Aragon: Le mouvement perpétuel*, ed. Jamel-Eddine Bencheikh, Alain Nicolas, and Henriette Zoughebi, 65–74. Paris: Stock, 1997.
Salvemini, Gaetano. *Mazzini*. Trans. I. M. Rawson. New York: Collier, 1962.
Santagostini, Mario. *Il manuale del poeta*. Milan: Mondadori, 1990.
Schulz, Gerhard. "The Stranger and the Blue Flower: Some Observations on Novalis (1772–1801)." In *Romanticism Today: Frederich Schlegel, Novalis, E. T. A. Hoffman, Ludwig Tieck*, ed. Reinhold Grimm, 27–43. Bonn: Inter Nationes, 1973.
Segre, Cesare. *Avviamento all'analisi del testo letterario*. Turin: Einaudi, 1985.
———. *Introduction to the Analysis of the Literary Text*. Trans. John Meddemmen. Bloomington: Indiana University Press, 1988.
Serrao, Achille. "From Language to Dialect: *De Calvianis quidam*." Trans. Thomas E. Peterson. *World Literature Today* 71, no. 2 (1997): 271–78.
Serres, Michel. *Le tiers-instruit*. Paris: Gallimard, 1991.
Seward, Barbara. "The Artist and the Rose." In *Joyce's "Portrait": Criticisms and Critiques*, ed. Thomas E. Connolly, 167–80. New York: Appleton-Century-Crofts, 1962.
———. *The Symbolic Rose*. New York: Columbia University Press, 1960.
Shearman, John. *Mannerism*. Baltimore, Md.: Penguin, 1967.
Singh, G. "Dante and Pound," *Critical Quarterly* 17 (1975): 311–28.
———. "Il Dante di Pound." *Testo* 11 (1986): 3–18.
Siu, R. G. H. *Ch'i: A Neo-Taoist Approach to Life*. Cambridge, Mass.: MIT Press, 1974.

Spagnoletti, Giacinto, ed. *Poesia italiana contemporanea 1909–1959*. Parma: Guanda, 1964.
Starobinski, Jean. "René Char and the Definition of the Poem." In *figuring Things: Char, Ponge, and Poetry in the Twentieth Century*, ed. Charles D. Minahen. Lexington, Ky.: French Forum, 1994.
Steiner, George. *In Bluebeard's Castle*. New Haven: Yale University Press, 1971.
Tabanelli, Giorgio. *Carlo Bo: Il tempo dell'ermetismo*. Milan: Garzanti, 1986.
Thovez, Enrico. *L'arco d'Ulisse: Prose di combattimento*. Naples: Ricciardi, 1921.
———. "Il Camaleonte." *Il pastore, il gregge e la zampogna: Dall'Inno a Satana alla Laus Vitae*, 149–61. Naples: Ricciardi, 1910.
Tynianov, Yuri. *The Problem of Verse Language*. Ed. and trans. M. Sosa and B. Harvey. Ann Arbor: Ardis, 1981.
Valeri, Diego. "Difficoltà del superlativo assoluto in poesia." In *Studi di varia umanità in onore di Francesco Flora*, 898–902. Milan: Mondadori, 1963.
Valesio, Paolo. *Gabriele D'Annunzio: The Dark Flame*. New Haven: Yale University Press, 1992.
Vittorini, Elio. *Conversazione in Sicilia*. Turin: Einaudi, 1975.
Waldrop, Rosemarie. *Against Language?* Hague: Mouton, 1971.
Watzlawick, Paul, ed. *The Invented Reality: How Do We Know What We Believe We Know?* New York: Norton, 1984.
Whitehead, Alfred North. *Science and the Modern World*. New York: Macmillan, 1967.
Wilden, Anthony. *The Rules Are No Game: The Strategy of Communication*. London: Routledge and Kegan Paul, 1987.
Zaccaria, Giuseppe. *Il Novecento letterario in Italia*. Milan: Vita e Pensiero, 1985.
Zambon, Vittorio. *La poesia di Diego Valeri*. Padua: Liviana, 1968.
Zanzotto, Andrea. *Aure e disincanti del Novecento letterario*. Milan: Mondadori, 1994.
———. *Fantasie di avvicinamento*. Milan: Mondadori, 1991.

INDEX

Accrocca, Elio Filippo, 152, 237
Adorno, Theodor, 37, 263n.34
Agamben, Giorgio, 231
Agrarian culture, 133, 214
Albisola, Giancarlo, 127
Aleramo, Sibilla, 74, 186–87
Alighieri, Dante, 3, 4, 5, 10, 16, 19, 21, 36, 68, 73, 89, 104, 163, 211, 213–14, 237
Allegory, 6, 44, 53, 60, 95, 96, 205, 220, 225, 237, 257n.18
Anacreon, 36, 109–10, 115, 122
Anacreonta, 109–10, 127
Anacreontic rose, 36, 109–27
Anceschi, Luciano, 28, 176; *Linea lombarda* (ed.), 33, 121
Apollinaire, Guillaume, 47–48, 59, 60, 161–62, 169, 195
"L'après-midi d'un faune" (Mallarmé), 39
Aragon, Louis, 205–6
Artaud, Antonin, 44–45, 93, 141
Asor Rosa, Alberto, 146
Audisio, Nella, 107

Babel, Isaak, 215–16
Bacchus, 109, 110
Bachelard, Gaston, 154
Balestrini, Nanni, 218–19
Ballerini, Luigi, 152–53
Bandini, Fernando, 182
Banfi, Antonio, 191–92, 300

Barbarini, Berto, 26–27
Barile, Angelo, 133–34
Baroque, ix, 94, 106, 110, 113, 115, 117, 118, 147, 148, 172; and neobaroque, 123
Barthes, Roland, 163, 183, 185–86, 249n.6; *Writing Degree Zero*, 161
Bassani, Giorgio, 30–31
Bataille, Georges, 141
Bateson, Gregory, 286n.6
Baudelaire, Charles, 37–38, 40, 45, 47, 67, 90, 94, 198
Bellezza, Dario, 33, 86
Bellintani, Umberto, 81
Bembo, Pietro, 10
Bemporad, Giovanna, 196
Benjamin, Walter, vii
Benussi, Cristina, 56
Bertolucci, Attilio, 31, 162, 164–67, 177, 292n.11; *La camera da letto*, 166–67
Bertolucci, Bernardo, 127
Betocchi, Carlo, 95–96, 101
Bettarini, Mariella, 201
Bigongiari, Piero, 74, 98, 105–7; *Moses*, 106
Bloom, Harold, 147
Blumenberg, Hans, 93
Bo, Carlo, 140
Bobbio, Norberto, 65, 259
Bodei, Remo, 153
Bodini, Vittorio, 116–18
Boeri, Mirella, 203

Boine, Giovanni, 41, 143; *Frantumi*, 132–33
Bonnefoy, Yves, 54
Bontempelli, Massimo, 25, 56, 61
Bonvesin de la Riva, 19
Borgese, Giulio Antonio, 57
Brecht, Bertolt, 15
Breton, André, 50, 51
Brevini, Franco, 113
Brindisi, Rocco, 123
Brown, Norman O., 18
Buddhism, 42
Budigna, Luciano, 227
Buonarroti, Michelangelo, 125
Burke, Kenneth, 185
Buttita, Ignazio, 112
Buzzi, Paolo, 70

Cacciatore, Edoardo, 224–25, 226, 238
Calvino, Italo, 141, 162, 285n.51
Campana, Dino, 27, 73, 74–75, 138, 262n.28; *Canti orfici*, 74, 191
Campo, Cristina, 126
Caproni, Giorgio, 44, 128, 130, 137–40, 143, 162, 164, 237
Cardarelli, Vincenzo, 17, 61, 129
Carducci, Giosue, 8, 13, 21–22, 24
Carpe diem, 36, 41
Carrieri, Raffaele, 80–81
Catholic church, 7, 40, 90, 129, 152, 167, 214
Catholicism, 32, 83
Cattafi, Bartolo, 123–25
Catullus, 68, 156
Cavalcanti, Guido, 4, 104
Cavalli, Patrizia, 202
Ceccardi, Ceccardo Roccatagliata, 130–31, 139, 143
Celan, Paul, 107–8
Cendrars, Blaise, 48
Cerruti, Marco, 77, 264n.48
Char, René, 53–54, 169–70
Christianity, 103, 108, 133, 159, 177, 182
Ciabatti, Gianfranco, 221–22
Claudel, Paul, 43–44, 54, 132, 251n.28; *Cinque grandes odes*, 44
Clementelli, Elena, 17, 196

Cocteau, Jean, 45
Comi, Girolamo, 88–89, 100
Command message, 2–3, 196, 223
Compass-card (*rosa dei venti, roses des vents*), 16, 44, 45, 153, 211, 237–38
Connotation, 5–6, 15, 37, 119
Constructivism, 53, 135, 169, 230, 232, 236
Conte, Giuseppe, 141–43
Contini, Gianfranco, x, 4, 163
Copioli, Rosita, 199–200
Corra, Bruno, 26
Corazzini, Sergio, 3, 57, 73
Correspondences, 37, 143
Corti, Maria, 6, 19
Coviello, Michelangelo, 33
Crepuscolarismo, 57, 58, 60, 68, 69, 70, 74
Croce, Benedetto, 2, 3–4, 41, 57, 70, 259
Cucchi, Maurizio, 236
Curtius, Ernst, xiii, 93, 223

D'Alcamo, Ciullo, 4, 189, 235
Da Lentini, Giacomo, 4
D'Annunzio, Gabriele, 9, 10, 11–13, 18, 23, 24–25, 29, 56, 60, 65, 70, 71, 73, 77, 80, 163, 220
Da Todi, Jacopone, 32
Debenedetti, Giacomo, 95
De Libero, Libero, 29–30
Della Casa, Giovanni, 68
Della Corte, Carlo, 32–33
De Martino, Ernesto, 214
Denotation, 5–6, 15, 37
De Robertis, Domenico, 19–20
De Robertis, Giuseppe, 95
De Stael, Madame, 7; *Corinne*, 8
Desnos, Robert, 50
Detienne, Marcel, 199
Dialects and dialect poetry, 4, 85–86, 92, 110–14, 128, 130, 140, 174–75, 180, 182, 207–9, 214, 225
Di Giacomo, Salvatore, 91, 110–12, 269n.17, 275n.8
Dissonance, 139, 143
Dolce stil nuovo, 104, 220
Dossi, Carlo: *La villa delle rose*, 13
Duchamp, Marcel, 50
Duse, Eleonora, 71

Eco, Umberto, 152; *The Name of the Rose*, 3
Éluard, Paul, 180; *La rose publique*, 51
Enantiosis, 14, 145, 180
Encyclopedic, 161–83 passim
Erba, Luciano, 33, 158, 253n.46

Fallacara, Luigi, 98, 99–100; *Primo vere*, 27
Fascism, 3, 65, 76, 77, 192, 209, 214, 227
Feminine, the, 44, 183; beauty, 46, 75; consciousness, 228; voice, 184–204
Feminism, 157, 290n.43
Flora, Francesco, 14
Florence, 73, 81, 97, 102–4, 128, 132, 134, 135, 140, 146, 164, 212
Fogazzaro, Antonio, 23
Folgore, Luciano, 59
Fontecedro, Emanuela, 202
Fortini, Franco, 17, 83, 135, 211–14, 218, 221, 261, 278n.35; *La poesia delle rose*, 211, 212–13, 216, 306–7n.22, 308n.33
Foscolo, Ugo, 79, 110–11, 127, 137, 186; "Le grazie," 11–12, 19–21; "De' sepolcri," 20
Frabotta, Bianca Maria, 157
Francis of Assisi, Saint, 11, 189
Frederick II, Emperor, 174
Free verse (*verso libero*), 41, 156
French poetry, 35–55
Frezza, Luciana, 198
Futurism, 14, 47, 58, 59, 70, 74, 161

García Lorca, Federico, 45, 116, 118–20, 278n.35
Gargani, Aldo, ix, 184–85
Gatto, Alfonso, 17, 28, 29, 98, 120–22, 123, 148–49
Gautier, Théophile, 38–39, 42
Genoa, 129, 131, 136, 137–38, 140
Gerbino, Giovanni, 26
Giambene, Renata, 126–27
Giotti, Virgilio, 155, 160
Giudici, Giovanni, 81–84, 143
Giuliani, Alfredo, 183
Gobetti, Piero, 65
Goethe, Johann Wolfgang von, 6, 7
Goffredo, Giuseppe, 112, 226
Golden Age, 193, 205
Gómez de la Serna, Ramón, 56

Góngora, Luis de, 120, 278n.35; *Polifemo*, 118
Govoni, Corrado, 3, 57–58, 73
Gozzano, Guido, 3, 25, 56, 58, 61, 64–66, 70, 73, 129
Graf, Arturo, 9
Gramsci, Antonio, 4, 128
Grande, Adriano, 136–37
Guglielmi, Giuseppe, 226–27
Guglielminetti, Amalia, 58–59
Guidacci, Margherita, 158–59
Guillén, Jorge, 114–15, 276n.14

Hays, Gregory, 265n.57
Heine, Heinrich, 158, 186
Hellerstein, Nina, 251n.28
Heraclitus, 136, 226
Hermetics and hermeticism, ix, 14, 29, 49, 58, 75, 97–106, 122, 140, 166, 170, 207, 221, 226
Homer, 89, 112
Huidobro, Vicente, 50

Ignatius (Saint) of Loyola, 93
Illness, 67, 68, 72, 86, 101, 229
Italy, 132; idea of, 143; Risorgimento of, 206; post-Risorgimento period of, 128; unification of, 8
Iterativity, 29, 46, 82, 113, 168–69, 210

Jahier, Piero, 41, 54, 131–32, 143
Jakobson, Roman, 240n.16
Jesus Christ, 6, 32, 45, 63, 90, 95, 106, 112
Jimenez, Juan Ramón, 45, 99, 252n.35
Joyce, James: *A Portrait of the Artist as a Young Man*, 149
Judaism, 77, 108, 158

Keats, John, 186
Kemeny, Tomaso, 235–36
Kenner, Hugh, 243n.43
Kenosis, 230
Korzybski, A., 88, 163
Kristeva, Julia, 18, 243–44n.49

Laforgue, Jules, 14, 41–43, 45, 198
Lawrence, D. H., 141, 142

Leopardi, Giacomo, 7–8, 17, 22, 55, 66, 79, 100, 109, 127, 150, 172, 182, 185, 186, 187, 188, 190, 202, 238, 306n.16; "Imitazione," 8, 154, 170–71; "L'Infinito," 241n.22; "Il sabato del villaggio," 21; *Zibaldone*, 21
Leopardism, 17, 204
Leto, Gabriella, 198–99
Levi, Primo, 157–58, 160
Liguria, 81, 128–43, 283–84n.28
Linea lombarda (ed. Anceschi), 33, 121, 164, 176, 215
Locus amoenus, 101
Lombardy, 81, 90, 128, 138
Longhi, Roberto, 31
Lorca. *See* García Lorca
Lotman, Yuri, 160
Lucania, 170, 172, 174, 214
Lucchese, Romeo, 129–30
Lucini, Gian Pietro, 13, 14, 243n.38
Lumelli, Angelo, 233–35
Luperini, Romano, 221, 224
Lupi, Dania, 202–3
Luzi, Mario, 29, 39, 40, 74, 81, 98, 101, 102–4, 105, 164, 205; *Un brindisi*, 104

Machado, Antonio, 45
Macrí, Oreste, 99–100, 106
Madrigal, 90, 120, 132
Majorino, Giancarlo, 217–18
Mallarmé, Stephane, 11, 14, 16, 18, 38–40, 41, 42, 43, 45, 46, 47, 51, 67, 100, 104, 120, 198, 236, 278n.35
Mandelstam, Osip, 143
Mannerism, 6, 75, 81, 127, 203
Mantero, Manuel, 114, 276n.14
Manzoni, Alessandro, 7; "In morte di Carlo Imbonati," 147
Maraini, Dacia, 183
Marin, Biagio, 92–93, 162
Marino, Giambattista: "Elogio della rosa," 9
Marinetti, Filippo Tommaso, 59
Martini, Fausto Maria, 69
Mary, Virgin, 4, 6, 7, 31, 32, 44, 50, 87, 90, 92, 96, 149–50, 188
Mascioni, Grytzko, 85
Mathematics, 171, 173
Mazzini, Giuseppe, 129, 133, 206

Mengaldo, Pier Vincenzo, 17, 270n.25, 271n.43, 272n.52, 282n.20
Menicanti, Daria, 191–2
Merini, Alda, 107
Michelstaedter, Carlo, 17, 144, 264n.48; *La persuasione e la rettorica*, 77
Milan, 13, 62, 146, 174, 225
Miller, Henry, 141
Modesti, Renzo, 33, 176
Montale, Eugenio, 17, 41, 55, 64, 65, 97, 98, 100, 116, 134, 137, 139, 145–47, 148, 160, 163, 170, 180, 207; "L'anguilla" (The Eel), 150; *Ossi di seppia*, 14, 283–84n.28
Monstration, 111, 115
Monti, Vincenzo, 7
Morante, Elsa, 190–91; *Alibi*, 190
Mörike, Edvard, 126
Mysticism, 29, 36, 100, 108
Mystic rose, 3, 94, 193
Myth and legend, 85, 101, 141, 143, 153, 159, 172, 179, 199, 212

Naples, 91–92
Narrativity, 31, 203, 269n.17
Navigation, metaphor of, 51, 67, 153
Negation, 14, 37, 97, 131, 137, 159, 224, 226, 232
Negri, Ada, 70–73
Neo-avant-garde, 33, 49, 212, 218–21
Nerval, Gerard de, 35–36
New Lyricism, the (*I nuovi lirici*), 28–29, 74, 263n.31
New Rationality, the, 224, 236
Nietzsche, Frederich, 74, 185
Novalis, 7, 15
Novaro, Mario, 130, 134
Il Novecento, 61, 62
Noventa, Giacomo, 85, 162, 207–9
I Novissimi, 218, 220

Olson, Charles, 200, 302–3n.55
Onofri, Arturo, 23, 89–90, 100
Orelli, Giorgio, 176–77, 179
Orlando furioso (Ariosto), 166
Orphism, 16, 27, 36, 43, 45, 89, 225
Ossola, Carlo, 93, 108, 239n.2, 269–70n.24
Otium, 223–38 passim

Pagliarani, Elio, 218, 220–21
Palazzeschi, Aldo, 3, 55, 60; 257n.18
Pan, the Panic, 24, 140, 141
Papini, Giovanni, 3, 133
Parini, Giuseppe: "La Educazione," 146–47
Paris, Renzo, 235
Parronchi, Alessandro, 81, 104–5
Pascoli, Giovanni, 9–11, 13, 18, 21–24, 28, 31, 56, 68–69, 70, 79, 82, 84, 112, 115, 121, 163, 169, 179, 182, 222, 241n.26, 291n.6; "L'Avvento," 207; *Primi poemetti*, 23; "Il sabato," 21
Pasolini, Pier Paolo, 17, 31, 112, 130, 132, 201, 209–11, 212, 264n.51, 275n.8, 282–83n.20, 305n.12; *Poesia in forma di rosa*, 156, 210, 292n.11
Pavese, Cesare, 155–56, 160
Pea, Enrico, 95
Peirce, Charles S., 239n.4
Pellico, Silvio: *Le mie prigioni*, 1–2
Penna, Sandro, 116, 156, 160
Perse, Saint-John, 137; *Amers*, 50; *Anabase*, 49; *Chronique*, 49
Petrarca, Francesco, 4, 11, 21, 24, 38, 175, 187, 240n.11; *Il Canzoniere*, 5, 8
Petrarchism, 5, 71, 94, 105, 176
Petrocchi, Giorgio, 134
Piccolo, Lucio, 115–16
Pierro, Albino, 174–76, 179
Piersanti, Umberto, 182
Pindar, 89
Pirandello, Luigi, 128
Pitigrilli, 65
Poe, Edgar Allan, 36–37, 40, 93–4
Poésie pure, 14, 162
Ponge, Francis, 52–53
Porta, Antonio, 218; "La rose," 219–20
Porta, Carlo, 162
Postmodern, 56, 255–56n.2
Pound, Ezra, 15, 54, 80; *Pisan Cantos*, 16
Pozzi, Antonia, 17, 191
Pozzi, Giovanni, viii, 5–6, 78, 240nn. 11, 13, 262n.28, 290n.41
Prayer, 73, 101, 108, 216, 226, 229; secular prayer, 88, 100
Praz, Mario, 68; 243n.36
Prostitution, 60, 73, 169, 217

La quarta generazione, 121, 123
Quasimodo, Salvatore, 28, 78–80, 163, 207; *Oboé sommerso*, 14; *Lirici greci*, 79

Raboni, Giovanni, 216–17, 247n.40
Ramat, Silvio, 150–51
Recursiveness, recursivity, 13, 17, 54, 98, 145, 146, 168, 187, 192, 211, 241n.22, 286n.2. *See also* Wonder, recursive
Rebora, Clemente, 17, 41, 62–63, 66, 282n.14; *Frammenti lirici*, 132
Relativism, 47, 56
Report message, 2–3, 196, 223
Reverdy, Pierre, 49, 54, 253n.46
Rhetoric, ix, 18, 61, 77, 144–60 passim, 226
Rilke, Rainer Maria, 14–15, 87–88, 91, 108
Rimbaud, Arthur, 18, 27, 40–41, 43, 67, 161
Risi, Nelo, 215–16
Riviera Ligure, 129, 130, 131
Romagnoli, Sergio, 283–84n.28
Roman de la rose, 4, 27, 48, 113, 205, 224
Rome, 128, 133, 173, 174, 186
La Ronda, 62
Ronsard, Pierre de, 102
Rosai, Ottone, 81
Rosarium philosophorum, 211
Rosselli, Amelia, 74, 214, 227–30; "Il soggiorno in inferno," 228, 231
Rosselli, Nello, 207
Rose window, 16, 44, 47, 87, 90
Rosicrucianism, 89–90
Rossi, Tiziano, 154–55

Saba, Umberto, 75–77, 78, 95, 163
Sacrament, ix, 43, 80, 88, 91, 95, 108
Saint-Pol-Roux, 243n.38
Sala, Alberico, 122–23
Sanesi, Roberto, 200–201
Sanguineti, Edoardo, 74, 84–85, 222
Sappho, 79–80, 111
Saussure, Fernande de, 1, 2; *Anagrammes*, 33
Savonarola, Girolamo, 221
Savoy monarchy, 128, 131
Sbarbaro, Camillo, 17, 41, 134–36, 139, 145, 282–83n.20; *Trucioli*, 132, 134–35
Scapigliati, 13, 67–68

Scataglini, Franco, 26–27, 112–14, 115, 182
Schopenhauer, Arthur, 42, 77
Scotellaro, Rocco, 214–15, 238
Segre, Cesare, 241n.22, 246n.27
Sereni, Vittorio, 139, 162, 164, 167–70, 191; *Gli strumenti umani*, 168–69
Seriality, 33, 71, 261n.18
Serra, Renato, 95, 133–34
Serrao, Achille, 85–86
Severini, Gino, 59, 257n.13
Seward, Barbara, 287n.15
Shakespeare, William, 5
Shelley, Percy Bysshe, 186
Sinisgalli, Leonardo, 17, 28, 52, 162, 170–74, 177, 179, 215
Socialism, 207, 214, 222, 227
Soffici, Ardengo, 3, 60, 133, 185
Solmi, Sergio, 17, 83, 100–102; *La rosa gelata*, 101
Slataper, Scipio, 41; *Il mio Carso*, 63
Spanish Civil War, 52
Spatola, Adriano, 235
Spaziani, Maria Luisa, 17, 30, 192–96
Spitzer, Leo, 93
Squatriti, Fausta, 231–32
Starobinski, Jean, 54
Stein, Gertrude, 62
Steiner, George, 294n.42
Stevens, Wallace, 62
Stochastic events, 16, 50, 146, 222; defined, 286n.6
Surrealism, 14, 50, 106, 123, 206, 222, 227
Swedenborg, Emanuel, 37
Symbolism, 14, 25, 27, 39–40, 58, 68, 69, 70, 77, 95, 100, 102, 127, 143, 145, 152, 163, 166, 183
Synesthesia, 74, 98, 104, 151

Tarozzi, Bianca, 203
Tasso, Torquato, 68
Tassoni, Luigi, 127
Testori, Giovanni: *Diadèmata*, 32
Thovez, Enrico, 23, 69–70, 242–43n.36
Tolstoy, Leo, 77

Tommaseo, Niccolo, 7, 37; *Canti del popolo greco*, 79
Tondelli, Pier Vincenzo, 86
Topos, topoi, vii–x, 6, 13, 17, 93, 115, 148, 189, 196, 223–24, 231
Transumption, 147–48
Tuscany, 82, 111, 128, 216
Tynianov, Yuri, 144

Ungaretti, Giuseppe, 14, 17, 39, 41, 55, 93–95, 98, 108, 152, 163, 201, 207, 269n.24

Valeri, Diego, 14, 90–91
Valéry, Paul, 14, 17, 294n.42
Valesio, Paolo, 147–50, 160
Varese, Claudio, 21
Verlaine, Paul, 38, 198
Veronese Riddle, 78
Vico, Giambattista, 21, 63, 185
Vergil, 4, 36, 189
Villa, Dario, 236
Villa, Emilio, 225–26
Violets and roses, 19–34, 148, 187
Vittorini, Elio: *Conversazioni in Sicilia*, 83
Vivaldi, Cesare, 146
Viviani, Cesare, 153–54
La Voce, 60, 62, 95
Vociani, 74, 75
Volponi, Paolo, 182, 196–97

Weak thought (*pensiero debole*), 201
Wonder, 49, 63, 100–101, 130, 158, 191; recursive, 17, 34, 78, 118, 230; extensive, 8, 17, 34, 88, 230
World War I, 47, 56, 60, 63, 131
World War II, 30, 48, 52, 121, 131, 162, 168, 189, 206, 214

Zaniboni, Lucio, 127
Zanzotto, Andrea, 92, 162, 177–82, 189, 264n.51, 269n.21, 305n.12; *Dietro il paesaggio*, 177–78; *IX Ecloghe*, 181
Zeichen, Valentino, 232–33

Thomas E. Peterson is professor of Italian at the University of Georgia. His numerous articles have focused on Dante, Tasso, and twentieth-century Italian narrative and poetry. His books include *The Paraphrase of an Imaginary Dialogue* (1994), *Alberto Moravia* (1996), and *The Ethical Muse of Franco Fortini* (UPF, 1997).